Introduction to
Tribal Legal Studies

TRIBAL LEGAL STUDIES SERIES

SERIES EDITOR: Jerry Gardner (Cherokee), Tribal Law and Policy Institute

This series began as a collaborative initiative between the UCLA Native Nations Law and Policy Center and four tribal colleges. It is designed to promote education and community empowerment through the development of resources for and about tribal justice systems.

American Indian tribal court systems deal with a wide range of difficult criminal and civil justice problems on a daily basis. Culturally based legal training is one of Indian Country's most pressing needs, as tribes assume responsibility for a growing number of government functions, such as child welfare and environmental control, and tribal courts continue to expand as the primary sources of law enforcement and dispute resolution for tribal communities. This book series is designed to develop legal and technical resources for tribal justice course offerings and materials, so that they reflect community thought, philosophy, traditions, and norms, and serve to strengthen tribal government and leadership.

BOOKS IN THE SERIES
1. *Introduction to Tribal Legal Studies* (2004), by Justin B. Richland and Sarah Deer
2. *Tribal Criminal Law and Procedure* (2004), by Carrie E. Garrow and Sarah Deer
3. *Sharing Our Stories of Survival: Native Women Surviving Violence* (2007), edited by Sarah Deer, Bonnie Clairmont, Carrie A. Martell, and Maureen L. White Eagle
4. *Introduction to Tribal Legal Studies*, second edition (2010), by Justin B. Richland and Sarah Deer

EDITORIAL REVIEW BOARD

Introduction to Tribal Legal Studies

SECOND EDITION

JUSTIN B. RICHLAND
and
SARAH DEER

ALTAMIRA
PRESS

A division of
ROWMAN & LITTLEFIELD PUBLISHERS, INC.
Lanham • New York • Toronto • Plymouth, UK

Published by AltaMira Press
A division of Rowman & Littlefield Publishers, Inc.
A wholly owned subsidiary of The Rowman & Littlefield Publishing Group, Inc.
4501 Forbes Boulevard, Suite 200, Lanham, Maryland 20706
http://www.altamirapress.com

Estover Road, Plymouth PL6 7PY, United Kingdom

British Library Cataloguing in Publication Information Available

Library of Congress Cataloging-in-Publication Data
Richland, Justin B. (Justin Blake), 1970–
    Introduction to tribal legal studies / Justin B. Richland and Sarah Deer. — 2nd ed.
      p. cm. — (Tribal legal studies series ; 4)
    Includes bibliographical references and index.
    ISBN 978-0-7591-1210-0 (cloth : alk. paper) —
    ISBN 978-0-7591-1211-7 (pbk. : alk. paper) —
    ISBN 978-0-7591-1940-6 (electronic)
    1. Indians of North America—Legal status, laws, etc. I. Deer, Sarah, 1972– II. Title.
KF8205.R53 2010
340.5'273—dc22   2009030791

Printed in the United States of America

Contents

Foreword

THE INSPIRATION for this series of textbooks on Tribal Legal Studies comes from many places, but the multiple paths have led to a common outcome. Jerry Gardner, series editor, has long worked in the Native tribal court and law-training field. Over the years, he and colleagues have provided numerous weekend, weeklong, and one- to four-day seminars to tribal legal personnel from all over the United States. The goal was to offer information and training so that tribal governments could build and improve their courts and legal departments. Many tribal communities and leaders realized that exercising sovereignty required the capability to manage disputes and exercise law and order on Native reservations.

Many tribes want to include traditional methods of legal resolution, emphasizing restorative justice rather than the punitive methods that predominate within U.S. law and court systems. If tribal communities are going to exercise sovereignty, they must do so in ways that emphasize their cultural values and maintain order and commitment among tribal members. Tribal communities have too long lived under legal and court regimes that did not express their sovereignty or their ways of managing and sustaining social and cultural relations. The task of educating Native leaders and court personnel about federal, state, and tribal law is of paramount importance, as Native governments and communities work toward more effective governments that will express Native values and protect Native rights.

Jerry Gardner and his colleagues found that weekend and short seminar courses were useful for many, but did not provide enough depth and breadth for the needs of a well-trained legal and court staff. Consequently, in an effort to provide more sustained information and training, a curriculum for Native legal studies was created at the New College in northern California in the 1980s. This experiment lasted only briefly, as few tribal people wanted to travel to California and stay away from their home reservations for the sustained periods necessary to complete a couple years of coursework.

Joining with faculty at UCLA such as Carole Goldberg and Duane Champagne, a new Tribal Legal Studies strategy was formed. This project was initially funded through the U.S. Department of Education by way of a FIPSE (Fund for the Improvement of Post-secondary Education) grant. A course curriculum was created for four Native-controlled community colleges: Salish Kootenai College, Diné College, Northwest Indian College, and Turtle Mountain Community College. For five years, from 1998 to 2003, courses were delivered and curricula revised. Our plan was to deliver the courses in the heart of Indian Country, where the people lived and the Native legal issues and institutions were day-to-day events. During the FIPSE grant, Turtle Mountain Community College was successful in winning several large Department of Justice grants for developing project courses and curricula, which provided assistance with the first two Tribal Legal Studies textbooks.

A major difficulty in delivering Tribal Legal Studies courses for tribally controlled community colleges was the scarcity of funds for appropriately trained legal personnel, as well as a dearth of curriculum materials. The Tribal Legal Studies Series addresses the latter problem. The textbook series includes federal, state, and tribal legal information in lesson formats that heretofore were not available. Students are encouraged to research the legal culture and norms of their own traditions and include them in solving the legal issues of their contemporary communities. We hope to provide information that will make students more aware of legal and cultural issues necessary for them to understand and serve the interests of their Native communities and governments.

Students are encouraged to follow multiple paths through this Tribal Legal Studies Series. Some may wish to continue their education by enrolling in law school—but now armed with training in Native legal principles and knowledge that few law schools offer. We think such law students will approach the law in a more sophisticated manner and will be better prepared to interpret and understand American law in ways that will serve Native communities. Other students may wish to use the courses in preparation for assuming the responsibilities of political office, for gaining skills necessary to fulfill tribal or Bureau of Indian Affairs jobs, or for training to serve in tribal courts or as community legal advocates. Community members who have greater understanding of federal, state, and tribal law will be better tribal citizens and will be in a much better position to evaluate and strengthen Native courts, law, constitutions, government organization, and policies.

It is our sincere hope and belief that the Tribal Legal Studies Series will lead to better-educated tribal citizens, leaders, and policy makers and will support and help strengthen Native tribal governments and legal institutions that express Native values and understandings that will produce greater capabilities for exercising and protecting Native sovereignty.

Duane Champagne
(Turtle Mountain Band of Chippewa)
July 2009

Preface to the Second Edition

THE PUBLICATION of the Tribal Legal Studies Series is the culmination of a dream of many people throughout Indian Country to formalize and institutionalize tribal legal education through collaboration between tribal justice systems and tribal colleges. We are pleased to offer this new revised edition, which includes many new excerpts as well as the most up-to-date case law on tribal jurisdiction.

Since the publication of the first edition in 2004, the Tribal Law and Policy Institute (TLPI) has continued to work with a variety of organizations, including the University of California, Los Angeles (UCLA) Native Nations Law and Policy Center and several tribal colleges to develop, pilot, and implement Tribal Legal Studies curricula at tribal community colleges. This endeavor was initially funded through a grant from the U.S. Department of Education's Fund for the Improvement of Postsecondary Education (FIPSE) to UCLA. This project would not have been possible without the dedication and commitment of both Duane Champagne, UCLA professor of sociology and long-term director of the UCLA American Indian Studies Center, and Carole Goldberg, UCLA professor of law and director of the UCLA Joint Degree Program in Law and American Indian Studies.

The Tribal Legal Studies program has been designed to increase tribal college course offerings and to provide a Legal Studies certificate program, a two-year Associate of Arts (A.A.) degree and/or Associate of Applied Science (A.A.S.) degree in Legal Studies, and a possible four-year Bachelor of Arts (B.A.) degree in Legal Studies.

The project is designed to prepare students for employment with tribal governments and tribal court systems as judges, advocates (prosecutor, defender, or civil advocate), paralegals, victim advocates, court-appointed special advocates (CASA), court administrators, court clerks, probation officers, social service personnel, law enforcement personnel, and other positions related to the administration of justice in Indian Country. The target audience for the program includes students who plan a career working for tribal courts or governments, students with a specific interest in careers such as paralegals and victim advocates, professionals working in tribal government, and students planning further careers in law. The courses in the program are also available as in-service training for current tribal employees and the community at large. Moreover, the program serves as a gateway to those students who become interested in law school or other higher education opportunities.

Since 1998, TLPI and our partners have developed a series of courses, including:

- Introduction to Tribal Legal Studies
- Tribal Criminal Law and Procedure
- Tribal Family and Juvenile Justice Systems
- Legal Research and Writing
- Violence against Native Women
- Tribal Constitution and Code Development
- Trial Skills Development
- Federal Indian Law
- Tribal Civil Law and Procedure
- Tribal Legal Studies Internships

Tribal Legal Studies courses have also been offered through distance learning in collaboration with the Tribal Learning Community and Educational Exchange (TLCEE), UCLA Extension, and TLPI.

These textbooks and related curricula are designed to enhance American Indian and Alaska Native communities and tribal justice systems in at least three different dimensions. First, they empower tribal court staff (current and future) to provide leadership and shape their own futures and their communities by providing them with the legal knowledge, cultural knowledge, and advocacy skills needed to successfully complete this program and to go on to law school and other higher education opportunities. Second, they promote tribal self-determination and enhance tribal sovereignty by strengthening, improving, and empowering tribal justice systems and thereby building tribal capacity to create positive change and promote social and economic community development. Third, they strengthen the links between tribal courts and tribal community colleges by enriching the tribal college legal curriculum, enhancing their capacity to meet the needs of their communities, serving as gateways to higher education, and building partnerships between tribal colleges and mainstream institutions.

It has been clear that the success of the Tribal Legal Studies project requires the formalization of the design, development, and printing of Tribal Legal Studies textbooks and instructor guides for each of the Tribal Legal Studies courses. Moreover, we anticipate that the printing of these textbooks and the accompanying instructor guides will greatly facilitate the dissemination of the Tribal Legal Studies curriculum to other tribal colleges and colleges with programs throughout Indian Country. We hope that the printing of these textbooks and instructor guides will thereby benefit all of Indian Country.

> Jerry Gardner (Cherokee), Series Editor
> Executive Director, Tribal Law and Policy Institute
> June 2009

Tribal Legal Studies Textbook Series
Volume 1: Introduction to Tribal Legal Studies
Volume 2: Tribal Criminal Law and Procedure
Volume 3: Sharing Our Stories of Survival: Native Women Surviving Violence

Notes on Law, Non-Indian Anthropologists, and Terminology

Notes on Law

Local Case Law

We have included tribal case law that has been published in case reporters or on the Internet. Please note that some of the cases may have been overturned by subsequent decisions and therefore should not be used as legal authority without conducting necessary legal research. Only a select few tribes are represented in this text. We encourage readers, students, and instructors to consult local tribal case law (if available) to supplement the materials in the text. We have done major editing on some of the cases to facilitate the educational value. For example, we have edited most footnotes and citations out of the tribal case law. In addition, portions of case law that are irrelevant for this textbook are omitted so that students can focus on the issues at hand.

Practitioners should always consult the original cases and read them in their original context before using or citing them as law. Many of the cases include references to other tribal law. It is important that this textbook not be used as a replacement for necessary legal research.

We do not include long portions of text from federal or state case law because this is a textbook concentrating on tribal law. References to federal and/or state case law are kept to a minimum, except where the law has impact for tribal judicial systems (for example, the *Oliphant* decision holding that tribes can no longer assert criminal jurisdiction over non-Indians).

Tribal Statutes

We have included some tribal statutes (often called tribal codes)—usually tribal statutes that have been published on the Internet. We have indicated the date of enactment of these statutes whenever that information was available. These tribal statutes, however, may have been revised, supplemented, and/or overturned by subsequent tribal legislative actions. Consequently, tribal statutes included here should not be used as legal authority without conducting necessary legal research. Again, only a select few tribes are represented. We encourage readers, students, and instructors to consult local tribal statutes (if available) to supplement the materials in the text.

Practitioners should always consult the full tribal statutes and read them in their original context before using or citing as law. References to federal or state laws are kept to a minimum, except where the law impacts tribal judicial systems (for example, the Indian Child Welfare Act).

Note on Non-Indian Anthropologists and Historians

We have used a few reports or accounts from non-Indian anthropologists or historians. We realize that these accounts may not always be consistent with the beliefs and/or legal procedures of Native peoples. Nevertheless, we include them as a starting point for discussing traditional methods of dispute resolution and crime control among indigenous peoples. We encourage readers, students, and instructors to read critically and form independent analysis of the passages.

Note on Terminology

It is important to note that there are a number of difficult issues with regard to the use of particular terminology while discussing tribal legal systems. David E. Wilkins provides an excellent analysis of these terminology issues at the beginning of his book *American Indian Politics and the American Political System* (2002) as set forth below.

> Throughout the book, several terms are used interchangeably in referring to indigenous peoples in a collective sense—*tribal nations, tribes, Alaskan Natives, indigenous nations,* and *indigenous peoples.* But when I

refer to individual indigenous persons, I use only *Indian* or *American Indian*. Of all the terms most used, *Indian* is easily the most problematic (though some argue that the term *tribe* is pejorative and hints strongly of colonialism), and I use it with some hesitation for two reasons: first, because of its obvious geographical inaccuracy, and second, because it erroneously generalizes and completely ignores the cultural diversity evident in the hundreds of distinctive indigenous nations of North America, each with its own name for itself. One could thus argue that continued usage of the term attests to surviving vestiges of colonialism.

Nevertheless, the terms *Indian* and *American Indian* remain the most common appellations used by indigenous and nonindigenous persons and institutions, and so it is used in the text when no tribal name is specified. I have, moreover, intentionally avoided using the phrase *Native American*, despite that term's popularity among mainstream academics in recent decades, since it causes more confusion than the one it purports to replace, as it can be applied literally to any person born in the Americas. The expressions *Native peoples* and *Native nations* may be less confusing, but these terms and the intriguing phrase *First Nations*, which are all popular in Canada and among some Alaskan indigenous groups, have never quite caught on in the United States among indigenous nations or policy makers.

What complicates matters, of course, is that there is no single term that is acceptable by all indigenous people all the time, and even people within specific native communities sometimes disagree on which name they prefer (e.g., Navajo or Diné; Chippewa, Ojibwe, or Anishinabe; Iroquois or Haudenosaunee) and on whether they would rather be identified as tribal communities (which emphasizes their kinship affiliation) or as national entities (which, while not discounting kinship ties, tends to place greater emphasis on an independent political character and a right to engage in diplomatic relations with other nations or states, like the United States or other polities).

Of course, federal law and policy have vacillated on these terms as well. But we shall see that despite assimilative efforts, federal lawmakers continue to recognize the sovereign character of indigenous communities regardless of whether they are called *tribes* or *nations*.[1]

We agree with Wilkins's analysis of the terms mentioned. We have determined, however, that by alternating these terms in this book, the student or reader will get a clearer understanding of the diversity that each individual and/or nation has in regards to their identity. The terms to be used interchangeably are:

- Indian, Native, Native American, indigenous
- tribes, nations, governments
- traditions, customs, values, beliefs

It is expected that these terms will assist in the learning and comprehension of this textbook.

Note

1. David E. Wilkins, *American Indian Politics and the American Political System* xviii–xix (2002).

Acknowledgments

THIS BOOK is a result of collaboration between the Tribal Law and Policy Institute (www.tlpi.org) and the Native Nations Law and Policy Center at the University of California, Los Angeles (www.law.ucla.edu/nativenations).

The first edition was made possible in part by a grant from the U.S. Department of Justice, Office of Justice Programs, Bureau of Justice Assistance under Grants #2001-DD-BX-0059 and #2009-MU-BX-K003. Points of view or opinions expressed in the document are those of the author(s) and do not necessarily represent the official position or policies of the U.S. Department of Justice. The first edition was also made possible in part under a grant from the Fund for the Improvement of Postsecondary Education (FIPSE), U.S. Department of Education. However, those contents do not necessarily represent the policy of the Department of Education, and you should not assume endorsement by the federal government.

The Tribal Law and Policy Institute (TLPI) is an Indian-owned and -operated nonprofit corporation organized to design and deliver education, research, training, and technical assistance programs that promote the improvement of justice in Indian Country and the health, well-being, and culture of Native peoples. TLPI operates the Tribal Court Clearinghouse (www.tlpi.org)—a comprehensive online resource for information concerning tribal justice systems, including a searchable database of tribal court opinions.

Many TLPI staff members and consultants assisted with the development of the Tribal Legal Studies Series and this *Introduction to Tribal Legal Studies* textbook—including Neal Axton, Stephanie Kena Lopez, Elton Naswood, Natalie Stites, Diane Payne, and copyeditor Dr. George Boeck.

The second edition would not have been possible without the continued efforts of TLPI staff and consultants, including Heather Valdez Singleton, Lavern Yanito Dennison, Lou Sgroi, Mona Evan, Bonnie Clairmont, Arlene Downwind-White, Maureen L. White Eagle, Jessica Marisol Allen, Melissa Taylor, Carrie A. Martell, Carrie Garrow, Pat Sekaquaptewa, Abby Abinanti, Joseph Flies-Away, Judy Leaming, Terrilena Dodson, Ryan Rash, Erik Stegman, and Jennine Stebing, along with ongoing support from UCLA Native Nations Law and Policy Center, especially Duane Champagne, Carole Goldberg, and DeAnna M. Rivera. Thanks also to Thomas Hart, University of Miami law student.

The TLPI Board of Directors has played a critical role in guiding and supporting the project: President Abby Abinanti (Yurok), Vice President David Raasch (Stockbridge-Munsee), Secretary-Treasurer Margrett Oberly Kelley (Osage/Comanche), Evelyn Stevenson (Salish/Kootenai), Ed Reina (Pima/Maricopa), Patricia Sekaquaptewa (Hopi), and Michael Jackson (Tlingit/Haida).

Justin Richland: I would like to thank Jerry Gardner, Duane Champagne, Carole Goldberg, Sarah Deer, and everyone at the Tribal Law and Policy Institute for heading up what is such a worthwhile project, and for allowing me to participate. I would also like to thank my friends and colleagues in the Department of Criminology, Law, and Society, and the Department of Anthropology at the University of California–Irvine for giving me the support necessary to complete this work. Finally, I would like to thank my wife, Lindsey, and son, Silas, for just plain putting up with me.

Sarah Deer: I would like to thank my parents, Jan and Montie Deer, my grandparents, Isaac "Kelso" and Wanda Lee Deer, and my patient husband, Neal R. Axton. Thanks also to the faculty and staff at William Mitchell College of Law for their generosity and support.

*Further information and resources concerning the Tribal Legal Studies Series is available on the Tribal Court Clearinghouse (www.tlpi.org) and on the Tribal Legal Studies website (www.triballegalstudies.org).

Credits

THE FOLLOWING copyrighted material has been reprinted with permission of the copyright holder.

Alfred, Taiaiake. *A Conversation with Atsenhaienton: Responsibility*, in Peace, Power, Righteousness: An Indigenous Manifesto (1999). Copyright 1999 by Oxford University Press. All rights reserved.

Atwood, Barbara Ann. *Tribal Jurisprudence and Cultural Meanings of the Family*, 79 Nebraska Law Review 577 (2000). Copyright 2000 by the University of Nebraska Law Review. All rights reserved.

Basso, Keith. Wisdom Sits in Places: Landscapes and Language Among the Western Apache (1996). Copyright 1996 by the University of New Mexico Press. All rights Reserved.

Becker, Bidtah, and Paul Spruhan. *Navajo Nation Judiciary*, 2 Tribal Law Journal (2002). Copyright 2002 by the Tribal Law Journal at the University of New Mexico School of Law. Permission also granted by the authors. All rights reserved.

Begay, Manley A., et al. *Development, Governance, and Culture*, in Rebuilding Native Nations: Strategies for Governance and Development (Miriam Jorgensen, ed.) (2007). Copyright 2007 by the Arizona Board of Regents. Reprinted by permission of the University of Arizona Press. All rights reserved.

Bluehouse, Philmer. *Is it "Peacemakers Teaching" or is it "Teaching Peacemakers"?* 20 Conflict Resolution Quarterly 495 (2003). Copyright 2003 by John Wiley & Sons, Inc. All right reserved.

Llewellyn, Karl N., and E. Adamson Hoebel. *The Cheyenne Way: Conflict and Case Law*, in Primitive Jurisprudence (1941). Copyright 1941, 1968 by the University of Oklahoma Press. All rights reserved.

Mayo, Massey K., and Jill E. Tompkins. *Ethical Duties*, in A Guide for Tribal Court Law Clerks and Judges (2007). Copyright 2007 by Massey K. Mayo and Jill E. Tompkins. All rights reserved.

McCarthy, Robert. *Civil Rights in Tribal Courts: The Indian Bill of Rights at Thirty Years*, 34 Idaho Law Review 465 (1993). Copyright 1993 by the Idaho Law Review. Permission also granted by the author. All rights reserved. (The views expressed are those of Mr. McCarthy and do not necessarily represent the opinion of the United States Department of the Interior.)

McCoy, Melody. *When Cultures Clash: The Future of Tribal Courts*, 20 Human Rights 22 (1993). Copyright 1993 by the American Bar Association. Permission granted by the author. All rights reserved.

Melmer, David. *Boarding School Victims Want Reparation*, Indian Country Today, April 23, 2003. Copyright 2003 by Indian Country Today. All rights reserved.

Melton, Ada Pecos. *Indigenous Justice Systems and Tribal Society*, 79 Judicature 126 (1995). Copyright 1995 by Judicature: The Journal of the American Judicature Society. All rights reserved.

Mindell, Carl, and Alan Gurwitt. *The Placement of American Indian Children: The Need for Change*, in The Destruction of American Indian Families (1977). Copyright 1977 by the Association on American Indian Affairs. All rights reserved.

Old Coyote, Henry. *Family and Clan Structure*, in Respect for Life: The Traditional Upbringing of Native American Children (Sylvester M. Morey and Olivia L. Gilliam, eds.) (1974). Copyright 1974 by the Myron Institute/ Orion Society. All rights reserved.

Porter, Robert, Odawi. *Strengthening Tribal Sovereignty Through Peacemaking: How the Anglo-American Legal Tradition Destroys Indigenous Societies*, 28 Columbia Human Rights Law Review 235 (1997). Copyright 1997 by the Columbia Human Rights Law Review. Permission also granted by the author. All rights reserved.

Red Cloud Indian School. *Tiospayes* (1972). Copyright 1972 by the Red Cloud Indian School, Inc. All rights reserved.

Richland, Justin. *What Are You Going to do With the Village's Knowledge? Talking Tradition, Talking Law in Hopi Tribal Court*, 39 Law and Society Review 235 (2007). Permission granted by the author. All rights reserved.

Rusco, Elmer. *Civil Liberties Guarantees under Tribal Law: A Survey of Civil Rights Provisions in Tribal Constitutions*, 14 American Indian Law Review 269 (1990). Copyright 1990 by the American Indian Law Review. All rights reserved.

CHAPTER 1

What Is Law? Legal Norms, Structures, and Practices

OR MOST non-Native people in the United States and elsewhere, the question of how law shapes who they are and how they identify themselves is one that doesn't usually occupy their thoughts. Unless they are somehow involved with the legal system—for example, are a party to a lawsuit, are in prison, or are even doing something more mundane like getting a driver's license—non-Native people don't often think of law as impacting their everyday lives. However, for citizens of tribal nations, and others who identify as American Indian (or Native American, Indigenous, Aboriginal, First Nation, etc.), awareness of the many ways their lives are impacted by law—both the law of their tribal nation and that of the non-Native state that often encompasses it—is virtually inescapable.

In one way or another, Native peoples often have law in mind. This is, of course, true when they think about the institutions, practices, and beliefs originally imposed on them through European and U.S. colonization. But it's also true, in a sense, when they are reflecting on their relationship to the institutions, practices, and beliefs of their tribes' unique cultural heritage. And it's even true when they think about the ways these two spheres of human thought and action—Native and non-Native—confront each other in contemporary tribal life. One purpose behind the writing of this book is to ask about the particular orientation tribal citizens have to law—both their own and others'. But this book also goes further. An additional purpose is to ask what this tribal orientation to law means for understanding the status of tribal nations in the

United States today. Finally, but perhaps most importantly, this book is designed to ask how studying tribal law can give us insight into the institutions, practices, and beliefs that shape the everyday lives of tribal people.

To have these as our goals means that we have as one of our basic premises the belief that studying tribal law is an important way to understand the values and identities of tribal peoples today. It is also a way to address the damage done to tribal communities and cultures as a result of centuries of colonization and oppression by European and U.S. powers. We believe that research into tribal law reveals how Indian people have endured this oppression by living according to their own ideas about identity and society.

We are not the first to think in this way. For many Native scholars and practitioners, tribal law is seen as key to the exercise and expansion of tribal sovereignty—the capacity of a tribal people to express their cultural values and to live according to them. As Carey N. Vicenti, the former chief judge of the Jicarilla Apache Tribe, said of tribal courts:

> The real battle for the preservation of traditional ways of life will be fought on the bold promontory of guiding human values. It is in that battle that tribal courts will become indispensable. It is in the tribal court that the competing concepts regarding social order, and the place of the individual within the family, the clan, the band, and the tribe, will be decided.[1]

Additionally, as Frank Pommersheim, chief justice of the Cheyenne River Sioux Tribal Court of Appeals, explains, the power of tribal courts and tribal legal systems also serves to protect tribes against further loss of sovereignty:

> It is the wisdom and integrity of tribal law and tribal courts, properly and consistently informed by tradition and evolving contemporary tribal standards, that will stand as the best bulwark against federal encroachment. Without this continuing development, there can be little expectation for [tribal] stability and equilibrium.[2]

In writing this book, we follow these and other tribal leaders in thinking that studying tribal law offers an understanding of how tribes have survived as unique peoples with distinct cultural heritages. Thus the readings and discussion questions in this text demonstrate how some tribal legal actors have confronted non-Indian efforts to diminish their tribal sovereignty by studying and strengthening their tribes' law and legal systems. But before turning to those materials, the next section in this chapter describes our basic understanding of law and legal systems in general to lay a foundation for how and why we approach tribal law in the ways we do in the rest of the text.

If you are a tribal citizen, as you read the remainder of this chapter, ask yourself whether the study of your laws might benefit your tribe. Also consider whether such a study might improve tribal members' capacity to live and define their identity by their own norms, practices, and structures.

What Is Law?

If someone were to ask you, "What is law?" what would you think of first? Maybe you would think of a specific value that is an important principle in your community. Maybe you would think about some rule that all children are taught from the time they are small—for example, "Do not kill," "Do not steal," or "Keep your promises." But is law simply a value or norm? In many societies, there is a norm for being polite and friendly to other people. But would you call this norm a law? When someone is rude to you, you might think he or she is being impolite, but would you say they are breaking a law?

Maybe you would think that law is about the people, places, and processes you deal with when you break the law. In some cultures, if you break a law, you could be arrested or given a ticket by a law enforcement officer. You might have to go before a judge in court, where lawyers argue about whether or not you broke the law, and a judge or jury decides if you are guilty or not guilty. If they decide that you did break the law, you might have to go to jail, pay a fine, or both. But what if you live in a society that historically or traditionally did not have police, lawyers, judges, or courts and jails? Would you say that your society historically or traditionally had no law?

Scholars who study law in societies have looked at all of these kinds of things, which together form what is called the *legal system* of a society or culture. These scholars analyze legal systems by studying the norms, structures, and practices that make up its parts. Figure 1-1 illustrates this.

FIGURE 1.1. Tribal Legal Systems

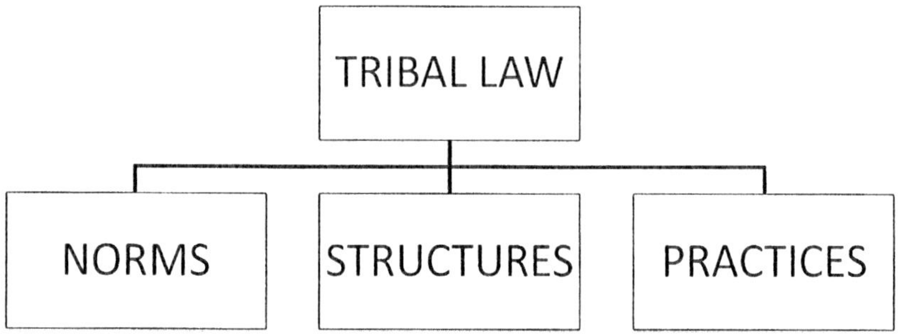

For our purposes, *norms*, *structures*, and *practices* can be defined as follows:

- *Norms* are those values and beliefs held by a community about the proper and improper ways to act toward other people, places, and things. In law, there are two kinds of norms:
  - *Substantive norms:* the norms about everyday life that legal actors think about when deciding how to handle a dispute or wrongdoing (e.g., "Do not murder," "Do not steal")
  - *Procedural norms:* the norms that legal actors must themselves follow when handling a dispute (for example, in Anglo-American trials, a lawyer is not allowed to talk to members of the jury outside the courtroom before the trial has ended; otherwise, the jurors might be biased and their decision unfair)
- *Structures* are the roles played by people during the operation of a legal system and the institutions in which those operations occur. These "structures" seem relatively permanent and do not usually change very much over time. Thus, the roles of lawyer, judge, jury, witness, bailiff, defendant, and plaintiff, as well as the institutions of the U.S. Congress, the Supreme Court, the trial court, and the prison, can all be understood as parts of the structure of the Anglo-American legal system.
- *Practices* are what legal actors actually do when undertaking the operations of the legal system. In some legal systems, the practices of filing written complaints in court, making oral arguments, and examining witnesses are all practices of lawyers. Police practices include obtaining search warrants, interrogating suspects, making arrests, and testifying in court.

It is possible to look at any legal system in any society and see it as the interaction between legal norms, structures, or practices. Those norms in a society that are enforced by legal structures and practices are thus "legal" norms. Likewise, those structures that are involved in the enforcement of legal norms, through the use of legal practices, are "legal" structures, and so on. The norms, structures, and practices that are considered legal may differ depending on the culture and society from which they come. With this understanding of law and legal systems, we can now discuss why it is important to study law generally, and more specifically why it is important to study tribal law.

Why Study Law?

A good rationale for studying law comes if we understand what the law means to the many people quoted in this book. Most of the authors whose works are included in this text had some formal training in and experience with the philosophies and practices of Anglo-American law. In most instances, this training and experience is matched by their understanding of the unique legal heritages of their tribal communities.

For jurists trained and experienced in Anglo-American law, the law is a fundamental element organizing American society and defining American identity. For them, the term *law* means the way in which societies express who they are and the ways of life they value as a people. Certainly there are ways of life and values that are not expressed by the laws of the United States. For example, there are U.S. citizens who identify themselves as Catholics, and Catholics share values that concern how they live their lives—what they do on Sundays, how they express their faith in their God, and even what they eat, wear, read, and watch on television. There are other U.S. citizens who identify themselves as Jews and whose values and ways of life lead them to believe and do very different things than what Catholics do. Yet these different groups of citizens recognize themselves and each other as Americans because they also share values and ways of life expressed in the laws and the legal systems of the United States. People in these groups have no problem being Catholic or Jewish and still being American at the same time.

Some people in America complain that U.S. laws do not represent their values. We hear this complaint when people protest the actions of the U.S. Supreme Court or Congress about such issues as abortion, the death penalty, or prayer in school. But it is precisely because Americans and jurists in Anglo-American law think the law *should* represent their values that they will argue with each other for changes to laws that they feel are unjust, unfair, or even unconstitutional.

"Studying law," for Anglo-American jurists, means studying the fundamental elements of American social organization and identity. It also means evaluating whether the norms, practices, and structures that make up the U.S. legal system interact in a way that protects the valued ways of life of all American citizens. Moreover, it means evaluating whether the political and legal leaders are exercising their power and authority in ways that actually reflect and protect the values and ways of life of all American people.

When legal scholars trained in Anglo-American law turn to studying the law of other societies, they are usually looking for many of the same things. First, they might explore just the norms, practices, and structures that make up the official legal system. They may also study the ways in which political and legal leaders use the legal system to exercise their power and authority.

But they might also be interested in understanding a more fundamental law of that society. For example, they might want to know how the people of that society identify themselves as a people and how they express the ways of life they value. Legal scholars exploring these questions are also often interested in evaluating whether a society's official legal system and its leaders are effective in representing all its members and protecting all their valued life ways.

It would seem that people trained in Anglo-American law would thus understand and appreciate the laws of tribal people. Unfortunately, this often has not been the case. In general, people trained in Anglo-American law have not understood or respected the laws of tribal people. Only more recently, with an increase in the numbers of Indian lawyers and Indian legal scholars, has understanding and appreciation of tribal law in North America improved. Studying tribal law is a critical first step in correcting the negative work on tribal law. Tribal law has much to offer legal scholarship in general, and much positive work has yet to be accomplished. Such studies are an important part of the effort to help ensure that tribal communities have strong legal systems that incorporate their members' values.

Anglo-American legal scholars and practitioners have historically failed to recognize the law of American Indian and Alaska Native societies. Their legal training has given them an understanding of law as an expression of a people's fundamental values, but because of prejudicial, ethnocentric beliefs, they have not always been able to see how these tribal societies could have a legal system that did not mirror systems based on Anglo-American or European law.

One of the problems has to do with the fact that Anglo-American scholars and practitioners trained in Anglo-American law are taught to see law as separate and distinct from religion, culture, and other aspects of everyday life. Consequently, they are often unable to see law in societies where there might not be the same kind of separations between law, life, and religion. Remember that law in the United States serves as a main unifying identity of Americans as a people, primarily because American citizens usually have very different ethnic, religious, and cultural backgrounds. If the law of the United States were not separate from religion (at least in principle, if not always in practice), the religion and culture of some citizens would be imposed on others. This imposition is exactly what the founders of the United States were trying to escape in Europe.

Unfortunately, the ideals of tolerance and respect have not always been practiced in Anglo-American law in its treatment of Indian tribes. Tribal nations do not always distinguish law from spiritual beliefs and cultural practices, which can be confusing to non-Natives. And because Anglo-American legal scholars did not recognize tribal government structures, tribes were seen by non-Indians as being "lawless." Viewing tribal nations as lawless provided the United States with justification for imposing its own legal standards and norms on tribes.

On the few occasions when these scholars and practitioners did recognize Indian tribes as having something like law, they very often claimed this law to be inferior to those in the Anglo-American legal system. Characterizing Indian tribal law as "savage" or "backward," Anglo-American jurists justified U.S. policies designed to diminish the norms, structures, and practices that made up the culture and identity of Indian tribes. They used this as justification for "civilizing" Indians by forcing them to live according to Anglo-American ways of life. This was at least part of the thinking behind the federal policies and legislation that led to the allotment of tribal lands and the establishment of Indian boarding schools. In all these actions, agents of the federal government argued that it would be in the best interest of Indians if they were forced out of using their "irrational" traditions, languages, and land-use practices and made to assimilate (or adopt) the values, practices, and laws of Anglo-American society. That is, these practices were put in place to destroy tribal law and unique tribal identities and to replace them with U.S. norms, structures, and practices.

Fortunately, the idea that American Indian and Alaska Native tribes and communities have no law or only inferior law is being taken less and less seriously. This is largely because of the increase in the numbers of legal scholars, practitioners, and legislators of American Indian descent. Indian jurists, who very often have one foot in the world of their tribe and the other in the non-tribal world, are taking what they have learned from their Anglo-American legal studies and using it for the benefit of their tribe. For them, as well as for the non-Indian legal professionals working in Indian Country, this project has meant understanding that law is an expression of the unique values and social identity of tribal people that does not have to look like Anglo-American law. Ottawa legal scholar Matthew L. M. Fletcher explains:

> Tribal courts and tribal common law have made an impressive comeback in the latter half of the 20th century and beyond. Well over 200 tribes now have a functioning tribal court system and most of the remaining tribes are in the process of developing a tribal court system. And these tribal courts are not necessarily copies of state and federal courts.[3]

How to Study Tribal Legal Systems

The tribal jurist starts first by researching the norms, structures, and practices of the tribe in order to discover the fundamental values of tribal members and their identity as a tribe. When this research concerns norms, structures, and practices that express the values and identity of a society, it results in an understanding of the law of the tribe. This is true even when that law is expressed as elements of tribal custom, tradition, and culture that look nothing like the norms, structure, and practices of Anglo-American law.

Focusing on norms, structures, and practices is one good way to study
tribal legal systems. It is also a way to review research that has been done by
European and Euro-American scholars claiming to describe these systems. We
can even see how these scholars sometimes misunderstand and misrepresent
tribal law in their work because they fail to properly study all three of its parts
and how they interrelate. Ethnocentrism often prevents academics from seeing legal systems in tribes when they do not look like the European and Euro-
American justice systems they were trained in.

To understand how this is possible, consider the following statement
regarding the Ojibwa people:

> All old men are called 'gʉttci anʉcʉnaːbe "ancient, elder," and are accorded
> a conventional respect. Along with all of the mature males of the village,
> they constitute the council, the "smoking place." Councils are called by
> any interested citizen to discuss anything that may appeal to him as of
> communal import. . . . The council arrives at some general agreement,
> but it can discipline dissenters in no other way than by tacit ostracism. A
> persistent dissenter can break way with impunity, living isolated or estab-
> lishing another village. There is no social instrument to pursue him; only
> the medicine of the jealous "wise man."[4]

We can see that the Ojibwa did (and still do) have their own traditional
system for resolving disputes. The Ojibwa system plays the same important
role that European legal systems played in their societies. Ethnocentric scholars who only look for structures like courts with judges and codes, and for
practices like trials and imprisonment, would totally miss these uniquely
Ojibwa legal traditions and might misrepresent the Ojibwa as having no law
at all. When studying tribal legal systems, it is very important not only to
examine tribal norms, structures, or practices but also to develop a picture of
how they all interact. If you fail to do this, you can run into misunderstandings and misrepresentations.

It is also the case that given both the incredible cultural diversity of Native
peoples in the United States, Canada, and other countries around the world
and the legacies of colonization, what law looks like for one tribal nation is
often very different than what law looks like in another. Thus, for example,
in some tribal communities, elders and other traditional leaders are asked to
participate in adversarial courts as witnesses or consultants to a tribal judge.
In other tribes, special legal structures have been designed to address disputes
by relying on norms and practices more consistent with the tribe's unique legal
heritage. In still others, an intertribal court has been set up so that certain kinds
of conflicts and disputes are addressed by judges and rules devised by agree-

ment among several historically independent tribal nations. It is certainly true that most tribal nations with legal systems like these have constitutions that authorize the creation of tribal councils charged with the responsibility of drafting and enacting tribal laws. Their constitutions also authorize the creation of courts in which those laws are argued by lawyers and tribal judges, and the laws are then enforced by tribal police who arrest offenders and monitor tribal jails. Thus there are some common norms, structures, and practices among the laws of these tribes. And when these legal systems are put in place, they change the ways in which the tribe's traditional legal system operates. But it is very important to note that, alongside those common threads, each tribe's unique legal heritage persists, and continues to shape and be shaped by the operation of their contemporary tribal law.

So, when we study contemporary tribal legal systems, it is very important neither to ignore a tribal nation's unique legal heritage nor to study *only* the tribe's traditional law. To do the latter would overlook the tribes' new legal system simply because it is not part of their heritage. This approach ignores the fact that many tribal members are affected by the new legal system, no matter how foreign its origins may be. Therefore, the approach we take is to suggest that it is critical to develop a good understanding of the legal norms, structures, and practices of both the tribe's traditional legal system and its newer legal system. Only by studying all of these elements of tribal law will it be possible to understand how the entire legal systems of tribal nations serve their communities' interests and strengthen their sovereignty.

Where and How to Look for Tribal Legal Systems

There are three major resources for finding tribal law: contemporary legal documents, traditions and oral law, and academic studies.

The first suggested resource is one that anyone trained in Anglo-American law would use (even to study non-Native law): legal documents, including tribal constitutions, legislation, and tribal court case opinions. In order to find the most up-to-date and authoritative information on tribal legal systems, we must first look to the contemporary tribal legal documents in which both traditional and nontraditional legal norms, structures, and practices are being represented and relied upon by tribal lawyers, legislators, and judges in the exercise of their tribal legal authority. This will provide some of the best information about the ways in which the traditional legal system and the newer legal systems of the tribe interact. Later, we will provide examples of tribal legal documents, including constitutions and codes, that will demonstrate how tribal nations are balancing their unique legal heritage and their contemporary concerns.

The second source for tribal law is not one that non-Native lawyers would typically take, but one that should be familiar to almost any member of a tribal nation. One of the most important—but too often and easily overlooked— places to look for tribal legal systems is not a "place" at all, but people. There are many people in any tribal community who have knowledge about the traditional and contemporary ways of life in the community. These elders and other community members can be sources of information about legal norms, structures, and practices. They can also give useful information about how effectively legal traditions are being used in combination with the newer tribal legal systems. Community members often have an important perspective on how their traditional and contemporary ways of life are being respected or ignored in the actual operation of their tribal legal system. It is crucial that the study of tribal legal systems include talking with community members, because ultimately it is their values and lives that are affected by those systems.

The third resource we suggest for finding tribal law is the one that is perhaps the most controversial: academic studies of tribal legal systems and other aspects of tribal life. These sources are controversial because they are often the work of anthropologists and other non-Native social scientists who are viewed by some tribal peoples as having misapplied or misrepresented their cultural heritage. We are well aware of this and ultimately feel that only members of the particular tribe being represented in those studies can adequately judge the value of the research in question. Nonetheless, it has been our experience that such research can be valuable.

Indeed, we believe that it is not only academic research directly examining a tribe's traditional and contemporary legal systems that can serve as a good source for finding tribal law. In addition, academic research that studies tribal oral traditions, social structures, ceremonial practices, and members' everyday lives can be equally significant sources (again, as determined by tribal members).

To give one example, consider a potentially helpful study that describes a tribe's ceremonial system, revealing that certain men or women were responsible for the proper performance of a particular ceremony. Say this research also reveals that when a tribal member violates this ceremony (maybe by misusing a headdress or altar), that person would be brought before those leaders. Like a judge (though not exactly), these leaders would give guidance to this person on how to act properly in the future. By describing these aspects of the norms, structures, and practices involved in this ceremonial performance, a study like this one would reveal important operations of this tribe's system for handling social violations—an important part of the work of any legal system. Laguna author Leslie Marmon Silko writes, "[T]here is no better way to uncover the deepest values of a culture than to observe the operation of that culture's system of justice."[5]

Other information might be found by looking at research that describes a tribe's kinship system or the ways in which a tribal community divides people into groups of relations. For example, if a tribe's kinship system groups people into matrilineal clans, these people might have certain duties and obligations to each other requiring them to share food, to help in performing clan ceremonies, or to take care of clan children and elders. If two people from the same clan are in a dispute, perhaps because one feels that the other violated some of these duties and obligations, the clan leader may be expected by the tribes' kinship system to help them resolve that dispute. Studying kinship in this way can thus also reveal aspects of tribal legal systems.

By studying the academic research conducted on all aspects of tribal life, it is possible to begin to understand a tribe's legal norms, structures, and practices, whether they are similar to or different than European and Anglo-American laws and legal systems. Of course, using academic research as a source of information must be done carefully. Very often these scholars lacked an understanding of tribal life, or were otherwise biased, so they did not accurately describe the norms, structures, and practices that contributed to tribal legal heritages. Nonetheless, academic research can be a good source of information if it is recognized that it usually tells a part of the story or history. For a student of tribal law to succeed using academic research, he or she must analyze different academic resources on the same tribe, while also talking with tribal members about their own understanding of their tribal legal traditions.

In the next chapter, we will explore in greater detail the three different sources for finding tribal law.

Questions

1. What are some advantages to using anthropology and sociology to study tribal law? What are some disadvantages?
2. How would you go about studying tribal law through the people in a community? What would be involved in embarking on such a process?
3. Besides family law, where and how could kinship structures be applied to tribal judicial systems?

In Your Community

1. List some norms, structures, and practices for your own tribe.
2. What is the word for "law" in your language? Does the word for "law" or "justice" give you any insight into the beliefs of your tribe?
3. Identify the existing legal structures that are in active use in your community (district court, appellate court, peacemaker court, etc.).

Glossary

Anglo-American: Someone or something of English American origin. The Anglo-American legal system is the system used by the majority of non-Indian legal systems operating in the United States today.

Assimilate: To make similar; to cause to resemble. A tribal government is "assimilated" when it looks and operates exactly like an Anglo-American government.

Clan: A social group made up of a number of families with a common ancestor. Matrilineal clans are organized on the basis of descent through female ancestors. Patrilineal clans are organized on the basis of descent through male ancestors.

Ethnocentric: Belief in the superiority of one's own ethnic group.

Jurist: A person who works in the field of law such as scholars, lawyers, and judges.

Kinship: Biological and social relationships.

Legal actor: A person who participates in the legal system.

Legal system: Any system for addressing antisocial behavior or resolving disputes.

Norms: Values and beliefs held by a community about the proper and improper ways to act toward other people, places, and things. See also *procedural norms* and *substantive norms*.

Ostracism: Banishment from society.

Practices: What legal actors actually do when undertaking the operations of the legal system.

Procedural norms: The norms that legal actors must themselves follow when handling a dispute.

Promontory: High point; prominent place.

Structures: The roles played by people during the operation of a legal system and the institutions in which those operations occur.

Substantive norms: The norms about everyday life that legal actors think about when deciding how to handle a dispute or wrongdoing (e.g., "Do not murder," "Do not steal").

Tribal sovereignty: The power of a tribal people to express their own norms, practices, and structures.

Suggested Further Reading

Russel L. Barsh, *The Nature and Spirit of North American Political Systems*, 10 American Indian Quarterly 181 (1986).

Robert B. Porter, *The Tribal Law and Governance Conference: A Step towards the Development of Tribal Law Scholarship*, 7 Kansas Journal of Law and Public Policy 1 (1997).

Wenona T. Singel, *Cultural Sovereignty and Transplanted Law*, 15 Kansas Journal of Law and Public Policy 357 (2006).

Notes

1. Carey N. Vicenti, *The Reemergence of Tribal Society and Traditional Justice Systems*, 79 Judicature 134, 137 (1995).

2. Frank Pommersheim, *Braid of Feathers: American Indian Law and Contemporary Tribal Life* 97 (1995).

3. Matthew L. M. Fletcher, *"A Perfect Copy": Indian Culture and Tribal Law*, 2 Yellow Medicine Review 95–118 (2007).

4. Ruth Landes, *Ojibwa Sociology* (1937).

5. Leslie Marmon Silko, *Yellow Woman and a Beauty of Spirit: Essays on Native American Life Today* 20 (1996).

CHAPTER 2

Studying Tribal Law and Contemporary Tribal Legal Documents

"written laws,"

AS DESCRIBED in the previous chapter, perhaps the best place to begin a study of tribal legal systems is to review the most current body of written laws of the tribe that is the object of your investigation. These existing laws often provide guidance as to the contemporary norms, practices, and structures that members of the tribe have, over the years, felt it important to enshrine, or include, in the basic texts that make up their legal system. These include a tribe's constitution, its legislation (codes, statutes, ordinances, and resolutions), and its case opinions. It is true, however, that contemporary tribal laws do not always reflect the actual legal principles of the tribal communities. As this textbook will explore later, the current laws of some tribes originated from outside sources, such as the U.S. government or non-Indian attorneys. Therefore, contemporary tribal documents should be approached with some caution and studied in a larger context.

The written tribal laws used in this textbook can be divided into three general categories:

1. *Constitutions:* Most tribal governments have a written constitution that provides the foundation for all other aspects of their legal system, including their statutory and case laws. Generally speaking, if a tribe's statutory or case law conflicts with the terms of the tribe's written constitution, that

statutory or case will be considered unconstitutional and therefore invalid.

2. *Statutory law:* Tribal legislatures, like all legislatures, regularly pass laws in accordance with the powers and limitations spelled out in their constitution. These laws may be called *statutes*, *codes*, *ordinances*, or *resolutions*, but can generally be referred to as a tribe's "statutory law."

3. *Case law:* Some tribes have courts that issue written opinions when they decide cases. These written opinions, which often interpret the force and effect of a tribe's constitution or statutory law and apply them to the facts of the case they are deciding, is what is often called tribal "case law."

Each of these textual forms of tribal law is valuable for different reasons. Tribal constitutions are important for revealing the fundamental principles that bind the tribe—though again, many tribal constitutions reflect the heavy influence of non-Native legal sources (e.g., the Bureau of Indian Affairs or other federal agencies). Tribal statutory law or legislation is valuable because it reveals particular substantive areas of tribal life for which the tribe has deemed it necessary to create and enact written law. This might include laws related to crime, business development, environmental protection, family relations, and so forth. Finally, tribal case law is valuable because it sheds light on how tribal judges are applying the other kinds of law (constitutions, statutory law, other cases, as well as traditional law) to the lives and actions of tribal members. Because a court decision arises out of a particular set of facts, it is possible to understand how the laws are used in real-life situations of tribal members and the people they come in contact with.

Though we will be considering some examples of tribal constitutions and statutory law, case law will be the most used form of tribal law throughout this text to illustrate fundamental issues concerning contemporary tribal legal studies. This is true because tribal judges who write decisions often describe a specific set of circumstances in the lives of their fellow tribal members, explain the relevant statutory or constitutional law that governs tribal life, and then provide a decision that applies those laws to the facts of the circumstances of tribal disputes. Because they provide a picture of not only tribal law but also the complex details of everyday tribal life, tribal case opinions are particularly valuable for the purposes of a tribal legal studies text, and thus will be given the most attention in this one.

The first excerpt below is from the Constitutions and Bylaws of the Nez Perce Tribe, and it includes the preamble, purpose, qualifications for membership, and formation of the General Council of the Tribe. The original version of the Nez Perce Tribal Constitution was ratified by the General Council in 1948. It has since been amended five times, most recently in 1999. As you read this excerpt, consider how the provisions of the Nez Perce Constitution relate to the organization of your tribe, or a tribe near where you live. Are there similarities and differences?

CONSTITUTION AND BYLAWS

The Nez Perce Tribe

Preamble

We, the members of the Nez Perce Tribe, in order to exercise our tribal rights and promote our common welfare, do hereby establish this Constitution and Bylaws.

Article I: Purpose

The purpose of this Constitution and Bylaws shall be to protect and promote the interests of the Nez Perce Indians to develop cooperative relations with the Bureau of Indian Affairs and other federal agencies, and to cooperate with the State and local governments.

Article II: Name

This tribal organization shall be called "The Nez Perce Tribe."

Article III: Territory

The jurisdiction of the Nez Perce Tribe shall extend to all lands within the original confines of the Nez Perce reservation boundaries as established by treaty; and extra-territorial jurisdiction for the purposes of protecting the rights of the Nez Perce Tribe as guaranteed by treaties with the United States of America; and also to such other lands as may be hereafter acquired by or for the Nez Perce Indians of Idaho.

Article IV: Membership

Section 1.

The membership of the Nez Perce Tribe shall consist as follows, provided they have not lost or do not hereafter lose their membership under the terms of any tribal membership ordinance:

(A) All persons whose names appear on the official Nez Perce Tribal Membership Roll of December 3, 1956, as corrected by any action of the Secretary of the Interior.

(B) All children who are of at least one-fourth (¼) degree Nez Perce Indian ancestry born to a member of the Nez Perce Tribe, provided that an application for enrollment is filed with the Nez Perce Tribal Executive Committee within eighteen (18) years after birth.

(C) Person adopted into the Tribe under the terms of a tribal membership ordinance.

Section 2.

The Executive Committee of the Tribe shall have power to make rules, subject to approval by the Secretary of the Interior or his authorized representative, governing the adoption of new members or the termination of membership in the Tribe.

Article V: The Tribal General Council

Section 1.

The qualified voters of the Tribe as defined in Section 5 of this Article, shall constitute the Tribal General Council. There shall be two meetings of the Tribal General Council annually, which shall take place on the first Friday and Saturday in May and on the last Friday and Saturday in September.

Section 2.

The Tribal General Council shall on the first day of the May, 1983 Tribal General Council meeting, upon being called to order by the Chairman of the Tribal General Council, elect a Chairman, a Secretary, three (3) Election Judges and a Resolutions Committee of not more than four (4) members. Election of Tribal General Council officers shall thereafter be held on the first day of September Tribal General Council meeting. Provided however, that the terms of the adoption of this amendment, shall be extended until the election of their successors in September, 1984.

Section 3.

The officers of the Tribal General Council, elected under Section 2 of this Article, shall hold office for one year and until their successors have qualified.

Section 4.

(A) It shall be the duty of the Chairman of the Tribal General Council to preside over meetings of the Tribal General Council.

(B) It shall be the duty of the Secretary of the Tribal General Council to take minutes and record all action of the Tribal General Council.

(C) It shall be the duty of the Chairman and the Secretary of the Tribal General Council to prepare the agenda for every meeting of the Tribal General Council subject to amendment from the floor.

(D) It shall be the duty of the Election Judges to pass on the eligibility of members to vote in the General Council, to supervise all elections and decide all election disputes, subject to the provisions of any Tribal Election Ordinance, and to certify the election results as attested to by the Chairman of the Tribal General Council.

Section 5.

Any enrolled member of the Nez Perce Tribe who is eighteen or over shall be entitled to vote in General Council Meetings or Elections.

Section 6.

The Resolutions Committee shall have the power, between meetings of the General Council, to meet for a total of not to exceed ten days annually for the purpose of considering suggestions, problems and complaints from the people concerning tribal affairs. If the Resolutions Committee find any such suggestions, problem or complaint to merit its presentation to the Nez Perce Tribal Executive Committee, it shall do so. The Nez Perce Tribal Executive Committee shall be required to place such item or items on the agenda of its next regular meeting or to call a special meeting for the consideration of such item or items. The item or items shall be automatically placed on the agenda of each regular NPTEC meeting thereafter until final disposition has been made. A report in writing of the action taken at each meeting shall be mailed or delivered to each member of the Resolutions Committee within seven (7) days after each meeting. Nothing herein contained shall be construed as depriving a member of the right to appeal directly to the Nez Perce Tribal Executive Committee.

The next excerpt comes from a tribal statute from the Susanville Indian Rancheria in northeastern California. Tribal statutes are sometimes referred to as *ordinances* or *codes*. As with constitutions, tribal statutes often start with a preamble, explaining what the tribal government is attempting to do in passing this law and with what authority. It is then followed by a list of definitions to help tribal officials and citizens understand the law when they want to act in ways that might be affected by its terms. This excerpt concludes with a statement of the policy considerations that were made by the tribal General Council when drafting and passing this statute.

The excerpt thus reveals that this statutory law was drafted and passed by the General Council of the tribe in 1969, pursuant to the constitution and bylaws of the Susanville Indian Rancheria, for the purpose of regulating the assignment and use of tribal lands within the boundaries of the rancheria's reservation. The right to control the use and distribution of land is a fundamental element of the sovereign powers of any government. The Susanville Indian Rancheria Assignment Ordinance is a good example of how one tribal government is seeking to exercise that sovereign authority through the statutory law.

ASSIGNMENT ORDINANCE

Susanville Indian Rancheria]

I. Preamble

The General Council hereby enacts this assignment ordinance in accordance with Article V, Section 1, of the Constitution and Bylaws of the Susanville Indian Rancheria, Lassen County, California, approved by the Secretary of the Interior on March 10, 1969.

II. Definitions

Wherever used in this assignment ordinance the terms defined in this Article shall have the following meaning:

A. *Assignment* means a formal right to use Rancheria land subject to the conditions set forth in this assignment ordinance.

B. *Assignee* refers to the holder of an assignment.

C. *Area Director* means the Area Director, Bureau of Indian Affairs, Sacramento Area Office, Sacramento, California, who is the authorized representative of the Secretary of the Interior.

III. General Assignment Policy

A. Assignments made and approved pursuant to the Assignment Ordinance of January 12, 1963, and not relinquished or canceled are recognized as binding and are hereby ratified.

B. An assignment does not vest title to assigned land in the assignee but is a use right granted to him by the General Council, which may not be sold or inherited and which terminates upon relinquishment or cancellation of the assignment or upon the death of the assignee.

C. An assignment may not be transferred, assigned, or exchanged without the approval of the General Council.

D. In the event of an assignee's death, the General Council shall give preference in reassignment of the property to the surviving spouse or children provided they are otherwise eligible to receive an assignment under the provisions of this assignment ordinance. A surviving spouse who is ineligible for an assignment under the provision of this assignment ordinance but who is responsible for the care of minor children shall be granted the privilege of occupancy of the property for such period of time as determined proper by the General Council.

E. An assignee may relinquish his assignment at any time by giving written notice to the Business Committee.

F. Leases, easements or rights-of-way of Rancheria lands are subject to Federal laws and regulations and may be granted only with the consent of the General Council and the approval of the Secretary of the Interior or his authorized representative.

G. Improvements of the following character placed on the assigned land by the assignee shall be considered as personal property which may be removed, sold, bequeathed, willed or inherited at the discretion of the assignee: houses, garages, barns, sheds, interior fences, crops, household items and personal belongings. Other improvements such as exterior fences, underground water and sewage systems, trees shrubs, and betterments of similar nature attached to the land, even though placed on the property by the assignee, shall be considered part of the real property belonging with the land and shall remain on the assignment unless their removal is authorized by the General Council.

H. Houses originally constructed by the Government and located on assignments become a part of the personal property belonging to the assignee living in these houses.

I. If the assignment is relinquished or canceled, the removable improvements of the assignee defined in paragraphs G and H of this Article must be removed or otherwise disposed of within one hundred and eighty (180) days after formal written notice to him by the Business Committee; otherwise said improvements become a part of the real property, title in them vests with the land, and they become available for assignment along with the land.

J. During the absence of the assignee, said assignee may with the prior approval of the General Council allow another Indian who is eligible to receive vacant promises for a period not to exceed one year; provided, that the General Council may grant successive extensions of like duration. The assignee at his discretion may or may not charge the approved occupant rent for the use of the premises under terms mutually agreed upon between them.

K. The General Council may in its discretion grant privileges of temporary occupancy to Indians not having a valid assignment or to such other classes of persons as may be defined by the General Council. Terms of such temporary occupancy shall be defined by the General Council and the approved occupant; provided, that said terms shall be reduced to writing and shall include the following covenants:

1. That the approved occupant agrees to pay a certain monthly rental to the Secretary-Treasurer for deposit in the Rancheria account.
2. That the approved occupant agrees not to commit any of the violations set forth in Paragraph A, Article VI (Procedures for Canceling Assignments and Removing Persons from Rancheria), of this assignment ordinance.
3. That any violations of the foregoing two covenants shall be grounds for removal of the approved occupant in accordance with provisions of this assignment ordinance.
4. That the approved occupant may attend all meetings of the General Council as a guest and without voting privileges.

L. Except for those persons who are qualified under paragraphs D, J, or K of this Article or who are in residence with an assignee as one of the members of that assignee's household, no person shall reside on the Rancheria who is not eligible for assignment under provisions of this assignment ordinance. All persons in residence on the Rancheria in violation of this prohibition are hereby declared to be trespassers.

The next excerpt comes from an Alaska Native tribal environmental statute. When the Native Village of Venetie codified its natural resources law in 1994, it included interviews with community elders in order to establish legislative intent. Consider how these statements from the elders provide context for the formal statutory language.

PROTECTION OF THE ENVIRONMENT AND NATURAL RESOURCES ORDINANCE (94-93)

Native Village of Venetie Tribal Government

WHEREAS, the Native Village of Venetie Tribal Government (IRA), exercising its inherent authority as confirmed by Article III, "Governing Body," of its Constitution, desires to protect the environment and natural resources of the areas used by members of the Tribe;

NOW THEREFORE BE IT RESOLVED THAT the Native Village of Venetie Tribal Government Ordains and Enacts the following Tribal Ordinance:

Section 1. Explanation by Tribal Members

(b) *Josesph Tritt:* Do you think the Tribe should protect lakes, streams and creeks?

Lincoln Tritt: Yes. I think it is very important because life out here is all a cycle. Every little piece, living thing out there makes the circle whole. You get dd [*sic*] of the microscopic plants from the water and the fish got nothing to eat. So your [*sic*] destroying the good part of the life cycle and all these things that are out there are not a nuisance or anything. They are there to do their part in keeping life forms. If we interfere with that, we interfere with life.

Josesph Tritt: Explain how different kind of contamination or pollution can have on some small game, fish and larger animals like caribou, moose, bear and sheep. Let me rephrase that question. Compared to when you were much younger does waste material in surrounding villages becoming a problem?

Lincoln Tritt: When I was younger, when we go out hunt, camp, or whatever, we go out there and we eat the meat or fish, or whatever, and we could just leave the bone there, cause we know eventually they will decompose and go back into the ground. But then later on, when they start introducing plastics, cans, and stuff like that, well, we did the same thing with them. We left them there to deteriorate, but then we came back about 20 years later and they were still there. Then we start realizing that these things don't go away, and by the time we found out, we had garbage piled all over the place.

(c) *Josesph Tritt:* Describe or explain a way our people could keep their traditional hunting and fishing, or trapping areas clean?

Lincoln Tritt: One thing is, in these past 50 or 60 years or something, since the white man started teaching us, they have always taught us that our ways were wrong. So we have to get back to learning our own system. We have to get back our system, the way our people fought and solve things and work. Other words, we have to change our whole values around to where we start valuing ourselves, our society, and most of all the belief and the great spirit that our people had. That was the one thing that keep them alive all these years.

(d) *Josesph Tritt:* Do you think in 20 to 30 years from now, we as a Tribe will have more problem with waste and contamination to our land?

Lincoln Tritt: There's no other way. There is no way around it, unless we can do something now. It's always going to, grow. Like I said, there's no way we can make all these garbage and all these contaminants disappear. You can move them around, but it'll always be there. And everyday, every year your adding more and more and it's going to be one big problem.

(e) *Josesph Tritt:* Do you think the Tribe should control surface rights when constructing building or individual housing units? Or, should those rights be given to granting agencies like the State of Alaska, Federal, or Agency Branch?

Lincoln Tritt: I think the Tribes should do that because the Tribes know the land more than any of these Federal and State agencies. We have proof that many times we came up with a lot of things that they did not even think about. So, I think the Tribe should have strict control on all these, because they are very aware of their land.

(f) *Josesph Tritt:* Describe or explain a way our people could keep their traditional hunting, fishing, or trapping areas clean.

William Tritt: Why don't they pick up after themselves? Everybody should take responsibility. We went to "Vatr'agwangwaii" that time and we took along cokes and candies. We brought back the empty cans and empty candy wrappers and I put them into a plastic bag and brought them back in my pack. Just simple things. Just throwing the cans away anywhere just like that, I think that is too much. That is not protecting the environment.

(g) *Josesph Tritt:* In general area of discussion, what do you think about our land and traditional sites? What would be your greatest concern? And could you explain in a short statement what area on the land is your greatest concern?

William Tritt: Like I said before, our land is very sacred to us. Our forefathers, they keep the land the way God made it for us. It is now up to us to preserve our land and historical sites and our culture.

(i) *Josesph Tritt:* Describe or explain a way our people could keep their traditional hunting, trapping, and fishing areas clean.

Ernest Erick: Do not throw things into the water. Pick up your fish when you are done. Clean up the area so the next person could use it. Pull out your fishing traps. Clean up the area. Respect it because your forefathers has used the area. I already explained it in Gwich'in, but I am explaining it in English too, just in case. Trapping area, fishing area, pick up your empty oil containers, your empty gas container. Pick up your Styrofoam cups. Clean the area.

(l) *Amos Frank:* If the non-resident go fishing, hunting, or trapping, we need to talk to them about the traditional law and how to take care of themselves and he or she need to know about the native rules and what he need to know how to survivor. All that they need to know and about the law and regulation and punishment, or not really punishment, but scold them to remember, not to break any law or regulations. . . . We should put a big sign that will say, "Bring your trash back to village."

(p) *Josesph Tritt:* Compared to when you were much younger, are waste material in the areas surrounding the village becoming a problem?

Gideon James: Yes, there again I remembered when I was a little boy, I remembered that there is hardly any trash or hardly any waste that I can recall. Anything today that is at our dump site, or anywhere in our trash cans are brought to us from outside. There is a lot of stuff that are in our dump site. Sometimes it needs to be controlled as far as how to get rid of it and how we control which items need to be thrown away. But here again, if we continue just wait until the State or Federal Government to do something about this we are wrong, you know. We must as a land owner, we must protect ourselves from this type of a mismanagement of our land, or you know, danger, or contaminate our land. So we must identify this type of different type of waste materials and start controlling this waste materials in this areas that we used for dump sites. And lots of things that I said but enough on the dump site part that are brought to us from the outside and lots of things that are recyclable we can always send them back to where they come from.

(q) *Josesph Tritt:* What do you think about teaching our kids in school about recyclable materials?

Gideon James: When I was a little boy, like I said, there was hardly any trash that I remembered around the village. This is about 30 years ago, over 30 years ago. 40 years has past now that you look at our dump sites. There has been a huge amount of trash that been accumulated. So, I don't hold the Tribes, or I don't blame the Tribes for accumulating that type of trash in the immediate area. But, I blame the influence on the outside that have make it happens. So and actually half of the blame lays with the people that are responsible for creating some of these trash that we have today. So, and in knowing that explain that I know for the next 30 or 40 years from now our kids today that are 10, 12, or 13 years old will have to deal with it in next 40 or 50 years from now. So, right now, we must introduce to our school right here in Arctic Village and Venetie that we need to explain to our kids some of these recyclable materials are and identify. I need to make them aware that this type of recyclable materials we will keep it to minimum over the years and keep it in school, so by the time we get to adulthood, and also by the time they get out of school, and also by the time they start their life apparently that these things take to minimum and worst part is the dump. So, and I think if we don't do that, so we are going to continue to accumulate lots of trash and eventually will cause contamination so it is good that we must introduce this recyclable materials for school.

(s) *Ernest Erick:* We have to keep the water and air clean. If we stand up with one another and have respect for our land then we will have a clean or happy air and water. If we as the Tribal Government Tribes and work together and keep our land and air clean and we could do it and really have respect for our land and protect our land. We should protect all the streams and creeks and keep it clean we will have better life to live on.

Edward Sam: If we don't do it and if we don't take care of it now or keep the land clean and later on in the future our children will end up with the trash or what? That is not very nice.

(u) *Edward Sam:* Well, it will be pretty hard to tell people to keep the area clean. We just can't make a person do it. If you throw a cigarette out on the street and expect you to pick it back up, or I can't make you to pick up the cigarette butt right? It is a individual commitment and you got to trust somebody on this one. It got to be an individual commitment. Set a strict rules. Who ever go out trapping and I make a strict rules and tell the person about the rules. And it is up to that person to keep the area keep. We just can't tell each individual to pick up your trash, or bring your trash back to the village, so let us make strict rules. We will not know where all he or she will travel in the woods. If we tried to tell him about the trash and he might tell us to leave him alone or might say keep away from me. So that is why you make sure it is all right for a individual to know that he or she should know about the strict rules is to clean up the area.

(v) *Ernest Erick:* Compared to when you were much younger, are waste material in this area in the village becoming a problem?

Pete Peter: Yes. That is because there was no Ordinance on littering. That was the attitude towards littering. There was no law against it and people dump their trash even before they hit the dump site. It was okay like. That was the attitude a long time ago. This was because there was no Ordinances back then. If we write an Ordinances and have it all written down, we will not have that problem.

Section 2. Findings

The Native Village of Venetie Tribal Government (IRA) ("Tribal Council") finds that:

a. It has governmental authority over the lands within the boundaries of the Venetie Reservation;
b. It owns in fee simple title the lands within the boundaries of the Reservation;
c. Pollution of the land and water of the Reservation and of lands and waters outside of the boundaries of the Reservation poses a threat to the health and welfare of the Tribe and its members;
d. Littering in the villages and at campsites, in addition to being unsightly, poses a threat to the fish and animals upon which the Tribe and its members depend;
e. The village dumpsites have not been managed as well as they should have been over the past years, and there are old batteries and other hazardous materials that are in the dumps that should not have been placed there;
f. It is necessary to protect the environment and natural resources of the Reservation and of the lands and waters outside of the Reservation in

order to protect the health and welfare of the Tribe and its members; and

g. It is important to the health, welfare, and economy of the Tribe and its members that all materials which can be recycled are in fact recycled.

Section 3. Purposes

The Tribal Council wishes to:

a. Protect the lands and waters of the Reservation and outside the boundaries of the Reservation so that pollution and littering do not adversely affect the health, welfare, and safety of the Tribe and its members.
b. Ensure that the village dumps are constructed and managed in a manner that assures the health, welfare, and safety of the Tribe and its members.
c. Adopt and implement a comprehensive recycling program.

Section 7. Pollution

(a) There shall be no pollution of any lands or waters within the scope of this Ordinance. This includes, but is not limited to, dumping of oil, fuel, or gas on the ground, or in the water.

(b) No materials shall be burned except paper, wood and similarly combustible materials. In no event shall plastics be burned.

(c) Human waste shall be buried in one place well away from any waters.

(d) Each oil or fuel spill must be reported to Tribal Council and appropriate action will be taken to have area cleaned.

(e) The Tribal Council shall study the effects of hazardous materials to humans and establish permanent rules to control the handling and transport for safety of hazardous materials.

(f) Waste water will be separate from human wastes and be dumped at proper locations inside toilet.

Section 8. Operation of the Village Dump

(a) The village dump in each village shall be the sole depository of all trash and hazardous materials.

(b) The Tribal Council shall enter into a study to determine the best way to manage the village dumps. The study shall include, but not be limited to:

1. Whether the existing location of the dumps is the best location, and if not, where the dumps should be located;
2. How best to manage hazardous wastes (such as old batteries) and other wastes (such as used oil);
3. The most appropriate design for the dumps;
4. Any changes to the design or management system of the current dumps; and
5. How the Council can finance the operation of the dump.

(c) Pending completion of the study, the Council shall manage the dumps in the following manner:

1. A special shed shall be set aside for the storage of hazardous and other wastes.
2. If economically feasible, a fence shall be constructed around the dump and a manager shall be hired to manage the use of the dumps.

Section 9. Recycling

(a) All materials which can be recycled shall be recycled. These include, but are not limited to, aluminum cans, Styrofoam cups, and glass bottles.

(b) A recycling center shall be established at the village dump or at some other location if the Tribal Council so determines. All recyclable materials shall be brought to this center.

(c) The Tribal Council shall develop a program to determine the best use of recycled materials. This program shall include, but need not be limited to, the reuse of these materials in the village, the sale of these materials (such as aluminum cans) off-Reservation, and how the proceeds from any such sale could be best used (such as allowing the children to be responsible for recycling cans and keeping any proceeds).

(d) The Tribal Council shall enter into a study as to what shall be done with the old equipment in the villages. Upon completion of the study, the Council shall designate a person to implement the study, including making plans to get rid of any equipment the study finds cannot be used.

The last excerpt for this chapter comes from a written opinion of the Colville Confederated Tribes Court of Appeals. This document expresses rules and provisions that outline how the tribes' unique customs and traditions are expected to be used in combination with legal norms, structures, and practices more recently acquired from Anglo-American legal sources. The task of integrating these two sources of law is one of the most important aspects of contemporary tribal legal systems. We will see how this is accomplished with examples of tribal legal documents, including tribal constitutions, codes, and opinions throughout this book.

LAURIE WATT V. COLVILLE RESERVATION COURT OF APPEALS

Confederated Tribes of the Colville Reservation Court of Appeals*

Before Chief Justice Dupris, Justice Bonga, and Justice Stewart.
The opinion of the court was delivered by: Dupris, C. J.

Summary of Proceedings

On November 21, 1996 the appellant, Laurie Watt, entered a guilty plea to the charge of driving without a valid license. The Court entered a sentence of jail and fine, with some of the sentence suspended on conditions. The appellant filed this appeal from the Judgment and Sentence. . . . Oral Arguments were heard on September 19, 1997. The Court of Appeals found at the Oral Arguments that the Appeal should be dismissed.

Facts

The appellant [Laurie Watt] entered a guilty plea to the charge of Driving Without A Valid License. The prosecutor's office made a recommendation of a fine of $500.00 with $200.00 suspended and sixty (60) days in jail with fifty-five (55) days suspended. The appellant's attorney recommended the appellant be allowed to work community service hours [instead] of the jail time because of extenuating circumstances regarding the care of the appellant's young child. The Trial Court did not accept these recommendations.

---

* Confederated Tribes of the Colville Reservation Court of Appeals, *Laurie Watt v. Colville Reservation Court of Appeals*, 25 Indian Law Reporter 6027 (1998).

Issue

The appellant argues that the Trial Court abused its discretion by not allowing her to serve her jail term through community service contrary to Tribal custom and tradition.

Discussion

Did the Trial Court Abuse Its Discretion by Not Substituting Community Service [Instead] of Jail Time, Contrary to Tribal Custom and Tradition?

The Court of Appeals must review two things in this appeal: (1) whether there is a custom or tradition regarding the use of community service [instead] of jail time; and (2) whether the Trial Court abused its discretion in failing to allow the appellant community service [instead] of jail time.

As to the first question, there is nothing on record to support the appellant's argument regarding custom and tradition. Appellant cites no authorities regarding the nature of punishment prior to the statutory law of the Tribes. [The appellant argued that the Justices were presumed to know what the law is, and this included custom and tradition. The burden is on the Court, the appellant contends, and not the appellant. This argument is totally without foundation and is rejected by this Court.] At best the appellant has supported her arguments with suppositions of what she believes custom and tradition is regarding punishment. She has failed to meet even a minimum burden of showing what is custom and tradition. . . . Next we decide whether the Trial Court abused its discretion by failing to allow community service [instead] of jail time in this case. In reviewing for an abuse of discretion it is not the Appellate Panel's duty to decide . . . the sentence of the appellant. We cannot substitute what we would have ordered [instead] of what the trial judge ordered just because we may have ruled differently.

The record must show a clear abuse of discretion between the facts of the case and the sentence entered by the trial judge. We must be shown that the record does not support the trial judge's findings. . . . The record . . . shows that the sentence is well within the statutory limits for the offense charged. The appellant has not met her burden on this issue either.

We hold that this appeal shall be dismissed. . . . It is so Ordered.

Stewart, J., Concurring

The Colville Tribal Court started in the early 1940's as a Court of Justice. There was only one judge for years on end. Albert Orr was a quiet, soft-spoken man, and treated every one who came to his court with dignity and respect. The officers were expected to tell the truth and the defendants knew they could not pull anything on the Judge, because everyone knows what was going on within the Reservation.

There weren't many jury trials. The first time I was in Court as an officer was 1962. The person on trial asked for a jury and was able to pick his own jury. So, he called for friends from Idaho, Yakima, Spokane, and maybe a couple of local people. The standard reading went something like this: "you can be represented by a tribal member as long as it is not an attorney." There was no Court of Appeals until into the 1970's, as I remember it.

As the times changed so did the Court. The Colville Tribal Court took the lead, in many ways, being one of the bigger reservations in the State. The laws were changing, and the Court was closed down and only started again after the Tribes saw what was happening with our people. Both Okanogan and Ferry County courts were swamped with cases. The sheriff did not have money to send full-time officers to take care of the Reservation, so the Tribal Council took back jurisdiction over tribal members from any tribe.

In 1971 I was working for Highway Safety on a grant from the Department of Transportation out of Washington D.C. This Reservation in the mid-1970's had the highest fatality rate of any place in Washington State between Omak and Coulee Dam. I was keeping record at the time, and decided we should have some kind of driver's license for the five hundred (500) Tribal employees who drove Tribal vehicles. Fifty percent of our drivers did not have any kind of a state driver's license. There were five program directors who did not have a license. I started a program to teach people to drive, and made every employee who drove have a Tribal license. The first year the Tribes saved $1,000.00 on insurance.

By this time we had one full-time judge, Frank LaFountaine, and needed a part-time judge to fill in while Judge LaFountaine was on vacation. I was asked to fill in as judge for a couple of weeks. By then we had lawyers and a public defender, and we were starting to be a real Indian court, a Court of Law.

This brings us up to date to the case in question. The Court of Appeals started out having a few cases a year. I remember when we had five appeals cases in one year and that seemed to be a lot. I could see every one needed to have the right to appeal, though.

The public defender we have at this time is a compassionate person, well able to make sure the people he represents are protected under the law. I wouldn't have it any other way. Just a few years ago if we had twenty-five cases a week we thought we had a full caseload. Now it is not unusual to have twenty-five cases in one day. The whole Court staff, and the Police Department, Prosecutor's Office, Probation Office, as well as the Public Defender's Office (and maybe a few departments I have forgotten to give credit to) are all over-worked.

Quite often the public defender will get stuck in a pattern, take the easy way out, and file any number of cases saying "arbitrary and capricious," yet when the Court of Appeals says "enough!" he can write really in-depth on an issue. He can write something to be proud of.

This case is one of his new ideas, well worth thinking over. From what I remember, the Tribes did not have jails to hold people in who violated the law. He is right. It reminded me of when I first worked in Law and Order as a new Game Warden and officer. The Fish and Game Committee sat me down and said: "You are new to the job, but we have had Tribal police for hundreds of years before the white man came. We didn't have much law breakers, but we did have some. The worst thing that would happen in the old days was, a young buck would ride his horse through the camp too fast. Some of the Elders would call him out and say, 'Don't do that again.' It usually worked, but some times he would do it again. The same Elders would call some of the other young men and say, 'Take him out back of the camps and beat him up.' If he did it again, the Elders would tell the young people to take him out and kill him."

Our old laws like those I was told about do not work because the world is changing. We still must protect our people from the ones who do not obey the law, or accept it as the Tribes write it up. The Colville Tribes has one of the leading Courts. We have to set the standards, not only for our own people, but because we have laid the foundation for the smaller tribes to use as guidelines for their courts.

We, as the Court of Appeals' Justices for this Tribe, cannot control what the federal courts, or the state courts, or the county courts do. We are responsible to this Tribe to set standards for the cases to build on from where we are now. If the standard for a cement foundation is one bucket of water, three shovels of sand, and a shovel of cement is working and has worked for years, we cannot be led down the path of change by putting too much water or sand, and a half a shovel of cement to keep our foundation from crumbling.

A law without a penalty is only advice. The penalty of the law is the cement of the foundation. Contempt of court comes in many forms, e.g., not wearing a dress coat, or a tie, or not speaking loud enough to be heard. Other examples include not following a court order to pay a fine, even if it is community service, or not obtaining a driver's license, or driving without a license. This all falls within contempt for the Court.

The Probation Department reported that defendant Watt did not comply with past court orders; the officers arrested her several years ago for no valid license. The Trial Court gave her a fair and just sentence, and yet a case that should not have been filed in the Court of Appeals has cost the Tribes thousands of dollars at this time.

The briefs from the Prosecutor's Office listed most of the reasons. No insurance for an unlicensed driver is high on the priority list. I feel if we let a chosen few get away with disregarding Court orders, we are not putting our finger in the leak that could wash out the dam of violations and erodes away the hard-earned foundations that have been laid for years. I did not mean this to be this long. Please forgive my rambling and simple way of putting things on paper. I feel we can only uphold the Trial Court's decision. Let the majority rule in this case.

In the *Watt* decision above, there were two separate opinions, written by two different groups of judges on the Colville Confederated Tribes Court of Appeals. The first was written by Justice Dupris, which represented both Justice Dupris's decision and the decision of Justice Bonga. Justice Stewart wrote the second opinion. Since the first opinion represented the decision of two of the three judges, it is called the majority opinion and it is the law. The second decision is a concurring decision. This means that Justice Stewart agreed with the majority decision, but he wanted to write some words of his own. In the majority opinion, the justices reject an argument that the tribal court who heard this case first (the trial court as opposed to the appeals court) made a mistake by not sentencing Watt to community service. She claimed that tribal custom and tradition does not include jail time.

The excerpts in this chapter were selected to provide a sample of different kinds of contemporary written tribal law. Tribal law is constantly expanding and changing—and more tribal governments are using their traditional language in today's codes. In the next chapter, we will explore the role of language, culture, and spiritual beliefs in tribal law.

Questions

1. Do you think the qualifications for membership in the Nez Perce tribe and the organization of its General Council have their origins in the unique legal heritage of the Nez Perce or in an Anglo-style law that has been imposed on them by the U.S. government?

2. What kinds of rights to land are regulated in the Susanville Indian Rancheria Assignment Ordinance? Does it provide for individuals to have rights to *own* or *sell* rancheria lands? Explain why you think the assignment ordinance does or does not provide rights to own or sell rancheria lands.
3. The Venetie tribal code includes commentary and explanation from tribal leaders. Do you think this is an effective way of including tribal values in tribal codes?
4. Laurie Watt argued that her jail time was a violation of tradition and that the trial judge abused his discretion. Why did the justice writing the majority opinion disagree with her? Do you agree with the majority decision's conclusion?
5. Now consider Justice Stewart's concurring opinion in the *Watt* case. How is the concurring opinion different from the majority opinion? Why do you think he related what he was told by the Fish and Game Committee back when he was a game warden? Did he follow their advice? Why do you think he wanted to write a separate opinion if he was only going to agree with what the majority decided?

In Your Community

1. What kinds of modern legal documents are available for study in your tribe? Is there a constitution? Statutes? Case law? How do you go about getting access to these documents?
2. Do your tribe's legal documents reflect the cultures and values in your tribal community? If not, what would need to change in order to ensure that the tribal laws reflect your culture?

Glossary

Amendment: An alteration, addition, or change in law.

Appellant: A person or party who appeals a court's decision.

Assignment: The act of transferring an interest in property or some right (such as contract benefits) to another.

Codified: Written down; organized; arranged.

Covenant: A promise in a written contract or a deed of real property.

Discretion: The power of a judge to make decisions on various matters based on his or her opinion, within general legal guidelines.

Easement: The right to use the real property of another for a specific purpose.

Fundamental: Basic; core; essential.

Jurisdiction: Legal authority.

Legislative intent: The purpose for which a law is passed.

Preamble: An introductory statement or preliminary explanation as to the purpose of a law.

Relinquish: To give up a possession, claim, or right.

Title: A comprehensive term referring to the legal basis of the ownership of property.

Vest: To give to a person a fixed and immediate right of title.

Suggested Further Reading

Felix S. Cohen et al., *On the Drafting of Tribal Constitutions* (2006).

Robert D. Cooter, *American Indian Law Codes: Pragmatic Law and Tribal Identity*, 56 American Journal of Comparative Law 29 (2008).

Eric D. Lemont, ed., *American Indian Constitutional Reform and the Rebuilding of Native Nations* (2006).

Pat Sekaquaptewa, *Key Concepts in Finding, Definition and Consideration of Custom Law in Tribal Lawmaking*, 32 American Indian Law Review 319 (2008).

CHAPTER 3

Tribal Law in Customs and Traditions

ONE OF THE most important ways in which legal and social science scholars study tribal law is by examining tribal traditions. Tribal traditions often reveal critical information about the norms, structures, and practices of a tribal people—thus providing clues to the legal systems of tribal governments. As most tribes in North America had no formal systems of writing prior to contact with Europeans, information concerning their creation, their history, their fundamental values, and their most important ways of life have been passed by word of mouth from one generation to the next.

There are two major ways in which we can study tribal traditions. The first is through stories, along with the manner and circumstances in which they are told by tribal peoples to each other. Elders and storytellers have a sacred role in many indigenous cultures, because they have gained the respect and trust to tell the stories that carry this critical knowledge. Furthermore, telling these stories is usually one of the ways in which these people use their knowledge to help resolve disputes or otherwise correct the improper behavior of their relatives and other tribal members. Thus, stories about the legendary acts of tribal heroes, the mischievous behavior of Coyote or Raven, or important places and events in tribal history are also almost always stories designed to teach the people listening to them about tribal values and proper ways of living. In this way, oral traditions and their telling are not just a source of tribal law—they are also some of the basic ways in which tribal law is practiced. This is still true for many tribes today. As such, stories remain some of the most critical ways in which tribal peoples learn and remind themselves about the norms, structures, and practices that make up their legal system.

The second way to study tribal traditions is by reviewing historical or ethnographic resources. Of course, because these are often written by nontribal citizens or by scholars who did not grow up in the communities they study, their explanations must always be analyzed for possible inconsistencies or misunderstandings.

The following excerpts demonstrate how some legal and social science scholars and tribal leaders explain tribal legal traditions. In the first, the Honorable Robert Yazzie, tribal citizen and chief justice (emeritus) of the Navajo Nation Supreme Court, and James W. Zion, former solicitor general for the Navajo, have written about Navajo law, focusing specifically on Navajo traditional law. The second, written by Professor Rennard Strickland, a citizen of the Cherokee tribe and former dean of the University of Oregon School of Law, describes the nature of traditional law among the Cherokee. The third excerpt considers one oral tradition and storytelling practice in the Apache community of Cibecue, Arizona. Written by anthropologist Keith H. Basso, it suggests how stories about places and their names on the reservation are often told by community members to remind their relatives about proper and improper behavior. Finally, Justin Richland, an anthropologist and legal scholar, describes a moment of interaction in Hopi tribal court where efforts by a Hopi judge to incorporate Hopi customs and traditions into his Anglo-style legal proceeding were met with resistance. He explains that just because a tribe values the introduction of custom and tradition into its contemporary legal system, not all members of a tribe may agree on the ways in which that integration should take place.

NAVAJO LEGAL THINKING AND INSTITUTIONS

James W. Zion and Robert Yazzie[*]

Navajo norms, values and moral principles are stated in the Navajo language and preserved in Navajo creation scripture, origin stories, ceremonies, songs, stories, and maxims. The Navajo creation scripture relates the journey narratives which led the people to their current homeland.

---

[*] James W. Zion & Robert Yazzie, *Indigenous Law in North America in the Wake of Conquest*, 20 Boston College International and Comparative Law Review 55 (1997).

Navajo social stories about mythic creatures, particularly Coyote and Horned Toad, are another means to record values as legal principles. Songs are also used as legal teaching tools.

The Navajo language is very sophisticated. Many Navajo words and phrases express concepts which are difficult to render in another language. They are descriptive and provide vivid word pictures. Navajos do not use religious or sexual swearing, but one phrase which is used, *shash kheyadae*, means "from the bear's den!" The Navajo word for a lawyer, *agha'diit'aahii*, means "someone who pushes out with words." It describes someone who is bossy, not a very nice person in Navajo thinking.

There are several Navajo maxims to urge good action or describe bad acts: in the marriage ceremony, the couple is urged, *hazho' sokee'*—"stay together nicely." An elder who speaks to a child will say, *hozhigo*—"do things in a good way." Of a wrongdoer, Navajos will say, "He acts as if he had no relatives" (showing the importance of social controls).

The word *k'e* is important in Navajo relationships; it is what makes the Navajo legal institutions of the clan and civil leader work. It is very difficult to translate this word into another language because it has deep connotations in order to urge persons to go along with the group. It is an aggregation of deep feelings which urge respect and solidarity with the group. The word speaks to reciprocal relationships where there are duties and obligations to both the individual and the group. The maxim which expresses Navajo individuality and freedom is, "It's up to him." Navajos believe in a greater degree of freedom than the Western concept of individuality, but individuality is still exercised in the context of the well-being of the group.

There is a special kind of k'e called *k'ei* or clanship. Navajos are matrilineal. They are "born of" their mother's clan and "born for" their father's clan. Thus, they trace relationships beyond blood ties or immediate biological family. The clan is the Navajo legal institution.

Navajos had both war leaders and civil leaders. Traditional civil leaders are selected by group consensus and they have authority only for as long as they benefit the group. The Navajo civil leader's authority is not coercive, but persuasive. That is, he or she compels others through urging and example, not through power and force. The Navajo leader is not merely an "advisor" or a "mediator," however, nor a "chief" in the sense of someone who can command another.

A traditional civil leader is a planner. The Navajo concept of civil leadership authorizes justice planners for the traditional Navajo legal institution. A justice planner is a *naat'aanii*. The word itself describes a person who speaks wisely and well. Wisdom comes from experience and knowledge of the ceremonies, and speech is valued as a virtue. The Navajo language tends to be very precise, so words are important. A traditional story about one naat'aanii says that he was "able to talk the goods in." This phrase refers to the talent for planning the leader had, and how his wisdom was used for community success. Navajo planning, *naat'aah*, is very pragmatic and a plan is the product of considering every aspect of a problem through talking it out in a group setting.

What happens when there is a dispute? The person who claims injury demands *nalyeeh*. The word is translated as "restitution" or "reparation," but it is an action word which demands compensation for an injury and an adjustment of relationships between an "offender" and a "victim." Who is the judge? It is not a naat'aanii, but the persons who are involved in the dispute. The persons who have "standing" by being within the "zone of dispute" in Navajo common law include relatives and clan members of the parties. The procedure used to resolve the dispute is "talking things out," and the Navajo word for "trial," *'ahwiniti*, means "where they talk about you."

How does the "trial" work? The person who demands nalyeeh seeks the assistance of a relative to get a naat'aanii to summon the participants to talk things out. The particular naat'aanii will often be a blood or clan relative because horizontal[1] legal institutions operate within relationship groups. The session always opens with a prayer, and it is often held after a meal. Prayer is a means of summoning supernatural assistance. It focuses the minds of the participants on the purposes of the gathering. Prayer is a powerful and compulsive word. It brings in the supernaturals, not simply as witnesses (as with the European oath) but as participants and agents for action.

Following the prayer, each person in the group has an opportunity to speak. The opinions and feelings of both the "victim" and the "perpetrator" are important, as are those of their relatives. For example, in a talking out session held to discuss the paternity of a child, the child's grandparents resolved the putative father's denial of paternity by pointing out that they (as the parents of the couple) knew about the sexual relationship all along and there was no doubt the child was theirs.

After such discussions take place, the naat'aanii expresses an opinion about the dispute in "the lecture." This translation in English is unfortunate because what the naat'aanii says is not simply a lecture on abstract moral principles. It often relates to Navajo creation scripture through its many examples and maxims of the right way to do things. A Navajo naat'aanii is not a "neutral," as with American [Alternative Dispute Resolution] mediation, because he or she is summoned to guide the parties, not as a decision-maker, but as a guide or teacher. The naat'aanii's opinion about the right way of doing things is important to the parties. The "lecture" or opinion is also important for the process of naat'aah or planning.

The first step of making a plan is to carefully identify the problem. The Navajo word for it is *nayee*, which literally translated means "monster." A "monster" is something which gets in the way of life, a barrier, an impediment, or an obstacle to be overcome. In Navajo creation, there were monsters who walked the earth, and the Hero Twins who slayed them went through a long process of learning, preparation, trial and seeking assistance to be able to slay them. The naat'aanii helps the parties identify the causes of trouble and uses Navajo wisdom and experience in the lecture to guide them. The parties then develop a plan of action to end the dispute through consensus and agreement. That plan describes the duties of each participant to mend relationships.

The end goal and the result is *hozho nahasdlii*, which is the new relationship and attitude of the parties. It is the product of the process. It means, "now that we have done this, we are again in a state of hozho." The term *hozho nahasdlii* is used to conclude a prayer. Unlike the European prayer-termination word, *amen*, it does not mean "may it be so." It means "It is so." Although *hozho* is very difficult to translate, it refers to the wholeness of all reality and the connections of everyone and everything. It involves the supernaturals, who are actually present to be a part of the process. It uses values of k'e solidarity and respect to reach a conclusion or state of being among everyone where each one interrelates in a proper way with the others.

A final decision often involves a transfer of goods to the injured person, to compensate for actual injury and to serve as a symbol of a good relationship. The amount or value of the compensation can include "a little extra" to show the seriousness of the act or injury. An agreement to deliver goods (such as jewelry, sheep, horses or money) also has the effect of showing the innocence of the victim, as with the open and visible delivery of horses to compensate for a rape, or a husband's act of giving nalyeeh to a wife to make up for an assault.

Relatives are an important part of the final agreement or "judgment." The relatives of someone who has injured another are responsible to help pay nalyeeh or help the parties with the immediate dispute. They are "traditional probation officers" in the sense that if they pay valuable goods to a victim and that person's family, they will "keep an eye on" the offender to prevent future misconduct.

These are only a few of the legal principles and procedures used in traditional Navajo dispute resolution. They work, because Navajos value relationships and respect the traditions which are expressed in the Navajo language and religion. Navajo justice is egalitarian, consensual and builds on the interdependence of people in clans and families. Traditional Navajo law had no need for civil rights or constitutional protections, because the Navajos did not need protection from authority figures in vertical institutions.

TRADITIONAL LAW WAYS AND THE SPIRIT WORLD

*Rennard Strickland**

To the Cherokees law was the earthly representation of divine spirit order. They did not think of law as a set of civil or secular rules limiting or requiring actions on their part. Public consensus and harmony rather than confrontation and dispute, as essential elements of the Cherokee world view, were reflected in the ancient concepts of law.

The ongoing social process could not, in the Cherokee way, be manipulated by law to achieve policy goals. There was no question of man being able to create law because to the Cherokee the norms of behavior were a sovereign command from the Spirit World. Man might apply the divinely ordained rules, but no earthly authority was empowered to formulate rules of tribal conduct.

The Cherokee law was centered in the priestly complex of the native tribal religion. The recitation of laws was a high religious ceremony. Among the ancient Cherokees there was an office of tribal orator, a priest who was sometimes called the "beloved man." The orator's duties included, among others, the delivery of the laws of the Cherokees at the annual *busk*, or first-fruit celebration. Dressed in the orator's costume and wearing the wings of a raven in his hair, the lawgiver must have been an impressive and important figure. John Haywood, in *Natural and Aboriginal History of Tennessee*, reported observations of the recitation of the law:

> The great beloved man or high priest addresses the warriors and women giving all the particular and positive injunctions, and negative

* Rennard Strickland, *The Fire and the Spirits: Cherokee Law from Clan to Court* 10–12 (1975).

precepts they yet retain of the ancient law. He uses very sharp language to the women. He then addresses the whole multitude. He enumerates the crimes they have committed, great and small, and bids them look at the holy fire, which has forgiven them. He presses on his audience by the great motives of temporal good, and the fear of temporal evil, the necessity of a careful observance of the ancient laws.

When the orator spoke the law, he was reading the meaning of history and tradition contained in the tribal *wampum*. He held the ancient and sacred wampum belts in his hand. At the earliest periods the laws were interpreted from divining crystals, whose surface might picture the events of the forthcoming year. In later times wampum beads of varying shades were strung together to symbolize events and customs of the Cherokees. Even today the Kee-too-wah Cherokees are said to continue to read their ancient laws from many of the same belts used by the beloved men in Haywood's time.

The law was read but once a year. The law was simple, and the people knew the law. The reading was more symbolic than informative but served, no doubt, as a reminder that the Cherokees were a people governed by the laws of the Spirits. Each year among the Cherokees there was a "great festival of the expiation of sins," at which all crimes except murder were forgiven after the expiration of a year. The Cherokees felt that "the heart cannot be weighed down with all the sorrows of the past years," and thus the new year feast was a time of absolution at which "the divine fire is appeased for past crimes."

The fire itself and the smoke of the fire are agents and act to grant the pardon. No Cherokee who retains a grudge or notion of revenge can participate in the renewal festival, which is a time of "joy and gladness" when the fire has "sanctified their weighty harvest." At this feast the Cherokees "rejoice exceedingly at this appearance of the holy fire, and it is supposed to atone for all their past crimes, except murder." . . .

These are the postulates commonly accepted by the traditional Cherokee:

1. The fire is central to life. Fire and smoke are agents of Being. Spirit Beings created the world. These Beings, who possess emotional intelligence similar to that of people control the destiny of people, who, in important aspects of life, is subordinate to the souls of the Spirit Beings. Our social order is patterned after the system of the creating Spirits. Divine Spirit retribution is always a grave danger. Displeasure may or may not be vented immediately. The Spirits allow both supernatural and secular aspects in their divinely ordained world.

2. Matrilineal clan is the primary social unit, whose purity of blood must be safeguarded at all times.

3. War and peace are separate activities which require two distinct political organizations, as well as dual obligations for all men and women.

4. Priests, as leaders of the peace organization, have been given secrets which will guard the welfare of the tribe.

5. Popular consensus is essential to effective tribal action. Leadership depends upon popular support, which may be withheld to prevent action. Withdrawal of factions may provide the solution when agreement by consensus is impossible. Social harmony is an element of great value.

6. Society is divided into separate classes and ranks which were created by the Spirits. There is no significant stigma and only limited privilege attached to class membership. All classes, both men and women, are of great value socially and have important and useful roles in Cherokee society.

7. All natural resources are free or common goods. Food supplies and wealth items are privately owned but are to be shared. Property is to be used but not accumulated, for wealth is not a desired social goal. All people are to be honored regardless of physical and personal limitations.

8. Marriage is a temporary state and may be dissolved, at will, by either party. While marriage exists, sexual fidelity is expected.

9. There is a supernatural world to which the ghosts of all people desire to go. Actions on earth, either one's own or those of a clan brother or sister, may prevent passage into the afterworld, or Nightland. Duties of blood and oaths, are, therefore, highly regarded.

STALKING WITH STORIES

Keith H. Basso[*]

This chapter focuses on a small set of spoken texts in which members of the community of Cibecue express claims about themselves, their language and

[*] Keith H. Basso, *Wisdom Sits in Places: Landscape and Language Among the Western Apache* 38–41, 51–57 (1996).

their lands on which they live. The statements that interest me, which could be supplemented by a large number of others, are the following.

> The land is always stalking people. The land makes people live right. The land looks after us. The land looks after people. (Annie Peaches, age 77, 1978)

> Our children are losing the land. It doesn't go to work on them anymore. They don't know the stories about what happened at these places. That's why some get into trouble. (Ronnie Lupe, age 42, chairman, White Mountain Apache Tribe, 1978)

> We used to survive only off the land. Now it's no longer that way. Now we live only with money, so we need jobs. But the land still looks after us. We know the names of the places where everything happened. So we stay away from badness. (Nick Thompson, age 64, 1980)

> I think of that mountain called Tséé L/igai Dah Sidilé (White Rocks Lie Above In A Compact Cluster) as if it were my maternal grandmother. I recall stories of how it once was at that mountain. The stories told to me were like arrows. Elsewhere, hearing that mountain's name, I see it. Its name is like a picture. Stories go to work on you like arrows. Stories make you live right. Stories make you replace yourself. (Benson Lewis, age 64, 1979)

> One time I went to L.A., training for mechanic. It was no good, sure no good. I start drinking, hang around bars all the time. I start getting into trouble with my wife, fight sometimes with her. It was bad. I forget about this country here around Cibecue. I forget all the names and stories. I don't hear them in my mind anymore. I forget how to live right, forget how to be strong. (Wilson Lavender, age 52, 1975)

If these statements resist easy interpretation, it is not because the people who make them are confused or cloudy thinkers. Nor is it because, as one unfortunate commentator would have us believe, the Western Apache are "mystically inclined and correspondingly inarticulate." The problem we face is . . . a barrier to constructing appropriate sense and significance that arises from the fact that all views articulated by Apache people are informed by their experience in a culturally constituted world of objects and events with which most of us are unfamiliar. What sort of world is it?

Or, to draw the question into somewhat sharper focus, what is the cultural context in which Apache statements such as the foregoing find acceptance as valid claims about reality?

More specifically still, what is required to interpret Annie Peaches's claim that the land occupied by the Western Apache is "always stalking people" and that because of this they know how to "live right"? How should we understand Chairman Lupe's assertion that Apache children sometimes misbehave because the land "doesn't go to work on them any more"? Why does Nick Thompson claim that his knowledge of place-names and historical events enable him to "stay away from badness"? Why does Benson Lewis liken place-names to pictures, stories to arrows, and a mountain near Cibecue to his maternal grandmother? And what should we make of Wilson Lavender's recollection of an unhappy time in California when forgetting place-names and stories caused him to forget "how to be strong"? Are these claims structured in metaphorical terms, or are they, given Western Apache assumptions about the physical universe and the place of people within it, somehow to be interpreted literally? . . .

As we shall see, most of these premises are grounded in an unformalized native model of Western Apache storytelling which holds that oral narratives have the power to establish enduring bonds between individuals and features of the natural landscape, and that as a direct consequence of such bonds, persons who have acted improperly will be moved to reflect critically on their misconduct and resolve to improve it. A native model of how stories work to shape Apaches' conceptions of the landscape, it is also a model of how stories work to shape Apaches' conceptions of themselves. Ultimately, it is a model of how two symbolic resources—language and the land—are manipulated by Apaches to promote compliance with standards for acceptable social behavior and the moral values that support them. . . .

Without exception, and usually in very graphic terms, historical tales focus on persons who suffer misfortune as the consequence of actions that violate Apache standards for acceptable behavior. More specifically, "'ágodzaahí" stories tell of persons who have acted unthinkingly and impulsively in open disregard for "Apache custom" (ndee bi 'at'ee) and who pay for their transgressions by being humiliated, ostracized, or killed. Stories of the 'ágodzaahí variety are morality tales pure and simple, and, when viewed as such by the Apaches—as compact commentaries on what should be avoided so as to deal successfully and effectively with other people—they are highly informative. For what these narratives assert—tacitly, perhaps, but with dozens of compelling examples—is that immoral behavior is irrevocably a community affair and that persons who behave badly will be punished sooner or later. Thus, just as 'ágodzaahí stories are "about" historical events and their geographical locations, they are also "about" the systems of rules and values according to which even Apaches expect each other to organize and regulate their lives. In an even more fundamental sense, then, historical tales are "about" what it means to be a Western Apache, or, to make the point less dramatically, what it is that being an Apache should normally and properly entail.

To see how this is so, let us consider the texts of two historical tales and examine the manner in which they have been interpreted by their Apache narrators. . . .

It Happened at Tséé Chiizh Dah Sidilé (Coarse-Textured Rocks Lie Above In A Compact Cluster)

> Long ago, a man became sexually attracted to his stepdaughter. He was living below Coarse-Textured Rocks Lie Above In A Compact Cluster with his stepdaughter and her mother. Waiting until no one else was present, and sitting alone with her, he started to molest her. The girl's maternal uncle happened to come by and he killed the man with a rock. The man's skull was cracked open. It was raining. The girl's maternal uncle dragged the man's body up above to Coarse-Textured Rocks Lie Above In A Compact Cluster and placed it there in a storage pit. The girl's mother came home and was told by her daughter of all that had happened. The people who owned the storage pit removed the man's body and put it somewhere else. The people never had a wake for the dead man's body. It happened at Coarse-Textured Rocks Lie Above In A Compact Cluster.

Narrated by Benson Lewis, this historical tale deals with the crime of incest, for sexual contact with stepchildren is considered by Western Apache to be an incestuous act. According to Mr. Lewis, the key line in the story is the penultimate one in which he observes, "The people never had a wake for the dead man's body." We may assume, Lewis says, that because the dead man's camp was located near the storage pit in which his body was placed, the people who owned the pit were also his relatives. This makes the neglect with which his corpse was treated all the more profound, since kinspeople are bound by the strongest of obligations to care for each other when they die. That the dead man's relatives chose to dispense with customary mortuary shows with devastating clarity that they wished to disown him completely.

It Happened at Ndee Dah Naaẕiné (Men Stand Above Here And There)

Long ago, a man killed a cow off the reservation. The cow belonged to a white man. The man was arrested by a policeman living at Cibecue at Men Stand Above Here And There. The policeman was an Apache. The policeman took the man to the head army officer at Fort Apache. There, at Fort Apache, the head army officer questioned him. "What do you want?" he said. The policeman said, "I need cartridges and food." The policeman said nothing about the man who had killed the white man's cow. That night some people spoke to the policeman. "It is best to report on him," they said to him. The next day the policeman returned to the head army officer. "Now what do you want?" he said. The policeman said, "Yesterday I was going to say HELLO and GOOD-BYE but I forgot to do it." Again he said nothing about the man he arrested. Someone was working with words on his mind. The policeman returned with the man to Cibecue. He released him at Men Stand Above Here And There. It happened at Men Stand Above Here and There.

This story, narrated by Nick Thompson, describes what happened to an Apache who acted too much like a white man. Between 1872 and 1895, when Western Apaches were strictly confined to their reservations by U.S. military forces, disease and malnutrition took the lives of many people. Consequently, Apaches who listen to this historical tale find it perfectly acceptable that the man who lived at Men Stand Above Here And There should have killed and butchered a white man's cow. What is not acceptable is that the policeman, another Apache from the same settlement, should have arrested the rustler and contemplated taking him to jail. But the policeman's plans were thwarted. Someone used witchcraft on him and made him stupid and forgetful. He never informed the military officer at Fort Apache of the real purpose of his visit, and his second encounter with the officer—in which he apologized for neglecting to say "hello" and "good-bye" the previous day—revealed him to be an absurd and laughable figure. Although Western Apaches find portions of this story amusing, Nick Thompson explains that they understand it first and foremost as a harsh indictment of persons who join with outsiders against members of their own community and who, as if to flaunt their lack of allegiance, parade the attitudes and mannerisms of white men.

So far my remarks on what Western Apache historical tales are about have centered on features of textual content. This is a familiar strategy and certainly a necessary one, but it is also incomplete. In addition to everything else—places, events, moral standards, conceptions of cultural identity—every historical tale is also about the person to whom it is directed. This is because the telling of a historical tale is almost always prompted by an individual's having committed one or more social offenses to which the act of narration, together with the tale itself, is intended as a critical and remedial response. Thus, on occasions when 'ágodzaahí stories are actually told—by real Apache storytellers, in real interpersonal contexts, to real social offenders—these narratives are understood to be accompanied by an unstated message from the storyteller that may be phrased something like this: "I know that you have acted in a way similar or analogous to the way in which someone acted in the story I am telling you. If you continue to act in this way, something similar or analogous to what has happened to the character in the story might also happen to you."

This . . . message is just as important as any conveyed by the text of the storyteller's tale. For Apaches contend that if the message is taken to heart by the person at whom it is aimed—and if, in conjunction with lessons drawn from the tale itself, he or she resolves to improve his or her behavior—a lasting bond will have been created between that individual and the site or sites at which events in the tale took place. . . . [T]o understand more clearly what the idea involves, let us examine the circumstances that led to the telling of a historical tale at Cibecue and see how this narrative affected the person for whom it was told.

In early June 1977, a seventeen-year-old Apache woman attended a girls' puberty ceremonial at Cibecue with her hair rolled up in a set of pink plastic curlers. She had returned home two days before from a boarding school in Utah where this sort of ornamentation was considered fashionable by her peers. Something so mundane would have gone unnoticed by others were it not for the fact that Western Apache women of all ages are expected to appear at puberty ceremonials with their hair worn loose. This is one of several ways that women have of showing respect for the ceremonial and also, by implication, for the people who have staged it. The practice of presenting oneself with free-flowing hair is also understood to contribute to the ceremonial's effectiveness, for Apaches hold that the ritual's most basic objectives, which are to invest the pubescent girl with qualities necessary for life as an adult, cannot be achieved unless standard forms of respect are faithfully observed. On this occasion at Cibecue, everyone was following custom except the young woman who arrived wearing curlers. She soon became an object of attention and quiet expressions of disapproval, but no one spoke to her about the cylindrical objects in her hair.

Two weeks later, the same young woman made a large stack of tortillas and brought them to the camp of her maternal grandmother, a widow in her mid-sixties who had organized a small party to celebrate the birthday of her eldest grandson. Eighteen people were on hand, myself included, and all of us were treated to hot coffee and a dinner of boiled beef and potatoes. When the meal was over, casual conversation began to flow, and the young woman seated herself on the ground next to her younger sister. And then— quietly, deftly, and quite without warning—her grandmother narrated a version of the historical tale about the forgetful Apache policeman who behaved too much like a white man. Shortly after the story was finished, the young woman stood up, turned away wordlessly, and walked off in the direction of her home. Uncertain of what had happened, I asked her grand- mother why she had departed. Had the young woman suddenly become ill? "No," her grandmother replied. "I shot her with an arrow."

Approximately two years after this incident occurred, I found myself in the company of the young woman with the taste for distinctive hairstyles. She had purchased a large carton of groceries at the trading post at Cibecue, and when I offered to drive her home with them she accepted. I inquired on the way if she remembered the time her grandmother had told us the story about the forgetful policeman. She said she did and then went on, speaking in English, to describe her reactions to it. "I think maybe my grandmother was getting after me, but then I think maybe not, maybe she's working on somebody else. Then I think back on that dance and I know it's me for sure. I sure don't like how she's talking about me, so I quit look- ing like that. I threw those curlers away." In order to reach the young woman's camp, we had to pass within a few hundred yards of Men Stand Above Here And There, the place where the man had lived who was arrested for rustling in the story. I pointed it out to my companion. She said nothing for several moments. The she smiled and spoke softly in her own language: "I know that place. It stalks me every day."

"WHAT ARE YOU GOING TO DO WITH THE VILLAGE'S KNOWLEDGE?": TALKING TRADITION AND TALKING LAW IN HOPI TRIBAL COURT

*Justin B. Richland**

The courtroom interactions analyzed in this paper come from approxi- mately 30 hours of audio recordings of property dispute hearings before the

* Justin B. Richland, *What Are You Going to do With the Village's Knowledge? Talking Tra- dition, Talking Law in Hopi Tribal Court*, 39 Law and Society Review 235–71 (2005).

Hopi Tribal Court collected by the Hopi court as part of its official record, from 1995 to 2002. Additionally interviews of Hopi tribal members (including legal professionals and lay members), Hopi tribal court archival research, and ethnographic observation of Hopi courtroom proceedings were also conducted by the author over 27 months of fieldwork on the Hopi Reservation conducted since 1996, a period that included a 13 month stay from November 2001 to December 2002. . . .

A Dispute over Property Inheritance before the Hopi Tribal Court

The dispute that is of particular interest here emanated from a conflict between three sisters ("petitioners") and their aunt ("respondent") over their competing claims to an orchard worked by the petitioners' grandfather (also the respondent's father). The petitioners, who still live in the village where the land is located, claimed to have inherited the property from their mother upon her death, because she was the primary caregiver of their grandfather at the time of his death (Affidavit in support of Petition for Injunctive Relief, *James v. Smith*, CIV-018-94, 1994). According to them, Hopi custom and tradition dictate that property left intestate by a decedent should go to the person who showed the most commitment to its maintenance and to the support of its late owner (ibid.). They claim that this person was their mother, respondent's younger sister, and that upon their mother's death (also following custom), this property—like all women's property—should go to them, her daughters (ibid.).

The respondent, however, claimed that in 1954 she and her husband, an Apache man (and not a Hopi tribal member), were taken by her father to the field in question and told that she was to inherit the property upon his death (Answer to Amended Petition and Counter Petition to Quiet Title and for Injunctive Relief, *James v. Smith*, CIV-018-94, 1994). The respondent claims that because this land is an orchard, traditionally worked by the husband, it does not constitute the kind of clan lands that are inherited through the mother. Consequently, she contended that tradition requires that her father's intent to pass the land to her must prevail (ibid.). The petitioners counter this, arguing that regardless of the father's prior statements, tradition holds that the respondent has lost her claim to this land when she failed to return to show any commitment to it's maintenance, and when she married a non-Hopi man and left the reservation to live with him (Response to Answer/Counter Petition, *James v. Smith*, CIV-018-94, 1995). . . .

A Hearing on Custom and Tradition

The stretch of talk analyzed below was audio recorded by the court clerk in the winter of 1997, but was not observed by this analyst. The tribal Judge presiding was a Hopi man with 28 years experience on the Hopi bench. A fluent Hopi speaker, and deeply involved in the traditional practices of his village, the judge did not, however, come from the village where the dispute arose.

In some significant ways this hearing was highly unusual for a court based on a system of adversarial adjudication. . . . Departing from the normal examination processes of the Hopi tribal court, the judge played a central role in the questioning of the elders. . . .

Judicial efforts to control the frame of the elders' testimony were initiated almost at the very outset of the proceedings. In his introduction, the judge commented explicitly about the issues to which the elders were to speak, specifically asking the witnesses to testify how often, according to tradition, someone no longer living in the village is required to return to her land if she is to maintain possession of it. Consider first lines 002–011.[2]

(1) Judicial Efforts to Frame the Relevant Issues for Witness Testimony

002 Judge: *Pam   hapi pay   **yephaqam   hak   ayo'***
In that way truly now   somewhere here someone to there
In that manner someone may go over

003 *Yangqw   ayo'   sen   naala hoyok-hoyokni*
From here   to there perhaps alone move- will move
S/he might move away from here alone

004 *Niikyangw pi   pay   naat pi   piptu**ngwu***
But   truly now still   truly return+**HAB**
But s/he continues to come back regularly . . .

007 ***Hiisakis***   *sen   pam pas   pew   pìpte'*
How often perhaps she   much to here return
How often must s/he return

008 *Put pay naat*
It   now still
And still—

010   *Tutuyqawngwu*   *put tuutskwat*
             maintain control over **+HAB**   it   land
             Ah . . . have the right over others in that land

011   *Himu'ytangwu*
             Have as a posession**+HAB**
             To have ownership of it . . .

Focusing on the grammatical and discursive structure of this stretch of talk, notice the use of the indefinite terms[3] *yephaqam* (somewhere here) and *hak* (someone) at line 002. Here the judge was setting up the facts for elders to review as hypothetical events similar but not identical to the actual facts of the dispute. Then in lines 007–011, he posed his question, employing at lines 010 and 011, verbs inflected with the habitual aspect marker -*ngwu*.[4] The Indefinite + HABITUAL construction exemplified here is used repeatedly by this judge throughout his questioning of all the witnesses. As one native speaker explained to me, the form is often used in Hopi discourse by someone, usually an authority figure, to "admonish" another to change some problematic behavior.

When the judge employed the Indefinite + HABITUAL construction in his questions, he was projecting a metadiscursive frame proposing that elders testify about . . . generalized principles of tradition. And if we turn now to line 014, we see that witness 3 produced just such a principle, employing a similar construction. . . .

(2) Testimony of Witness 3: Part I

014 Witness 3: *Pu' pam angqw*   **suushaqam** *pìtu***ngwu**
             Then s/he from there **for once**   return**+HAB**
             Then s/he should return once in a while. . . .

But in the very next line, 015, the elder shifted referents, and using the demonstrative *I'* (this) started referring to the actual woman disputant and actual facts of the dispute.

(3) Testimony of Witness 3: Part II

015 Witness 3: **I'**   *pay*   *qa*   *hìsat,*   *sutsep*   *papki*
             This now   not sometime always   return
             This one [the woman disputant] never came back frequently . . .

[I]n response at lines 038–040, the Judge rejected this testimony.

(5) Rejecting Witness 3's Testimony

038 Judge: *Pay nu' ayanwat as   umuy tuuvìngta*
            Well I that way *CntrFct* you   ask
            I asked you in a different way instead.

039   *Pay   qa hakìy   pas   itam aw suuk aw taykyahkyàngw*
            Well not someone Intens   we   to   one to   look
            We are not to look at some one person

040   *turta put yu'a'totani*
            Let it   will talk
            As we talk about this.

It is at this turn that the witness seems to realize that the judge's use of
the Indefinite + HABITUAL construction is not simply initiating a topic
for her testimony, framing what would be deemed some of the possibly
relevant information she could speak to, but was in fact working as a
much more complete . . . constraint on her talk, compelling her to speak
only of principles of tradition and expressly not to the particularities of
this dispute.

   The witness then began to challenge the judge and his efforts to control her talk. At lines 059–061, she questioned why the judge only wanted
testimony on generalized principles of custom.

(6) Witness Resistance to Metadiscursive Constraints
on Her Testimony: Part I

058 Witness 3: *Noqw my understanding is*
               But
               But my understanding is

059   *Sùupan   as   ima yep   naami   hìntsakqw*
              It seems as if *CntrFct* these here to oneself   be doing
              Because these [people] here are in dispute

060   *Sùupan   as   itam pumuy- pay pumuysa engemyaqw*
              It seems as if *CntrFct* we   them   well those   for the
                 benefit of
              I thought we were [doing this] only for them-

061   *Kur   hapi pay pas itam sòosokmuy engemya.*
                     Perhaps truly well *Ints* we   all of them for the benefit of
                     But appears [to me] now we are doing this for all.

In response, the judge asserted at line 062 that he is asking for *umuh-navotiy* (your traditions).

(7) Restating the Constraints

062 Judge: *Pay puy umuhnavotìy   itam umumi   tungla'yyungwa*
               Well   your knowledge we from you   be asking
               We are asking you for your traditions

[He] then explained that testimony on the facts had been completed. . . .

(8) Justifying the Constraints

067 Judge: *Hak̟   pumuy put maqahqat*
               Someone them it   give
               As to who gave it [land] to them

068   *Pu' hisatnihqat*
               Then at that time
               And when that happened

069   *Pam pì   pay paas   yuk̟ìwta.*
               It truly well thoroughly finished
               That has all been done.

It is this final comment that prompted another elder witness to pointedly question the very purpose of the hearing. . . .

(9) Witness 4 Questioning the Purpose of the Hearing

070 Witness 4: *Noqw i' hìntìqw   yep pay aw paas   yuk̟ìwtaqw*
               But it for what purpose here well to thoroughly finished
               Then why when this has all been done

071   *Pas   pìw itam aw hìntsatskya*
               Intend also we to being done
               that we are even doing anything about it . . .

(10) Questioning the Judge's Interest in Village Tradition

074 Witness 4: *Um it ķitsoķit- um navotìyat   uma hintsatsnaniqe oovi*
                 You this village you knowledge your will be doing   therefore
                 What are you—What are you going to do with the village's
                     knowledge

This tense interaction continued, and after the judge reiterated his search for clarity on principles of tradition, it ended when witness 4 finally announced [his opposition] at lines 087–090.

(11) Thwarting the Hearing

087 Witness 4: *Nu' aw   wuuwaqw*
                 I   toward think in that way
                 When I think of it,

088   *it   yep* [village name] *navotiyat ķitsoķit navotiyat*
                 this that [village name]   knowledge
                 this village's traditional way

089   *Put pay kya   so'on haķ   pas hin*
                 It   now perhaps not someone very something
                 That is something that probably no one

090   *pas navoti'ytani*
                 very will have as knowledge
                 will know very much about.

What these spates of interaction reveal is the considerable difficulty posed by the judge's demand that the witnesses speak only to custom and tradition in the form of generalized statements rather than in application to the particularities of the dispute.

Questions

1. Does the article by Chief Justice Yazzie and Mr. Zion describe aspects of Navajo traditional law that could be called legal practices? What do the authors say about how Navajos traditionally "talk out" disputes?
2. Why is Navajo language important in discussions about Navajo common law?

3. In the Strickland account of traditional Cherokee law, what is the difference between law and religion? Is there any difference? Is it important to separate law from religion?
4. What do the Apache people in Basso's excerpt mean when they say they are being "stalked" with stories?
5. Do you think the stories in Basso's excerpt are "laws" for the Apache people? Why or why not?
6. Why do the Hopi tribal judge and the elder witnesses argue over the uses of tradition in the Hopi proceeding described by Richland? Who do you think is right, the judge or the elders?
7. Do you think Basso and Richland might be missing something in their discussion of Apache and Hopi traditions because they are not citizens of the tribes they study? Is there anything positive that comes from an outsider studying the unique legal heritage of a tribe like the Hopi or Apache? What do you think?

In Your Community

1. Can you think of a story told by members of your tribe? Describe the meaning of the story, who usually tells the story, when it is told, and to whom they tell the story. Do these descriptions give you any information about the norms, structures, and practices of your tribal law?
2. Have you ever been taught a lesson through a story? If so, describe how this story has helped shape your behavior.

Glossary

Absolution: Setting free from guilt.

Aggregation: Several things grouped together.

Anthropologist: A person who studies anthropology—the social science that studies the origins and social relationships of human beings.

Coercive: Restrained by force.

Connotations: A set of associations implied by a word in addition to its literary meaning.

Consensus: General agreement.

Cylindrical: In the shape of a cylinder.

Egalitarian: Marked by social equality.

Ethnographic: Relating to the branch of anthropology that deals with the scientific description of specific human cultures.

Faction: A group of people with similar political goals.

Indictment: An accusation of wrongdoing.

Injunction: A legal command to prohibit someone from doing a specific activity.

Maxim: A saying that is widely accepted.

Metadiscursive: A stretch of talk or discourse whose subject is the talk or discourse of which it is a part.

Metaphorical: Using one thing to represent another; symbolic.

Morality tales: Stories relating the beliefs on what is right and wrong.

Paternity: The state of being a father; fatherhood.

Penultimate: Next to the last.

Perpetrator: One who commits an offense or crime.

Postulate: Fundamental element; basic principle.

Precepts: Rules of personal conduct.

Probation: Staying out of jail under supervised conditions.

Putative: Generally regarded as such; supposed.

Reciprocal: A relationship that involves mutual giving and receiving.

Remedial: Intended to improve or make right.

Textual: Relating to a written text.

Suggested Further Reading

Thomas Biolsi & Larry J. Zimmerman, eds., *Indians and Anthropologists: Vine Deloria, Jr., and the Critique of Anthropology* (1997).

Larry Evers et al., eds., *Native American Oral Traditions: Collaboration and Interpretation* (2001).

Wolfgang Fikentscher, *The Sense of Justice and the Concept of Cultural Justice*, 34 American Behavioral Scientist 314 (1991).

Matthew L. M. Fletcher, *Rethinking Customary Law in Tribal Court Jurisprudence*, 13 Michigan Journal of Race and Law 57 (2007).

Pat Sekaquaptewa, *Evolving the Hopi Common Law*, 9 Kansas Journal of Law and Public Policy 761 (2000).

Notes

1. Earlier in their article, Yazzie and Zion describe "horizontal systems" as kinship and clan-based. Horizontal systems are more egalitarian and less coercive than "vertical systems."

2. The portions of transcript provided in this paper from the 1997 Hopi hearing employ several conventions typical of linguistic anthropological and other discourse analytic studies (see Duranti 1997).

Thus, names of speakers occur in the left column. Hopi utterances are represented first in Hopi using an orthography from *Hopìikwa Lavàytutuveni: A Hopi Dictionary of Third Mesa Dialect* (1997). Utterances are represented one clause per line, with each clause then translated twice, first with a morpheme-by-morpheme translation and then a looser English gloss, which appears in italics. Portions bolded mark the forms explicitly discussed in the paper. Also note the following additional conventions:

001: Line numbers divide interactional discourses in a phrase-by-phrase progression, allowing for interlinear transcription.

HAB: Marks the Hopi habitual aspect suffix *-ngwu.*

SUBCL: Marks Hopi particles that are used in utterances to connect subordinate clauses to superordinate clauses.

Ints: Marks Hopi particles that are used as modifiers which intensify their object forms.

CntrFct: Marks a Hopi particle *-as* that is employed in counterfactual statements.

3. Generally speaking, indefinite terms (e.g., somebody, anybody, somewhere, anywhere, someone) are a class of lexical and grammatical forms used when reference is made to something that is held as unidentifiable. In Hopi usage, as will be explored, indefinite terms can be employed by speakers to make claims without specifically referring to actual people, places, or times (see *Hopìikwa Lavàytutuveni* 1997).

4. The habitual aspect is a grammatical category in that denotes a quality of the event described as characteristic of a period of time. In Hopi usage, *-ngwu* can give the sense that the event or state it characterizes is a customary behavior or occurrence, or is a generally true comment about the world (again, see *Hopìikwa Lavàytutuveni* 1997).

CHAPTER 4

Forms and Trends of Traditional Tribal Governments

W E CAN NOW turn our attention to more systematically exploring some of the main topics of tribal legal studies. As described
above, law and legal systems are a fundamental part of any government and its authoritative operation. Consequently, a useful way to begin
a study of the different features of tribal law is by reviewing the history and
contemporary character of tribal governments more generally. This is by no
means a simple task. The reasons for this are twofold.

The first reason is that the differences between Anglo-American and various tribal concepts of what constitutes the norms, structures, and practices of
government can make it difficult to know what should be included in a
description of the key elements of tribal government. The "no government"
myth was just as common as the "no law" myth among Anglo-American legal
scholars and social scientists studying tribal law and society in North America. A good example of this is the study by Mischa Titiev of the Hopi living in
the village of Old Oraibi.[1] Though Titiev describes a number of ceremonial
leaders, clan leaders, and even a village chief (called the *Kikmongwi*), he contended that the Hopi had no formal government because none of these individuals were recognized as having the power to force other villagers to act in
socially acceptable ways. But is this kind of coercive force a necessary element
of all governments? What about those societies where respected individuals
lead by example and instruction rather than force? What about those where

the main form of coercion is the force of public opinion—where acting contrary to social expectation is avoided because doing so will result in people (such as family relatives) not wanting to cooperate with you at times when such cooperation is crucial to your survival? Is it fair to say that societies like these have no governments?

The second reason that providing a general overview of tribal government is difficult is because of the differences among the more than five hundred tribal nations within the United States today. The historic and contemporary types of government represented in these tribal nations span the spectrum—from the small fishing villages of the Pacific Northwest and even smaller groups in coastal California, to the highly mobile and far-ranging bands of Dakota and Shoshone of the Great Plains and Great Basin regions, to the Pueblo theocracies of the Southwest, to the confederacies and constitutional governments of the Northeast and Southeast. And even where we might find similarities in the governments of tribes from the same general regions, a closer look at any specific tribe will reveal a unique set of traditions and historical accounts concerning the origins of the tribe, its government, and how that government has been affected through contact with other tribal and European nations and the founding of the United States.

This diversity is captured well by Deloria and Lytle, who, though writing about studying tribal law, could have easily been commenting on the study of tribal governments, when they wrote that: "One would have to cover nearly 400 ratified treaties and agreements . . . and over 250 tribal constitutions and charters. . . . Add to this massive accumulation the traditions and customs of 500 or more individual tribes and the task becomes formidable indeed."[2]

Consequently, neither a comprehensive overview of the various tribal governments currently in operation nor a sufficiently detailed analysis of a single tribal government is possible within the space allowed in this single volume. Despite these difficulties and constraints, we believe it is necessary to provide a general overview of the history and contemporary operation of tribal governments. While the diversity of tribal governments should never be ignored, it is nonetheless true that there are certain shared aspects of all these governments that can guide our discussion.

The first shared aspect is that all governments, regardless of their specific shape, can be understood as designed to perform certain functions. In his analysis of American Indian indigenous governments, Wilkins offers a good functional definition for tribal government:

> Regardless of which of the . . . indigenous governments we are describing, it is important to note that the leadership of every tribal nation across time has sought to provide for the community's defense and safety, has

allocated resources according to tradition and custom, has overseen domestic and foreign relations, and has, in general, provided for the basic needs and desires of their people.[3]

Generally, the fundamental functions of any government include (1) community defense, (2) allocation of resources, and (3) regulation of domestic and foreign affairs, such that the wants and needs of their people are met. All governments everywhere undertake these tasks, so it is possible, at least at this basic level, to analyze any government in terms of the ways in which it accomplishes this work. Figure 4-1 shows the functional definition of tribal government.

FIGURE 4.1. Functional Definition of Tribal Government

Function Definition of Tribal Government

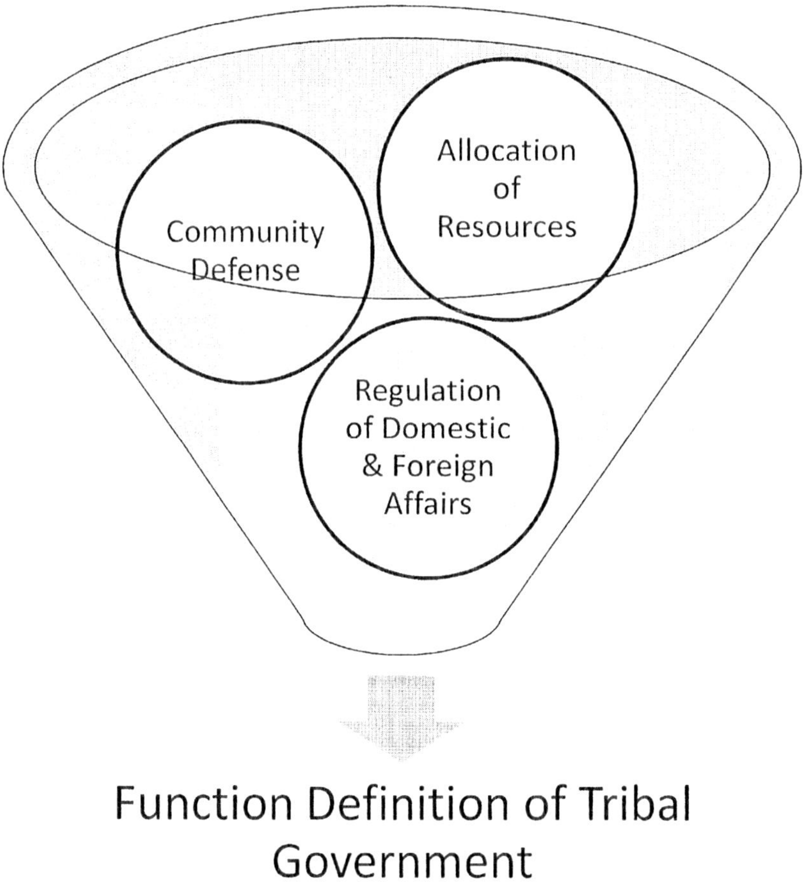

Furthermore, one way in which to understand how Anglo-American law defines the concept of sovereignty is to understand it as the right and capacity that the leaders of any people or nation have to accomplish these functions as they see fit, without interference from other nations and governments. We defined *tribal sovereignty* earlier as the power of tribal peoples to live by their own norms, structures, and practices. Combining these two definitions, we can understand this concept now as the right and capacity of tribal peoples and their governments to set these norms, structures, and practices for the purposes of cultural promotion, community defense, allocation of resources, and the regulation of domestic and foreign affairs without interference from other nations.

It is evident from the earliest treaties between the young U.S. federal government and different tribal leaders that American Indian tribes were treated as sovereigns with whom the United States could enter into government-to-government relationships. Such relationships implied that tribes were understood by federal authorities as having the full negotiating power, equal to the United States, to accept or reject the different terms of these treaties and the ways in which such agreements would guide their foreign affairs. As time went on and the U.S. federal government grew in strength, it increasingly acted in ways that treated tribes not as sovereign governments but as conquered peoples, subject to U.S. domination, with only a diminished sovereignty. Moreover, they treated tribal sovereignty as something that could still be reduced at any time, by the will of Congress. Indeed, it is against the backdrop of such domination and potential for further domination that the arguments regarding the sovereignty of tribal nations and their governments are voiced.

Using this functional definition for tribal government allows not only for analysis of very different governmental forms and practices but also for comparison and evaluation of those forms. Comparing and evaluating how well different forms of government fulfill their basic functions is part of the operation of every government. However, the concept that people belonging to a particular nation have a right to compare, evaluate, and reform their own government becomes much more complex when people foreign to that nation compare, evaluate, and try to reform its government. Very often, when outsiders evaluate and try to reform the governments of other people, they do so because they think their ways of governing are better by comparison, and they propose reforms to make those governments more like their own.

Sometimes aspects of the proposals made by outsiders may be well received by certain members of the nation being evaluated, especially if they have been invited by those members to propose reforms. Often, however, these proposals are seen as insensitive to the nation's history and governmental heritage. By focusing only on the basic governmental functions listed in our definition above, these foreign proposals can overlook all the other unique functions that each particular government fulfills for its people (such as its symbolic and religious functions). Such foreign proposals for reform may also be seen as an imposition on the affected nation's sovereignty, particularly where such proposals can be actually enacted without the consent of the people themselves. This was often the case in the European colonies created in Africa, Asia, and the Americas. These sentiments are felt by members of these nations, even in situations where the intentions of the outsiders making these proposals were really to improve their governments and their lives. This is precisely the situation that has arisen over the history of relations between tribal nations and the U.S. federal government.

There is, then, a second aspect shared by all tribal governments in the United States—their historic and continued subjugation to efforts by the U.S. federal powers to reform tribal government and society. Since the early 1800s and the foundational U.S. Supreme Court cases of federal Indian law, there has been recognition of a special relationship between tribes and the federal government, often referred to as the "federal trust relationship." The federal trust relationship can be interpreted differently from the perspectives of the federal government and the tribal governments. In the federal government's view, this relationship is based on the premise that, while tribes do retain sovereignty, they are nonetheless in "a state of pupilage"[4] to the United States, to be protected by federal authorities and dependent on them to learn the proper way to be participants in civil society and its government. Tribal governments often have a different perspective on the federal trust relationship, sometimes based on tribal kinship patterns and obligations.

This trust relationship has two significant elements. On the one hand, this relationship has been quite useful in protecting tribes and their sovereignty against intrusions by state governments and any authorities other than the federal government. Furthermore, this relationship means that the federal government itself, including Congress, has a duty to act only in the best interest of tribes and their people.

On the other hand, what has been taken as federal policy to be in the best interest of tribes and tribal peoples has usually come from what *non-Indians* thought was best for them, with little input from tribes themselves. As we shall see, this has often meant policies like those behind the Indian Reorganization Act of 1934, which worked to refashion tribal governments in the image of Anglo-American style constitutional democracy. Even the more blatant federal acts to seize and redistribute tribal lands were often justified as necessary for easing Indians into the new demands of "civil" society. Tribal removal efforts and the eventual settlement of tribes on reservations were policies justified as necessary to protect tribal peoples from the unscrupulous activities of expanding non-Indian populations encroaching on their former lands. Later, the allotment of reservation lands and even the termination of the federal trust relationship itself were explained as necessary to hasten the assimilation of tribal peoples to American culture and society. The belief was that Indians would only become truly "civilized" when they owned their own land, received proper non-Indian educations, and otherwise abandoned their tribal customs and traditions.

In summary, it is possible to provide an overview of the history and contemporary character of tribal governments along two different dimensions. First, we can analyze how different tribal governments originally operated to accomplish the basic governmental functions of providing for community defense, allocating resources, and regulating domestic and foreign relations. Second, we can analyze how U.S. federal policies imposed on tribes during the last two centuries have contributed to changes in how tribal governments accomplish those functions.

The following excerpt from Deloria and Lytle provides a good review of some of the basic features and functions of some of the various tribal governments that were in operation prior to and in the early years of the United States. These readings are useful primarily because they set the stage for better understanding the traumatic and often detrimental changes imposed on tribal governmental systems by U.S. federal policies seeking to recreate tribal governments in their image. In the next chapter, we will explore in more depth the changes made to these governments over the years of U.S. federal domination.

THE EVOLUTION OF TRIBAL GOVERNMENTS

*Vine Deloria Jr. and Clifford M. Lytle**

It is difficult to generalize about traditional forms of tribal government because there was such a great variety of Indian social groupings. Many tribes were loose confederations of hunting groups who spoke the same language and ranged over a broad expanse of territory. Such groups as the Shoshone and Paiutes, for example, were spread thinly in small groups over what is now the Great Basin area of the Western United States. The Sioux, as the French called them, or the Dakota, as the Indians called themselves, once ranged from the area near Wisconsin Dells, Wisconsin, to the Big Horn Mountains of Wyoming, a distance of nearly 1,300 miles in width. By

---

* Vine Deloria Jr. & Clifford M. Lytle, *American Indians, American Justice* 82–89 (1983).

contrast, small fishing villages in the Pacific Northwest were scattered independently among the many rivers of that region and had commercial and trading contacts but little political organization above the village or longhouse level. Some tribes, such as the Creek, were occasionally aggressive and incorporated smaller groups into themselves as a result of marriages or wars and eventually had to evolve a national organization to maintain themselves within their expanding territorial domain.

There were, of course, theocracies, such as the Pueblos of New Mexico and the Hopi of Arizona, who traced their form of government back to ancient times and organized their political and social life around a religious ceremonial year following basically religious rather than secular laws. The persistence of priesthood or influence of medicine men was not particularly significant in many tribes and if they followed theocratic forms it was only in deference to old prophecies that guided them in their migrations around the continent. The place of the religious leader should not be underestimated when speaking of the organization of the Indian tribe because most groups were highly sensitive to the admonitions of their holy people. But in comparison with the established clergy and priesthood that many societies have experienced, on the whole the tribes of North America were exempt from the absolute exercise of political powers by religious leaders.

It is best when discussing tribal political organizations to give some of the better-known examples of Indian institutions and see what function they played in the lives of people. Harold Driver describes the elaborate political structure of the Cheyenne as follows:

> The Cheyenne were governed by a civil council of forty-four chiefs, divided into five priestly chiefs, two doormen, and thirty-seven others. The priestly chiefs, who outranked the others, conducted tribal rituals, including the chief-renewal ritual performed every year when the group assembled. One of the five priestly chiefs presided at the meetings of the council of forty-four chiefs and manipulated the sacred medicines in the chief's medicine bundle; he was called the Prophet, and represented the mythical culture hero. The doormen were sometimes called upon to sum up the essence of the discussion and to render a decision for the group. When one of the five priestly chiefs retired, he chose his successor from the remaining thirty-nine members of the group; if he died so suddenly that he could not choose his successor, the surviving four priestly chiefs chose one for him. A priestly chief, on retirement, stepped down only to the rank of the undifferentiated thirty-seven chiefs; he did not have to leave

the council. If an undifferentiated chief died without choosing his successor, the entire council chose one for him. Each ordinary chief could serve only ten years, which explains why the rules of succession are so complicated. New chiefs were chosen on the basis of merit, and it was considered bad taste for a man to choose his own son. The personal qualities which constituted merit were control of temper and generosity.

None of the forty-four chiefs ever exerted any force to carry out the will of the civil council. Force was applied by the members of one of the six men's societies which the council selected on two important occasions: moving camp, and the tribal buffalo hunt. Moving camp was a military venture because there was always some danger of encountering an enemy. The tribal buffalo hunt was the most important occasion of the year, and teamwork was necessary to kill the maximum number of buffalo.

The two headmen and the two doormen of each of the men's societies formed a council of twenty-four war chiefs. A man could not be both a civil chief and a war chief. If a war chief was chosen as a civil chief, he must first resign his position of war chief before accepting that of civil chief. The council of war chiefs chose the war leader for each military raid; but, once the campaign ended, his authority terminated.

This rather formal organization complete with provisions for the replacement of chiefs, resignations, and the allocation of functions between war and peace would seem to suggest an institution similar between war and peace in most respects to those of the Western tradition. As the offices of chief were realized among the Cheyennes, however, they differ dramatically from political offices of Western peoples. The first duty of the chief was that he should care for the widows and orphans, and consequently, generosity was not simply a peripheral concern of the people when choosing a chief. Almost as important in the functioning of the office was the person's ability to act as a mediator in tribal disputes. A chief would often suffer loss himself as a means of resolving a dispute so that it would not disrupt the camp. Performing the function of a chief, therefore, was hardly the enriching experience that modern politicians enjoy when assuming their office.

Apart from their functions of making war, deciding when and where to move camp, authorizing the annual buffalo hunt, and ensuring that the annual religious ceremonies were held without incident, the role of the chiefs was to provide for the security and well-being of the people. Although chiefs were each charged with the responsibility of mediating disputes among the people, at times the council itself had to act to settle disputes. This duty was particularly true when a series of disputes had resulted in the killing of a person and the relatives sought revenge or demanded some additional form of compensation above that which had been offered by the slayer's relatives. On these occasions the council of chiefs had to satisfy the people and display the utmost wisdom in ensuring that justice was done and was perceived by everyone as settling the matter. Thus the function of the council was a conciliatory-judicial one rather than an executive function as one might initially perceive.

Many tribes considered the relationship between war and peace as critical to the successful operation of tribal harmony and provided for both war and peace functions. The Creeks, for example, as their confederacy grew larger, made provisions for distinct functions of war and peace. It is estimated that the Creek Confederacy had between fifty and eighty separate towns in the century before white contact; these towns represented the six language groups that composed the nation: Muskogee, Hitchiti, Koasati, Euchee, Natchez, and Shawnee. They divided these towns into red and white towns, red for war and white for peace. The white towns had all the councils, performed the adoption ceremonies, enacted the laws and regulations of the nation, and regulated the internal affairs of the confederation, including intertown relationships. No blood was supposed to be shed in the white towns and it was regarded as a serious offense to do so.

The red towns declared and conducted wars on behalf of the confederacy. They planned the military expeditions and conducted foreign relations on behalf of the nation. To prevent intraconfederacy disputes from fragmenting the tenuous alliance, ball games of some degree of ferocity were initiated matching towns against each other. Traditionally, red towns competed against white towns. To hear some tribal traditions about these ball games one would wonder whether a formal war would not have been more humane since these games made the average professional football game appear mild indeed.

Each town was governed by a head chief call a *micco*. He was appointed by a council of lesser miccos, generally from their group, and was given life tenure dependent upon his good behavior. Assisting him was a lesser personage called a *micco apotka*, who acted the role of an administrative assistant. The town itself was governed by a council of wise men and respected family heads called miccos who had basically the same function as the council of forty-four chiefs of the Cheyennes. When men became too old to serve in the council of miccos they were given the title of "beloved men" and acted as a very senior advisory group occupying places of honor at all councils and ceremonial occasions.

The warriors of each town were organized in a similar fashion with one acknowledged leader, called the *thlocco*, occupying the role of a war chief. The warriors were organized according to several particular ranks: the highest grade of warriors, who would be people well seasoned in the arts of war, were called *tastanagalgi;* of lesser rank were the *imala lakalgi*, who were less experienced; and they and the young men and relatively inexperienced warriors were called *imala laboskalgi*. The thlocco was the absolute leader of the nation during times of military emergency but his powers ended with the war and he reverted to town citizen until his office was needed again. In addition to these offices, the entire nation was divided into red and white clans and each clan was designated as a war or peace clan. By allocating these functions and allowing a certain amount of passage between offices as people matured, the Creeks produced some outstanding statesmen. Since the general posture of the nation, until it became involved with colonial intrigues of the European powers, was peaceful, the system tended to produce a stable and generally happy society.

The colonists had difficulty understanding the Creek system of government. They could not conceive why they had to make war against one well-known chief and trade peacefully or make peace with another. The European treaty commissioners always insisted on dealing with the "head" chief of the Creek Confederacy and, rather than learn the complicated system the Creeks used to allocate the functions of war and peace, began to insist on signing their treaties with the most influential miccos of the upper and lower towns of the Creek Confederacy. After a time these offices seemed to appear as a means of dealing with the Europeans and eventually the Creeks organized a council of kinds who were the miccos of the respective towns presided over by the miccos of the most important towns of the upper and lower halves of the nation. The Creeks thus evolved towards a European style of political organization because it was simpler to do so and because the preservation of the peace with the European powers made it necessary.

The Choctaws, another member group of the Five Civilized Tribes, so named because of their adaptability in developing institutions comparable in many respects to the European models, organized themselves along similar lines. Angie Debo has described the council process of the Choctaw Republic, which bears a striking similarity to both the Creek and the Cheyenne manner of organizing the tribe:

> Councils of the district were called by its Head Chief, and Councils
> of the entire Nation by the Head Chiefs acting in concert. Runners
> carrying bundles of sticks to reckon the time of meeting were sent to

summon all the town chiefs to the assembly. Apparently only these
officials were admitted to participate in the Council, but the common
people also came to listen to the speeches and to join in the inevitable
feasting, games, and dances. The Councils were distinguished by the
decorum with which they were conducted, and by the wild eloquence
of the native orators. The members were greatly influenced by the
judgment of the Head Chiefs and guided by their recommendations,
but the decision was democratic and in accord with the wishes of the
assembly.

The Council usually dealt with such matters of public policy as
peace, war, or foreign relations, but apparently it sometimes exercised
certain judicial power. It was not a legislative body, for the Choctaws
like other primitive people thought of law as a universal custom
rather than a legislative enactment.

In addition to the democratic nature of the Choctaw decision-making
process, two other important features may be discerned from Debo's
description. The first pertains to the seemingly limited role played by the
Head Chief, who appears to be a ceremonial leader rather than an executive; the second relates to the nonlegislative quasi-judicial nature of the
tribal councils' functions. Both these observations are important because
they testify to the fact that traditional tribal councils were charged with the
responsibility of ensuring domestic tranquility. They did not enforce a set
of laws, or even legislate them, but they did act in a mediation, taking on a
problem-solving role on behalf of the community, and they acted as an
intercessor for those people who sought public resolution of wrongs they
had suffered.

The most highly developed tribal government, as we have already
mentioned, was that of the Iroquois, who formed a five-nation alliance sym-
bolized by the Great Binding Law and the White Roots of Peace from the
great Tree of the Law, which symbolically represented peace to all who
would believe. The founding of the league of the Iroquois goes far back into
the past and basically involves the bringing of the Great Binding Law by
Dekanawideh and his spokesman, Hiawatha. Through subtle diplomacy
these two heroes convinced five separate groups to gather together as one
nation and to stand united against their foes, who at the time were pressing them severely. The Five Nations, now called the Six Nations with the
admittance of the Tuscaroras in the middle of the eighteenth century, continues today as a significant political force in contemporary Indian affairs.
The constitution that binds these groups together, however, is a most
involved and complicated document that provides for many contingencies

and demonstrates a finely balanced appreciation of the fierce pride the Indian nations have traditionally demonstrated.

The central decision-making body of the Iroquois Confederacy is a council, which has fifty seats filled by *rodiyaners* and presided over by the *Atotarho*, who is always an Onondaga. The council is divided into three separate bodies: the older brothers, who are Mohawks and Senecas; the younger brothers, who are the Cayugas and Oneidas; and the keepers of the fire, who are the Onondagas. Certain accommodations were made at the founding of the league to ensure the participation of the respective tribes. The Onondagas received 14 seats at the great council, the Mohawks 9, the Senecas 8, the Oneidas 9, and the Cayugas 10. The tribes, however, when voting each cast but one vote. Drawing upon the immediate disputes that had led these tribes to quarreling with each other, the constitution provided that no meeting would be considered legal unless the Mohawks were in attendance. The Senecas, who received only 8 seats at the council (and then shared these few with the Tuscaroras when they were admitted), were named the keepers of the western door and the war-making powers were vested in them.

The tribes are seated around a central fire during their deliberations, which must be held at least once in every year. The chiefs are further subdivided and they hold open discussions among these lesser groups so that all can hear the arguments and reasoning. In a highly complicated manner the subject under consideration is discussed by each of the tribes until it finally reaches the Onondagas, who have a final vote of "yes" or "no." The genius of this process is that the Onondagas, after having heard the subject analyzed from every possible standpoint, are then able to discern the general sense of the meeting and in effect place their imprimatur on a decision already basically the voice of the assembled people.

The constitution provides for various offices in the league; it establishes the clans that extend across the five nations and bind individual members together in a blood-extended family relationship; and it places ownership of the seats on the council, the rodiyaners, in the clan mothers so that women have a powerful voice in selecting the chiefs and consequently direct the affairs of the Six Nations in a fundamental way. The constitution also provides for adoption, emigration, rights of foreign nations, rights and powers of war, a definition of treason, protection of religious ceremonies, protection of the house, and funeral addresses. . . .

This important mediating function of the chief and the council provides a second interesting insight to be gained from examination of the traditional forms of tribal governments: the primary thrust of traditional government was more judicial than legislative in nature. As characterized by the National American Indian Court Judges Association (*Justice and American Indians*, p.

18), the system of private settlement of individual criminal offenses was nearly universal among Indian tribes. Unless an offense endangered the well-being of the tribe, the issue was to be settled privately among those affected. The process involved bargaining with a gift or some other form of propitiation or restitution serving as the basis for the settlement. Sometimes the aggrieved family or clan would insist that the wrongdoer join their group to replace the slain member, and the murderer was duty bound to respect their wishes. When the bargaining and negotiations failed, the chief would mediate and make every effort to preserve the peace. He provided the cement that held the tribe together peacefully. This adjudicatory nature of traditional tribal government stands in sharp contrast to the legislative orientation that the European influence would later introduce into Indian Country.[5]

Questions

1. Do you think that it is possible or necessary to provide some generalizations about the nature of all traditional tribal governments? Why or why not?
2. Do you think it is important to examine how tribal governments traditionally operated their government, even if the governments look very different today? Why or why not?

In Your Community

1. Do any of the general trends described by Deloria and Lytle match aspects of the original government of your tribe? Are there important elements to that government that the Deloria and Lytle reading do not capture?
2. When did U.S. federal officers or other foreign officials (e.g., Spanish, British, French, Russian) first come to your community? Do the records about those early encounters shed any light on the precolonial tribal government?
3. Were there any early efforts made by members of your government to adjust or adapt your government to meet federal expectations, as was observed in the Creek Nation?

Glossary

Functional: Describing something based on what it *does* rather than what it *is*.

Government-to-government: A relationship between equal or near-equal nations that prevents one from having control over the citizens of the other.

Mediator: One who reconciles differences in a dispute.

Negotiating power: The power the people in a dispute give the mediator and the dispute resolution process.

Subjugation: Being brought under control; conquering.

Theocracy: A government ruled by religious authority.

Unscrupulous: Without concern for the ethical treatment of others.

Suggested Further Reading

Duane Champagne, *American Indian Societies: Strategies and Conditions of Political and Cultural Survival* (1989).

Notes

1. Mischa Titiev, *Old Oraibi: A Study of the Hopi Indians of the Third Mesa* (1944).
2. Vine Deloria Jr. & Clifford M. Lytle, *American Indians, American Justice* 99–103 (1983).
3. David E. Wilkins, *American Indian Politics and the American Political System* 119 (2002).
4. *Cherokee Nation v. Georgia*. As used in this case, *pupilage* means being like a pupil or student, in need of instruction, guidance, and supervision from a teacher.
5. Deloria & Lytle, *American Indians, American Justice* 82–89.

CHAPTER 5

The History of Federal Indian Policy and the Changes to Tribal Governments

ROM THE federal perspective, U.S. policy toward Indians has always been justified in light of the federal trust relationship and the duty that the U.S. government owes to tribal peoples to protect their interests and welfare. However, more often than not, what has been held by federal agents to be necessary to protect the interests and welfare of tribal peoples has been determined primarily by non-Indians, with only minimal input from Indians and tribal nations themselves. Historically, most of the non-Indians who have affected federal policy regarding Indians have been convinced that what is best for Indian interests and welfare is to get them, ultimately, to adopt lifestyles and governmental operations more like those of American society.

Of course, at any particular period in the last two hundred years of federal Indian policy, how exactly to make Indians more like other American citizens has been handled differently. Sometimes the policy has been to isolate tribal nations in far-removed territories and reservations until these people and their societies could "evolve" into the democratic civil society that Euro-Americans have already attained. Other times, the policy has been assimilation—the breaking down of tribal communities and their collective land holdings to force tribal members to live like their more individualistic non-Indian neighbors—owning and farming private lands, sending their children to schools, and voting in state and federal elections. In the years of tribal reorganization

73

SCOTUS; always wanted
tribes to adopt Anglo ways!

• federal
trust
relationship

and more recent federal policies of tribal self-determination, the renewed recognition of tribal nations as viable sovereign entities is still based on the fact that support from the federal government comes only if tribes can show that they have governmental institutions that are sufficiently similar to U.S.-style political and legal institutions.

At many times in U.S. history, competing federal interests in increasing non-Indian access to tribal lands and natural resources and limiting tribal authority seemed so prominent that one has to wonder if the federal trust relationship was merely used as a (rather thin) cover under which these much more harmful activities could be undertaken. Nonetheless, the trust relationship has always been a cornerstone of federal policy toward tribal nations. Hence actions taken in the name of that policy are arguably still informed by a general belief that tribal welfare and interests are better served as the tribes adopt more Anglo-American-style governmental institutions.

This chapter offers a brief review of the history of federal policy toward tribes, focusing on a few significant periods. As you read the materials provided, consider how, even in the early years, when the Supreme Court was describing tribal peoples as possessing some degree of sovereignty, the Court was also planting the seeds for future federal policy that would try to force tribes to abandon their unique culture and governmental systems and to adopt Anglo-American social and political organization. Figure 5-1 presents the different eras of federal Indian policy.

EARLY RECOGNITION OF TRIBAL SOVEREIGNTY

*Patricia Sekaquaptewa**

In reviewing the foundational U.S. Supreme Court case law, there are two important things to focus on: (1) What is happening to tribal sovereignty (powers); and (2) What is happening to tribal rights in land. The early cases defined both tribal sovereignty and rights in land as means of justifying why tribes did not have the power to sell land without permission and why the U.S. Supreme Court would not hear cases brought by tribes in federal court. The early cases are essentially about the right to buy (or take) and sell Indian lands.

---

* Patricia Sekaquaptewa, *Early Recognition of Tribal Sovereignty* (2002) (unpublished classroom materials on file with the UCLA Tribal Legal Development Clinic).

FIGURE 5.1. The Different Eras of Federal Indian Policy

> **Colonial Period**
> (1492-1776)
> Trade, land cessions, and war

> **Confederation Period**
> (1776-1789)
> American Revolution, Articles of Confederation, Continental Congress, conflict
> between national and state government over management of Indian affairs

> **Trade and Intercourse Act Era**
> (1789-1835)
> Adoption of U.S. Constitution, Congress to exclusively regulate trade, relations,
> and land cessions, and enter into treaties with tribes

> **Removal Period**
> (1835-1861)
> Extinguishment of Indian title to eastern lands and removal of Indians
> beyond state boundary lines westward

> **Reservation Era**
> (1861-1887)
> Westward non-Indian settlement leapfrogs the Indian Territory to California,
> creation of reservations within states and territories, with resulting Indian Wars

> **Allotment Period & Forced Assimilation**
> (1871-1934)
> End of treatymaking, federal courts given some criminal jurisdiction over
> crimes committed by Indians in Indian Country, federal government individually
> allots tribal lands, and opens up remainder for non-Indian settlement

> **Indian Reorganization Act Period**
> (1934-1940)
> Allotment ended, tribes adopt constitutions and establish tribal
> councils and business committees

> **Termination Era**
> (1940-1962)
> Controversy over IRA, Congress passes a number of statutes subjecting some
> tribes to termination of federal supervision and subjecting them to
> state jurisdiction, many Indians relocated to urban centers

> **Self-Determination Era**
> (1962-Present)
> Revitalization of tribal entities and improvement of conditions on reservations,
> restoration of some tribes to federal recognition and supervision, passage of Indian
> Civil Rights Act, the Indian Self-Determination and Education Assistance Act,
> the Indian Child Welfare Act, Indian Tribal Government Tax Status Act,
> Indian Land Consolidation Act, Indian Gaming Regulatory Act

During the 1500s, the countries of Europe were simultaneously competing for newly discovered lands and wealth and debating about the rights of the indigenous peoples they were encountering. The principles derived from this competition and debate became part of the European international law. About three hundred years later, the young U.S. Supreme Court, in the case of *Johnson v. M'Intosh*, reached back to these principles to settle a dispute between two non-Indians over certain property. One of the parties claimed he acquired the land from the British government and the other claimed he acquired the same land from an Indian tribe. The Court had to justify why the title issued by the British government was better than the title issued by the Indians. In doing so, the Court first announced a "Doctrine of Discovery." According to this new doctrine, the first European power that "discovered" and claimed a particular territory then had the exclusive right to purchase the land from the Indians from that time forward. The Court reasoned that, in this particular case, the British discovered the land in question and had the exclusive right to purchase it from the Indians. The party who then received title to this land from the British government legitimately owned the land. When the new American government was established, it inherited all the discoverer's rights from the British, including the exclusive right to buy land from the Indians.

In 1831, the Cherokee Nation asked the U.S. Supreme Court to stop the State of Georgia from executing laws that would do away with the Cherokee government and seize its lands. The Cherokee argued that they had treaties with the United States that protected their government and lands. The Court found that it could not help the tribe, stating that it only had authority under the U.S. Constitution to hear disputes between "foreign nations" and "states," and the tribe could not be considered a foreign nation. The Court constructed a new category for tribes—the category of "domestic dependent nations":

> Though the Indians are acknowledged to have an unquestionable, and, heretofore, unquestioned, right to the lands they occupy, until that right shall be extinguished by a voluntary cession to our government; yet it may well be doubted, whether those tribes which reside within the acknowledged boundaries of the United States can, with strict accuracy, be denominated foreign nations. They may more correctly, perhaps, be denominated domestic dependent nations. They occupy a territory to which we assert a title independent of their will, which must take effect in point of possession, when their right of pos-

session ceases. Meanwhile, they are in a state of pupilage. Their relation to the United States resembles that of a ward to his guardian.
They look to our government for protection; rely upon its kindness
and its power; appeal to it for relief to their wants; and address the
president as their great father. (*Cherokee Nation v. Georgia* 30 U.S. |5
Pet.| 1 |1831|)

By the mid-1800s, U.S. law recognized that tribes were domestic
dependent nations with limited sovereignty and the right to occupy and use
(but not necessarily to sell) their aboriginal lands. Even then, these were
considered serious blows to tribal sovereignty and rights in land. Nevertheless, these early cases formally recognized tribal governmental status under
U.S. law, thus paving the way for modern federal–tribal, government-to-
government relations.

The Taking of Tribal Lands and Resources

Whatever your political views on these issues, it is undeniable that most
of the federal–tribal relationship has been, and continues to be, defined
by the taking of tribal land and resources. The taking of tribal land, in the
past, has seriously undermined the integrity and functioning of tribal government. There were three major interrelated processes for taking tribal
land throughout the years: (1) by negotiating treaties where the Indians
"ceded" their homelands to the federal government in exchange for lesser
lands farther away, to the west of the non-Indian communities; (2) (after
treaty-making was banned by Congress in 1871) by negotiating agreements with a tribe to cede more land, followed by Congress passing a law
approximating the agreement; and (3) by implementing the General
Allotment Act and related acts that cut up tribal lands into individual
plots, giving each Indian family a small "farm" and opening up remaining tribal lands to non-Indian homesteaders. In some states (for example,
California and Alaska), tribal lands were effectively confiscated and
turned into public domain lands without any compensation whatsoever.
Between 1887 (the General Allotment Act) and 1934 (the Indian Reorganization Act), Indian landholdings were decreased by 90 million acres
(American Indian Lawyer Training Program, *Indian Tribes as Sovereign
Governments* 9 |1988|).

LAW AND LEGISLATION

*Carole Goldberg**

Treaty-Making between the United States and the Indians

Between the founding of the nation and 1871, when Congress banned further Indian treaties, the United States entered into hundreds of agreements, most of them embodying the following terms:

1. a cession (giving up) of Indian land, in exchange for a reservation or grant of land set aside for the Indians' permanent and exclusive use and occupancy;
2. acknowledgement that the tribe retains the rights of self-government, but that the tribe has also come under the "protection" of the United States;
3. provision for water, hunting, fishing, and gathering rights for the Indians in lands set aside for them, and sometimes hunting and fishing rights in ceded territories as well;
4. assertion of federal control over matters involving non-Indians in areas reserved for the Indians, including trade and crimes between Indians and non-Indians, with such control to supersede state authority; and
5. provision of needed supplies and services by the United States.

Congress eventually abandoned treaty-making with Indian tribes because the House of Representatives did not like the fact that it was excluded from the treaty-making process. Under the United States Constitution, treaties are signed by the president and ratified by a two-thirds vote of the Senate. After 1871 Congress dealt with Indian affairs through legislation, in which both houses of Congress participate. This change of method did not alter the legal status of Indian nations.

Some Indian tribes have never entered into treaties with the United States, either because the Senate refused to ratify treaties that were negotiated or because the tribes' first contact with the United States occurred late in the nineteenth century. Nevertheless, the terms of Indian treaties have

---

* Carole Goldberg, *Overview: U.S. Law and Legal Issues*, in *The Native North American Almanac* 470–73 (Duane Champagne, ed., 2001).

served as the model for federal law applicable to all tribes, perhaps because the treaties represent a form of consent to limited tribal incorporation within the American political system. Absent such consent of the governed, American political theory views governmental power as unjust and illegitimate. The treaties are thus a means to justify the authority of the federal government over Indian lands and people.

Indian Policy of the New American Government

The earliest Indian policy of the American government, embodied in legislation known as the Trade and Intercourse Acts (first adopted in 1790 and reenacted with amendments many times thereafter), sought to preserve peace between Indians and land-hungry settlers by ruling out most contact between the two groups. Among other things, the acts restricted non-Indian entry into Indian lands, regulated trade with the Indians, limited the introduction of alcoholic beverages into Indian Country, and punished interracial crimes involving Indians and non-Indians. One of the most important features of the Trade and Intercourse Acts was the prohibition on transfer of Indian lands without federal approval. Some states, notably New York and Georgia, resisted this policy, and continued to make their own Indian treaties. Land transfers resulting from these agreements have been the source of many modern Indian land claim cases, such as the successful suit brought by the Oneida of New York. In that litigation, the Oneida challenged treaties with the state of New York that date back to 1793, claiming that the transfer of land to the state was invalid because the federal government never gave its consent. The United States Supreme Court agreed, and found that the passage of time had not weakened the Oneida claims, in part because the state of New York and the United States had done their best to discourage and prevent claims in the past.

The federal policy of physically separating Indians and non-Indians, as embodied in the Trade and Intercourse Acts, began to weaken in the early decades of the nineteenth century, as settler pressure for westward expansion swelled. The crisis was most acute in the lands of the Cherokee, where gold was discovered in the late 1820s. In 1829 Georgia enacted laws purporting to extend its authority onto Cherokee lands and to abolish the Cherokee government. Throughout the 1820s the Cherokee adopted a constitution and tribal laws modeled on the U.S. system, and abolished traditional legal regimes such as the blood feud, which entailed retaliation for the death of a clan member by killing a member of the killer's clan. Treaties with the United States promised the Cherokee a permanent homeland and self-government on that part of their ancestral lands that was located in

Georgia. Nevertheless, neither Congress nor the president was willing to challenge Georgia's actions on behalf of the Cherokee. Faced with the prospect of losing their rights, the Cherokee Nation sued in federal court. Chief Justice John Marshall issued decisions in two Cherokee cases (*Cherokee Nation v. Georgia* and *Worcester v. Georgia*) that acknowledged the sovereign powers of Indian tribes and the absence of state authority in areas set aside as tribal homelands. These opinions could not, however, protect the Cherokee against the rising tide of American settlers when the president of the United States and the Congress were unwilling to stand behind treaty promises.

Through a series of laws and coerced treaties in the 1830s to the 1850s, the federal government demanded the "removal" of the Cherokee as well as other eastern and midwestern tribal groups to an area west of the Mississippi River that was established for Indian settlement, known as Indian Territory. As a result, most of the Cherokee were forced to leave their ancient homelands to move to the Indian Territory. Thousands of Cherokee lost their lives in what has become known as the Trail of Tears. In many of these treaties, the United States promised the tribes that the land set aside for them in the Indian Territory would never become part of a state or territory without their consent, and would never be subject to state law. Several times during the first half of the nineteenth century, Congress actually came close to establishing the Indian Territory as an American state exclusively for Indian people, but the legislation never passed both houses of Congress, partly because some Indian groups opposed the idea. By the end of the nineteenth century, the government broke its promise to keep Indian Territory separate from the states when the Indian Territory was reorganized first as part of the Territory of Oklahoma and later as part of the state of Oklahoma. Some of the eastern Indians who hid or refused to move at the time of removal later had their remaining lands declared reservations; thus there are now federally recognized Cherokee and Choctaw tribes both in Oklahoma and on the East Coast.

Tribal Governments Undermined by the Reservation System and Allotment

Through the second half of the nineteenth century, as pressure from non-Indians made even the existence of Indian Territory politically unfeasible, the federal government embarked on a policy of concentrating Indians on reservation lands where they could be "civilized" and assimilated. The Office of Indian Affairs was established to act as administrator of these new reservations; initially as part of the War Department, the office came under the Department of Interior in 1849.

In the course of administering reservation life, this Office of Indian Affairs came to dominate, weaken, and drive underground tribal government and legal systems. With tribal economies disrupted by the move to reservations, much of the Indian administration's power came from its control over the necessities of life, such as food and shelter. The Office of Indian Affairs established Courts of Indian Offenses and Indian Police, staffed with handpicked Indians, to replace traditional sources of law and authority. The judges and police thus enforced a Code of Indian Offenses, drafted by the Indian Affairs administrators, that prohibited many traditional cultural and religious practices, including the Ghost Dance (part of a largely religious movement), the destruction of an individual's personal property at death, Indian games of chance, and polygamy. Agents of the Office of Indian Affairs on each reservation (called *superintendents*) also designated tribal leaders who were willing to sign leases of tribal land and otherwise cooperate in pursuing the assimilationist goals of federal policy. Many traditional tribal functions, such as the allocation of land-use rights and the organization of agriculture, were taken over by the superintendents.

The weakening of tribal government and legal systems accelerated in the last decades of the nineteenth century, when Congress enacted laws requiring the allotment (division) of communally held lands on many reservations into individually owned parcels, thereby eliminating a defining element of tribal life. The parcels were to be held in trust (protected from being taxed or sold) by the federal government for a brief period of time, after which they were to be freely owned by the individual Indian. The state federal purpose of imposing allotment was to transform Indians into individualist farmers. Allotment diminished tribal powers by withdrawing lands from tribal control and reducing the total acreage under Indian ownership. The federal government sold off "excess" lands that it did not deem necessary for allotment, and the parcels allocated to individual Indians often found their way into non-Indian hands, either through fraud or tax sales. Eighty-six million acres, over 60 percent of the Indians' land base, was lost during the allotment era (approximately 1886–1934). Another legacy of allotment is the fact that some modern reservations have large numbers of non-Indian residents, living on once-allotted land that they now own. These non-Indian residents often wish to be free from tribal authority, even though they are living within the boundaries of an Indian reservation.

Congress formally abandoned the policy of allotment in 1934 and extended the trust period for existing allotments indefinitely. Thus, many previously established allotments remain held in trust by the federal government. Through inheritance, many of these allotments are now owned by hundreds of people, which makes it extremely difficult to use the allotments

efficiently. Congress has attempted to find some way to return these allotments to tribal ownership. The United States Supreme Court has refused to
allow such transfers, however, unless the United States or the tribes compensate all of the allotment owners for their fractions of ownership rights.

Allotment laws frequently abrogated treaty promises to the Indians.
But when tribes challenged these laws in the U.S. Supreme Court, they lost
on the grounds that the United States was free to act as it thought was best
for Indians, even though that meant violating treaty promises. The U.S.
Supreme Court has said that Congress may abrogate Indian treaties just as
it may abrogate treaties with foreign countries, even though Indian tribes
are not in the same position as foreign countries. For example, Indian tribes
are unable to appeal to international bodies or to military force if the United
States unilaterally abandons a treaty promise. Nevertheless, there are some
constraints on Congress when it contemplates violating an Indian treaty.

If the treaty has created property rights (including the rights to hunt
and fish), the U.S. Supreme Court has said that Congress must compensate the tribe for any rights it loses when the treaty is abrogated. The
Sioux claim against their loss of the Black Hills, part of their ancestral
lands, is based on this principle. To the disappointment of many Sioux,
however, this principle provides only monetary compensation, not a return
of land. Some groups of Sioux have refused to accept the money, insisting
that they are entitled to reclaim their ancestral lands in accordance with
their treaty rights.

The Indian Reorganization Act and Federal Recognition of Tribal Governments

In 1934, Congress adopted the Indian Reorganization Act, now referred to
as the IRA. The IRA provided a way for tribes to form tribal councils and
business committees, to draft and adopt constitutions, and for Congress and
the president to formally recognize a tribal government as a government.
It is difficult to overestimate the influence of this law on the development
of modern tribal governments. Whether contemporary tribal governments
were coerced to accept or rejected the terms of the act, most tribal governments today will find that their tribal council structure, business council
structure, and/or provisions in their constitutions have elements of the IRA
or related provisions in them. Often, even non-IRA tribes are dealt with
"through the lens of the IRA" by federal officials and others.

THE EVOLUTION OF TRIBAL GOVERNMENTS

Vine Deloria Jr. and Clifford M. Lytle[*]

Tribal Government in Modern Perspective

Modern tribal government can trace its inception, although not its fruition, back to the New Deal administration of Franklin Delano Roosevelt. When the federal government finally awakened to the fact that the Indian allotment policy had been a failure, resulting in the loss of a substantial portion of the Indian land estate and the impoverishment of the people, Congress, at the urging of the president and the secretary of interior, Harold Ickes, initiated a new Indian policy by enacting the Indian Reorganization Act of 1934 (IRA, 48 State. 984). Part of the catalytic force behind this measure was the 1928 Meriam Report, which described the failure of the federal government to provide for Indians. . . .

The Indian Reorganization Act became important because it directed national policy from a deliberate effort to extinguish tribal governments and customs to a goal of establishing self-government and providing it with sufficient authority and powers to represent the reservation population in a variety of political and economic ventures. The act did not enumerate the powers of the new governments established under its provisions. Indeed, Felix S. Cohen noted that "the act of June 18, 1934 had little or no effect upon the substantive powers of tribal self government. . . . [It] did bring about the regularization of procedures of tribal government and modification of the relations of the Interior Department to the activities of tribal government" (Cohen, pp. 129–130).

The IRA, then, signaled an attitudinal change toward Indians and tribal governments. It provided an opportunity to revitalize tribal governments that had been submerged by the failure of either the legislative or the executive branches of the federal government to articulate the proper relationship that in fact existed between the Department of Interior and the Bureau of Indian Affairs in their trustee capacity and the tribal governments, which, for better or for worse, were the successors to the gatherings of chiefs and headmen who had signed the treaties on behalf of their nations three-quarters of a century before. In addition to terminating the destructive allotment system, the IRA afforded tribes an opportunity to organize

---

[*] Vine Deloria Jr. & Clifford M. Lytle, *American Indians, American Justice* 99–103 (1983).

for their common welfare and to adopt written constitutions that would be formally approved by the secretary of the interior and that granted them status as federally chartered corporations.

The tribes who agreed to accept the provisions of this act could employ their own legal counsel (with the approval of the Secretary of the Interior) and even issue charters of incorporation for business purposes. More important, the act established a special fund from which the secretary of interior could make loans to tribally chartered corporations for economic development purposes. Tribal members were extended the opportunity to vote on whether or not they wanted to participate in the benefits and accept the responsibilities of the IRA, but this vote was to be a one-time opportunity. If a majority of the tribe voted against participation, it could not reconsider this decision at a later date. Tribes had two years to accept or reject the IRA. Within that period 258 elections were held; 181 tribes accepted the terms of the act while 77 tribes registered a negative vote. Even these provisions were significantly vague. The act read that the Indians on every reservation could vote on this opportunity and in some cases, indeed a substantial number of cases, there was more than one tribe living on the reservation in question. Consequently, we derive the new "consolidated" or "confederated" tribal names from the elections held under this act and these bodies then assumed the political status their predecessor entities once possessed. Thus, out of these IRA elections we find the Three Affiliated Tribes of the Fort Berthold Reservation, who formerly were the Mandans, Gros Ventres, and Arickaras; the Confederated Salish and Kootenai of the Flathead Reservation; and the Confederated Colville tribe, which was formerly a large number of Indian bands occupying that reservation.

Another difficulty involved with the act concerned the sequence in which the elections were to be held. The Secretary of Interior was authorized under the IRA to transfer federal surplus and submarginal lands to the use of Indians who were landless. Once these lands were transferred, and this case occurred with some frequency in California, an election could be held by those Indians who moved onto the land to adopt the provisions of the IRA and to approve a constitution. The question subsequently arose whether a tribe had to have land before it could adopt a constitution or whether a constitution could be approved with the idea of receiving a transfer of land. While these questions did not seem pressing at the time, over the years, as new groups were considered for recognition by the Interior Department, they became major barriers for small groups of Indians achieving federal status and joining in the benefits conferred by the act. Some Indian scholars believe that this question has never been satisfactorily handled in the decades since the IRA has become a reality.

When the Indian Reorganization Act was passed in 1934, the first impression was that it would bring about a monumental change in Indian affairs. While there was little new substantively in the act that could not be found in miscellaneous solicitor's opinions or memos of the Interior Department rulings, the act did lay the foundation for a resurrection of tribal government and power. The bureaucratic stranglehold and paternalistic orientation of the BIA were substantially modified. Administrative centralization was replaced by decentralized power in tribal governments. Once these initial positive changes had become institutionalized, however, continuing efforts to reform the bureaucratic stance of the government toward the tribes declined and a mass of additional, sometimes conflicting, opinions and memos accumulated to handicap the tribes in their further development efforts.

The political damage that had been inflicted upon tribal governments for so many decades in the past could not be undone overnight. The traditional forms of tribal government had been dormant for too long and much of the religious undergirding of the informal customs had been badly eroded. The format that emerged under the 1934 Act was almost a carbon copy of the structured, legalistic European form of government. Since tribal governments were floundering, the Bureau of Indian Affairs seized the initiative and drafted a model constitution that could be used by tribes as a starting point for their written documents. This model constitution in most cases became the final product, which should not be surprising since Congress in passing the IRA required that all constitutions be approved by the Secretary of Interior before becoming operational (25 U.S.C. 476), and homogeneity rather than usefulness consequently became the virtue.

Secretarial approval of constitutions, by-laws, selection of legal counsel, and most tribal resolutions proposing land use and civil and criminal codes was in effect a veto power on the activities of the newly formed tribal governments. In some instances these restrictions were necessary. It was difficult if not impossible, for example, for reservation Indians to check the credentials of attorneys seeking to be the legal counsel of the tribe. In most instances the secretarial veto proved helpful in directing the tribes toward adequate legal representation, but in some cases the integrity of the attorney in opposing the policies of the lower-level bureaucrats was sufficient evidence to delay or disapprove his or her contract. It can certainly be argued that, given the inexperience and impotency of tribal governments during these formative years, BIA assistance to the tribes was needed. But the agency utilized this secretarial approval requirement along with other powers as a basis for maintaining control over tribal affairs. In fact, processes and problems that had formerly been handled by community consensus were now formalized and required tribal resolutions and secretarial approval.

The efforts to revitalize tribal governments continued with limited success throughout the 1930s and 1940s. Although the exercise of power by tribal governments took on the appearance of increasing sophistication, these developments came at the expense of certain tribal traditions and informal customs that had served the communities well for nearly three-quarters of a century. Indians, consciously or not, adopted the whites' legalistic perspective on government. The 1950s, however, posed a significant threat in tribal development. The Eisenhower administration initiated a policy of "termination," initially discussed during the early years of the Truman administration, designed to eliminate the reservations and assimilate the Indians into the mainstream of the white social and economic systems. Termination was a contemporary version of allotment since it divided the tribal assets on a per capita basis and then required the individual tribal members to forfeit their federal rights to services and supervision. The Bureau of Indian Affairs, as it had during the allotment days, played a major role in terminating the tribes and selling off the tribal land estates.

In the overall scheme of things, however, the Eisenhower "termination" policy was but a momentary, though totally destructive, digression from the continuing resurgence of tribal government development. In the two decades following the Eisenhower years, tribes were once again placed in a position to seize the initiative that had begun in the 1930s to exercise self-governing powers. The social programs of the 1960s, the New Frontier and the Great Society social welfare legislation, enabled the tribal governments to be sponsors of federally funded programs, and tribal governments rapidly expanded to take advantage of these opportunities. Soon each tribe had developed its own massive bureaucracy to deal with the multitude of programs for which it was eligible. Although the IRA had enabled tribes to charter organizations for the purpose of economic development, few tribes had any experience in operating complicated subsidiaries. The first thought of many tribes during the 1960s was to designate the tribal council as the housing authority, the economic development corporation, and even sometimes the school board. But it was quickly apparent to both tribes and the federal funding agencies alike that this kind of institutional response was fraught with complications. Consequently, HUD [the U.S. Department of Housing and Urban Development], EPA [the Environmental Protection Agency], and other federal agencies required tribal councils to charter separate housing authorities and nonprofit development corporations. One of the major problems to arise in these efforts to develop subsidiary institutions was the fact that many programs needed to provide in-kind matching grants and materials and the tribal council had control of and responsibility for tribal property and income. In order to make certain that their people derived every possible service and program for which they were eligible, tribal governments were burdened with responsibilities far in excess of anything conceived during the IRA's formative years.

Self-Determination: Reallocating Control and Funding from the Bureau of Indian Affairs to Tribal Governments

In 1975, Congress adopted another very important law—the Indian Self-Determination and Education Assistance Act (Public Law 93-638). This act transferred significant amounts of control and funding from the Bureau of Indian Affairs (BIA) and other federal agencies to tribes as "subcontractors" to open and manage their own service agencies and providers. These service agencies and providers included everything from tribal government divisions, such as courts, to tribal social services and counseling services to hospitals. The act also provided for a demonstration project for some tribes to assume complete control (known as "compacting tribes") over all their federal funds and services.

There have been serious problems with the implementation of the act. One of its inherent contradictions has been the reinforcement of the federal trust responsibility to tribes, which requires federal oversight and control of the funding to tribes, while simultaneously seeking to promote tribal independence and self-determination as subcontractors or compacters.

You may be more familiar with this act as the source of your tribe's annual federal "638," "contract," or "compact" funds. Each year, your tribal council passes a resolution prioritizing its most important budget requests (or negotiates a compact, for compacting tribes). The BIA and your tribe then negotiate which items on the list will be funded and how much funding the tribe will receive for each item. Because these 638 funds are often a primary source of funds for key tribal agencies or service providers, it is important to understand from where and how this funding flows into your tribe.

FEDERAL SELF-DETERMINATION AND SELF-GOVERNANCE POLICIES, 1970–TODAY

Carole Goldberg[*]

In an address he gave in 1970, President Richard Nixon announced a new direction for federal Indian policy. He repudiated the policy of termination dating from the 1950s, and also rejected initiatives from the 1960s "War on Poverty" that had enlarged federal bureaucratic management and oversight. Instead, he gave his support to policies that would support tribal self-determination and self-governance.

Congress endorsed this new policy direction in 1975 with passage of the Indian Self-Determination and Education Assistance Act (Public Law 93-638). This act enabled Indian nations to make contracts with the federal government for the purpose of taking over a share of the administrative responsibilities and resources previously handled by the BIA. Contracts under the Self-Determination Act have affected education, law enforcement, forest management, and many other functions on reservations.

Partly to calm Indian nations' fears of termination, the Act specifically preserved the federal trust responsibility and the Federal–Indian relationship. What this meant in practice, however, is that the BIA retained some control over which contracts received funding. The tribes submitted lists of contracts to be funded in priority order, and the BIA made decisions based on those lists. Furthermore, when contracted activity involves federal trust resources such as land, timber, fish, or water, the BIA must approve all decisions made by the contracting tribe.

Implementing the Self-Determination Act has been hampered by resistance from the BIA, which has stood to lose power and jobs. Another problem with the act has been the bureaucratic burden that has accompanied each contract. Because these contracts put Indian nations in the position of carrying out administrative responsibilities of the federal government, a host of federal laws and regulations regarding civil rights, employment, labor, and other matters have to be followed, and several layers of BIA officials have to oversee compliance. Tribal bureaucracies have had to grow to keep up with all the rules and requirements.

---

[*] Carole Goldberg, *Federal Self-Determination and Self-Governance Policies, 1970–Today* (2002) (unpublished material on file with the UCLA Native Nations Law and Policy Center).

Critics of the self-determination policy have complained that it did not achieve any meaningful transfer of power from the federal government to the Indian nations. For example, according to George Esber, "In essence, the United States is agreeing to legal compliance with the self-determination policy by granting Indian participation in Anglo activities. This is not equivalent to the governance of Indian affairs as Indian undertakings." Nonetheless, the Self-Determination Act at least moved federal policy in the direction of greater autonomy for Indian nations, and handed tribes some significant resources to use for redevelopment.

To remedy some of the problems associated with contracting under the Self-Determination Act, Indian nations led a reform effort that produced amendments to the act in 1988 authorizing the Tribal Self-Governance Demonstration Project. Under this project, twenty (later thirty) Indian nations went beyond contracting for specific BIA services, and received large blocks of federal funds to manage themselves. Self-governance "compacts" between the federal government and participating Indian nations authorized these nations to move money among programs, prioritize spending, redesign services, and be responsible for their own choices. Funding for the compacts was allocated from existing BIA funds, with reference to amounts the tribe would have received absent the agreement. To qualify for participation in the Self-Governance Demonstration Project, Indian nations had to develop a spending plan and demonstrate sound fiscal management and a history of successful administration or prior 638 contracts. As in the Self-Determination Act, Congress reaffirmed and continued its trust responsibility within the new funding framework.

The self-governance initiative received strong support from tribal leaders. According to Professor Robert Porter, "The Indian nations appreciated the negotiated and respectful manner in which Congress was withdrawing the BIA from their daily affairs. While the project preserved the trust responsibility, it allowed the Indian nations to develop governmental competence without fear of losing federal funds."[1] Self-governance policy unquestionably put more money with fewer bureaucratic restrictions in the hands of tribal governments. Most important, it defined the federal–tribal relationship on the basis of mutual consent as reflected in compacts.

In 1994, Congress passed the Tribal Self-Governance Act, which established the self-governance policy on a permanent basis. Under this permanent legislation, up to twenty additional tribes may join the compacting process in any given year, and compacts may include Interior Department programs outside the BIA, such as national parks on or near reservations. The federal government's trust responsibility remains in the form of an annual "trust evaluation," in which the secretary of interior checks to see if any trust assets, such as land or water, are in imminent jeopardy. If such conditions exist (for example, if a tribe clear-cuts its own forest), the secretary can unilaterally reassume federal responsibility. The terms of the trust evaluation are established in the compact itself, however, giving the Indian nations a greater measure of control over how it is conducted. It is not an easy matter to reconcile the federal government's ongoing treaty and other trust obligations with a true policy of self-determination for Indian nations.

Questions

1. Which U.S. policy do you think had the most harmful effect on tribal governments?
2. Why did Congress abandon treaty-making with Indian tribes? Do you think the abandonment of treaty-making was harmful to tribal governments?
3. How did the Office of Indian Affairs further the erosion of tribal sovereignty?
4. Do you think that the General Allotment Act had an impact on the internal legal systems of tribal governments? Why or why not?

In Your Community

1. Research the following questions about your tribe's history of contact with the United States:
   - Was your tribe removed or placed on a reservation?
   - Was the land of the tribe allotted?
   - Does the tribe have a constitution that was written following the Indian Reorganization Act?
   - How have these policies affected the way the tribe currently operates its government?
2. Research the following issues about your contemporary tribal government:
   - Is your tribe a "contracting tribe" or a "compacting tribe"?
   - What does a typical annual "Tribal Priority Allocation" request include for your tribe?
   - How much federal government supervision or control comes with the 638 funds?

Glossary

Abrogated: Abolished by authority.

Allotment: An assigned portion. The Allotment Act (also known as the Dawes Act) authorized the U.S. president to allot (divide) portions of reservation land to individual Indians.

Blood feud: A feud in which members of the opposing parties murder each other.

Cede: To yield; surrender; give up ownership or responsibility.

Cession: Something ceded.

Doctrine of discovery: The legal theory that the Europeans gained title to the land in North America because they "discovered" the land.

Domestic dependent nations: A legal status describing tribal nations that retain some sovereignty but are also dependent on the United States for guidance and protection.

Individualistic: Relating to the character of persons as individuals rather than as members of a community.

Paternalistic: Like a father; benevolent but intrusive.

Ratified: Formally approved by authority.

Self-determination: Sovereignty; the right of a people to make their own laws and be governed by them.

Trust relationship: A special legal relationship between the United States and Indian tribes, in which the U.S. government has a duty to protect and oversee affairs pertaining to tribes.

Suggested Further Reading

Matthew L. M. Fletcher, *The Original Understanding of the Political Status of Indian Tribes*, 82 St. John's Law Review 153 (2008).

Francis P. Prucha, *Documents of United States Indian Policy* (3rd ed. 2000).

David E. Wilkins & K. Tsianina Lomawaima, *Uneven Ground: American Indian Sovereignty and Federal Law* (2002).

Note

1. Robert Porter, *A Proposal to the Handoganyas to Decolonize Federal Indian Control Law*, 31 University of Michigan Journal of Law Reform 899, 971 (1998).

CHAPTER 6

Introduction and History of Tribal Courts

THE REMAINDER of this book focuses more specifically on tribal justice systems, including the history and development of these systems (especially tribal courts), the changing scope of tribal power and authority in both criminal and civil law, and the use of nonadversarial and traditional forms of dispute resolution in many tribal justice systems across Indian country. The excerpts included in this text attempt to strike a balance between unique tribal legal heritages and the mandates of U.S. law. The effort to strike this balance is being made, in large part, out of a recognition that real tribal sovereignty comes only when tribal peoples incorporate their unique histories and traditions into the laws enacted to govern their communities today.

As the Hopi Appellate Court held:

> The customs, traditions and culture of the Hopi Tribe deserve great respect in tribal courts, for even as the Hopi Tribal Council has merged laws and regulations into a form familiar to American legal scholars, the essence of our Hopi law as practiced remains distinctly Hopi. The Hopi Tribe has a constitution, ordinances, and resolutions, but these Western forms of law codify the customs, traditions and culture of the Hopi Tribe, which are essential sources of our jurisprudence.[1]

As you read the different excerpts, ask yourself: Do the authors pay attention to how different tribal justice systems have tried to strike a balance between Anglo-American legal practices and their own tribal legal heritage? If so, how have these balances been achieved and maintained over time? What aspects of Anglo-American law do tribal courts usually adopt, and what aspects of their own tribal legal heritage do they usually turn to? Do all tribal justice systems make the same exact balance, or do they each adopt and keep different aspects of the Anglo-American and their own legal heritages?

We begin by looking at the history of tribal courts and how changing concepts and policies about the relationship between Anglo-American law and Native America's unique legal heritages have influenced the development of tribal justice systems over time. First, we will review the creation of Courts of Indian Offenses as explored by Vine Deloria Jr. and Clifford Lytle. The Courts of Indian Offenses are the predecessors of many tribal courts in operation today, but among a few tribes, they are still the only working courts. We will then read an article by Christine Zuni that reviews the historical development of modern tribal courts. Finally, we will review a U.S. Supreme Court case from 1896 in which the Cherokee Nation court system was recognized as a logical extension of sovereignty.

This brief history will reveal how the adversarial-style dispute resolution system of Anglo-American legal traditions was first introduced in Indian country primarily as a means to control and oppress, rather than actually serve, tribal nations. We will see, however, that the tribal citizens called to be judges of these courts sometimes relied on their customs and traditions to resolve disputes, even when they were forbidden to do so. We will see also how tribal courts were introduced as acts of self-government by some tribes, often in an effort to remedy the problems caused by Courts of Indian Offenses. This review will set the stage for following chapters that consider the operation of tribal courts today and the continued importance of relying on each tribe's unique legal heritage in the resolution of contemporary disputes.

COURTS OF INDIAN OFFENSES

Vine Deloria Jr. and Clifford M. Lytle[*]

During the early part of the nineteenth century when Indians were being pushed westward to the reservations, law and order in Indian Country was controlled by the military. At this time, the Bureau of Indian Affairs was a

---

[*] Vine Deloria Jr. & Clifford M. Lytle, *American Indians, American Justice* 82–89 (1983).

part of the Department of War. In 1849, with the creation of the Interior Department, the Bureau of Indian Affairs was transferred to this new department and Indian affairs were placed under civilian control. The military still continued to exercise some police functions on the isolated frontiers, but, in general, law and order was a responsibility of the Indian agents. . . .

Courts of Indian Offenses most probably began with the appeal by disputing chiefs to the agent as arbiter of problems that could not be resolved in the traditional tribal manner. . . . On some reservations the early councils were both judicial and legislative and exercised, after the influence of the chiefs had declined, executive powers also. Courts of Indian Offenses mark the first evolution away from one body holding all three political powers in its hands to the tripartite arrangement we see on many reservations today.

The development of the Indian police also played a critical role in this movement toward independent institutions. Unable to rely upon the traditional chiefs to carry out their instructions, many of which were anathema to the old people, the agents early began to enroll Indians as agency policemen. This new group enabled the agent to control the Indians without having to rely upon the presence of federal troops, which in many cases might have created an unpleasant incident or a war. Although the rise of Courts of Indian Offenses certainly indicated the increasing application of the white laws over the Indians, they were not wholly without respect among the Indians. Manuelito, one of the most respected and beloved of the Navajo war chiefs, served for a time as an Indian policeman and performed duties in a Court of Indian Offenses.

The allotment policy considerably increased the need for the Courts of Indian Offenses. In order to break up the traditional family groupings on many reservations, allotments were deliberately mixed so that family members might have their lands scattered all over the reservations. The idea behind this bureaucratic hodgepodge was to encourage the younger generation to move away from the elders and to begin farming on their own. The result of the application of the idea was that it became difficult if not impossible for communities that were dependent on tribal customs to conduct some of their ceremonies because the clan or family was so dispersed. The Courts of Indian Offenses then served to provide them with some forum in which a modicum of justice could be realized. Subsequent sale of allotments and the settling of white purchasers within the reservation borders made it virtually impossible to do anything except rely on these courts for redress.

In 1883 the Courts of Indian Offenses were made a regular part of the Bureau of Indian Affairs activities on the reservations. The status of these courts was never very clear since Congress frequently did not appropriate sufficient funds to make them effective, and they were described, in the only case to deal directly with their legality, *United States v. Clapox*, 35 Fed. 575 (D.C. Ore. 1888), as "mere educational and disciplinary instrumentalities by which the Government of the United States is endeavoring to improve and elevate the condition of these dependent tribes to whom it sustains the relation of guardian." One commentator, Rice, suggested that the Courts of Indian Offenses "derive their authority from the tribe, rather than from Washington," but this attempted justification has never become a popular explanation because of the documented abuses of Indians in these courts by the agents.

These courts have become known as CFR courts since they operated under the written guidelines as set down in the Code of Federal Regulations. But when surveying the literature concerning their operation it is difficult to determine whether they were really courts in the traditional jurisprudential sense of either the Indian or the Anglo-American culture or whether they were not simply instruments of cultural oppression since some of the offenses that were tried in these courts had more to do with suppressing religious dances and certain kinds of ceremonials than with keeping law and order. The sacred Sioux ceremony of "keeping the soul," eloquently described in *The Sacred Pipe* by Black Elk to Joseph Epes Brown, which was basically a condolence rite, was banned by these courts on the Dakota reservations to the consternation of the people.

Although the CFR courts were staffed by Indian judges, they served at the pleasure of the agent, not the community. The Indian agent appointed his judges as a patronage exercise, which rewarded the Indians who seemed to be assimilating while depriving the traditional people of the opportunity to participate in this vital function of the community. Even though the judges invested a good deal of energy and prestige in serving on these courts, too frequently the ultimate decision rested with the Indian agent, who often acted as though the people had no right to understand the reasoning behind his arbitrary decisions. Interestingly, there was never any real statutory authority for the establishment of the CFR courts and their legitimacy was rationalized under general powers that were lodged in the office of the commissioner of Indian affairs. At its zenith, the CFR court system was operating on about two-thirds of all reservations. With the authorization of the IRA corporate form of tribal government, all but a few tribes assumed judicial functions as a manifestation of self-government and rid themselves of this hated institution. Since these courts did not have the sanction of the whole tribal community, even the most beneficial parts of their operations have been eyed with suspicion by Indians and historians alike.

RULES FOR INDIAN COURTS

Thomas J. Morgan*

Offenses: For the purpose of these regulations the following shall be deemed to constitute offenses, and the judges of the Indian court shall severally have jurisdiction to try and punish for the same when committed within their respective districts.

a) Dances, etc.—Any Indian who shall engage in the sun dance, scalp dance, or war dance, or any other similar feast, so called, shall be deemed guilty of an offense, and upon conviction thereof shall be punished for the first offense by with withholding of its rations for not exceeding ten days or by imprisonment for not exceeding ten days; and for any subsequent offense under this clause he shall be punished by withholding his rations for not less than ten nor more than thirty days, or by imprisonment for not less than ten nor more than thirty days. . . .

c) Practices of medicine men.—Any Indian who shall engage in the practices of so-called medicine men, or shall resort to any artiface [sic] or device to keep the Indians of the reservation from adopting and following civilized habits and pursuits, or shall adopt any means to prevent the attendance of children at school, or shall use any arts as a conjurer to prevent Indians from abandoning their barbarous rites and customs, shall be deemed to be guilty of an offense, and upon conviction thereof, for the first offense shall be imprisoned for not less than ten nor more than thirty days: Provided that for any subsequent conviction for such offense the maximum term of imprisonment shall not exceed six months. . . .

Misdemeanors

That if an Indian refuses or neglects to adopt the habits of industry, or to engage in civilized pursuits or employments, but habitually spends his time in idleness and loafing, he shall be deemed a vagrant and guilty of a misdemeanor, and shall, upon the first conviction thereof, be liable to a fine of not more than five dollars, or to imprisonment.

---

* Report of August 27, 1892, in House Executive Document No. 1, part 5, vol. II, 52nd Cong., 2nd sess., serial 3088, pp. 28–31.

LEGAL HISTORY OF TRIBAL COURTS

*Christine Zuni**

A. General Overview

The history of tribal dispute resolution predates both state and federal courts. This history is as different from the history of state and federal courts as the Indian culture and value system are different from the dominant culture and its value system. The history of tribal court is dominated by the federal–tribal relationship.

While it may be said that all tribes have their own unique history, generally the history of the development of tribal court systems is similar. In addition to the tribal court systems that we will speak of, several tribes, including several of the Pueblos of New Mexico, operate entirely within a "traditional" system. A mirror to reflect the Anglo-American jurisprudence model, whether in whole or in part, is missing; it has never been there. Under such tribal systems the methods and the ends of dispute resolution differ. In the case of non-traditional tribal courts, federal law interjected Anglo-American laws and concepts irrespective of the difference between traditional law and Anglo-American law and the gulf between the two. Recognizing that a gulf exists is the first step towards understanding the impact Anglo-American law and its concepts of justice has had on native peoples. This sobering recognition is also instrumental to comprehend the challenges facing modern day tribal court systems, structured in the Anglo-American mode, struggling to remain relevant to, or at least respectful of, native social and political thought. Interestingly, a similar challenge faces traditional systems, as they seek to maintain traditional aspects of their systems, while "modernizing" their operations to meet increased and changing demands. External mandates premised on the Anglo-American jurisprudential model of justice press on these systems as well.

B. History

Prior to 1871, when treaty-making with tribes ended, the federal policy was one of respect for tribal self-government and traditional forms of tribal jus-

---

* Christine Zuni, *Strengthening What Remains*, 7 Kansas Journal of Law and Public Policy 18 (1997).

tice. Congress recognized this right through treaties. Tribes retained sole jurisdiction over Indians and concurrent jurisdiction over criminal conduct by non-Indians. In *Worcester v. Georgia*, the United States Supreme Court ruled that the state of Georgia had no jurisdiction over Indians within Indian country, unless Congress expressly authorized it. There was no limitation on tribes in terms of their ability to use traditional forms of judgments, i.e., restitution, banishment, and death.

From 1871 to 1934 the federal policy was to end tribal self-governance. This was the period in which the General Allotment Act was enacted and Indian lands were divided into individual holdings, with the remainder opened to settlement, and Indians subjected to state law. In 1883, Courts of Indian Offenses were created to replace tribal forums of justice. The purpose of these courts was to "educate" and "civilize" the tribes. The imposition of agency-appointed chiefs, judges, and law enforcement officers served to weaken traditional tribal law and procedure. In 1885, Congress passed the Major Crimes Act, to extend federal court jurisdiction over felony criminal offenses committed by Indians on Indian reservations. Congress was spurred by *Ex Parte Crow Dog* in which Crow Dog, the accused murderer of Spotted Tail (both Brule Sioux), was convicted of murder in the First District Court of Dakota, Dakota Territory, and sentenced to death. The Supreme Court found the district court to be without jurisdiction, finding Crow Dog was subject to the jurisdiction of his tribe and not to the United States or its general laws. The traditional remedy included reconciliation and an ordered gift. In *Talton v. Mayes*, the Court found that the Bill of Rights under the United States Constitution, providing protections for criminal defendants, did not apply to tribal criminal proceedings. This was the precursor to the Indian Civil Rights Act of 1968. The effect of this period was the weakening of traditional governments and law, as well as the loss of 90 million acres of tribal land to non-Indians from the date the General Allotment Act was passed to 1934.

From 1934 to 1953, the federal policy sought to restore tribal self-government, which included the creation of tribal courts. The Indian Reorganization Act (IRA) was passed by Congress in 1934 to accomplish this purpose. Under the Act, tribes could adopt written constitutions. Model constitutions were provided and contained provisions whereby tribal councils could create tribal courts to replace Courts of Indian Offenses. Many tribes adopted these model constitutions. Not all tribes which organized under the IRA adopted constitutions and a number of tribes did not organize under the IRA. The model constitutions and model codes limited criminal jurisdiction of tribal courts to minor offenses, subjected laws and ordinances to Interior Department approval, and limited sentencing powers of tribal courts to a maximum period of six months, imprisonment for criminal offenses.

From 1953 to 1968, the federal policy was to terminate the federal trust responsibility and transfer jurisdiction to states. One purpose of the policy was to eliminate tribal courts. Although most tribes and their court systems survived termination, tribal councils were discouraged from efforts to develop more effective tribal courts. The structure of courts remained unchanged and tribes were forced to bear greater funding burdens. Congress also passed Public Law 280 which allowed state courts to assume criminal and civil jurisdiction over Indians within Indian country without tribal consent. *Williams v. Lee* upheld tribal court jurisdiction in non–Public Law 280 states over civil disputes by non-Indians and Indians within Indian country. Tribal court criminal jurisdiction remained limited. Yet, federal jurisdiction under the Major Crimes Act and the General Crimes Act was not vigorously exercised. The tribal codes developed by the Interior Department and adopted by tribes remained basically unchanged since 1934.

In 1968, the Indian Civil Rights Act (ICRA) was passed and the federal policy of recognizing tribal powers of self-government, including the authority to establish court systems for administering justice, was once again reaffirmed. The Indian Civil Rights Act, however, provided no federal funding to enable tribes to restructure or improve their court systems. Moreover, it permitted federal courts to review by writ of habeas corpus the legality of detention by order of an Indian tribe. The Act required tribal courts to afford criminal defendants many of the basic due process rights made applicable to federal and state courts under the United States Constitution. It placed requirements on tribal self-government which reflect Anglo-American principles of justice. The Act also limits the sentencing power of tribal courts for criminal offenses to one year or a $5,000 fine upon conviction.

From 1968 to the present, Congressional policy has been to promote tribal self-government and increase funding for court operations. However, many courts are currently operating on tribal and federal funds which are not nearly comparable to similarly situated state courts. Tribal courts are under-funded and under-staffed because many tribes lack funds to adequately supplement federal funds to assist courts with the development of the court system and expanded tribal jurisdiction. Recent U.S. Supreme Court decisions have taken criminal jurisdiction over non-Indians and non-member Indians from tribal courts at a time when both live, work, and are routinely present on reservations. Criminal jurisdiction over non-member Indians was restored by Congressional amendment to the Indian Civil Rights Act in 1992. Some tribes prosecute major crimes listed under the Major Crimes Act due to the lack of federal enforcement.

The United States Supreme Court recently found a tribal court lacked jurisdiction over a civil dispute between non-Indians in Indian country. Many tribes have amended their tribal codes, moving away from the Code of Indian Offenses and the IRA model codes, but some still employ codes whose major criminal and civil provisions have not changed since they were first adopted under the IRA.

In 1993, President Clinton signed tribal courts legislation into law. The legislation provided for federal appropriations to be made available to tribal courts for their exclusive use. Tribes still await these appropriations.

A central proposition in federal Indian law governing tribal nations, and hence tribal judicial systems, is that Indian nations retain vestiges of their original sovereignty and therefore have residual authority to govern their own affairs. Their sovereign qualities were initially recognized by the federal government when it negotiated treaties with Indian nations as it did with other foreign nations. Thus, the power to establish and maintain tribal judicial systems is an inherent, retained power that was never surrendered.

TALTON V. MAYES, 163 U.S. 376 (1896)

United States Supreme Court

[The appellant was prosecuted in Cherokee tribal court for murder. He challenged his conviction in federal court, claiming that the Cherokee court did not comply with the U.S. Constitution.]

By treaties and statutes of the United States the right of the Cherokee nation to exist as an autonomous body, subject always to the paramount authority of the United States, has been recognized. And from this fact there has consequently been conceded to exist in that nation power to make laws defining offences and providing for the trial and punishment of those who violate them when the offences are committed by one member of the tribe against another one of its members within the territory of the nation. . . .

The case in this regard therefore depends upon whether the powers of local government exercised by the Cherokee nation are Federal powers created by and springing from the Constitution of the United States, and hence controlled by the Fifth Amendment to that Constitution, or whether they are local powers not created by the Constitution, although subject to its general provisions and the paramount authority of Congress. The repeated adjudications of this court have longs since answered the former question in the negative. . . .

The existence of the right in Congress to regulate the manner in which the local powers of the Cherokee nation shall be exercised does not render such local powers Federal powers arising from and created by the Constitution of the United States. It follows that as the powers of local self government enjoyed by the Cherokee nation existed prior to the Constitution, they are not operated upon by the Fifth Amendment, which, as we have said, had for it sole object to control the powers conferred by the Constitution on the National Government.

Questions

1. How were non-Indian methods of dispute resolution introduced into tribal governments?
2. What was the origin of the Courts of Indian Offenses?
3. According to Deloria and Lytle, why were the Courts of Indian Offenses really just "instruments of cultural oppression" rather than courts serving tribal people?
4. According to the readings, did all tribal people "hate" the Courts of Indian Offenses, or did some actually work for them? Why do you think such respected leaders as Manuelito of the Navajo worked as Indian judges in these courts?
5. Were you surprised by the "Rule for Indian Courts" as established in 1892? What was the intent of those rules?
6. In *Talton v. Mayes*, the U.S. Supreme Court recognized that the Cherokee nation has the power to "make laws . . . and provid[e] for the trial and punishment of those who violate them." However, the case also reminds us that the Cherokee nation is "subject to the paramount authority of the United States." Are these two notions contradictory? How does the Court recognize tribal courts today?

In Your Community

1. Was or is your tribe under the control of a Court of Indian Offenses?
2. Does your tribe or nation currently have its own court system? When was it created?
3. Check the date of its creation with Zuni's general history of tribal court development. According to Zuni, what was the leading federal Indian policy at the time your tribe or nation's court was created?

Glossary

Adversarial: Having opposite sides or interests.

Anathema: Something that is intensely disliked.

Anomalous: Out of the ordinary.

Appropriation: A legislature's setting aside for a specific purpose a portion of money raised by the government; a governmental taking of land or property for public use; taking something wrongfully.

Arbiter: A person chosen to decide a disagreement.

Code of Federal Regulations (CFR): The compilation of all the rules and regulations put out by federal agencies.

Dispute resolution: The process of resolving a disagreement between persons about their rights or their legal obligations to one another.

Jurisprudence: Legal philosophy.

Modicum: Small, moderate amount.

Nonadversarial: Not having opposing interests against.

Patronage: The privilege of some public officials to give out jobs on their own discretion, without going through civil service procedures.

Tripartite: Divided into three parts.

Writ of habeas corpus: A judge's order requiring that someone holding a person bring that person to court.

Suggested Further Reading

Russel Lawrence Barsh & J. Youngblood Henderson, *Tribal Courts, the Model Code, and the Police Idea in American Indian Policy* (1976).

Duane Champagne, *American Indian Values and the Institutionalization of IRA Governments*, in *American Indian Policy and Cultural Values: Conflict and Accommodation* 25–34 (Jennie Joe, ed., 1987).

Comment, *Tribal Self-Government and the Indian Reorganization Act of 1934*, 70 Michigan Law Review 9555 (1972).

Vine Deloria Jr., ed., *The Indian Reorganization Act: Congresses and Bills* (1992).

Graham D. Taylor, *The New Deal and American Indian Tribalism: The Administration of the Indian Reorganization Act, 1934–1945* (1980).

Carey Vicenti, *The Reemergence of Tribal Society and Traditional Justice Systems*, 79 Judicature 134 (1995).

Note

1. *Hopi Indian Credit Association v. Thomas*, 1996.NAHT.0000007 (1996) at www .versuslaw.com.

CHAPTER 7

Tribal Justice Systems Today
General Overview and Comparison

NOW THAT WE have briefly reviewed the history of tribal court development, we can look at how they are working in tribal nations today. The first reading is from an article prepared by Melody L. McCoy, a member of the Cherokee Nation of Oklahoma and an attorney with the Native American Rights Fund. She provides an overview of tribal courts and describes some of the general norms, structures, and practices that are common to their operation. In addition to reviewing the kinds of cases that tribal courts hear these days, McCoy also takes up the question of the balance being struck by tribal courts between tribal custom and tradition and Anglo-American law as sources of substantive and procedural law in the resolution of the disputes coming before them.

Then we turn to a piece prepared by Ho-Chunk Professor Mary Jo Hunter that introduces some factors tribes consider in selecting tribal judges. This excerpt provides important insight into the very complex considerations that tribal governments and legislators must make when they are developing a tribal legal system.

As you read the excerpts in this chapter, think about the contemporary challenges faced by tribal courts and consider how your community has dealt with those challenges.

WHEN CULTURES CLASH: THE FUTURE OF TRIBAL COURTS

*Melody L. McCoy**

Tribal courts exercise jurisdiction over nearly 70 million acres throughout the country—some in remote locations and others in or near urban areas. The tribes themselves vary widely, from the 200,000-plus-member Navajo Nation to bands with fewer than 50 members.

A typical tribal court system today consists of a trial court and at least an intertribal court of appeals. Most tribal courts have long had separate criminal and civil divisions such as juvenile and traffic. There is a broad range in their caseloads. In 1992 the Navajo courts processed over 85,000 cases; some smaller tribes heard fewer than 10. Most tribal courts are tribunals of general jurisdiction, meaning they can hear all types of claims and actions, even those that arise under federal or state law. As economic and leisure activities in Indian country increase, they handle more and more contract and tort cases in addition to domestic disputes and probate suits. Tribes today regulate zoning, water, wildlife, taxation, healthcare, employment, and most other subjects customarily covered by state or municipal law.

Generally, anyone can file a suit in tribal court, although a few tribes restrict access to tribal members or reservation residents. Most tribes have codified their procedural laws as well as their evidentiary laws and the codes govern such things as filing and service of process. Some tribal courts have written local rules of practice.

The territorial jurisdiction of tribal courts generally extends to the boundaries of the reservation or Indian lands, where state courts generally lack jurisdiction. In some instances, such as in Indian child adoption and custody matters, tribes may exert jurisdiction over activities outside the reservations. Some tribes (in North Dakota, Oklahoma, and Washington) have experimented with regional intertribal judicial systems, typically at the appellate level, designed to serve more than one reservation.

Tribal Court staffs include chief judges, probation officers, secretaries, administrators, paralegals, and assistants. The qualifications for judges are

* Melody L. McCoy, *When Cultures Clash: The Future of Tribal Courts*, 20 Human Rights 22 (1993).

usually codified. Most staff members are Indian and tribal members, and more courts are requiring the lawyers who practice before them be members of a tribal bar. Very few tribes prohibit any legal representation of parties in proceedings and many allow lay advocates. A few provide free or low-fee advocates, typically in criminal cases. Jury trials are required in some criminal cases and may be allowed in civil cases as well.

Thus, today's tribal courts tend to look and act much like the non-Indian courts. This is not surprising. Many similarities are the result of federal Indian policies which long have suppressed tribal self-determination. . . .

The similarities between tribal and non-Indian courts can be misleading. Contemporary tribal courts have inherited a great deal of non-Indian influence, but they are also heirs to a host of tribal traditions and customs that distinguish them from their non-Indian counterparts.

Traditionally, Indians resolved disputes by consensus, not by an adversary system, as do Anglo-Americans. In many ways, determinations by a single judge contradicts native custom. To accommodate this, some tribes have committees of elders or other individuals empowered to hear and resolve specific disputes within the community without any involvement by the tribal court. They may also be authorized to advise the tribal court.

But even in the courts, important tribal ways have been maintained. For example, in Alaska and the Southwest, some tribal courts conduct proceedings in their native language. In the Pacific Northwest, fishing tribes have traditional courts that handle only disputes related to rivers. And, in addition to its modern system, the Navajo Nation has a traditional Peacemaker Court based on the ancient practice of choosing a *Naatáanii*, or headman, who arbitrates or resolves disputes; tries to reform wrong-doers; and represents his group in its relations with other communities, tribe and governments. Some of the Pueblos in New Mexico have two courts—a contemporary secular court and a traditional religious one.

Tribal courts usually operate under written constitutions and legal codes. A few use a code embodied in federal regulations. But in the courtroom, these are mixed with unwritten traditional law. Traditional law is especially likely to be applied in the important areas of child custody and property distribution. The Chilkat Indian Village (Tlingit) court in southeast Alaska recently held a four-week trial on tribal laws protecting the village's religious objects.

Certain Anglo-American legal concepts such as plea bargaining are foreign to traditional Indian ideas of justice, which offer their own unique legal remedies. For instance, even the U.S. Supreme Court recognizes the ancient tribal right to "exclude" nonmembers from the reservation, usually for posing a significant threat to the community or flagrant violation of tribal law. Cultural values also manifest themselves in subtle ways; for example, prisoners may be granted special leave to attend funerals.

While centuries of non-Indian invasion, assimilation, and repression have all but eliminated many traditional tribal cultures, a new appreciation for harmony in Indian communities is affecting tribal justice systems.

TRIBAL COURT OPINIONS: JUSTICE AND LEGITIMACY

Mary Jo Hunter[*]

The training and background of the tribal judge or justice is connected to who is the creator of the tribal court. A tribe which has a tribal council that retains the authority over the judicial arm may select tribal court judges and justices by appointments. Such appointments may be made based on a variety of factors. Education may be a key factor in appointing the judge or justices. The tribal council may opt to utilize only law-trained individuals. It is apparent that the Winnebago Tribe of Nebraska appoints only law-trained judges to their lower and appellate courts. Such decisions are an attribute of tribal sovereignty and the tribe's inherent right to select the factors for their judicial officers. Other tribal councils may select only tribal members without requiring a law degree.

Other tribes, such as the Ho-Chunk Nation, have created new tribal constitutions which establish separate branches of government. Where a tribal court is created as a separate judicial branch, certain judicial positions may require specific training. In our case, the justices are elected by the tribal membership and are required to be tribal members. On the other hand, the lower court judges are appointed by the tribal legislature. Of the five judicial positions within the Ho-Chunk Nation, only the Chief Judge of the trial court and the Chief Justice of the appellate court are required to possess a law degree. The other three judicial positions are held by non-lawyers.

It is easily comprehensible that the decisions and opinions rendered by the varying tribal courts create an impression of many differences rather

---

[*] Mary Jo Hunter, *Tribal Court Opinions: Justice and Legitimacy*, 8 Kansas Journal of Law and Public Policy 142 (1999).

than similarities. Yet, an overview of such decisions establishes the wealth of tribal court knowledge being created by many tribal decisions.

Such an array of talent has initiated conversations on many fronts about the need for dissemination of opinions in a technologically advanced mode such as the Internet.

So, which is better as the tribal court judge or justice, the lawyer or the non-lawyer? Who is better equipped to oversee the tribal judiciary? And should that judge or justice be a tribal member? Or, is it better if the tribal judge or justice does not come from the tribal membership but is a non-member, or even a non-Indian? Such questions are important.

How decisions will be reached and how they are written is based in part on the answers to those questions. For example, the question was raised last year by Professor Pommersheim. He asked, how does a tribal court conceive of the basic principle of judicial review?

The way in which that principle is approached will vary depending on who is in that position. Questions which arise purely as a legal concept may be addressed by non-lawyers in an entirely different framework than a legal one. On the Ho-Chunk Nation Supreme Court, the tribal members have created an appellate court which requires two non-lawyer tribal members to sit as Associate Justices. It is my belief that their view is equal to, if not above, the views of the law-trained justice. It is my understanding that the judiciary could have been created in such away as to require only law-trained judges. Such was not the case. Tribal members wanted participation by tribal members in the judicial process. Therefore, the Associate Justices write decisions on a rotating basis with the law-trained Chief Justice. Their analysis of concepts such as tribal sovereign immunity may differ from the law trained Justice, but it is essential that their views are reflected in opinion writing. To do otherwise, does not respond to how tribal members decided that their judicial system would function. . . .

Many tribes today utilize their elders in elders circles or traditional courts. In such systems, it is useful to approach those charged with providing knowledge of traditions and customs with such questions. Unfortunately, there are tribal systems which do not have such readily available references. If they are available within a tribal court system, such consultations are necessary to establish the unique perspective of the particular tribe's customs and traditions. That perspective is one of the key elements supporting the need for tribal judiciaries. . . .

Obviously, how a tribal court will use and incorporate tribal traditions and customs is up to each tribe and those whom the members select for their judicial officers. Yet, it is an aspect of tribal judiciaries which we must nurture and strengthen. It is a method of memorializing our traditions and customs while dispensing justice. And the use of traditions and customs legitimates them for the world outside of our tribal judiciaries. Whether we consider that as important is not as relevant as whether we see the importance of drafting tribal court opinions which will be seen as legitimate and as fair dispensations of justice to both Indian and non-Indian alike.

Pi-na-gi-gi!

Questions

1. What are some of the ways in which tribal courts have been able to deal with the "culture clash" of Anglo-American courts?
2. What kinds of choices do tribes need to make in designing a tribal court system?
3. After reading the Hunter excerpt, what do you think is the best method for selecting a judge? Why?

In Your Community

1. What choices have been made in the design and development of your tribal court system? Would you have made different choices?
2. How are judges selected in your community? Would you change the process? If so, how?

Glossary

Adversary system: The system of law in the United States in which a judge acts as a decision maker between opposite sides.

Codified: Included in an official and formal statement of law such as a legal code or statute.

Plea bargaining: In Anglo-American criminal law, when a person accused of a crime is given an opportunity to reduce his or her potential punishment by agreeing before the trial to admit being guilty of the crime.

Probate: Handling the will and estate of a deceased person.

Secular: Not specifically relating to spirituality or religion.

Tort: A civil (as opposed to criminal) wrong.

Suggested Further Reading

B. J. Jones, *Tribal Courts: Protectors of the Native Paradigm of Justice*, 10 St. Thomas Law Review 87 (1997).

Mark J. Wolff, *Spirituality, Culture and Tradition: An Introduction to the Role of Tribal Courts and Councils in Reclaiming Native American Heritage and Sovereignty*, 7 St. Thomas Law Review 761 (1995).

William P. Zuger, *A Baedeker to the Tribal Court*, 83 North Dakota Law Review 55 (2007).

CHAPTER 8

Examples of Tribal Court Systems

W E NOW TURN to consider more closely the legal systems of the different tribal governments. Below are some excerpts from the *Tribal Law Journal* (a project of the University of New Mexico School of Law) that concern the structure and powers of various tribal judiciaries. Keep in mind that tribal laws are constantly changing (just like federal and state laws), and therefore the information in these excerpts should not necessarily be relied upon as current law.

Many tribal courts have developed their own statements concerning the development of their court. We have included one example—the Stockbridge-Munsee Community Band of Mohican Indians (which is posted on the official tribal court website).

The last excerpt is authored by former Navajo chief justice Tom Tso, who writes about the importance of designing a court system that first and foremost meets the expectations and needs of the people it serves. For the courts of the Navajo Nation, this means being ready to apply "traditional law" in the resolution of certain kinds of disputes among Navajo people, as well as bypassing the legal structures and practices that sometimes make Anglo-American-style courts confusing and frustrate Navajo people's efforts to get justice.

JUDICIARY OF THE OGLALA LAKOTA NATION

*Danielle Her Many Horses**

The courts of the Oglala Lakota Nation are subordinate to the Tribal Council. The Law and Order Code of the tribe authorizes the existence of the court system and details the powers granted to the court. The court system consists of the Oglala Sioux Tribal Court and the Supreme Court of the Oglala Sioux Nation. The Tribal Court at Pine Ridge has concurrent jurisdiction with federal and state courts to hear civil and criminal cases. The Supreme Court serves as the appellate court for all appeals from "final Orders and Judgments of the Oglala Sioux Tribal Court."

The Tribal Council appoints Tribal Court judges. There are six judges sitting on the Tribal Court: one Chief Judge, four Associate Judges, and one Special Judge. Only the Special Judge must be an attorney licensed by the State of South Dakota. The Supreme Court consists of four members: The Chief Justice, two Associate Justices and one Alternate Justice. Three justices sit per case on the Supreme Court. Of those judges that sit, two must be legally trained attorneys who are members of any state bar or the federal bar.

The Tribal Court system follows the doctrine of *stare decisis*. Tribal Court decisions are not handled in an ad hoc fashion. Supreme Court decisions are binding on the lower court.

---

* Danielle Her Many Horses, *Oglala Lakota Nation Profile*, 2 Tribal Law Journal (2002) at tlj.unm.edu/tribal-law-journal/articles/volume_2/oglala/index.php.

NAVAJO NATION JUDICIARY

*Bidtah Becker and Paul Spruhan**

The Navajo Nation operates a two level court system with trial courts and the Navajo Nation Supreme Court. There are presently ten districts

---

* Bidtah Becker & Paul Spruhan, *Profile of the Law of the Navajo Nation*, 2 Tribal Law Journal (2002) at tlj.unm.edu/tribal-law-journal/articles/volume_2/navajo/index.php (revised in 2009).

(Alamo, To'hojiilee, Aneth, Chinle, Crownpoint, Kayenta, Ramah, Shiprock, Tuba City, and Window Rock). The courts of the Navajo Nation have members of the Nation as judges, and this is significant because not all tribes have such a requirement.

Navajo does not require its judges to be trained in western law. Persons appointed to the bench must be able to speak Navajo and English and "have some knowledge of Navajo culture and tradition." This includes an understanding of the clan system, an understanding of religious ceremonies, and an appreciation of the traditional Navajo lifestyle. This requirement is vital because the judiciary is required to incorporate traditional teachings. The Navajo Codes states "[i]n all cases the Courts of the Navajo Nation shall apply any laws of the United States that may be applicable and any laws or customs of the Navajo Nation not prohibited by applicable federal laws."

1. Opinions

The Navajo judicial system follows a "common law" model uniquely adapted to accommodate the inclusion of unwritten "customary" or "traditional" Navajo law. Like state or federal courts, the Navajo courts may decide a case based upon motions of the parties or after briefing and oral argument at the appellate level. The Navajo Nation Supreme Court may take certified questions of law from district courts. Cases may be decided and published through written opinions by a certain justice. Opinions follow an American common law structure of questions or issues presented and holdings. The justices cite to previous Navajo opinions as precedent and may look to opinions from other jurisdictions or general practice treatises for guidance.

2. Navajo Fundamental Law

The Courts of the Navajo Nation are commanded to first apply statutes, to be interpreted using Navajo "Fundamental Law." If a statute is silent, the Navajo courts appeal to "Navajo Fundamental Law" Diné Bi Beenahaz'áanii, the uncodified traditional, customary, natural and common law of the Navajo people as an additional source of precedent. The Navajo Nation Supreme Court has likened Navajo Fundamental law to the "lex non scripta" or the unwritten law of English common law as described in Blackstone's Commentaries on the Law of England. The Court has stated that Navajo custom and traditions are law as part of a broader Navajo "Common Law."

One issue raised by the use of Navajo fundamental law is, how do persons not cognizant of traditional Navajo law present their arguments for or against its use? Aware of this issue, the Navajo courts have developed guidelines for discovering and implementing Navajo customs and judicial procedure by which to bring them before the court. "Where any doubt arises as to the customs and usages of the Navajo Nation the court may request the advice of counselors familiar with these customs and usages."

A litigant may demonstrate the fundamental law principle to be applied through recorded Navajo court opinions, learned treatises on the Navajo way, judicial notice, or the testimony of expert witnesses who have substantial knowledge of Navajo common law. The courts can look to custom which is "generally known throughout the community," and anthropological writings viewed from Navajo perspectives.

When custom is presented in one of these ways it appears the ultimate decision to apply them to the facts of the specific case lies in the district court judge's discretion.

Judicial notice of Navajo common law is appropriate "[w]here no question arises regarding custom or usage . . . if a custom is generally known within the community, or if it is capable of accurate determination by resort to sources whose accuracy cannot reasonably be questioned, it is proven." If a district court takes judicial notice of a particular custom as Navajo common law, the court is required to clearly indicate the custom upon which it relied. Clear references facilitate examination of an order by the Navajo Nation Supreme Court.

If expert witnesses are required, the courts have developed a unique procedure under the laws of evidence. In cases where Navajo custom is disputed the trial court is to hold a pre-trial conference with two or three expert witnesses appointed by the court. The parties to the litigation may only ask clarification questions. The experts can discuss how a particular Navajo custom should be applied in the case and should reach a consensus on the issue. The trial court then has discretion to allow the testimony of an expert on the relevant custom. Similar to the federal rules of evidence to qualify as an expert the trial judge must be satisfied that an individual is indeed an expert on Navajo common law. An expert may be qualified through reading or practice, through "familiarity with Navajo traditions acquired by oral education, or his adherence to a traditional way of life, or through his long-term interest in deepening his knowledge of Navajo custom, or through his status within the community as a person with a special knowledge of custom."

3. Peacemaker Court

The Navajo judicial system also includes a traditional peacemaking court, sometimes referred to as court-annexed traditional mediation. The foundational principle of the Peacemaker Court is *k'e*, or "respect, responsibility and proper relationships among all people." Through non-adversarial discussion between parties, peacemakers look to achieve *Hozho nahasdlii*, or a state realized at the end of journey. Peacemaking sessions are facilitated by Navajo persons who are bilingual and possess knowledge of traditional Navajo culture. Based upon traditional Navajo ceremonies that seek a common goal among groups of individuals, the Peacemaker Court assists disputants in the healing process by fostering a mutually beneficial agreement.

As mediation becomes more accepted in Anglo-American law, more non-Navajos may look to the Peacemaker Courts for guidance in organization and structure. Chief Justice Yazzie of the Navajo Supreme Court reminds us that the Peacemaker Court is "ODR" or "Original Dispute Resolution" as opposed to "ADR" or "Alternative Dispute Resolution."

MISSION STATEMENT

Stockbridge-Munsee Tribal Court*

It is hard to believe that the Stockbridge-Munsee Tribal Court is already eleven years old. Seemingly, it was only yesterday that the court began, perhaps because of the hard work that goes into developing and maintaining a court system is continuing.

In 1995 our community, through its elected council, made the decision to develop a tribal system of justice. Starting out slowly, with only a few tribal codes developed, the community recognized the need for the Tribe to have an internal mechanism for dispute resolution and enforcement of tribal laws. This mechanism is the backbone for tribal self-governance and an exercise of its sovereign rights.

After the Tribe's initial decision to begin its exercise of sovereignty through the establishment of a tribal court, the Tribal Council appointed the court's first judges who were sworn in August 11, 1995. The Court began hearing cases in January 1996, and soon recognized more needs for the community. It became very apparent that our community members, using the court, needed assistance to help them through the court processes. Therefore, the Court established a tribal court lay advocacy program where a number

---

* Stockbridge-Munsee Community, Band of Mohican Indians, *Tribal Court Mission Statement* (2008) at www.mohican-nsn.gov/TribalOffices/tribalcourt1.htm.

of our tribal members were trained through a program sponsored by the Wisconsin Tribal Judges' Association with the assistance of Wisconsin Judi care. This program trained lay people to provide legal representation to parties using, not only our tribal court but also all tribal courts in Wisconsin. Later, as the needs increased, the Court has organized additional trainings for the lay advocates, specific to the Stockbridge-Munsee Tribal Codes.

The Tribal Court began hearing more cases involving disputes between people in our community; the Court realized a need for a more traditional way to resolving these disputes rather than using the adversarial approach. As the Council's vision had provided, a peacemaker system was established. Although slow in starting, the Court now has several community members who have received some training and guidance in helping people resolve differences in a peaceful, healthy and respectful way. This approach is more in line with the Native American traditional practices used long before the introduction of the European adversarial system.

From its beginning, where the Court handled only a few types of cases, the Tribal Council has expanded the Court's jurisdiction to include many of the problems facing tribal communities. The Court now hears cases involving: Administrative appeals, probate cases, a youth code including youth in need, guardianship cases, termination of parental rights, adoptions, determination of paternity, truancy cases, juvenile delinquency, public peace and good order, financial responsibility, regulation of door to door sales, enforcement of the Tribe's natural resources code including fish and game regulations, regulation of tobacco sales, fireworks regulations, tribal land ordinance violations, housing codes, ATV regulations, curfew, and employee rights cases including employee preference disputes and enforcement of fair labor standards. The Court also hears requests for changing legal names, divorces, temporary restraining orders and domestic abuse protective orders, and the judges perform many marriages. This list will continue to expand.

In addition to the work being done in the tribal court, much work has been done outside the tribal court to enhance tribal systems of justice nation wide. The tribal judges have been extremely involved in developing respectful working relationships with the state courts of Wisconsin, developing training programs for tribal/state and federal judges throughout the country, and helping to develop long term Indian legal studies programs in tribal colleges. Tribal justice systems are not only becoming recognized as being competent, but are being recognized as being innovative in an overall picture of peace.

After nine years, the Court [is] continuing to look at ways to improve services to our community. The future of our tribal court is to continue to provide a community based system for dispute resolution and enforcement of our own laws. The Court's vision includes expanding our peacemaker system to include talking, healing, and/or sentencing circles. Also on the horizon is the establishment of a Youth Court using traditional circle concepts, a Wellness Court program to address alcohol and drug problems that may exist in our community, and expanded use of community service programs that will assist our elders.

The cultural sensitive nature of tribal courts is serving Indian people well. Having a cultural thread weaving throughout tribal codes and through tribal court processes is helping to make Tribal communities stronger. The Stockbridge-Munsee Tribal Court pledges to continue in this endeavor.

THE NAVAJO COURT SYSTEM

Tom Tso[*]

The Old and the New Way

A close look at the Navajo Tribal Government would reveal many characteristics that appear to be Anglo in nature. Actually, many concepts have their roots in our ancient heritage. Others are foreign to our culture but have been accommodated in such a way that they have become acceptable and useful to us. Ironically, the Navajo, whose governmental structure and operation are perhaps most like those of the Anglo world amongst United States Indian tribes, is the tribe that has no constitution. The Anglo world places much value on the written word and there is a tendency to believe that if things are not written down, they do not exist.

Navajos have survived since before the time of Columbus as a separate and distinct people. What holds us together is a strong set of values and customs, not words on paper. I am speaking of a sense of community so strong that, before the federal government imposed its system on us, we had no need to lock up wrongdoers. If a person injured another or disrupted the

[*] Tom Tso, *The Process of Decision Making in Tribal Courts*, 31 Arizona Law Review 225, 227–235 (1989).

peace of the community, he was talked to, and often ceremonies were performed to restore him to harmony with his world. There were usually no repeat offenders. Only those who have been subjected to a Navajo "talking" session can understand why this worked.

Today we have police, prosecutors, jails, and written laws and procedures. I am convinced that our Anglo-based system of law enforcement is no more effective than the ways we traditionally handled law enforcement problems. Our present system certainly requires more money, more facilities, more resources and more manpower. But we have this system now, and it works as well as those of our brother and sister jurisdictions. My point is that the Anglo world has said to tribes, "Be like us. Have the same laws and institutions we have. When you have these things perhaps we will leave you alone." Yet what the Anglo world has offered, at least as far as Navajos are concerned, is either something we already had or something that works no better than what we had.

The popular concept of tolerance in America is based upon its image as a melting pot, where everyone blends together to form an indistinguishable mixture. This is fine for people who come to this country and want to jump into the pot. The melting pot can, however, become a good place to hide people. When differences cause discomfort or problems, it can make everyone the same. The real measure of tolerance and respect for tribes may well be how successfully the outside world can coexist with tribes. We are part of the total environment of America and at least as important as the snail darter or the California condor. What a tragedy if fifty years from now a news commentator should report on how the government has set aside a preserve in the desert where nine Indians are being saved from extinction and how it is hoped they will reproduce in captivity.

As economic development plans progress, the Navajo Nation Courts are likely to face a wide range of issues. The jurisdiction statutes of the Navajo Nation provide that the tribal courts have jurisdiction over all civil causes of action where the defendant resides within the Navajo Indian Country or, regardless of residence, has caused an action to occur within the territorial jurisdiction of the Navajo Nation. Future litigation involving the land and resources of the Navajo Nation will no doubt challenge tribal court jurisdiction. In light of the decisions in *National Farmers Union Insurance Co. v. Crow Tribe of Indians* and in *Iowa Mutual Insurance Co. v. LaPlante*, however, these questions will be decided in the Navajo Nation Courts.

Beyond the jurisdictional issues, questions of what law will be applied in civil disputes are likely to arise. Whether federal law will attach in a specific case will depend on the facts. In cases where federal law does not apply, tribal common law and statutes will be used. The Navajo Uniform Commercial Code, Navajo Nation Corporation Code, Water Code, and Mining Code are examples of statutory provisions enacted to regulate on-reservation business ventures and the use of natural resources.

Non-Indians may have concerns about the impact of tradition and custom on case decisions. Navajo custom and tradition are unlikely to call for law entirely different from that expected in Anglo courts. They are more likely to supply additional factors to consider in an already familiar context. For example, the Anglo system is familiar with the concept of valuation and payment for the taking of land. Compensation for the loss of use to the surface user of land is an accepted concept in both Anglo and Navajo law. The difference will be in the valuation. Land that may appear to have little value to a non-Indian may be very valuable to a Navajo. It may have spiritual or historical value that has little to do with the income it can produce. The difficulty will be in assigning a dollar figure to values that have no measure in the market. This is not an impossible task. It is done every day in tort cases where damages are assessed for intangible harms like pain and suffering, intentional infliction of emotional distress, and loss of companionship.

Navajo courts will differ in the emphasis we place on the traditional relationship between Navajos and nature. We refer to the earth and sky as Mother Earth and Father Sky. These are not catchy titles; they represent our understanding of our place. The earth and sky are our relatives. Nature communicates with us through the wind and the water and the whispering pines. Our traditional prayers include prayers for the plants, the animals, the water and the trees. A Navajo prayer is like a plant. The stem or the backbone of the prayer is always beauty. By this beauty we mean harmony. Beauty brings peace and understanding. It brings youngsters who are mentally and physically healthy and it brings long life. Beauty is people living peacefully with each other and with nature.

Just like our natural mother, our Mother Earth provides for us. It is not wrong to accept the things we need from the earth. It is wrong to treat the earth with disrespect. It is wrong if we fail to protect and defend the earth. It would be wrong for us to rob our natural mother of her valuable jewelry and to go away and leave her to take care of herself. It is just as wrong for us to rob Mother Earth of what is valuable and leave her unprotected and defenseless. If people can understand that the Navajo regard nature and the things in nature as relatives, then they will easily see that nature and the Navajos depend upon each other. Understanding this relationship is essential to understanding traditional Navajo concepts which may be applied in cases concerning natural resources and the environment.

We Navajos find it difficult to separate our lives into fragments or parts. Our ceremonies are religious, medical, social, and psychological. The seasons tell us how to live and what ceremonies to have. The earth gives us our food, the dyes for our rugs and the necessities for our ceremonies. These may be seen as everyday things. Today, the earth gives us income and jobs from mining, from oil, and from the forests. Water and earth combine to give Navajo Agricultural Products, Inc. the ability to produce large amounts of food for the Navajo people. Snow and rain and proper runoff from the mountains give us lakes for fishing. These may be seen as commercial things.

We cannot separate our needs and our relationships in the same fashion. This is why our laws and judicial interpretations must accommodate both of these things. For example, our tribal law requires that persons who want to harvest or remove anything from the forests have a permit. An exception is made, however, for persons who need to gather plants and forest products for ceremonial purposes. In a recent Navajo Supreme Court probate case, the court held that any further division of the land would defeat the agricultural purposes of the land. Under Navajo common law, the parcel went to the heir who was best able to use the land for agricultural purposes. The other heirs were given set-offs in other items of the decedent's property. This case illustrates the Navajo Tribal Court system's ability to accommodate traditional values.

Conclusion

I have tried to give you a brief overview of the judicial decision-making process in the Navajo tribal courts, and to indicate some of the ways we attempt to accommodate the best from two cultures so that the Navajo Nation may proceed to develop within a framework that is familiar to us. We, the people, are a natural resource. Our culture and our history are natural resources. We are so related to the earth and the sky that we cannot be separated without harm. The protection and defense of both must be preserved. On the other hand, the dominant society views things in terms of separateness, of compartmentalization. For this reason, the Navajo Nation is best able to make the laws and decisions regarding our own preservation and development.

I have spoken of the Navajo experience, but I believe that much of what I have said applies to all Indian tribes. Understanding the challenges facing tribes is the first step toward meeting them. The process of making judicial decisions in the Navajo Nation reflects upon our response to these challenges.

Questions

1. Compare and contrast the different tribal courts in terms of their judicial (courts) and legislative (councils) functions.
2. What is meant by "common law"? How does it affect the tribal courts' decision-making process (if at all)?
3. How do the courts described in this chapter compare to the Anglo-American judicial systems?

In Your Community

1. In your opinion and experience, do you think the legal system of your tribe or nation "honors the expectations" of your people? Do you think the people of your tribe or nation enjoy "ease of access" to the courts?
2. With regard to the legal system of your tribe or nation, to what extent would "honoring the expectations" of your people mean resolving disputes by using the norms, structures, and practices of your people's customs and traditions whenever possible?

Glossary

Concurrent: Together; at the same time. In legal parlance, having the same authority.

Judiciary: The branch of government that interprets the law; the branch that judges.

Jurisdiction: The geographical area within which a court (or a public official) has the right and power to operate; the persons about whom and the subject matters about which a court has the right and power to make decisions.

Stare decisis: (Latin for "To stand by the decision.") A legal principle under which judges are obligated to follow the precedents established in prior judicial decisions.

Suggested Further Reading

Dennis W. Arrow, *Oklahoma's Tribal Courts: A Prologue, the First Fifteen Years of the Modern Era, and a Glimpse at the Road Ahead*, 19 Oklahoma City University Law Review 5 (1994).

Margery H. Brown & Brenda C. Desmond, *Montana Tribal Courts: Influencing the Development of Contemporary Indian Law*, 52 Montana Law Review 211 (1991).

Nell Jessup Newton, *Tribal Court Praxis: One Year in the Life of Twenty Indian Tribal Courts*, 22 American Indian Law Review 285 (1998).

CHAPTER 9

An Introduction to Balancing Tribal Legal Heritage and Anglo-American Law

THE DIFFERENCES between a tribe's unique legal heritage and Anglo-American legal norms, structures, and practices sometimes emerge in the context of contemporary tribal court proceedings. To understand how today's tribal court personnel (including judges, attorneys, and advocates) deal with these differences, it is helpful to consider how the personnel incorporate traditions into the modern context.

We return initially to Christine Zuni's article "Strengthening What Remains" to consider why she sees the use of "native concepts of justice" as an important element in the practice of today's tribal court personnel. Zuni provides a succinct review of the terms and issues central to the ongoing discussion over the use of what is often called "tradition" in tribal courts. She briefly defines some of the basic concepts repeatedly used in conversations of tribal legal heritage, including the notions of custom, customary law, common law, traditional dispute resolution, and peacemaking. She then offers a broad discussion of the main differences between Anglo-American and Indian worldviews and how these lead to very different concepts of justice.

Based on these differences, Zuni then argues that the imposition of Anglo-American legal norms, structures, and practices into tribal communities has caused considerable damage to the tribes' unique culture and sovereignty as a people. Only more damage will be caused, she argues, if tribal court personnel today continue to borrow principles and practices from Anglo-American law rather than turning to their own unique legal heritage as the source of contemporary tribal law and dispute resolution. Zuni concludes by considering some of the practical concerns raised by these issues, including how tribal legislatures can promote the use of their unique legal heritage and why tribal customs and traditions should be used in contemporary tribal court, even in cases where the disputants are not tribal members.

The next excerpt comes from an article on the education and experiences of a tribal judge from Laguna, William Bluehouse Johnson. The author, Cynthia Cheski, writes about how Judge Bluehouse handles the cultural and legal differences that he sees in his court, sometimes applying tradition, at other times applying state law.

This section lays a foundation for topics that are considered in more depth later in this volume. For now, think about how you might go about incorporating the customs and traditions of your people into the contemporary legal system of your tribe or nation. What choices would you have to make in the design or redesign of your legal system to promote the use of your people's unique legal heritage?

LEGAL HISTORY OF TRIBAL COURTS

Christine Zuni[*]

Tribal courts exist primarily to advance tribal people. However, as the historical development of tribal courts illustrates, this "service" was not always intended to serve the interests of the tribal community in preserving its own concepts of law. This was due to the various political and social agendas being pursued by the federal government through the use of tribal courts, none of which were particularly sensitive to the native worldview or philosophy. As tribal courts enter into a new period of development, we are at an opportune moment to critically appraise our systems and evaluate them using native ideals and taking into consideration the native worldview. It is the particular responsibility of native lawyers, practitioners, professionals, and advocates working within the tribal justice systems to assess the current situation of tribal courts and to determine the future course of tribal systems.

---

[*] Christine Zuni, *Strengthening What Remains*, 7 Kansas Journal of Law and Public Policy 18 (1997).

Preserving, strengthening, and incorporating our native concepts of justice, which include both native principles and laws as well as traditional methods and objectives of dispute resolution, are of particular importance in the appraisal of our tribal court systems. To the extent that tribal nations are similar, mutual exchange among them is useful; to the extent that tribal nations are different, this evaluation must be carried out on a tribal level. It is the intent of this paper to encourage that localized evaluation. This appraisal will consider the effect reliance on non-Indian law, both in the past and the present by tribal courts and lawyers, has had and continues to have on Indian nations.

The entire area of customary law, including methods of traditional dispute resolution, is currently a "high profile" area receiving attention from legal experts and researchers. Customary law is extremely important to the future development of tribal Justice systems. Those involved in the tribal judicial systems must begin to articulate their thoughts on, and address customary law. Courts in Indian country and the individuals involved in those courts play an influential role in controlling the extent to which the legal systems will embody customary law. All those involved in the judicial field at the tribal level, from lay people to legal professionals, must become involved in this discussion. The use and development of customary law in our legal system rises or falls on the position taken by the judiciary, the advocates, and the litigants. Despite all the helpful insights which may be gained from legal anthropologists and historians, tribal people are the ones familiar with the realities. We can distinguish the rhetoric from the practical truth, the ideal from the practice. And most importantly, we are the ones who, because we are most familiar with the problems, are instrumental in pointing to the practical solutions and methods which will succeed.

We find ourselves at a juncture in the development of our tribal court systems. Therefore, we need to take a moment to cast our thoughts over what has passed and why things have developed as they have. In this respect, it is critical to remember the history of tribal judicial systems development. As tribal courts expand their jurisdiction and develop, it is necessary not only to envision a destination, but also to change course if necessary to avoid the development of tribal justice systems by default. We must see to their future development by design. My ultimate vision is to see tribal justice systems develop into true indigenous justice systems, distinct from all others. To the extent that Indian nations are under real, or imagined, mandates to demonstrate some conformity, this can be accomplished without discarding or ignoring their own wisdom.

This paper is intended to encourage discussion and stimulate action and thought as well as to support the ongoing work in tribal courts in this area. We are involved in an ongoing process of developing an indigenous body of law and system of justice. We must pay particular attention to how we are going about the development of our court systems and look closely at what is developing. Incorporating customary law, whether wholly or partially, to our developing legal systems makes them truly unique to our individual tribes and reflective of the concepts we, as Indian people, have of law and justice.

The first question is, how do we go about answering this? There is no simple or easy answer. The first step is to begin consciously thinking about it, talking about it, and identifying those elements in our current systems where we have already incorporated principles of customary law and identifying other specific areas where we can incorporate the principles of customary law. The second step is to look at our systems to see where they are not meeting the needs of the community and to seek to incorporate methods which will more effectively meet those needs. As we look for viable methods, we should look first at tribal concepts and principles of dispute resolution which may assist in this effort and which complement our way of thought before we import other methods from outside. We should also look to adapt those methods which we import, or are mandated to follow, to fit our communities. I hope to encourage serious reflection on the present state of our court systems. Do such systems reflect native principles and values? Do they seek to incorporate and reinforce basic and important community values? Given the federal government's historic, and even its fairly recent agenda for tribal courts, a negative answer to this question is not surprising. However, I do not believe it is the intention of any tribal court system to merely mimic the Anglo-American system without thinking about developing a unique tribal justice system. There are enough similarities among tribes that we can discuss this matter collectively, yet the answers are as varied as the tribes themselves and thus lie within the tribal communities, not outside them. Once tribal people entered the legal profession, the move to turn the tribal justice system into our own tool began. My vision for tribal courts is the development of systems of justice which reflect the native society's concepts of law and harmony. While it is true that tribes are [under] federal mandates, there are ways of meeting those mandates while still maintaining tribal integrity in the design of the dispute resolution system.

From the beginning of contact to this day, we have faced the challenge of maintaining our ways. All of us here today face this common challenge in the development of our court systems. As native people in the United States we have a long history of resistance to the destruction of the ways of our people, and we have learned some hard lessons. . . .

Terms

Some of the terms used to discuss the development of justice systems based on Indian concepts follow. Because these terms are used interchangeably, I would like to attempt here to comment on them so that we will have a common understanding of the different terms. In reference to the law of native societies, commonly used terms are: *customary law*, *tribal common law*, *indigenous law*, and *native law*. In reference to traditional tribal methods of resolving disputes, *traditional dispute resolution*, *peacemaking*, and *peacekeeping* are common terms. *Custom*, *tradition*, and *practice* are widely used to refer to the source of both the law of native societies and the methods of dispute resolutions.

Customary Law, Common Law, Indigenous Law, and Native Law

All four of these terms refer to the same concept. However, in this category I have my own preference. Because *common law* is so closely associated in my legal-trained mind with the common law of England, I prefer using *customary law*, *indigenous law*, or *native law*. Generally, *customary law* is a law that is derived from custom. *Custom* in this sense means a long-established usage or practice which is considered unwritten law. Some additional requirements are that it has acquired the force of law by common adoption or acquiescence, and that it does not vary.

Traditional Dispute Resolution, Peacemaking, and Peacekeeping

Traditional dispute resolution refers to the methods of resolving disputes which were used by tribes prior to the existence of tribal courts. *Peacemaking*, a term used by particular tribes, i.e., the Navajo and the Iroquois, is a method of traditional dispute resolution.

Custom, Tradition, Practice, and Usage

Custom, as we use it in the discussions regarding justice based on Indian concepts, has the same narrow meaning as defined above: that is, long-established practices considered as unwritten law. The general meaning of *custom* includes those usages or practices common to many peoples or to a particular place as well as to the whole body of usages, practices, or conventions that regulate social life. It is important, however, to keep in mind the narrow definition which we use here.

Tradition is the method by which information and beliefs and customs are handed down by word of mouth or by example from one generation to another without written instruction. It also refers to the cultural continuity in social attitudes and institutions or to the pattern of thought or action passed down from generation to generation. In this sense, *tradition* may be said to refer more to the methods of resolving disputes and the methods by which native law is passed from one generation to the next. *Practice* and *usage* are generally used to describe custom, and so are, in essence, interchangeable with the word *custom*.

This is only a cursory examination of these words and their usage. As these words are used interchangeably, it is hoped that this will assist our communication. They are also English words. The meaning of *law* in the indigenous language is also important to consider.

Worldview and Tribal Court Development

The historical use and incorporation of non-Indian law has had negative effects on the development of judicial systems which are compatible with native societal concepts. The fact remains, however, that the Anglo-American approach to law is pervasive in most tribal court systems. Yet, the question why tribes would consider altering judicial concepts embodied in the Anglo-American system of justice will arise. The answer is simple. Native and non-native societies operate from two different worldviews. The Anglo-American system represents the worldview of Anglo-Americans. It is embedded in English history and law. Consequently, it should not be considered odd for Indian people to develop a system which is reflective of the native worldview, embedded in native history and law.

In comparing the general concepts of justice held by indigenous people of North America to the concepts of the Anglo-American system, I want to point out the fundamental differences in legal precepts or concepts that exist between indigenous concepts of law and relationships and Western or Anglo-American concepts of justice. The challenge Indian nations face today is developing justice systems which are relevant to the people and which meet community needs, and most importantly do not unilaterally substitute Western principles for indigenous concepts.

From initial contact native peoples experienced conflict in legal principles with the various colonizers. For example: with respect to the ownership of land, the native concept was that one cannot buy and sell the land; native law was oral and theirs written; many native societies were matrilineal while the colonizers' societies were patrilineal. Unless differences in worldview are articulated, it is difficult both to understand clearly the struggle in developing a native justice system within a system modeled after the Anglo-American system and to devise a method to do so. The displacement of native concepts and principles by the use and adoption of non-Indian law by Indian nations also becomes clearer by articulating the differences. The differences between indigenous views of justice and Anglo-American views of justice are fundamental. There are many different tribes, many different languages, yet there are some principles and common threads within our indigenous systems of justice. . . .

The Effects of Use of Non-Indian Law

The greatest danger in using non-Indian law is that, since it is not law that has evolved from native peoples themselves, it advances non-Indian approaches which do not necessarily provide the best way to resolve disputes or handle crimes and violations for a native community. A gulf between native people and non-Indian law occurs where non-Indian law introduces or reinforces views which are contrary to accepted values or precepts of the community. The Anglo-American system is in itself contradictory to native values in restoring harmony. Thus, the effectiveness of the methods and the law applied by the tribal judicial system in alleviating the problems it is responsible for addressing can be undermined by influence of Anglo-American principles. Courts and tribal lawyers must consider the difference between the federal and state governments and their approach to justice, and that of tribal governments in relation to the people they serve. While there are some similarities, there are also significant differences in terms of economic resources, function, and philosophy.

To the extent that tribal justice systems pattern themselves, not only in structure but in the law applied in their systems, after federal and state court systems, they surrender their own unique concepts of native law and participate, at a certain level, in their own ethnocide.

Law is a significant part of all cultures and, to the extent that Anglo-American concepts displace native concepts, native culture is changed. The use of non-Indian law perpetuates and interjects a way of thinking which should be carefully considered. While it may seem difficult to consider and argue cases based on a tribal perspective, this is the only way tribes can develop their own unique jurisprudence. If non-Indian law is not automatically used by tribal courts, or turned to as providing the definitive answer on all aspects of the law, Indian concepts will emerge.

Some would argue that there are reasons for the use of non-Indian law and that tribal courts are legitimized if they look and act like non-Indian courts. Non-Indian parties and lawyers are more comfortable in or with a system they can recognize. Others say that traditional law is too difficult or too controversial to apply.

Legitimization should not come at such a high price. Differences are to be expected by parties and lawyers when going into another jurisdiction. It is time that we begin to rethink the structure and foundation of tribal judicial systems and to infuse the tribal system with our own concepts of justice which more closely reflect our societal beliefs.

Practical Considerations

The Importance of Incorporating Customary Law Ways into Tribal Judicial Systems

Many tribal Constitutions and Codes mandate that custom and tradition be utilized by the tribal court. These provisions vary, but the majority of these provisions are quite strong regarding the preeminence that custom and tradition are to be given by the judiciary when considering matters before them. Even if no written provisions exist, recognition of the customary law of the tribe by the judiciary is possible.

Customary law is oral and primarily preserved in the native language. The predominance of English and the increasing number of tribal peoples who only speak English, the use of English in the tribal court, and the employment of persons external to the tribe as judges and advocates within tribal systems has diminished the use of native languages. This in turn affects the way in which thoughts and ideas are expressed. In integrating and relying on traditional law, courts and parties are likely to find themselves caught between English and the native language, unless everyone before the court is conversant in the native language. This raises at least two issues. One is insuring that a place is made for the use of native language in tribal court systems. The court has a responsibility to insure that qualified translators are available and utilized by the court for the benefit of both English and native speakers. The second issue is the interdisciplinary aspect of developing a court system based on native principles and traditional law. The court and lawyers must and should be working with others in the community who are recognized for their knowledge of the native language, of the history of the people, and of the legal traditions and teachings. In order to bring traditional law into the court, oral interviews and fieldwork may be required. It is important to recognize the work required in developing a tribal system which seeks to utilize traditional law. The work is slow and painstaking, with many detractors requiring great commitment, not only on the part of those involved in the court system, but of the leadership and the community. While outside forces and societal changes have impacted custom, it is important to distinguish between disuse of custom and custom which simply has not been recognized, but which, in fact, remains alive and intact.

The judiciary and advocates appearing before the court must use custom responsibly and must assume certain ethical obligations in its use. For instance, an advocate should be under the same obligation to report to the court both the favorable and unfavorable customary law on a particular matter, in the same manner they are responsible for reporting favorable and unfavorable case law. In addition, both the judiciary as well as the advocates should bear responsibility to search out applicable customary law before advocating or applying outside law.

The application of customary law to members of the tribe and non-members is a particularly important issue. Some courts decide whether it would be appropriate to apply customary law to tribal members based on their status as traditional and on their bicultural or assimilated status. They also make a distinction between members and non-members. This is an interesting distinction which will be addressed below.

A great deal of responsibility for the development of customary law as a solid foundation of tribal law lies with the tribal court system, primarily the judiciary and the parties before the court. The responsibility for the articulation and pronunciation of customary law lies with the judiciary, but I contend that the responsibility of presenting customary law to be considered by the courts belongs to the litigants.

The premise I begin with is that all tribes and their courts apply and draw upon customary law to some extent. Many, as they apply it in decision-making, may not stop to label it as such. This is what I want to stress here: the need for the tribal judiciary to consciously document its use, articulate it when applied and request parties to address customary law, and where it is applicable, to present customary law to the court. Applying customary law is not always easy for tribal court judges. It is often easier to apply state or federal law because it is written and because Western legal training leads us in that direction. On the other hand, because Indian tribes are oral societies, the customary law is contained in the oral tradition of the tribe. It is not written down. It is typically not codified. The sources of common law are the members of tribal society who were raised traditionally. In addition, non-legal research materials may provide information, as well as the personal experience and observation of community members. Western legal training does not necessarily prepare lawyers, both native and non-native, for this aspect of tribal court advocacy or judging.

How can the native court develop and encourage the use of customary law? One, courts can develop their own unique rules for customary law when it is at issue, or develop their own unique interpretation of the rules of evidence used by courts to accommodate the nature of customary law which might otherwise make it difficult or cumbersome to apply. Two, the court can call its own experts on customary law if customary law will assist the court to understand evidence (i.e., significant acts which symbolize something according to custom, such as paternity, or to determine a fact in issue, such as whether there was a marriage), or when customary law is in dispute. Basically, judges have a great deal of flexibility when they believe customary law will assist in understanding evidence or determining a fact in issue or when the judge needs expert guidance on what the customary law is.

Courts might want to consider developing unique rules or provisions which encourage the introduction of customary law, and clearly set out how customary law is to be addressed and presented to the court.

When Customary Law Is Not at Issue

When customary law is not at issue, i.e., where the custom is so widely known and accepted in the community, the court may consider recognizing the customary law on its own. This is known as *judicial notice* under the rules of evidence used by Anglo-American courts. The limitations on judicial notice generally apply only to adjudicative facts and exclude propositions of generalized knowledge under which common law rules are formulated. Tribal courts could set forth customary law not in dispute and widely known and accepted through its rulings. Indeed, recognition of customary law by constitution or code is strong support, if not a strong mandate, to do so.

Encouraging Use of Customary Law by Litigants

Because the court must be assisted by litigants in the development of customary law, the court might consider adopting unique rules which require litigants to plead the applicability or inapplicability of customary law, and require them to address relevant customary law, just as relevant state and federal law is routinely argued. Litigants would thus be required to determine whether customary law exists on a given matter, what that customary law is, and whether or not it is applicable and why it is or why it is not applicable.

Role of the Legislature

One of the roles of the tribal legislature is to provide for the use and development of customary law through legislation and to fund or support research of customary law at the tribal level. Codification of customary law is sometimes discussed, but the major emphasis is on assisting courts in its recognition. Because codification of customary law is not necessarily the answer, by incorporating customary law into legislation, its relationship to the oral tradition is changed. The primary method through which customary law will become a part of the tribal legal system is through the development of judge-made law and through the legislature's use of traditional legal concepts and precepts as the basis for legislation.

The tribe itself, however, must affirmatively decide that incorporation of customary law is desirable and encourage its use by considering its application itself as a foundation to its legislation. How much customary law will be incorporated will vary from tribe to tribe.

Participation by the Judiciary

Participation and interest of judges in incorporating customary law is critical. If there is no interest or if there is resistance on the part of the judiciary, incorporation of customary law and development of an indigenous body of law unique to a particular tribe will be minimal. The process of incorporating customary law into a formal legal system will not be easy and will take the work of the judiciary, the litigants, and the tribe. If an active approach is not taken to support customary law, customary law will give way to other influences, such as state and federal law devoid of indigenous thought.

Application of Customary Law

The application of customary law need not be limited to the indigenous population. If a comparison is made to the application of English common law, nowhere has its application been limited to only a certain group of people but has instead applied to all. Likewise, application of tribal customary law should know no distinctions among groups of people within the tribal jurisdictional boundaries. Where the customary law of two separate tribes come into conflict, say, for example, due to intermarriage, the principles to resolve conflicts of law could be applied, or developed by the tribal court itself.

Conclusion

Individual tribes face the challenge to develop an indigenous system of justice based on Indian concepts. Tribes do so in the face of imposed mandates, yet the spirit of resistance is alive. As judges, lawyers, and professionals working within the tribal justice systems, or as tribal leaders, we need to assure the responsibility for preserving the strength and good that is in our indigenous thought and refuse to blindly mirror the Anglo-American model.

CULTURES MEET ON THE TRIBAL CIRCUIT

Cynthia Cheski[*]

Long before laws were chiseled in clay or bound in books they were carried in the collective memories of families, tribes, and communities.

Although that tradition was long ago swamped by a tide of written codes and statutes, there are still judges in America who craft their rulings with their eyes on the law books and their ears open to the spoken wisdom of their people.

Judge William Bluehouse Johnson, 43, of the Tribal Court of Laguna Pueblo, New Mexico, is such a blender of traditions. He is the sole trial judge for about 7,000 people who are not only U.S. citizens, but also citizens of their sovereign tribe, within, but separate from, the United States.

Every day Johnson and his fellow Native American tribal court judges weigh the complexities, choosing state law for one case, custom for another, and mediation for a third.

Johnson didn't make up his mind about the law until he was 32 years old. He was born in Pueblo of Isleta, south of Albuquerque on the Rio Grande River, and had studied off and on at the University of New Mexico for years, finally earning a bachelor's degree with a pre-law concentration, and was accepted to law school after his second application and a summer preparation course at the University of Arizona.

His aim after graduation was to work in some capacity in Indian law, either as a practitioner for the Bureau of Indian Affairs or as counsel for a

---

[*] Cynthia Cheski, *Cultures Meet on the Tribal Circuit*, 20 Human Rights 25 (1993).

tribe. As things turned out, he became a judge before he even passed the bar exam.

While waiting to take the bar, Johnson worked part-time for the American Indian Law Center in Albuquerque. In early 1991, the Pueblo Indian tribe governor approached him with an offer: associate judge in tribal court.

His work load soon doubled after he became the judge at the Acoma Pueblo. "So now I'm working in two pueblos and the Indian Law Center. Between the three of them, I was finally beginning to make a full-time salary," he said, laughing.

By the spring of 1992, Laguna wanted a full-time, permanent judge. The council there gave Johnson a one-year contract and he left his other jobs.

Four days a week Judge Johnson presides over the court, hearing both civil and criminal cases. How to proceed with each one, which laws to use, is the touchy, unsettled, exciting part.

"First, there is the internal law of each tribe, derived from tradition and custom. This is Indian tribal law."

"There is law generated through the relationship between the U.S. government and Indian tribes. For instance, if a non-Indian commits a crime on a reservation, only the state or federal government can do anything."

"Then there is the Laguna Law and Order Code, which are ordinances that buttress the other laws."

Few Laguna residents exercise their right to a jury trial in Johnson's court, preferring his judgment. "The Indian psychology, the Indian sociology, is not to air your problems in front of your peers," he explains.

"They would rather trust one good person to hear it than have everyone sit there and hear them air their dirty laundry."

Although most litigants and defendants represent themselves, about 30 percent hire attorneys. Most outside counsel is unschooled in pueblo courts and laws, Johnson says, and many have no interest in learning. He usually applies state law for guidance in such cases.

Whether traditional or based in state law, Johnson knows that state courts only respect tribal court orders about half the time. He's trying to change that, in part through his memberships in the Indian Law section of the New Mexico state bar and also in the New Mexico Indian Bar Association.

Johnson sees deep irony in trying to apply traditional wisdom in a court based on an adversarial system of justice that is foreign to Native Americans.

"I end up doing a lot of equity," he said. "It's the old Indian way. A win-win situation. The Indian way of compromise. I can get parties to sit down and work it out. They're longer-lasting decisions and there's lot better compliance."

Questions

1. What are some of the advantages and disadvantages of designing a tribal court to function more like a traditional tribal dispute resolution system?
2. What are some of the advantages and disadvantages of designing a tribal court to function more like a non-Indian court system?
3. What are the functions or roles that tribal court should be expected to perform within tribal communities? Should preserving or strengthening a tribe's customs, traditions, and culture always be part of its responsibility?

In Your Community

1. Within your tribe's or nation's judicial system, what is the traditional philosophy of dispute resolution? Is there a traditional story (or stories) that explains this?
2. Interview a tribal judge in your community and learn about his or her experiences as a tribal judge. Attempt to find out their experiences with and their perspective of "traditional law."

Glossary

Common law: A system of law that is derived from judges' decisions rather than legislation.

Custom: Regular behavior (of persons in a geographical area or type of business) that gradually takes on legal importance so that it will strongly influence a court's decision.

Customary law: A law based on custom or tradition.

Ethnocide: The process of ridding a cultural group of its distinct ways of acting and believing.

Litigant: A plaintiff or defendant in a lawsuit.

Traditional dispute resolution: A nonadversarial style of resolving disputes through the use of cultural customs and traditions by tribal justice systems.

Worldview: The different beliefs, values, and meanings about the world that a particular society or people have that contribute to its unique culture, traditions, and ways of life.

Suggested Further Reading

Russel Lawrence Barsh, *Putting the Tribe in Tribal Courts: Possible? Desirable?* 8 Kansas Journal of Law and Public Policy 74 (1998).

Robert D. Cooter & Wolfgang Fikentscher, *Indian Common Law: The Role of Custom in American Indian Tribal Courts*, 46 American Journal of Comparative Law 509 (1998).

Matthew L. M. Fletcher, *Rethinking Customary Law in Tribal Court Jurisprudence*, 13 Michigan Journal of Race & Law 57 (2007).

CHAPTER 10

Introduction to Tribal Court Authority
Differences between Criminal and Civil Law

G IVEN THAT some of the contemporary powers of today's tribal courts have their origins in Anglo-American legal norms, structures, and practices, it is necessary when studying tribal courts to first look at how some of the basic powers of Anglo-American legal systems are organized and operate. This is true of one of the most basic characteristics of tribal court authority: the general practice of tribal courts to distinguish between their authority over matters of criminal versus civil law. Because this is an area heavily influenced by Anglo-American law, it is necessary to first understand what the terms *criminal law* and *civil law* mean in the Anglo-American legal tradition and how these two notions influence contemporary tribal legal norms, structures, and practices. A point to remember in this discussion is that differing cultures sort offenses into civil and criminal categories based on their own criteria, not on anything inherently civil or criminal in people's actions.

Criminal law concerns those norms or rules that, when violated, are considered offenses against the community as a whole rather than against an individual party. In Anglo-American law, for example, acts such as murder, theft, assault, and rape are considered acts that offend all of society. Since these acts are considered offenses against society as a whole, the criminal action is usually prosecuted by a governmental attorney and referred to as "The People," "The State," or "The Tribe" versus the accused defendant. Furthermore, the available remedies or sanctions in a criminal action include imprisonment, whereas imprisonment is not usually available as a remedy in a civil action (except through the court's contempt power to enforce court orders). Consequently, criminal law is sometimes called *penal law* because it imposes punishments on the accused if they are found guilty of violating the law. The reasons behind the punishments given under criminal law may vary, but they can include:

- an intent to deter future criminal activity;
- an attempt to inflict harm on the offender for the wrongdoing; and
- sometimes, an intent to rehabilitate the offender (teach him or her to be a better member of society in the future).

Civil law concerns those norms and rules that are supposed to be followed in the legal relationships that individual citizens or corporations have with each other or the government. These legal relationships include business contracts, family legal relationships created by marriage or adoption, property relationships such as ownership and leases, and the duties and obligations that arise between parties entering into these relationships. When these kinds of relationships are violated, they are considered to cause harm to the individual to whom a duty or obligation was owed. These laws give such individuals a *cause of action* (a legal complaint that they can bring to court) against the offending person and for which they can seek compensation. Civil law is also called *remedial law* because it is concerned with giving individuals a remedy to the loss or injury they may have suffered at the hands of the person or entity who violated their legal relationship.

The purpose behind the remedial judgments in civil law is to make up for what the offended party may have lost, usually in monetary terms. Such judgments are not usually designed to punish the person who broke the civil laws. However, there are occasions when civil judgments are awarded that are largely designed to punish the losing party. These judgments are called an award of "punitive damages" and often involve a very large sum of money above and beyond the amount paid to compensate for the actual loss to the offended party. Though these kinds of awards are fairly common, they can be controversial, in part because they are using civil courts and the civil system to impose punishments, but without the protections afforded to criminal defendants. In essence, such penalties blur the distinction between civil and criminal law.

Of course, a single activity can result in both criminal and civil violations. When that happens, two separate trials can be held. One trial—the criminal trial—will be held to decide whether the alleged offender is to be punished for committing a crime against society. Another entirely separate civil trial can also be conducted to decide whether the same offender is to be held responsible for remedying losses caused to certain harmed individuals.

To use a hypothetical situation to show how this works, imagine a woman named Jenny Johns who, while driving in California under the influence of alcohol, hits Mary Morris as she is walking across the street. Mary survives, but is paralyzed for life. Under criminal law, the State of California can prosecute Jenny for violating the state laws against driving while intoxicated. If so, the state would bring this criminal action to court in a case named *State of California v. Johns*. If Jenny is found guilty at this criminal trial, she could end up serving some time in jail. Note that Mary Morris is not named in the title of this case. She may be asked by the state attorney (called a *prosecutor* because he or she prosecutes the defendant) to be a witness in the trial, but otherwise she is not officially involved.

Under an entirely separate cause of action, Mary could file with the court a civil lawsuit against Jenny for the financial losses suffered as a result of being paralyzed, such as lost wages, medical expenses, and pain and suffering. The norms of civil law in California provide that, as a driver, Jenny owed a legal duty not to operate her car in a manner that is negligent, reckless, or in willful disregard for the safety of pedestrians and other drivers. At the civil trial, which would likely be titled *Morris v. Johns*, Mary and her lawyer would try to convince a jury or judge that Jenny harmed Mary by violating this duty by driving drunk and hitting Mary.

It is because criminal and civil legal activities are separated that we can talk about the Anglo-American legal system as divided between the criminal justice system and the civil justice system, each with their own separate (but similar) norms, structures, and practices. Furthermore, it is because of this division that the Anglo-American legal system makes a distinction between the power and authority that courts have to handle and punish criminal violations—criminal jurisdiction—from the power and authority that these courts have to handle and remedy civil violations—civil jurisdiction.

The difference between Anglo-American criminal and civil law is summed up well by William Geldart:

> The difference between civil law . . . and criminal law turns on the difference between two different objects that the law seeks to pursue—redress or punishment. The object of civil law is the redress of wrongs by compelling compensation or restitution: the wrongdoer is not punished, he only suffers so much harm as is necessary to make good the wrong he has done. The person who has suffered gets a definite benefit

from the law, or at least he avoids a loss. On the other hand, in the case of crimes, the main object of the law is to punish the wrongdoer; to give him and others a strong inducement not to commit the same or similar crimes, to reform him if possible, or perhaps to satisfy the public sense that wrongdoing ought to meet with retribution.[1]

Of course, different legal heritages around the world provide for different kinds of responses to the same normative violations. What might be considered a punishable offense (that is, a crime) that harms all of society in the Anglo-American legal system may, in the legal system of a different society, be treated as a remediable offense (that is, a civil violation) that causes a loss to an individual or family but not to the larger community. Professor Pat Lauderdale explains this concept:

> The closest approximation to the law-ways or common law of most indigenous North Americans is civil law. Civil law is more amenable to incorporating essential problems of unity and collectivity. It has the potential to provide a more equitable, less oppressive arena in which to negotiate and regulate major social problems, including those of a violent nature. The civil process has the potential to consider the positions and perceptions of the victim and the offender. This process focuses upon the paying of damages and the receipt of compensation reflecting both the problematic behavior of the offender and the suffering endured by the victims. Civil proceedings can carry far less degradation to the parties involved and de-emphasize the moral condemnation or stigma of criminal sanctions.[2]

Cultural differences existed between the Anglo-American legal system and the unique legal systems of American Indian tribes and Alaska Native villages. In the early years of the U.S. republic, these differences created problems for the punishment of crimes committed between Indians and non-Indians, and many early treaties between the United States and specific tribes outlined how such crimes were to be handled. As the exertion of U.S. federal power over American Indians became more intrusive, the distinction between criminal and civil law as observed in Anglo-American legal traditions was more fully imposed on tribes, often disregarding the tribe's own legal system and ways of handling specific offenses, including even those that arose between their own members. Today, this distinction has been incorporated into the organization and operation of many contemporary tribal legal systems. As a result, the authority that tribal courts now have to hear and decide criminal legal matters is very different from their authority to hear and decide civil legal matters, and both powers are different from the authority over these matters that tribes had prior to U.S. domination.

Introducing Jurisdiction

In the next few chapters, we will consider the history and current status of the powers that American Indian tribes have to handle matters of criminal and civil law, or what is called their criminal and civil jurisdiction. The term *jurisdiction* refers to a government's power to exercise authority over all persons and things within its territory. There are many different kinds of jurisdiction and many different terms describing the kinds of governmental power being exercised, the legal matters over which jurisdiction is being exercised, and whether that power is shared by other governmental bodies.

Whether or not a court in the Anglo-American legal system has power and authority over a particular conflict is determined by looking at three types of jurisdiction:

- *Personal jurisdiction* is the power of a court over a particular person.
- *Subject matter jurisdiction* is the power of a court to hear a specific type of case, that is, the type of activity and legal norms that the conflict concerns (e.g., murder, traffic violations, divorces).
- *Territorial jurisdiction* is the power of a court to hear a case that occurs within a specified area of land (such as a tribe's reservation).

For courts to have the power to hear and decide any particular case (often called its "adjudicatory" power), that case must usually involve some combination of individual persons, places (territorial location), and/or subject matter over which that particular court has jurisdiction. Although this notion is one that comes from Anglo-American law, it has become a central feature of contemporary tribal law as well—under the federal rules, tribal courts today can only assert their adjudicatory jurisdiction over cases involving certain individuals, territory, and subject matter.

Exclusive jurisdiction and *concurrent jurisdiction* are terms that refer to whether or not governmental powers overlap one another. Jurisdiction is said to be exclusive when only one government can exercise power over a particular case, set of circumstances, or individuals. For example, crimes committed by non-Indians on Indian reservations are under the exclusive jurisdiction of the federal government in many states. Tribal courts have exclusive jurisdiction over some matters, such as child welfare cases involving an Indian child living on a reservation.

Concurrent jurisdiction occurs when two different governments have power over a legal matter at the same time. For example, drinking establishments (e.g., bars) are often governed by multiple governments. The same drinking establishment might be regulated by tribal, state, and federal laws, for example. In some criminal cases, both the tribe and the federal or state government has power to prosecute the defendant. This shared power is one kind of concurrent jurisdiction.

Questions

1. In Anglo-American legal tradition, what is the difference between civil and criminal law?
2. Describe a situation in which a single act could be subject to both criminal and civil penalties.
3. Do you agree with Professor Lauderdale that civil law is the closest approximation to the law-ways or common law of most indigenous North Americans? Why or why not?
4. What are the three kinds of jurisdiction that need to be addressed in order to know if a court has jurisdiction? Define them.

In Your Community

1. What were some of the normative violations that were treated as criminal violations and civil violations according to your tribe's unique legal heritage?
2. How do you think the way your tribe handled these violations compare to the ways in which Anglo-American law addresses them?
3. How does your tribe address these violations in their contemporary legal system?
4. Do you agree with the way in which your tribe handles these violations today? Why or why not?
5. Research your tribe's legal codes (if possible) for statements that express the jurisdiction of your tribal court (if your tribe has one). If your tribe has no legal codes or no tribal court, try to write such a statement yourself. What should it say? Why?

Glossary

Cause of action: Facts sufficient to support a valid lawsuit; the legal theory on which a lawsuit is based.

Civil justice system: The network of courts and tribunals that deal with laws concerned with civil or private rights and remedies, as contrasted by criminal laws.

Criminal justice system: The network of courts and tribunals that deal with criminal law and its enforcement.

Jurisdiction: A government's power to exercise authority over persons and things within its territory.

Negligent: Failing to exercise a reasonable amount of care in a situation that causes harm to someone or something. It can involve doing something carelessly or failing to do something that should have been done.

Penal law: Law that provides for a penalty.

Prosecutor: The public official who presents the government's case in criminal law.

Reckless: Lacking proper caution; careless of consequences; negligent.

Redress: To set right; to remedy; to compensate; to remove the cause of a grievance or complaint.

Remedial law: A law passed to correct a defect in a prior law; a law passed to provide or modify a remedy.

Willful disregard: Acting in a manner known to be wrong; intentional or deliberate disregard of notice.

Suggested Further Reading

Michael Cousins, *Aboriginal Justice: A Haudenosaunee Approach*, in *Justice as Healing: Indigenous Ways* (Wanda D. McCaslin, ed., 2005)
Frank Pommersheim, *The Crucible of Sovereignty: Analyzing Issues of Tribal Jurisdiction*, 31 Arizona Law Review 329 (1989).

Notes

1. William Geldart, *Introduction to English Law* 146 (D. C. M. Yardly, ed., 9th ed. 1984).
2. Pat Lauderdale, *Indigenous North American Jurisprudence*, 38 International Journal of Comparative Sociology 131–48 (1997).

CHAPTER 11

Criminal and Civil Violations in Tribal Legal Traditions

A S MENTIONED EARLIER, what constitutes a crime or civil violation in one society or legal heritage does not always constitute a crime or civil violation in another. Thus, what one society accepts as the proper way to respond to acts such as murder, rape, divorce, or adultery is not always the way in which people from another society would respond to those acts. In some societies, the responses to these offenses appear to be more about providing remedies to the harmed individuals or families, while in others the responses are clearly meant to punish the offender. Even within societies and cultures, different people have different concepts about what acts constitute crimes or civil offenses. These concepts can also change over time.

Furthermore, what actually constitutes a remedy or a punishment to such violations can differ dramatically from society to society. Punishments designed to remove an offender from the community may involve imprisonment in some societies, while it involves banishment or exclusion in others. Sometimes different ideas of appropriate punishments arise in very closely related cultures and societies. For example, both the United Kingdom and the United States treat murder as a crime. However, many U.S. states allow the imposition of the death penalty for murder, but Britain does not.

In many tribal societies, there is a general belief that punishing offenders is something best left to a spiritual or supernatural authority. The idea that human beings could judge and punish others in some official manner was, at least in some societies and for some violations, considered to be highly improper.

Thus, among the Hopi, people who mistreated their relatives or were selfish with their food and other resources would not always be punished directly by a family or clan leader. Instead, they would be warned that if they did not change their ways, they would be struck ill with sicknesses caused by the supernatural powers punishing them for their bad behavior. If the person continued to act antisocially, they might be called out in public ceremonies and threatened directly by these spirits as they are being embodied by ceremonial participants. Other times, it was the human misuse of spiritual and supernatural forces, a phenomenon often called "witchcraft" by scholars, that would be the ultimate form of social violation in need of punishment.

The division between criminal and civil violations in Anglo-American law is also something that does not often hold true for American Indian tribes and their unique legal heritages. Sometimes remedial compensation to a victim's family was the way a person who killed someone was expected to respond. In other situations, acts that at one time were considered civil violations in Anglo-American law, such as adultery, were, among tribes such as the Ojibway, grounds not only for monetary compensation but also for severe physical punishment. Thus, violations treated as crimes under Anglo-American law were often treated as civil violations in tribal law, and vice versa, and tribal law often made no distinction between violations that would be punished and those that would be remedied.

Consequently, there was very often little distinction between the power and authority that tribal leaders had to handle criminal matters and the power and authority they had to handle civil matters. There was, in short, no distinction between tribal criminal and civil jurisdiction. The differences between these views of crime and punishment and the Anglo-American norms, structures, and practices are quite dramatic. Indeed, it was just these kinds of beliefs that led some non-Indian scholars to perpetuate the myth that "Indians have no law," as we discussed earlier.

In this chapter, we will read some excerpts from studies that describe the legal systems of American Indian tribes prior to intrusion by the U.S. federal government. We start with an excerpt from *The Cheyenne Way*, a famous study of the Cheyenne legal heritage conducted by legal scholar Karl N. Llewellyn and anthropologist E. Adamson Hoebel. This study is famous for introducing the "trouble case" method to the anthropological study of law and culture. It works by studying stories of actual offenses and how they were handled by the Cheyenne communities of the time to shed light on the norms, structures, and practices that make up the Cheyenne legal heritage. We will read an excerpt considering one such case to see what insights it offers into the ways in which the Cheyenne legal system responded to the offense of "individual hunting." Then we will turn to an excerpt from Joan Ryan's 1995 study entitled "Doing

Things the Right Way," based on her discussions and interviews with Dene Elders in Lac La Marte, Canada. The passage entitled "What Happened to the Person Who Broke the Rules" includes the norms, structures, and practices surrounding rule breakers.

Given that these passages were written by European or Anglo-American scholars based on their conversations with tribal elders about events and practices long past, it is possible that the picture they paint of these tribal legal systems is somewhat distorted. These studies tend to represent tribal legal systems as static and unchanging, with little recognition that different members of these tribes may have had competing views about what constituted a normative offense and how such offenses should be handled. Keep this in mind when you read these articles. Despite these shortcomings, the excerpts do reveal some fundamental differences between, on the one hand, the norms, practices, and structures of these tribal legal systems and the way they handled offenses and, on the other hand, the ways in which these same offenses are treated as crimes in the Anglo-American legal system. As you read them, compare the offenses that are considered remediable and those that are punishable by these tribes to those treated as crimes or civil violations in Anglo-American law.

THE TRIBAL OSTRACISM AND REINSTATEMENT OF STICKS EVERYTHING UNDER HIS BELT

Karl N. Llewellyn and E. Adamson Hoebel*

Once, at a time when all the Cheyenne tribe was gathered together, Sticks Everything Under His Belt went out hunting buffalo alone. "I am hunting for myself," he told people. He was implying that the rules against individual hunting did not apply to him because he was declaring himself out of the tribe—a man on his own.

All the soldier chiefs and all the tribal chiefs met in a big lodge to decide what to do in this case, since such a thing had never happened before. This was the ruling they made: no one could help Sticks Everything Under His Belt in any way, no one could give him smoke, no one could talk to him. They were cutting him off from the tribe. The chiefs declared that if anyone helped him in any way that person would have to give a Sun Dance.

---

* Karl N. Llewellyn & E. Adamson Hoebel, *The Cheyenne Way*, in *Primitive Jurisprudence* 9–12 (1941).

When the camp moved, Sticks Everything Under His Belt moved with it, but the people would not recognize him. He was left alone and it went to his heart, so he took one of his horses (he had many) and rode out to the hilltops to mourn.

His sister's husband was a chief in the camp. This brother-in-law felt sorry for him out there mourning, with no more friends. At last he took pity on his poor brother-in-law; at last he spoke to his wife, "I feel sorry for your poor brother out there and now I am going to do something for him. Cook up all those tongues we have! Prepare a good feast!"

Then he invited the chiefs to his lodge and sent for his brother-in-law to come in. This was after several years had passed, not months.

When the chiefs had assembled, the brother-in-law spoke. "Several years ago you passed a ruling that no one could help this man. Whoever should do so you said would have to give a Sun Dance. Now is the time to take pity on him. I am going to give a Sun Dance to bring him back in. I beg you to let him come back to the tribe, for he has suffered long enough. This Sun Dance will be a great one. I declare that every chief and all the soldiers must join in. Now I put it up to you. Shall we let my brother-in-law smoke before we eat, or after?"

The chiefs all answered in accord, "*Ha-ho, ha-ho* [thank you, thank you]. We are very glad you are going to bring back this man. However, let him remember that he will be bound by whatever rules the soldiers lay down for the tribe. He may not say he is outside of them. He has been out of the tribe for a long time. If he remembers these things, he may come back."

Then they asked Sticks Everything Under His Belt whether he wanted to smoke before or after they had eaten. Without hesitation he replied, "Before," because he had craved tobacco so badly that he had split his pipe stem to suck the brown gum inside it.

The lodge was not big enough to hold all the chiefs who had come to decide this thing, so they threw open the door, and those who could not get in sat in a circle outside. Then they filled a big pipe and when it was lighted they gave it to Sticks Everything Under His Belt. It was so long since he had had tobacco that he gulped in the smoke and fell over in a faint. As he lay there the smoke came out of his anus, he was so empty. The chiefs waited silently for him to come to again and then the pipe was passed around the circle.

When all had smoked, Sticks Everything Under His Belt talked. "From now on I am going to run with the tribe. Everything the people say,

I shall stay right by it. My brother-in-law has done a great thing. He is going to punish himself in the Sun Dance to bring me back. He won't do it alone, for I am going in, too."

After a while the people were getting ready for the Sun Dance. One of the soldiers began to get worried because he had an ugly growth on his body which he did not want to reveal to the people. He was a good-looking young man named Black Horse. Black Horse went to the head chiefs asking them to let him sacrifice himself alone on the hilltops as long as the Sun Dance was in progress.

"We have nothing to say to that," they told him. "Go to the pledger. This is his Sun Dance."

Black Horse went to the brother-in-law of Sticks Everything Under His Belt, who was a brother-in-law to him as well. "Brother-in-law," he begged, "I want to be excused from going into the lodge. Can't you let me go into the hills to sacrifice myself as long as you are in there, to make my own bed?"

"No," he was rebuffed, "you know my rule is that all must be there."

"Well, brother-in-law, won't I be all right if I set up a pole on the hill and hang myself to it through my breasts? I shall hang there for the duration of the dance."

This brother-in-law of his answered him in these words, "Why didn't you take that up when all the chiefs were in the lodge? I have agreed with them that everyone must be in the lodge. I don't want to change the rule. I won't give you permission to go outside."

Then Black Horse replied, "You will not make the rules my way. Now I am going to put in a rule for everybody. Everyone in there has to swing from the pole as I do."

"No," countered the brother-in-law. "That was not mentioned in the meeting. If you want to swing from the pole, that is all right, but no one else has to unless he wishes to."

When they had the Sun Dance everyone had a good time. Black Horse was the only one on the pole, and there were so many in the lodge that there was not room enough for all to dance. Some just had to sit around inside the lodge. Though they did not dance, they starved themselves for four days. This dance took place near Sheridan, Wyoming, seven years before Custer. I was only a year old at the time, but what I have said here I was told by Elk River and others. We call this place "Where the Chiefs Starved Themselves."

"WHAT HAPPENED TO THE PERSON WHO BROKE THE RULES?"

Joan Ryan[*]

Some people did not follow the rules and were dealt with in a variety of ways. Some offences were minor and some major. Minor offences were dealt with by the senior male within the small camps. Major ones required a gathering and a public admission of guilt, restitution, and a process of reconciliation.

A minor offence might be a small theft. For example, elders reported that when youths stole some bannock, they were ridiculed and shamed. The person from whom they stole would pin the bannock on their jackets and everyone in camp would know they had stolen it and would laugh at them. This was considered to be a "deterrent"; it was unlikely the youth would repeat his or her theft because they would not want to face ridicule again.

A more serious offence, but not a major one, would be the theft of an animal from a trap. This offence would be reported to the head man *(k'aowo)* in camp and he would then speak "harsh words" to the person who had stolen the fur. The thief would be asked to acknowledge his theft and to return the fur (or another of equal value) to the person from who it had been stolen.

If the offender refused to do this, the senior people gathered and confronted him. He was placed in the centre of a circle and people gave him "hard words" about his inappropriate actions. They demanded he acknowledge his guilt and promise to return the fur. This stressed the importance of restoring harmony within the community, reconciliation with the person he had offended and compensation through replacement of the fur. Once that was done, no further action was taken and no further mention of the offence was made.

Failure to behave properly, while on a hunt or while trapping, had serious consequences and was considered a serious offence. If a person mistreated an animal, for example by breaking its bones, no one would hunt or trap with him again. Nor would they provide him with meat. Such actions put the group at risk, a risk people were not willing to take. The offender would be shunned. This made life very difficult for him because it is extremely hard to hunt or trap without a partner.

---

[*] Joan Ryan, *Doing Things the Right Way: Dene Traditional Justice in Lac La Martre, N.W.T.* (1995).

OJIBWA SOCIOLOGY

*Ruth Landes**

On the obligations that a widow or widower must pay to the [patrilineal clan] of their deceased spouse:
The [patrilineal clan] affects marriage inasmuch as [patrilineal clan]-mates may not marry, and consistently with this, after-death mourning by the spouse and arrangement for remarriage are phrased in [patrilineal clan] terms. Actually it is the immediate family which acts, and in so doing [clan] boundaries are often lost sight of. The important [clan]-phrased rite is the reinstatement ceremony of the widowed spouse. When a man, for example, has died, his [clan] says that his wife has "destroyed," *c.iwanatciat*, him, and that consequently she must compensate his [clan]-mates. It is worth remarking in passing that murder cannot be compensated this way, but can be satisfied only by feud. However, the Central Algonkians from whom the Ojibwa have borrowed heavily practiced compensation for murder as an alternative to settlement by blood feud. The southern Ojibwa seem likewise to have practiced compensation for murder as well as the neighboring Dakota. It is possible that the Canadian Ojibwa borrowed the "compensation" idiom from the same sources that gave them their [clan] system.

The widow is thus "indebted" to the [clan] of her deceased husband and the members call her *nji~ga'm*, "my debtor." A man can also use this term to a joking relative, implying thereby that he "owns" her, i.e., has definite sexual rights to her. During her period of mourning, the widow must occupy herself with collecting goods for repaying her creditors, *gi.we' ni ge'*. She must do this chiefly through her own exertions, though close relatives always help. There must be no suspicion that a lover has aided, and surely not a [clan]-mate of the deceased. In this way she not only pays her bill, but "she shows her respect to the parents of her dead husband," and proves that she is a faithful soul worthy of being retained in marriage by the [clan], i.e., married to a [clan]-mate of the deceased husband. . . .

When the surviving spouse flirts during the period set aside for mourning, or neglects to pay the debt, or gets married without having passed through the releasing-rite, the [clan]-mates of the deceased punish her by stripping the offender of his-her property and by physical injury such as slicing off part of an ear. Invariably, the offender submits quietly to the punishment; and he is

---

* Ruth Landes, *Ojibwa Sociology* 44–45, 48–50 (1937).

often ostracized for the remainder of his life unless he moves to another locality. These "|clan|-mates" are actually members of one side of the bilateral family, though in default of these, unrelated |clan|-mates may act. It is considered presumptuous of an unrelated |clan|-mate to act before a close relative does. Besides by the |clan|-mates, the misbehaving widow (widower) is punished supernaturally by the shade of her husband; and several instances were advanced to show the kinds of supernatural revenge. Thus (Bat'is) Baptiste did not giwenige for his dead wife, and straightway married again. Shortly after, he became mortally ill, and called in an Indian doctor, *tcicsaki*, named Bob Mo:jə to divine the cause of the illness. Bob divined that it was caused by the jealousy of his unappeased deceased wife. Bob was own son to the deceased. Baptiste shortly died. Sometimes the deceased "takes away his (her) children" from the unfaithful spouse, and so they die. Sometimes when she is walking by herself, she will be followed by the shade of the vengeful deceased, who will take her away temporarily—i.e., cause her to faint—and ultimately he will take her away permanently. One faithless widow was pushed into her own fire by the shade of the injured husband, and was burnt to death. . . .

Twenty or twenty-five years ago, at Little Fork, Tom M'Ginnis died. At the reinstatement ceremony, four years later, his father's brother led his (Tom's) wife up to Tom's younger brother Bob, seated her there, and said "they would not let her go." Had she not complied, she would have been cut up about the ears and hair in punishment, because levirate and sororate obligations were not to be slighted. When Bob died, she was again to giwenige but she did not because at her husband's deathbed she was requested in marriage by a brother of Bob's. It is not invariable, however, that such an invitation relieves a "debtor" of obligation; but in this case the M'Ginnis' took matters into their family hands. It may be noted that a person can always escape these obligations by leaving the locality; but he will always be held at any time wherever the relatives of the deceased find him.

At Bear's Pass Andrew Williams became a widower. His father-in-law solicited him early for another daughter. So during his mourning period, while he was collecting goods, Andrew supported his prospective wife by sororate.

Mrs. Wilson said that her adopted mother had instructed her about this ceremony, and had given her gifts towards the payment of the debt. "She gave me a cedar mat and helped me make moccasins. Off and on she gave me a shawl that cost eight dollars, yards of print, a quilt, beads, ribbon." Also, Mrs. Wilson's mother helped her. Members of the debtor's bilateral family usually help "if they are not too stingy, because they like to see the right thing done."

Kavanaugh had another view of Mrs. Wilson's repayment. Mrs. Wilson had given birth to Albert about a year after the death of her husband. At that time she offered the indemnity wealth to the [clan]-mates of her husband. These suspected that she had broken the mourning with a Finn, the putative father of Albert. So when she came to them, they asked her why she was in such a hurry to pay them, and if "any one" (i.e., a lover) had financed her. They embarrassed her thoroughly. "I saw her when she came out of the wigwam. She did not marry for a long time after. And everybody sure said she was in a hurry to make the giwenige."

Questions

1. What is the primary purpose of punishment for wrongdoing? Are there ways to deter future crimes or to help offenders from committing future crimes without punishment?

2. As described in these readings, what kinds of punishment and remedies do these tribal communities seem to rely on most? Do you think these were effective responses to crime, given the ways in which many of these communities operated and were organized?

3. In the Dene passage, the crime of animal cruelty is treated more seriously than the crime of theft. Is this distinction the same in Anglo-American law? What different worldviews might account for differences in categorizing crimes?

4. Why do you think exclusion and compensation were the ways in which tribes like the Cheyenne and the Sioux responded to murder? Do you think these responses were effective? Do you think they would be effective in U.S. society? Explain your answers.

5. Do you think exclusion and compensation for crimes like murder, rape, and assault would be effective responses to crimes committed in tribal societies today? Why or why not?

In Your Community

1. Find out some behaviors that are considered offenses according to your people's legal heritage. According to that legal heritage, what were the appropriate responses (punishments or remedies) when such offenses were committed? How do these responses compare to the way in which such offenses are treated by Anglo-American law?

2. Locate someone knowledgeable about your tribe's legal heritage and ask this person about ways in which your tribe responded to offenses such as

murder, theft, and adultery. Do members of your tribe still respond this way to these offenses? Do you think these are or were effective responses? Explain.

Glossary

Banishment: Requiring someone to leave a country; driving out or removing someone from his or her home and society.

Bilateral family: Two sides or both sides of the family.

Ethnographic studies: The field of descriptive anthropology.

Indebted: Owing gratitude or recognition to another.

Ostracized: Exiled; excluded from a group by common consent.

Patrilineal clan: A group united by relations or descent through the fathers' line.

Retribution: The dispensing or receiving of reward or punishment, especially in the hereafter; something given or exacted in recompense.

Suggested Further Reading

Sidney Harring, *Crow Dog's Case* (1994).

Steven M. Karr, *Now We Have Forgotten the Old Indian Law: Choctaw Culture and the Evolution of Corporal Punishment*, 30 McGeorge Law Review 1221 (1999).

Stephanie J. Kim, *Sentencing and Cultural Differences: Banishment of the American Indian Robbers*, 29 John Marshall Law Review 239 (1995).

CHAPTER 12

Tribal Criminal Jurisdiction

THE LAST CHAPTER reviewed the responses of three different American Indian legal systems to certain kinds of criminal offenses and how those responses differed from the Anglo-American legal system. This chapter will review the limitations that have been imposed on the criminal jurisdiction of Indian tribes and nations during the history of their relations with the U.S. federal government.

Tribal criminal jurisdiction refers to the power and authority that American Indian and Alaska Native tribal courts have to prosecute certain kinds of persons accused of committing certain kinds of crimes in certain locations and, if these people are found guilty, to punish them. Generally speaking, this jurisdiction has been recognized as part of the inherent sovereign power that tribes had to regulate the people and affairs in their territory, as independent nations prior to their domination by the United States.

As explained earlier, criminal jurisdiction is a very important element of the right to self-governance, because it gives tribes the power to protect their people, culture, and nation. If a tribe has jurisdiction over a criminal case, this ensures that their law, based on their values and beliefs, will be applied to the actions of a wrongdoer. This is especially important given the differences between tribal criminal justice and Anglo-American criminal justice discussed in the previous chapter.

Over the history of tribal relations with the United States, however, limitations have been placed on the criminal jurisdiction that tribes and their courts can exercise. These limits have been justified as arising from the loss of certain inherent sovereign powers that tribes suffered by virtue of being conquered by the United States. It is a combination of each tribe's unique legal heritage, the federal limits imposed on that heritage, and how tribes have dealt with those limits that shapes the contemporary face of tribal criminal jurisdiction. As a result, criminal jurisdiction in Indian country can be a confusing maze of rules and restrictions.

The purposes of this chapter are to

1. provide an overview of the limitations placed on the exercise of tribal criminal jurisdiction;
2. address mechanisms or methods for preserving tribes' criminal jurisdiction; and
3. examine how tribal courts have addressed questions regarding jurisdiction.

"Indian Country" as Defined in Federal Law for the Purposes of Criminal Jurisdiction (18 U.S.C. 1151)

In order to make laws that affect tribes, the U.S. government has defined what land areas these laws will impact. The U.S. government defines this area as "Indian Country." The definition of Indian Country is in 18 U.S.C. 1151:

> (a) All land within the limits of any Indian reservation under the jurisdiction of the United States Government, notwithstanding the issuance of any patent, and, including rights-of-way running through the reservation,
> (b) all dependent Indian communities within the borders of the United States whether within the original or subsequently acquired territory thereof, and whether within or without the limits of a State, and
> (c) all Indian allotments, the Indian titles to which have not been extinguished, including rights-of-way running through the same.

Note that the U.S. Supreme Court, in the case *Alaska v. Native Village of Venetie Tribal Government, et al.* (522 U.S. 520 [1998]) recently gave a narrow interpretation to the term "dependent Indian communities" as used in the above definition. In that case, the Court explained that the term refers to a limited category of Indian lands that are neither reservations nor allotments and that satisfy two requirements: (1) the lands must have been set aside by the United States for the use of the Indians as Indian lands; and (2) the lands must be under federal superintendence. The Court then concluded that the lands at issue in that case did not constitute "Indian Country" over which the Native Village of Venetie tribal government could assert criminal jurisdiction. Those

lands had once been part of the Neets'aii Gwich'in Indians' reservation surrounding the village of Venetie, but after that reservation was extinguished by
the Alaska Native Claims Settlement Act of 1971, the Native corporation created by ANCSA to govern the region took title to the land, but not in a way,
the Court said, that maintained its status as Indian Country. The effect of that
decision was to disqualify the vast majority of lands held by Alaska Native corporations as Indian Country over which Native governments could exercise
criminal jurisdiction.

Federal Authority over Crimes between Indians and Non-Indians: The General Crimes Act (18 U.S.C. 1152)

In the early years of the republic, federal treaties and statutes regarding tribal
criminal jurisdiction primarily concerned the prosecution of offenses arising
between Indians and non-Indians. In much of this early legislation, such
"interracial" crimes became the jurisdiction of the federal courts.[1]

The Indian Country Crime Act—more commonly known as the General
Crimes Act, 18 U.S.C. 1152—gave federal courts criminal jurisdiction over
interracial crimes committed in Indian Country. This law, enacted in 1817,
provides as follows:

> Except as otherwise expressly provided by law, the general laws of the
> United States as to the punishment of offenses committed in any place
> within the sole and exclusive jurisdiction of the United States, except the
> District of Columbia, shall extend to the Indian country.
>
> This section shall not extend to offenses committed by one Indian
> against the person or property of another Indian, nor to any Indian com-
> mitting any offense in the Indian country who has been punished by the
> local law of the tribe, or to any case where, by treaty stipulations, the
> exclusive jurisdiction over such offenses is or may be secured to the
> Indian tribes respectively.

Under this law, non-Indians committing crimes against Indians in Indian
Country were subject to federal prosecution. Cases in which Indians committed crimes against non-Indians in Indian Country were, by this law, still under
the subject-matter jurisdiction of the tribe if tribal law handled them first.
Tribes continued to have jurisdiction over all crimes committed by Indians in
their territory, regardless of the victim. This was true because tribal criminal
jurisdiction was seen as part of a tribe's inherent sovereign power to maintain
social order among its members within its territorial boundaries.

Federal Jurisdiction over Indian Defendants: The Major Crimes Act (18 U.S.C. 1153)

The Major Crimes Act was passed by the U.S. Congress in 1885 as a response to *Ex Parte Crow Dog*, 109 U.S. 556 (1883). *Ex Parte Crow Dog* was an important case concerning tribal criminal jurisdiction. The U.S. Supreme Court held that, in the absence of federal statutes limiting tribal criminal jurisdiction, tribes possessed complete, inherent, and exclusive criminal jurisdiction in Indian Country. *Ex Parte Crow Dog* interprets the General Crimes Act as excluding crimes between two Indians and thereby upholds exclusive tribal criminal jurisdiction over crimes between Indian defendants and Indian victims.

The Major Crimes Act grants federal courts criminal jurisdiction over Indians who commit any of the designated offenses. It grants federal courts, instead of state courts, exclusive jurisdiction when the listed offenses are committed by an Indian against the person or property of another in Indian Country. But the federal government has concurrent jurisdiction with tribal courts. It is important to note that the Major Crimes Act does not strip tribal courts of their jurisdiction to handle the same offenses. Many tribal courts do not pursue the Major Crimes Act's offenses, but that is often due to the misconception they do not have the authority, the belief that the federal courts will handle the offenses, or lack of resources. But as tribes revise their tribal codes, more and more are incorporating and prosecuting these major crimes.

As set forth below from Russell's account of the *Crow Dog* case, the Supreme Court's decision, along with a misrepresentation of tribal society as "lawless," led to the passage of the Major Crimes Act of 1885. This Act was the first assertion of federal criminal jurisdiction over crimes committed by Indians against Indians in Indian Country, and it constitutes a major inroad into the exclusive criminal jurisdiction that tribes previously had.

MAKING PEACE WITH CROW DOG'S GHOST: RACIALIZED PROSECUTION IN FEDERAL INDIAN LAW

*Steve Russell**

Crow Dog killed Spotted Tail on the Great Sioux Reservation in 1881. Both parties were Brule. While Crow Dog had a self-defense claim to litigate,

---

* Steve Russell, *Making Peace With Crow Dog's Ghost: Racialized Prosecution in Federal Indian Law*, 21 Wicazo Sa Review 61 (2006).

there was never any doubt that he in fact committed the homicide. He was called to account within the Brule justice system and ordered to make substantial payments to Spotted Tail's family. Since Crow Dog apparently posed no ongoing danger to the peace of the reservation, that would have been the end of the matter.

Public opinion was not disposed to let that be the end of the matter because the media of the time portrayed Spotted Tail as an assimilationist Indian and Crow Dog as a rebel. Indians might call the differences between the two men tactical rather than strategic, but the public perception was otherwise. So it was that Crow Dog was indicted in a U.S. territorial court, tried, convicted, and sentenced to hang by the neck until dead for the homicide of Spotted Tail.

Crow Dog's writ of habeas corpus arrived in the Supreme Court as a case of first impression: do United States courts have inherent jurisdiction over a crime by one Indian against another on Indian land? The Court held that the United States has no such jurisdiction, and Crow Dog escaped the noose. To hold otherwise, said the Court, would be to try Indians:

> Not by their peer, nor by the customs of their people, nor the law of their land, but by superiors of a different race, according to the law of a social state of which they have an imperfect conception, and which is opposed to the traditions of their history, to the habits of their lives, to the strongest prejudices of their savage nature, one which measures the red man's revenge by the white man's morality.

One wonders whether the Court understood that it was "the red man's revenge" that preserved Crow Dog's life while "the white man's morality" wanted to kill him, but the law spoken seems plainly correct. If Indian nations were not separate sovereigns in the sense of criminal law, then it is unclear how they could have the sovereignty to cede to the United States the land it claimed then and claims now under numerous and often conflicting cession treaties. The blind paternalism of the opinion is an artifact of the times, but the holding is a plain victory for tribal justice, albeit coupled with a statement that Congress could extend federal jurisdiction upon Indian land if it chose.

Congress accepted the Court's invitation with alacrity in the Major Crimes Act. Within a month of the act's passage in 1885, Kagama killed Iyouse in the Hoopa Valley Reservation and Indian sovereignty was once more put to the test. The paternalism of *Crow Dog* survived in *United States v. Kagama;* the dominance of Indian sovereignty did not. Leaving aside that the *Crow Dog* opinion practically invited the Major Crimes Act, it seems clear in hindsight that the United States had to have authority over the persons of

Indians in order effectively to assert authority over Indian land not ceded by treaty and therefore, from the Indian point of view, reserved forever for exclusive Indian use.

Intrusion of State Jurisdiction in Indian Country: Public Law 280 (18 U.S.C. 1162)

To make matters of tribal criminal jurisdiction even more confusing, in 1953 Congress passed Public Law 280, legislation that transferred to certain named states the federal jurisdiction over crimes occurring in the Indian Country located within their borders. Public Law 280 did not take away powers from tribes, but this legislation did add yet another layer of complexity to the picture of criminal jurisdiction—one where the question of whether a tribe, a state, or the federal government has the power to prosecute a crime depends on who committed the crime (Indian or non-Indian) and where it was committed (Indian Country or not, and in what state). The impact of this statute (and others like it) varies from state to state and from tribe to tribe.

Upholding Tribal Sovereignty: *United States v. Wheeler*, 435 U.S. 313 (1978)

The U.S. Constitution protects individuals against double jeopardy, which prohibits a citizen of the United States from being prosecuted twice for the same crime by the same government. In *United States v. Wheeler*, 435 U.S. 313 (1978), the defendant was prosecuted and convicted in the Navajo Nation's tribal courts and then in federal court for the same crime. The defendant claimed the later federal prosecution violated his right against double jeopardy, but the U.S. Supreme Court ruled that the source of the power to punish offenders is an inherent part of tribal sovereignty and not a grant of federal power. Thus, because the two prosecutions were by separate sovereigns, the Navajo Nation and the United States, the subsequent federal prosecution did not violate the defendant's right against double jeopardy.

No Tribal Criminal Jurisdiction over Non-Indians: *Oliphant v. Suquamish Indian Tribe*, 435 U.S. 191 (1978)

As far back as original contact, tribal governments had exercised criminal jurisdiction over non-Indians, but in 1978, the U.S. Supreme Court, in *Oliphant v. Suquamish Indian Tribe*, 435 U.S. 191 (1978), put an end to the ability of tribes to do so. Oliphant was a non-Indian charged with a criminal offense in the Suquamish Tribal Court. He challenged the tribe's jurisdiction, arguing that the tribe did not have criminal jurisdiction over non-Indians because this power had been given up to the federal government. The Supreme Court agreed with Oliphant.

The Court reasoned that attempts to exercise criminal jurisdiction over non-Indians was a relatively new phenomenon and that few tribes had had anything resembling a court until recently, and thus criminal jurisdiction over non-Indians was not a power practiced historically. The Court also stated that, although Congress never expressly removed criminal jurisdiction over non-Indians, according to congressional history, it was implicit in its legislative actions. According to the Supreme Court, any criminal jurisdiction over non-Indians that tribes exercised in the past was lost by submitting to the overriding sovereignty of the United States.

Criminal Jurisdiction over Nonmember Indians: *Duro v. Reina*, 495 U.S. 676 (1990) and Congressional Duro-Fix

Only six years after the *Oliphant* decision, the ability of tribal courts to exercise criminal jurisdiction over nonmember Indians was challenged. Duro was an Indian, but not an enrolled member of Salt River Pima-Maricopa Indian Community. At a hearing in 1984 before the Salt River Tribal Court, Duro challenged the tribal court's jurisdiction over his misdemeanor prosecution. The tribal court ruled that *Oliphant* concerned criminal jurisdiction over non-Indians, not nonmember Indians, and thus that it had jurisdiction over the defendant, but Duro appealed this decision through the federal courts.

Six years later, the U.S. Supreme Court, in *Duro v. Reina*, 495 U.S. 676 (1990), extended the logic of *Oliphant* to find that, because of their domination by the United States, tribes also no longer possess criminal jurisdiction over offenses committed by nonmember Indians, even when such crimes are committed in Indian Country. The Court ruled that the power to prosecute nonmember Indians had been surrendered by tribes in their submission to the overriding sovereignty of the United States. Thus, the tribes had no criminal jurisdiction over nonmember Indians. Or, put another way, tribes had criminal jurisdiction *only* over their own enrolled members.

The *Duro* decision, however, prompted Congress to restore tribal criminal jurisdiction over nonmember Indians by amending the language defining the "powers of self government" in the Indian Civil Rights Act of 1968 (25 U.S.C. 1301), as meaning "the inherent power of Indian tribes, hereby recognized and affirmed, to exercise criminal jurisdiction over all Indians." These Indian Civil Rights Act (ICRA) amendments are commonly referred to as the

"Congressional *Duro*-Fix." This *Duro* fix was initially enacted by Congress on a temporary basis in 1990 (Public Law 101-511) and then made permanent in 1991 (Public Law 102-137). The amendments recognized that tribes do have jurisdiction over nonmember Indians and that this power was inherent and had never been stripped from the tribes.

Nonmember Indians, however, challenged the Congressional *Duro*-Fix. They contended that it was a delegation of federal authority rather than recognition of inherent tribal sovereign authority (despite the clear congressional intent). If the federal courts were to agree that the Congressional *Duro*-Fix was a delegation of federal authority, then it would be a violation of double jeopardy (being prosecuted for the same crime twice) for nonmember Indian defendants to be charged in both federal and tribal court. Furthermore, if it were to be held that the tribe is prosecuting the nonmember Indian through delegated federal authority, then the tribe would not be a separate sovereign.

If prosecution of nonmember Indians in both federal and tribal courts were to have been prohibited, it would have greatly limited the ability of tribal courts to exercise their inherent sovereign authority through the ability to take immediate action when a criminal offense occurs. Tribal courts would have been forced to either (1) hold off on prosecution of nonmember Indians until after the federal government made a prosecutorial decision or (2) commence a tribal prosecution, which would have prohibited any later federal prosecution. In a recent affirmation of the tribal position in the U.S. Supreme Court, the Court ruled 7 to 2 on April 19, 2004, in *U.S. v. Lara*, 541 U.S. 193 (2004), that double jeopardy does not apply since the tribe acted in its capacity as a sovereign authority when it prosecuted the nonmember Indian. In effect, the Court held that the Congressional *Duro*-Fix was recognition of inherent tribal sovereign authority rather than a delegation of federal authority. It should be noted, however, that the decision did not address all possible challenges to the tribal criminal prosecution of nonmember Indians. It is likely, therefore, that nonmember Indians will continue to challenge tribal criminal jurisdiction over them.

The Criminal Jurisdiction Maze

The jurisdictional maze set forth by the above legislation and U.S. Supreme Court cases is summarized in table 12-1.

Tribal Criminal Jurisdiction Today: Working within the Limits

The standing U.S. Supreme Court case law is clear. Tribal courts do not possess criminal jurisdiction over non-Indians who commit crimes within tribal

TABLE 12.1. General Scope of Criminal Jurisdiction in Indian Country

| Race | Type of Crime | |
	"Major" Crime (as defined by Major Crimes Act)	All Other Crimes
Indian perpetrator, Indian victim	Federal (under Major Crimes Act) and tribal jurisdiction	Tribal jurisdiction
Indian perpetrator, non-Indian victim	Federal (under Major Crimes Act) and tribal jurisdiction	Federal (under General Crimes Act) and tribal jurisdiction
Non-Indian perpetrator, Indian victim	Federal (under General Crimes Act) jurisdiction	Federal (under General Crimes Act) jurisdiction
Non-Indian perpetrator, non-Indian victim	State jurisdiction	State jurisdiction

* This general criminal jurisdiction chart does not apply to jurisdictions where Public Law 280, 18 U.S.C. 1162, or other relevant federal statutes have conferred jurisdiction upon the state.

borders. Many reservations have considerable non-Indian resident and tourist populations, so at first glance such a limitation would seem to severely hamper the inherent power of tribal nations to maintain peace and order on their land. While this remains a good argument against the *Oliphant* decision, tribal nations have had some success in addressing this problem by coming up with creative legal formulas for dealing with the problems caused by non-Indians in ways that do not involve their criminal jurisdiction. In this section, we will consider some of those alternatives, review some tribal legal codes in which these alternatives have been enumerated, and read some tribal cases that consider a tribe's criminal jurisdiction.

These excerpts reveal the ways in which tribal jurisdiction is being asserted by different tribes today. As you read these excerpts, think about how these tribes have tried to assert their power to regulate offensive behavior on their reservation in light of the federal limits placed on their criminal jurisdiction.

TRIBAL EFFORTS TO ADDRESS PROBLEMS PRESENTED BY THE LACK OF TRIBAL CRIMINAL JURISDICTION OVER NON-INDIANS

*Jerry Gardner**

The United States Supreme Court held in *Oliphant v. Suquamish Indian Tribe*, 435 U.S. 191 (1978), that tribal courts no longer have criminal jurisdiction over non-Indians, unless Congress delegates such power to them. This decision has presented substantial problems for Indian Nations and tribal court systems in maintaining law and order in their communities and in making it clear to the non-Indians who live in Indian country or who travel to Indian country that they are not above the law.

The following is a partial list of some of the methods that tribes have developed and attempted to implement in order to address the problems presented by the lack of criminal jurisdiction over non-Indians.

1. *Police Power to Arrest and Hold for Another Jurisdiction:* Although tribal courts do not have the power to criminally prosecute non-Indians, Indian Nations still have the inherent sovereign authority—or policing power—to stop and detain all persons (including non-Indians) suspected of criminal activity. This power includes the authority to hold that person for state or federal agencies that do have the power to criminally prosecute them.

2. *Police Power to Arrest and Take to the Reservation Boundaries:* Although tribal courts do not have the power to criminally prosecute non-Indians, Indian Nations still have the inherent sovereign authority—or policing power—to stop and detain all persons (including non-Indians) suspected of criminal activity. This power includes the authority to take that person to the jurisdiction or reservation boundaries.

3. *Exercise Power of Exclusion or Banishment:* Indian Nations have inherent sovereign authority to exclude (or banish) persons (including non-Indians).

4. *Exercise Jurisdiction through Consent or Stipulation of Non-Indians:* Although it is subject to legal challenge, some tribes have continued to

---

* Jerry Gardner, *Tribal Efforts to Address Problems Presented by the Lack of Tribal Criminal Jurisdiction over Non-Indians* (1997) (Tribal Law and Policy Institute, used with permission).

exercise criminal jurisdiction over non-Indians through the stipulation or consent of the non-Indians.

5. *Decriminalize Certain Actions (or Create Infractions System):* Many Indian Nations have changed their tribal codes to make certain minor offenses (such as traffic offenses) into civil actions (or infractions) rather than criminal actions. This is accomplished by removing the possibility of imprisonment (and other criminal language and provisions) from the tribal code provisions for these offenses.

6. *Prosecute through Civil Action:* Many actions (such as child abuse) can be handled as a criminal and/or civil action. Consequently, tribes handle the offense as a civil action when a non-Indian is involved.

7. *Use Civil Forfeiture Laws:* Many Indian Nations have expanded the use of civil forfeiture laws to handle offenses involving non-Indians. For example, a non-Indian who is stopped for an alleged driving while intoxicated offense can have their vehicle impounded and be required to appear at a civil forfeiture hearing in order to recover the vehicle.

8. *Use Civil Contempt Power:* Tribal courts still maintain the power to punish—through the court's contempt power—anyone (including non-Indians) who violates court orders.

A PRIMER ON TRIBAL COURT CONTEMPT POWER

Matthew L. M. Fletcher[*]

Defining "Civil Contempt" in General

Professors Shoben and Tabb offered a "model case" exemplifying coercive civil contempt:

> A court determines in a divorce proceeding that certain out-of-state property held in the husband's name should be deeded to the wife. The husband refuses to obey the order directing him to make the conveyance.

[*] Matthew L. M. Fletcher, *A Primer on Tribal Court Contempt Power* (2008) (prepared for the Michigan Indian Judges Association May 16, 2008, meeting).

The court may jail the husband until he complies. The imprisonment is not punishment for past disobedience; it is to compel an act in the present for the benefit of the wife. The husband has the "jail keys in his pocket" because he will be out of jail as soon as he makes the conveyance. This imprisonment is coercive civil contempt.

The distinction between criminal contempt and coercive civil contempt is a critical one for tribal courts. Tribal courts have no criminal jurisdiction over non-Indians, while they may have civil jurisdiction over non-Indians. As such, in theory, tribal court would not be able to issue criminal contempt penalties to non-Indians, but would be able to issue coercive civil contempt penalties to non-Indians. According to the Hopi Tribe appellate court:

> It is important to determine whether an instance of contempt of court is either civil or criminal for the following reasons: (1) according to federal law, there is no right to a jury trial for civil contempt; (2) civil contempt judgments are not appealable if they are considered non-final judgments; (3) a non-Indian can be found in civil contempt, but it is questionable whether a non-Indian can be found in criminal contempt; . . . (4) the burden of proof differs, in accordance with the different burden of proof for any civil or criminal offense.

What is the difference? It is no simple feat to find a clear distinction. The United States Supreme Court has not provided very clear guidance on this question. According to Justice Scalia:

> At common law, contempts were divided into criminal contempts, in which a litigant was punished for an affront to the court by a fixed fine or period of incarceration; and civil contempts, in which an uncooperative litigant was incarcerated (and, in later cases, fined) until he complied with a specific order of the court. Incarceration until compliance was a distinctive sanction, and sheds light upon the nature of the decrees enforced by civil contempt. That sanction makes sense only if the order requires performance of an identifiable act (or perhaps cessation of continuing performance of an identifiable act). A general prohibition for the future does not lend itself to enforcement through conditional incarceration, since no single act (or the cessation of no single act) can demonstrate compliance and justify release. One court has expressed the difference between criminal and civil contempts as follows: "Punishment in criminal contempt cannot undo or

remedy the thing which has been done, but in civil contempt punishment remedies the disobedience."

The difference between criminal contempt and civil contempt lies in the purpose for which the contempt order is issued. The Oregon Supreme Court offered a succinct statement for purposes of distinguishing the two:

> Contempts may be civil or criminal. In a civil contempt the contemnor violates a decree or order of the court made for the benefit of an adverse party litigant. In a criminal contempt a court's process is violated or disobeyed and disrespect of the court is manifested.

The Hopi Appellate Court provided a definition of its civil contempt power in a recent case:

> [T]he court's civil contempt power is not considered statute based. Rather, courts have generally held that "[a] court's civil contempt power rests in its inherent limited authority to enforce compliance with court orders and ensure judicial proceedings are conducted in an orderly manner." Thus, regardless of whether a statute authorizes a court to use civil contempt, it is to the court's discretion whether such usage is appropriate. Further, unlike a criminal contempt order, a civil contempt order has no statutory limitation as to the extent of punishment issued by the court. Courts have generally held that imprisonment until the contemnor complies with the court's order is a permissible form of civil sanction for contempt.

The Hopi court also noted that there are limits to the court's civil contempt power, focusing on the purposes to which the incarceration penalty has:

> The court's use of civil contempt has limits. Though it is generally held that courts have the power to issue a civil contempt order that includes an indefinite jail term, such an order is permissible only as long as it is reasonable in coercing the disobedient party to comply. Thus, some courts have placed limitations on such an indefinite order. It is generally held that where the civil contempt order is unable to force compliance or the disobeying party has expressed a clear intention not to comply with the court order, then there is nothing to coerce and thus the sanction is actually criminal.

The Hopi court in that case held that the incarceration resulting from the lower court's civil contempt citation was "unable to coerce compliance" from the defendant, and then held that the civil contempt had moved into the territory of criminal contempt, a tribal code-based tribal court authority.

The Fort Peck Tribes Court of Appeals offered this analysis:

> We note at the outset that the first tier of the analysis, distinguishing between criminal and civil contempt, is no mere formality. In general terms, civil contempt is coercive in nature, forcing action (e.g. compelling a witness to testify; compelling disclosure of some kind) or it may be remedial and thus used to vindicate or protect the rights of a litigant. Civil contempt does not exist to punish the contemnor or to vindicate the court's integrity; it exists as a remedial sanction to be used to obtain compliance with the court's order or to compensate for damages sustained as a result of noncompliance.

On the other hand, "criminal contempt is a crime in the ordinary sense" and "criminal penalties may not be imposed on someone who has not been afforded the protections that the Constitution requires of such criminal proceedings.

EASTERN BAND OF CHEROKEE INDIANS V. AMUFLO TORRES

Eastern Band of Cherokee Indians, Cherokee Supreme Court[*]

All parties stipulated that defendant Torres is a citizen of the republic of Mexico (United Mexican States).

Defendant Torres was charged with driving while impaired and failure to stop for a stop sign on September 10, 2003. While released on bond for these charges, defendant on September 21, 2003 was charged with driving while impaired and driving while license revoked. Again, on pre-trial release, defendant was charged with second-degree child abuse of an

---

[*] Eastern Band of Cherokee Indians, Cherokee Supreme Court, *Eastern Band of Cherokee Indians v. Amuflo Torres*, 4 Cherokee Reporter 9 (2005).

enrolled member on November 13, 2003. During this time period, defendant was living at 4031 Wrights Creek Road (the residence of an enrolled member), which this Court takes judicial notice is located in Indian Country within the Qualla Boundary (the reservation of the Eastern Band of Cherokee Indians in North Carolina). . . .

We now turn to the issue of jurisdiction.

This is a case of first impression. The issue for decision is: Does the Cherokee Court, an independent tribal court of the Eastern Band of Cherokee Indians, a federally recognized Indian tribe, have jurisdiction to try and to punish the defendant Torres, a citizen of Mexico who is not an Indian, for violating the criminal laws of the Eastern Band of Cherokee Indians? We answer the issue, yes.

Our research does not disclose any authority directly addressing this issue. We consider that the better reasoned analysis requires and supports the conclusion that the Cherokee Court does have criminal jurisdiction over non-Indians who are not citizens of the United States, i.e. aliens.

In reviewing issues of jurisdiction the Court is guided by Chapter 7, Section 2 (2000) of the Cherokee Code. Section 2 (c) states: "The Judicial Branch shall not have jurisdiction over matters in which the exercise of jurisdiction has been specifically prohibited by a binding decision of the United States Supreme Court, the United States Court of Appeals for the Fourth Circuit or by an Act of Congress."

Our research does not disclose any Act of Congress specifically prohibiting the exercise of criminal jurisdiction by Indian tribal Courts over non-Indians who are not citizens of the United States. Nor do we find any such decision of the United States Court of Appeals for the Fourth Circuit.

The Supreme Court of the United States has addressed the criminal jurisdiction of Indian Courts in four opinions during the last twenty-five years. The Court has reviewed jurisdiction over non-Indian citizens of the United States, *Oliphant v. Suquamish Tribe;* jurisdiction over member Indians, *United States v. Wheeler*; and jurisdiction over non-member Indians, *Duro v. Reina, United States v. Lara*. Each of these cases specifically involved the rights of citizens of the United States. Throughout its extensive history of jurisprudence regarding Indian tribal sovereignty, the Supreme Court has never considered the powers and status of the Tribes with regard to non-citizens of the United States. The Cherokee Court, drawing upon history and references from precedent concluded that the Eastern Band of Cherokee Indians maintained the "inherent authority" to prosecute non-citizens of the United States. . . .

The Court in *United States v. Lara, supra*, re-affirms many of the principles supporting our decision in *Torres*, e.g., ". . . . The common law conception of crime as an offense against the sovereignty of the government"; "Indian tribes are unique aggregations possessing attributions of sovereignty over both their members and their territory." In several places the Court in Lara again refers to the interest of the United States in protecting citizens of the United States: ". . . whether the . . . Due Process or Equal Protection Clauses prohibit tribes from prosecuting a non-member citizen of the United States."; "non-member Indian citizens of the United States . . .", "We hesitate to adopt a view of tribal sovereignty that would single out another group of citizens, non-member Indians, for trial by political bodies that do not include them." Kennedy, J. concurring, states: "Lara, after all, is a citizen of the United States. To hold that Congress can subject him, within our domestic boundaries, to sovereignty outside the basic structure of the Constitution is a serious step. . . . The National Government seeks to subject a citizen to the criminal jurisdiction of a third entity . . . subject American citizens to the authority of an extra-constitutional sovereign. . . ." *Lara*, 541 U.S. 193 at 212. Justice Souter, in dissent, cites *Oliphant* for it's holding that "Indian tribes therefore necessarily give up this power to try non-Indian citizens of the United States. . . ."

Therefore, we hold that *Oliphant* does not control the *Torres* appeal. *Oliphant* concerns Indian tribal court jurisdiction of criminal cases against non-Indian citizens of the United States. *Torres* concerns Indian tribal court jurisdiction of criminal cases against non-Indian aliens of the United States.

We hold that the sovereign power of inherent jurisdiction of the Eastern Band of Cherokee Indians to try and punish non-Indian aliens of the United States has not been expressly terminated by Treaty, Act of Congress, or specifically prohibited by a binding decision of the Supreme Court of the United States or the United States Court of Appeals for the Fourth Circuit. . . .

The facts of this case demonstrate the necessity of preserving the criminal jurisdiction of the Eastern Band of Cherokee Indians over non-Indian aliens of the United States in order to protect the safety, health, economic development, liberty and the general welfare of the Eastern Band of Cherokee Indians and all other people who live, work or visit on Tribal lands. The records of the Cherokee Court disclose that aliens of the United States are seeking and receiving the protection of the Cherokee Court in criminal cases arising on the Qualla Boundary against enrolled members of the Eastern Band of Cherokee Indians. To allow criminal jurisdiction when an alien is the victim and deny jurisdiction when an alien is the perpetrator, would indeed be inconsistent with the status of the Eastern Band of Cherokee Indians as a dependant sovereign nation.

Questions

1. The Supreme Court's decision in *Ex Parte Crow Dog* can in some ways be read as a victory for the tribe and a recognition of its inherent criminal jurisdiction over its own members. But in other ways, the reasoning behind the Court's decision furthers the myth of the "lawless" Indian and can be seen as giving Congress a reason for acting to limit tribal criminal jurisdiction, as it did with the Major Crimes Act. Explain.
2. According to Russell, what were the "paternalistic" beliefs about Indians and federal law that were behind the passage of the Major Crimes Act? How was this a shift in U.S. federal policy toward Indians and tribal sovereignty?
3. Of the alternatives discussed in Gardner, which do you think would be the most effective in deterring offensive activities by non-Indians?
4. Do you think any of the alternatives described by Gardner could be as effective, or perhaps even more effective, than criminal punishment? Could this make these alternatives more effective in deterring crimes by non-Indians in tribal territory?
5. What factors does a tribal judge need to consider when exercising civil contempt power?
6. If Torres appealed his tribal conviction to the U.S. Supreme Court, what do you think the outcome would be?

In Your Community

1. If you are a member of a tribe, does your tribe have tribal land in a state listed in Public Law 280? If a member of your tribe commits a crime on tribal lands, where would that crime be prosecuted?
2. Does your tribal nation exercise authority over non-Indians? What kinds of statutory law are in place to protect the community from criminal acts committed by non-Indians?

Glossary

Alacrity: Cheerful eagerness; liveliness.

Concurrent: Parallel; noncompeting, as authority.

Conveyance: Transfer of title (ownership papers) to property.

Double jeopardy: Being prosecuted for the same crime twice by the same government.

Explicit: Fully developed or described.

Inherent sovereign power: National authority not derived from another; powers originating from the nature of government or sovereignty that are not dependent on being granted by another government.

Nonmember Indians: Indians who are not officially members of the tribe asserting jurisdiction over them.

Respondent: The person against whom an appeal is taken or against whom a motion is filed.

Suggested Further Reading

Christopher B. Chaney, *The Effect of the United States Supreme Court's Decisions during the Last Quarter of the Nineteenth Century on Tribal Criminal Jurisdiction*, 14 Brigham Young University Journal of Public Law 173 (2000).

Robert N. Clinton, *Criminal Jurisdiction over Indian Lands: A Journey through a Jurisdictional Maze*, 18 Arizona Law Review 504 (1976).

Sam Ennis, *Addressing the Oliphant in the Room: An Argument for the Constitutional Reaffirmation of Indian Tribal Court Jurisdiction over Non-Indians*, UCLA Law Review (forthcoming in 2009).

David Lest, *Crime and the Native American* (1999).

Kevin Meisner, *Modern Problems of Criminal Jurisdiction in Indian Country*, 17 American Indian Law Review 175 (1995).

Catherine Baker Stetson, *Decriminalizing Tribal Codes: A Response to* Oliphant, 9 American Indian Law Review 51 (1982).

T. Vollman, *Criminal Jurisdiction in Indian Country*, 22 University of Kansas Law Review 387 (1974).

Note

1. The term *interracial* was used during the time of these treaties and statutes to refer to non-Indian perpetrators and Indian victims. However, in ways that we shall explore more fully in later chapters on the Indian Civil Rights Act, many argue that it is not appropriate to speak of members of Indian tribes as members of an Indian "race" or ethnic minority. The contemporary legal understanding is that tribal (political) identity is more salient than racial identity. Furthermore, it is by virtue of their membership in a tribe, not their ethnicity, that American Indian people are owed special duties and obligations from the federal government.

CHAPTER 13

Tribal Civil Jurisdiction

A S YOU WILL recall, civil law in the Anglo-American legal system concerns those norms that govern the legal rights, duties, and obligations between individual citizens, corporations, and sometimes the government as they arise in the legal relationships created by business contracts, adoption, marriage, and property dealings. Violations of these norms are treated as harms to the individual, but not necessarily crimes.

The Anglo-American legal system has norms, structures, and practices that work to determine if there existed a legal relationship that has been violated, who is to blame for that violation, and how the offender can remedy the loss suffered by the harmed individual. The focus of civil lawsuits is on compensating an individual, a corporation, or the government for a loss. Such compensation is usually in the form of money, but it can also be in the form of an injunction or a declaratory judgment. There can be a punitive element to civil judgments, called "punitive damages." It usually involves a sum of money above and beyond what is deemed necessary to compensate someone for the actual loss suffered, and it is paid by the responsible party or parties because they acted in a particularly egregious way. This, however, is still not a criminal proceeding and thus does not, by itself, normally result in jail time.

Regulatory and Adjudicatory Jurisdiction

As with criminal jurisdiction, the U.S. government has imposed certain limits on the civil authority of tribal courts. However, the rules limiting civil jurisdiction are different than the rules limiting criminal jurisdiction. Because the

171

initial federal changes imposed on the scope of tribes' inherent civil jurisdiction were targeted against tribal regulatory (lawmaking) jurisdiction, not their adjudicatory (law-applying) jurisdiction, it is important to understand the distinction between regulatory powers and adjudicatory powers.

Regulatory jurisdiction is the authority a government has to make laws over people and things (that is, the power to regulate). While the adjudicatory jurisdiction of the Anglo-American government rests in legal courts and their authority to apply laws to conflicts and disputes, the lawmaking powers generally rest in the legislature or the regulatory agencies the legislature establishes. Examples of regulatory jurisdiction include hunting and fishing, environmental, tax, and zoning laws. Under the federal framework, tribal governments usually retain a significant amount of regulatory jurisdiction over their lands. The decision to legalize certain kinds of gaming, for example, falls under the broad general category of regulatory jurisdiction.

Anytime a government tries to make a law, it has to have jurisdiction over the people, territory, and subject matter that it hopes to regulate by that law. If the government lacks any one of these elements, then it lacks the regulatory jurisdiction required to make the law in question. Consequently, the authority of a tribal nation to exercise control over the people and activities on its territory can be as much altered by changes to the civil regulatory jurisdiction as it is by the changes we saw made to the criminal adjudicatory jurisdiction.

Federal Changes to the Scope of Tribal Civil Jurisdiction

The majority of limitations to tribal civil jurisdiction have addressed the powers of tribal governments to exert regulatory powers over the activities of nonmembers within tribal borders. At first, these limits extended only to the power tribes had to regulate non-Indians on non-Indian fee lands, but one recent case has hinted that these limits on the power to regulate nonmembers may extend to Indian trust land as well as nonmember fee lands. Furthermore, these limits on tribal civil regulatory jurisdiction have now also been extended to tribes' civil adjudicatory jurisdiction over non-Indians.

The federal government has limited certain segments of tribal civil authority, but has recognized additional authority in other areas. Even as the limitations just described were being imposed, the federal government was also authorizing tribes to assert regulatory jurisdiction concerning some activities on all lands within reservation boundaries, whether these activities were undertaken by Indians or non-Indians. For example, Congress and administrative agencies such as the Environmental Protection Agency (EPA) have passed laws and policies authorizing tribes to make laws regulating pollution and polluters within tribal territorial borders.

The initial twentieth-century parameters of tribal civil jurisdiction were set out by the U.S. Supreme Court in *Williams v. Lee*, 358 U.S. 217, 79 S.Ct. 269 (1959), and *Montana v. United States*, 450 U.S. 544, 101 S.Ct. 1245 (1981). These cases demonstrate the initial Supreme Court conceptions of the inherent tribal civil jurisdiction of tribes—and, in the *Montana* case particularly, the perceived limitations of tribal civil jurisdiction. The Court extended those limitations in its more recent decisions in *Strate v. A-1 Contractors*, 520 U.S. 438 (1997); *Atkinson Trading Co. v. Shirley*, 532 U.S. 645 (2001); *Nevada v. Hicks*, 533 U.S. 353 (2001); and *Plains Commerce Bank v. Long Family Land and Cattle Corp.*, 554 U.S. ___ (2008).

After reviewing these initial parameters, we will then consider the Supreme Court's response to efforts by the Oneida Indian Nation to reassert its regulatory civil jurisdiction over lands that had been illegally purchased by the State of New York in the late eighteenth century and which the tribe had repurchased in the 1990s, in *City of Sherrill v. Oneida Indian Nation of New York*, 544 U.S. 197 (2005). We will also examine the Court's decision in *Carcieri v. Salazar*, 555 U.S. ___ (2009), in which the Court considered whether the Narragansett Tribe, a federally recognized tribe, could have land taken into trust by the secretary of the interior pursuant to the Indian Reorganization Act, even though it was not federally recognized at the time that Act was passed in 1934. We will end this chapter by looking briefly at some examples from a federal case that concerns congressionally authorized tribal regulatory authority and considering some of the questions raised by these additions to tribal civil jurisdiction.

Of course, when studying any aspect of tribal legal authority, it is never enough to simply consider the changes imposed on that power by the federal government. Much of tribal civil jurisdiction concerns the power and authority of the tribe over its members and nonmember Indians—areas of tribal power with which the federal government has much less concern. Consequently, we also spend time reviewing how at least some tribes are choosing to exercise that authority, as well as their authority over non-Indians, in light of federal limitations. To ignore what tribal courts are saying about their own civil jurisdiction would be to erase by omission the very core of tribal sovereignty that tribes have been successfully defending and enriching (often in the face of federal opposition) since their origins. Keep in mind that tribal civil jurisdiction (and federal changes to that jurisdiction) is an extraordinarily complicated and ever-changing legal arena.

Federal Changes: Reducing Tribal Civil Jurisdiction

The primary question that the federal government has raised concerning tribal civil jurisdiction is whether or not tribes should have the power to make and apply their civil law to non-Indians. Generally speaking, tribal civil jurisdiction over their members and nonmember Indians has been far less controversial to the U.S. Congress and the Supreme Court. For example, it is a well-established principle of the federal law concerning tribes that anyone (Indian or non-Indian) who wants to sue an Indian for a claim arising within Indian Country must do so in tribal court, absent Public Law 280 or some similar federal authorization for state jurisdiction. The exclusive jurisdiction that a tribe has over civil causes of action between Indians in Indian Country comes from the fact that a tribe's power to make and apply civil law to people and things in its territory is a fundamental part of their inherent sovereign power as nations.

In the 1959 case, *Williams v. Lee*, the Supreme Court recognized the inherent civil jurisdiction of tribes, even over non-Indian activities, on tribal lands. In that case, Lee, a non-Indian trader on the Navajo Reservation, brought a civil suit against Williams, a Navajo man, to retrieve some items that the Navajo man had purchased on credit from the Ganado Trading Post. Lee brought his lawsuit in Arizona court, but Williams challenged the suit, claiming that only tribal court had jurisdiction over the dispute. Looking to both prior Supreme Court cases and U.S. treaties with the Navajo, the Supreme Court held that the Arizona court lacked adjudicatory jurisdiction over the civil dispute. "It is immaterial that [Lee] is not an Indian," the Court held, going on to argue:

> He was on the Reservation and the transaction with an Indian took place there. The cases in this Court have consistently guarded the authority of Indian governments over their reservations. Congress recognized the authority in the Navajos in the Treaty of 1868, and has done so ever since. If this power is to be taken away from them, it is for Congress to do it.[1]

This language stood as a strong statement that tribes retained inherent adjudicatory jurisdiction over all people, whether Indian or non-Indian, who are engaged in civil disputes arising on their tribal lands.

By 1981, in *Montana v. United States*, the Supreme Court began to whittle away at tribal civil jurisdiction over non-Indians. In this case, the Court found that the Crow Tribe did not have regulatory jurisdiction over non-Indians hunting and fishing on a state-owned river running through its reservation. The *Montana* opinion focused on the fact that the non-Indians in question were engaged in activities on non-Indian private property within the reservation (known as "fee lands").

The *Montana* decision did not completely eliminate tribal civil jurisdiction over non-Indians. Even after this decision, tribes appeared to still have civil regulatory jurisdiction over non-Indians on tribal lands (fee or trust) and member-owned lands (either fee or trust allotments). Furthermore, the *Montana* decision also described certain situations where tribes would continue to have civil regulatory jurisdiction over non-Indians on non-Indian fee lands. These situations include:

1. when the non-Indian had entered into "consensual relations" with the tribe or its members, such as through business contracts, commercial transactions, and leases; or
2. when the non-Indian was engaged in activities that threatened or directly affected the "political integrity, the economic security, or the health or welfare of the tribe."

Under these rules (known as the "*Montana* test"), non-Indian individuals or corporations working under business contracts with Indian tribes or tribal members—such as store owners—are still regulated by tribal civil laws, even if their stores are located on non-Indian fee lands. Also, non-Indians engaged in activities that are central to the tribal life will be subject to the civil regulations of tribes, whether they have contracts with the tribe or not. So, for example, even if non-Indian store owners—operating a reservation store on lands they own—do not have a contract with the tribe, their activities are central to the life of the tribe if they are the only store on the reservation or perhaps hire many tribal members. Under the *Montana* ruling, they might still be subject to tribal regulations.

Thus, the limitations to tribal civil jurisdiction announced in the *Montana* case, while substantial, were by no means a total erasure of the civil authority of tribes over non-Indians.

In more recent decisions, however, the Supreme Court has considerably expanded these limitations on tribal civil jurisdiction. In *Strate v. A-1 Contractors*, the Court extended the limitations on tribal regulatory jurisdiction in *Montana* to the tribe's civil adjudicatory jurisdiction as well. In that case, the Court wrote, "As to nonmembers, we hold, a tribe's adjudicative jurisdiction does not exceed its legislative [regulatory] jurisdiction."[2] While it still may have been possible after the *Montana* decision for tribal courts to address civil disputes involving non-Indians on non-Indian fee land, after *Strate*, this is much less likely.

Then, in *Atkinson Trading Co., Inc. v. Shirley*, the Court broadened the *Montana* limitations to tribal civil regulatory jurisdiction by making the situations under which tribes could still exercise that jurisdiction narrower. Under the *Atkinson* decision, for a tribe to exercise civil regulatory jurisdiction over a non-Indian on non-Indian-owned land, that regulation must be related or linked to the "consensual relationship" that a non-Indian enters into with a tribe or its members through contract, commercial transaction, or lease. Before the *Atkinson* decision, it may have been possible, for example, for a tribe to regulate how non-Indian tribal employees use the land they own within the reservation—say, to prohibit them from opening a liquor store—even though that store would not be operated through any commercial contract or lease with the tribe. In such a situation, the consensual relationship of being a tribal employee would give the tribe broad civil regulatory jurisdiction over other activities of these non-Indians. But after *Atkinson*, the tribe would be less likely to have regulatory jurisdiction in this situation, unless it could show that the liquor store threatened or had a direct effect on the health and welfare of the tribe (that is, that it met the second *Montana* exception listed above).

Most recently, in *Plains Commerce Bank v. Long Family Land and Cattle Corp.* (2008), the Supreme Court continued to expand the *Montana* limitations to tribal civil adjudicatory jurisdiction with regard to non-Indian conduct on non-Indian fee land, finding that a non-Indian bank could not be sued in tribal court for discriminatory practices against tribal members when it sold fee land on a reservation to another non-Indian. In this case, the tribal members, the Long family, complained in tribal court that they were discriminated against by the bank when it sold the fee land they had been leasing from it to a non-Indian at a rate better than one the bank had offered to them. The bank challenged the jurisdiction of the tribal court over it, claiming that because the tribe had no regulatory authority over its sale of the fee land to another non-Indian, then the tribe could not have adjudicatory jurisdiction. The Court agreed, and in doing so, additionally held that the bank's sale of land to non-Indians did not constitute the kind of "nonmember conduct within the reservation" over which a tribe has regulatory, and thus adjudicatory, jurisdiction.[3]

Using the same approach to tribal authority, in *Nevada v. Hicks*, the Court found that, under some circumstances, the *Montana* limitations to tribal civil jurisdiction may prohibit the tribes' civil authority over non-Indian activities on *all* tribal lands. The facts in this case are somewhat unique, insofar as they involved a civil lawsuit brought by a tribal member in tribal court against a Nevada state game warden who came onto tribal lands to follow up on a crime committed on state property. The uniqueness of these facts may mean that the decision in *Hicks* limits tribal civil jurisdiction only over state officers coming onto tribal lands. However, if applied more broadly, this decision could result in near-complete divestiture of the power of tribes to exert civil jurisdiction over non-Indians within their territory. It remains to be seen what effects this decision will have on future determinations of tribal civil jurisdiction. As we can see, though, these Supreme Court decisions appear to be moving in the direction of denying tribal court's the ability to exercise civil jurisdiction over non-Indians.

As you might expect, efforts by tribes to recoup their original civil jurisdiction over lands that had been illegally taken from them have also been met with hostility from the Supreme Court. In *City of Sherrill v. Oneida Indian Nation of New York*, the Court held that the Oneida Indian Nation could not claim that the fee lands within its reservation that it had repurchased in the 1990s were exempt from city and state property taxes, even though those lands had never been legally transferred from tribal control. In the late 1700s and early 1800s, the lands in question were part of 300,000 acres of aboriginal Oneida lands recognized as a reservation for them by the United States and the State of New York, which under the Non-Intercourse Act of 1790 could not be divested by the tribe without the approval of the U.S. government. But in 1805, these and other lands were purchased by the State of New York without federal government approval. Thus, when the Oneida Indian Nation of New York repurchased the lands in 1997 and 1998, it claimed that they had never legally become fee-simple lands and instead were returned to its sovereign authority, as Indian Country subject only to Oneida tribal civil regulatory jurisdiction. The tribe claimed the lands were not subject to taxation by the city or state of New York. The Supreme Court disagreed, arguing that so much time had passed since their purchase in 1805, with no effort made by the federal government or the tribe to assert their sovereign authority over the lands in question, that even with their repurchase by the tribe, the lands could no longer be considered "Indian Country" subject only to tribal regulatory jurisdiction. Thus, even claims by tribes to rectify limitations on their civil regulatory jurisdiction made through historic wrongdoing have fallen on deaf ears in the Supreme Court.

This trend toward restricting Indian Country has continued in Supreme Court opinions, most recently in *Carcieri v. Salazar* (2009). In that case, the secretary of the interior had taken into trust a thirty-one-acre parcel of land in Charlestown, Rhode Island, adjacent to the 1,800-acre reservation of the Narragansett Indian Tribe, which had been federally recognized since 1983. Under the Indian Reorganization Act (IRA), the secretary of the interior can acquire land and hold it in trust "for the purpose of providing lands for Indians."[4] The IRA defines *Indian* to include "all persons of Indian descent who are members of any recognized Indian tribe now under Federal jurisdiction."[5]

The State of Rhode Island and the City of Charlestown challenged the secretary of the interior's power to take the thirty-one-acre parcel into trust for the Narragansett, claiming that the IRA authorizes such actions only for tribes that were federally recognized at the time of the Act's passage, in 1934. The Supreme Court's majority opinion agreed with the petitioners, despite the fact that this analysis ignores that the plain meaning of the Indian Reorganization Act was to authorize the secretary of the interior to take land into trust on behalf of federally recognized Indian tribes. It also ignores the fact that the better definition on which to ground an analysis of the IRA's application to this case would be to apply the definition of *Indian tribe*, not *Indian*, since it involves the actions that the secretary of the interior has taken on behalf of the Narragansett tribe, not a particular Narragansett or other Indian individual. The definition of *Indian tribe* in the IRA does not refer to tribes "now" under Federal jurisdiction, nor does it impose any other kinds of time restrictions on who might count as a "tribe" under the Act. For this and other reasons, the Narragansett clearly meet the definition of a tribe under the IRA and would seem to be precisely the kind of Indian community for whom the secretary of the interior could hold, and in countless prior instances has held, land in trust for their benefit.

The decision in *Carcieri* threatens to significantly disrupt the status of tribal lands held in trust all across Indian Country. This is true because it reverses the long-standing practice of the secretary of the interior regarding taking land into trust for tribes. As a result, many federal Indian law scholars and tribal leaders are hoping Congress will step in and "fix" the harm of this opinion with new legislation amending the language of the Indian Reorganization Act.[6] Whether or not this happens, *Carcieri* stands for only the most recent in a still-growing line of cases demonstrating the open hostility of the U.S. Supreme Court to tribal sovereignty and jurisdiction at the dawn of the twenty-first century.

Adding to Tribal Civil Jurisdiction

Paradoxically, during the very same period that the Supreme Court has articulated specific limitations to tribal civil authority, the U.S. Congress and administrative bodies have sometimes issued seemingly contradictory laws and regulations that recognize (and encourage) inherent tribal authority over non-Indians. Certain congressionally authorized civil powers have been given to tribes to regulate and enforce various kinds of civil laws. The best examples of this have been in the arena of environmental law, where Congress and the EPA have been making and administering laws that give tribes the power to set and enforce pollution emission standards above the levels required by federal law.

It is these federal restrictions and expansions of tribal civil jurisdiction that constitute some of the fundamental changes to tribal civil authority since their domination by the United States. As you may already have noted, most of these changes were made very recently, and their full impact on tribal sovereign power has yet to be revealed. Nonetheless—or maybe because these developments are so recent—attempting to understand at least the basic ways in which the federal government is changing the scope of tribal civil jurisdiction is critical to any good analysis of tribal legal systems as they operate today.

Contemporary Tribal Civil Jurisdiction: The Exhaustion Doctrine

In order to understand the impact of federal limitations on tribal civil jurisdiction, it is essential to look at how tribal governments express their own understandings of their civil jurisdiction—both regulatory and adjudicatory— over the different persons and activities operating within their territory. Such an investigation can reveal how tribes contemplate the scope of their civil powers in light of (and sometimes in explicit disregard for) the changes imposed by the federal government. Perhaps even more importantly, it can also reveal how tribes understand the scope of these powers in terms of their own legal heritages. As sovereigns, tribes have never taken federal law as the sole or even primary source of their authority. Instead, tribal governments look first and foremost to their own histories and foundations to express and explain that power. Observing how tribal governments are defining their own civil authority thus fills in a picture only outlined (and sometimes poorly so) by federal law and reveals how tribes see their civil powers being applied to all members of their communities—non-Indian and Indian, member and nonmember.

There remains yet another reason why it is important to look at how tribal codes and the decisions by tribal courts describe tribal civil jurisdiction. Two significant decisions written in the mid-1980s by the Supreme Court have held that people bringing civil lawsuits for actions arising in tribal territory must always bring their complaints to tribal court first before challenging tribal civil jurisdiction in federal court. In *National Farmers Union Insurance Co. v. Crow Tribe*, 471 U.S. 845 (1985), a Crow Indian had been hit by a motorcycle in a school parking lot located on land owned by the state of Montana (non-Indian fee land) within the Crow Reservation. The individual filed a civil lawsuit in tribal court against the insurer of the school district. The non-Indian insurance company (National Farmers Union) failed to show up or respond to the complaint in the tribal court trial, and so lost the case. The tribal court ordered the insurance company to pay the plaintiff $153,000.

Instead of paying the damages ordered by the tribal court, the company filed a complaint in federal court, claiming that the tribal court did not have civil jurisdiction over its case (because they were non-Indians operating on non-Indian-owned land) and asking the federal court to stop the tribal court from enforcing its decision against them.

The Supreme Court found that the insurance company committed an error when it failed to show up in tribal court. It held that even when a non-Indian company or individual is seeking to challenge the civil jurisdiction of a tribal court, it must first raise those challenges in tribal court, not federal court. Furthermore, even if the tribal court at first rejects these challenges, the person making these claims must exhaust all their chances to appeal that rejection in the tribal legal system before coming to federal court. This is called the *exhaustion doctrine*. Among the reasons the Supreme Court provided to explain this doctrine were that

> the existence and extent of a tribal court's jurisdiction will require a careful examination of tribal sovereignty. . . . We believe that examination should be conducted in the first instance in the Tribal Court itself. Our cases have often recognized that Congress is committed to a policy of supporting tribal self-government and self-determination. That policy favors a rule that will provide the forum whose jurisdiction is being challenged the first opportunity to evaluate the factual and legal bases for the challenge. . . . Exhaustion of tribal court remedies, moreover, will encourage tribal courts to explain to the parties the precise basis for accepting jurisdiction, and will also provide other courts with the benefit of their expertise in such matters in the event of further judicial review.[7]

This decision did not mean that the insurance company had to pay the tribal court's judgment against it. But it did mean that federal courts would have to give tribal courts the first opportunity to determine the scope of their civil jurisdiction, even over non-Indians, before allowing anyone to challenge that jurisdiction. The non-Indian insurance company thus had to go back to the Crow tribal court and try to challenge its civil jurisdiction there.

The exhaustion doctrine was further supported by the Supreme Court's decision in *Iowa Mutual Insurance Co. v. LaPlante et al.*, 480 U.S. 9 (1987). This case involved an Indian who was injured while working on a ranch owned by the Blackfeet Indian tribe. He sued the non-Indian company insuring the ranch in tribal court and won. Instead of then challenging that decision and the tribal court's civil jurisdiction in the Blackfeet Tribal Court of Appeal, the insurance company again went first to federal court. The Supreme Court wrote:

> The federal policy of promoting tribal self-government encompasses the development of the entire tribal court system, including appellate courts.

At a minimum exhaustion of tribal remedies means that tribal appellate courts must have the opportunity to review the determinations of the lower tribal courts. . . . Until appellate review is complete, the Blackfeet Tribal Courts have not had a full opportunity to evaluate the claim and federal courts should not intervene.[8]

The implications of these decisions are significant. When federal courts are called to review the actions and jurisdiction of other courts, they are required to be very respectful of the decisions made by those other courts. In this context, when federal courts review whether a tribal court correctly asserted its jurisdiction over non-Indians, they must presume that these courts made the correct assertion, unless it appears that it was "clearly erroneous." It can be hard to show that a tribal court or judge made a clearly erroneous decision with regard to civil jurisdiction. A federal judge cannot just *think* the tribal court lacked jurisdiction if he or she wants to overturn tribal court civil jurisdiction; the federal judge would have to be *firmly convinced* that the tribal judge was wrong. In this way, the exhaustion doctrine protects tribal civil jurisdiction and even favors tribal courts, efforts to determine that jurisdiction over the efforts by federal courts.

Consequently, reviewing how tribal courts evaluate and explain their civil jurisdiction is important not just as an academic exercise—it is also fundamental to the procedures by which federal courts themselves have to determine tribal civil jurisdiction.

To end this chapter, we turn to a case from the Hopi Tribal Appellate Court that reveals how the issues raised in tribal courts regarding tribal civil jurisdiction are so much broader than those that have been the focus of federal concern. In this case, *Coin v. Mowa*, AP-005-095 (1997), a Hopi woman brought a civil lawsuit against a Hopi husband and wife from her village to whom she was related. In the course of this civil dispute, over the sale of a mobile home, the Hopi Appellate Court had to decide whether or not this conflict was a "family dispute," as defined by the Hopi Constitution. If it was, only the Hopi leaders from the parties' village, and not the Hopi tribal court, could exercise subject-matter jurisdiction to hear and resolve the matter.

Reading excerpts from this case will show how many complex issues of tribal civil jurisdiction can emerge, even when the civil disputes are between tribal members. In these situations, tribal courts are much less occupied with conforming to federal limits placed on their civil authority. Instead, they are concerned with the equally difficult task of expressing and exercising their contemporary civil powers in ways that are consistent with their own unique legal norms, practices, and structures. Any failure by tribal courts to show their members that their contemporary civil powers comport with the tribes' legal heritage can be as devastating to legitimate tribal authority as any violation of federal law. Including this case here is a reminder that tribal courts are always undertaking the difficult balancing act between satisfying tribal legal expectations and traditions on the one hand, and U.S. federal legal oversight on the other.

In the excerpt below, consider how tribal courts could turn to their own customs and traditions to argue for taking jurisdiction over non-Indian activities on non-Indian fee land within their reservation.

ROSALINE COIN V. AUGUSTINE MOWA JR. AND FREDA MOWA, HUSBAND AND WIFE RESPONDENTS

Appellate Court of the Hopi Tribe*

Before Sekaquaptewa, Chief Justice, and Lomayesva and Abbey, Justices

Opinion and Order

The primary issue in this appeal is whether the trial court erred in finding that it was devoid of jurisdiction over this contract dispute because of Article III, section 2 of the Constitution and By-Laws of the Hopi Tribe that reserves certain subject matter jurisdiction to the individual villages.

Factual and Procedural Background

The parties to this appeal are members of the Hopi Tribe, residing at Shungopavi Village. On May 10, 1994, the parties entered into an oral contract for the sale of a mobile home belonging to the respondents, Augustine Mowa Jr. and his wife, Frieda Mowa. The contract did not include the sale of any land. According to the terms of this contract, appellant Rosaline Coin was to pay $2,000.00 to the Mowas and pay the $172.07 outstanding loan payment to the lien holder, SPFS, Division of Bank of America. In addition to supplying the mobile home, the Mowas agreed to make needed

---

* Appellate Court of the Hopi Tribe, *Rosaline Coin v. Augustine Mowa Jr. and Freda Mowa*, 1997. NAHT.0000011 at www.versuslaw.com.

repairs to the mobile home. Pursuant to the contract, Coin paid $800 down payment to the Mowas with the remainder of the contract price to be paid in installments. Between May and December 1994, Coin made a total of six additional payments for the mobile home. During this time, the Mowas never made any effort to make the agreed repairs.

On January 25, 1995, the Mowas gave Coin a one-day notice to vacate the mobile home and expressed their intent to repudiate the parties' contract. Later that same day, Coin demanded a return of the money that she had given to the Mowas. Although not receiving her refund, Coin complied with the Mowas request and vacated the mobile home. On February 10, 1995, Coin filed suit for breach of contract. After filing their response, the Mowas filed a Motion for Change of Venue and Motion to Allow the Kikmongwi of the Village of Shungopavi to Judge the outcome of this Matter. In addition to this motion, Radford Quamahongnewa, as spokesperson for the Kikmongwi of Shungopavi, wrote a letter to the trial court judge expressing the Kikmongwi's desire to exercise his traditional authority and jurisdiction to handle the matter in a way traditional to the Village.

Although the Mowas' motion was entitled a motion to "change venue," the Mowas invoked Article III of the Constitution and By-Laws of the Hopi Tribe in their argument. Recognizing that the Mowas actually sought a dismissal of the action, the trial judge granted the Mowas' dismissal without prejudice pursuant to the Constitution and By-Laws of the Hopi Tribe, Article III, section 2(b). However, the trial judge specifically noted that Coin could re-file her complaint if the case was not resolved by the village of Shungopavi within four months of the order.

Coin appealed this order of dismissal on the grounds that: (1) the trial court erred in referring the matter to the jurisdiction of the Village of Shungopavi; (2) the trial court erred in determining that this was a family matter falling within the reserved jurisdiction of the Kikmongwi of Shungopavi pursuant to Article III, section 2(b) of the Constitution and By-Laws of the Hopi Tribe; (3) the trial court erred by not providing a proper hearing and basing its decision on evidence unsupported by foundation testimony; (4) the trial court erred in interpreting the Mowas' Motion for Change of Venue and Motion to Allow Kikmongwi of Village of Shungopavi to Judge Outcome of this matter as a motion to dismiss for lack of subject matter jurisdiction; (5) referring this matter to the Village of Shungopavi violated Coin's freedom of religion in violation of the Constitution and By-Laws of the Hopi Tribe, the Indian Civil Rights Act of 1968, and the United States Constitution; and (6) the trial court erred in finding that Radford Quamahongnewa, as a member of the Sun Forehead Clan, was a proper spokesperson for the Kikmongwi of Shungopavi.

Issues Presented on Appeal

Although appellant has raised a variety of grounds for appeal, the crux of appellant's argument is that the trial court had proper jurisdiction of this matter and erred when it dismissed the complaint. In essence, there are two threshold issues that must be addressed before any other issues become relevant: (1) whether the trial court erred in liberally construing the motion to change venue as a motion to dismiss; and (2) whether the trial court erred in finding that it was devoid of jurisdiction over this dispute pursuant to Article III, section 2(b) of the Constitution and By-Laws of the Hopi Tribe.

Discussion

The Trial Court Erred in Interpreting Article III, Section 2(B) of the Constitution and By-Laws of the Hopi Tribe as Precluding Tribal Court Jurisdiction over This Cause of Action

Having appropriately decided to consider the jurisdictional issue, the trial court considered the language of Article III, section 2 of the Constitution and By-Laws of the Hopi Tribe. This provision provides in pertinent part that: The following powers which the Tribe now has under existing law . . . are reserved to the individual villages:

a. To appoint guardians for orphan children and incompetent members.
b. To adjust family disputes and regulate family relations of members of the villages.
c. To regulate the inheritance of property of members of the villages.
d. To assign farming land, subject to the provisions of Article VII. Constitution and By-Laws of the Hopi Tribe Art. III, § 2.

This narrow reservation of powers to the individual villages should be contrasted with the broad grant of power to the Tribal Court in Ordinance 21:

[T]he Hopi Tribal Court shall have jurisdiction over all civil actions where there are sufficient contacts with the Hopi Indian Reservation upon which to base the exercise of jurisdiction, consistent with the constitution and laws of the Hopi Tribe and the United States. It is the intent of this section to authorize the broadest exercise of jurisdiction consistent with these limitations. (Hopi Ordinance 21, § 1.7.1)

Because of this broad grant of power to the Tribal Court and the narrow reservation of subject matter jurisdiction to the individual villages, there is a presumption that the Tribal Court has jurisdiction over disputes not described in Article III. The trial court considered whether any of these provisions encompassed the present dispute and concluded that this was a "family dispute" within the meaning of Article III. Accordingly, the court dismissed the complaint.

The Hopi Tribal Court Had Jurisdiction over This Contract Dispute

Having decided the appropriate standard of review, it is necessary to interpret the Hopi Constitution. Article III specifically reserves certain subject matter jurisdiction to the individual villages. Before the trial court, the parties assumed that a dispute must fall within one of the four enumerated categories before the Hopi Tribal Court would be divested of jurisdiction. The current contract dispute relating to a mobile home (not including the land) does not invoke the villages' jurisdiction to appoint guardians for orphan children or incompetent members, to regulate the inheritance of property, or to assign farming land. However, the Mowas argued, and the trial court agreed, that this was a family dispute within the meaning of Article III.

In their brief, the Mowas argue that, "[t]hough the Petitioner and Respondents are not brother and sister they do share relatives common among them as members of the Village of Shungopavi and also by Clan relations." The Mowas are correct that Article III, section 2(b) should be interpreted broadly to encompass the Hopi concept of family. Nonetheless, the Mowas interpret Article III too broadly.

Under the Mowas' interpretation of Article III, the individual villages would have jurisdiction over all disputes between village members. Article III of the Constitution and By-Laws of the Hopi Tribe is designed to allocate subject matter jurisdiction between the individual villages and the Tribal Courts. According to the Mowas' definition of "family dispute," it is difficult to imagine any dispute that would not be handled by the villages. Because this definition would not properly allocate jurisdiction between the villages and the Tribal Court, it is not the proper definition of the term "family dispute." Rather, Article III contemplates disputes in which the parties' familial relations are an essential factor giving rise to the underlying cause of action. In this case, the underlying cause of action is the alleged breach of a contract to purchase a mobile home for a given price. This agreement does not depend upon the parties' familial relations. At no point do the parties seek to affect their familial ties. This is a contract dispute, not a conflict over matters related to the parties' family status. Therefore, this is not a "family dispute" within the meaning of Article III, section 2(b) of the Hopi Tribal Constitution. . . .

Finally, the Mowas introduced statements at both the Tribal Court and appellate court level by the Kikmongwi of Shungopavi expressing his desire to adjudicate the dispute. The Kikmongwi's desire to hear the case is not controlling in the constitutional analysis of subject matter jurisdiction under Article III. Hence, the Tribal Court erred in dismissing the complaint for lack of subject matter jurisdiction under Article III of the Constitution and By-Laws of the Hopi Tribe. Because of the conclusion that the trial court erred in dismissing Coin's complaint on constitutional grounds, there is no need to address Coin's other arguments on appeal.

Order of the Court

For the foregoing reasons, the judgment of the Tribal Court is REVERSED and this case is REMANDED to the Tribal Court for proceedings consistent with this opinion.

Questions

1. What are different kinds of relief that can be granted in a civil case?
2. What is regulatory jurisdiction, and how is it different from adjudicatory jurisdiction?
3. Given the trend of the U.S. Supreme Court in limiting tribal civil jurisdiction over non-Indians, what strategies can tribal governments take that will best protect their authority?
4. In your opinion, is there any difference between civil powers that come from a tribe's inherent sovereignty and those that were granted to tribes via congressional authorization? Explain.

In Your Community

1. Find out if there are any lands owned by non-Indians within the territory of your tribe. Also find out if there are any state highways running through the tribal territory. Finally, find out the size of the non-Indian population living within tribal territory. Based on this information, do you think that the federal limits on tribal civil jurisdiction negatively affect

the power of the tribal government to ensure the health and welfare of tribal society?

2. Who handles civil disputes in your tribal judicial system? Is the court system the best way to handle noncriminal disputes between tribal members?

Glossary

Civil law: Law relating to private rights and remedies (as opposed to criminal law).

Clearly erroneous: In Anglo-American law, a standard that appellate courts must apply when deciding whether to uphold or overturn a decision by a lower court. *Black's Law Dictionary* defines this standard as one whereby "a [lower court's] judgment is reversible if the appellate court is left with the firm conviction that an error has been committed."

Congressionally authorized: Sanctioned by the U.S. Congress and its administrative bodies asserting their authority over non-Indians.

Declaratory judgment: A judge's decision (about a real problem with legal consequences) that states the rights of the parties or answers a legal question without awarding any damages or ordering that anything be done.

Divestiture: The act of divesting; the compulsory transfer of title or disposal of interests upon government order.

Exclusive jurisdiction: That power that a court or other tribunal exercises over an action or over a person to the exclusion of all other courts; that forum in which an action must be commenced because no other forum has the jurisdiction to hear and determine the action.

Exhaustion doctrine: When a non-Indian company or individual is seeking to challenge the civil jurisdiction of a tribal court, it must first raise those challenges in tribal court, not federal court. Even if the tribal court first rejects these challenges, the person making these claims must exhaust all chances to appeal that rejection in the tribal legal system before coming to the federal court.

Immaterial: Of no substantial consequence; unimportant.

Implied divestiture: A doctrine that tribes have been divested of powers without any direct action from the U.S. government.

Inherent sovereign power: National authority possessed without its being derived from another; a right, ability, or faculty of doing a thing, without receiving that right, ability, or faculty from another; powers originating from the nature of government or sovereignty.

Injunction: A judge's order to a person to do or refrain from doing a particular thing. An injunction may be *preliminary* or *temporary* (until the issue can be fully tried in court), or it may be *final* or *permanent*.

Non-Indian fee lands: Lands located within the tribes' territorial borders but owned by non-Indians.

Nonmember fee lands: Lands within Indian Country not owned by or held in trust for the tribe or its members.

Tribal civil jurisdiction: The power and authority that American Indian and Alaska Native tribal courts have to prosecute certain kinds of persons accused of committing certain kinds of crimes in certain locations and, if these people are found guilty, to punish them.

Suggested Further Reading

D. F. Coursen, *Tribes as States: Indian Tribal Authority to Regulate and Enforce Federal Environmental Law and Regulations*, 23 Environmental Law Reporter 10579 (1993).

Jerry Gardner & Ada Pecos Melton, *Public Law 280: Issue and Concerns for Victims of Crime in Indian Country* (U.S. Dept. of Justice, Office for Victims of Crime, 2000).

Carole Goldberg-Ambrose, *Planting Tail Feathers: Tribal Survival and Public Law 280* (UCLA American Indian Studies Center, 1997).

James R. Hintz, Wilson v. Marchington: *The Erosion of Tribal Court Civil Jurisdiction in the Aftermath of* Strate v. A-1 Contractors, 20 Public Land & Resources Law Review 145 (1999).

G. William Rice, *Employment in Indian Country: Considerations Respecting Tribal Regulation of the Employer–Employee Relationship*, 72 North Dakota Law Review 269 (1996).

Catherine T. Struve, *How Bad Law Made a Hard Case Easy:* Nevada v. Hicks *and the Subject Matter Jurisdiction of Tribal Courts*, 5 University of Pennsylvania Journal of Constitutional Law 288 (2003).

Melissa L. Tatum, *Civil Jurisdiction: The Boundaries between Federal and Tribal Courts*, 29 Arizona State Law Journal 705 (1997).

Notes

1. 358 U.S. 217, 223 (1959).
2. 520 U.S. 438 (1997) at 453.
3. *Plains Commerce Bank v. Long Family Land and Cattle Corp.*, 540 U.S. ___ (2008).
4. 48 Stat. 985, 25 U.S.C. 465.
5. 25 U.S.C. § 479.
6. See, e.g., Colette Routel, Testimony before the United States House Committee on Natural Resources, April 1, 2009.
7. 471 U.S. 845, 856–857 (1985).
8. 480 U.S. 18, 16–17 (1987).

CHAPTER 14

Tribal Kinship and the Law

A MONG MEMBERS of a tribal community, kinship is one of the main ways that the norms, practices, and structures that make up a tribe's legal heritage are expressed and exercised. The relationships created by birth, marriage, and adoption carry not only close emotional ties but also very often the most important sets of duties, obligations, rights, and prohibitions that order tribal social life. An individual's relationships to the people in one's family bring certain responsibilities and expectations regarding caregiving, food production and distribution, the inheritance of property, and sometimes access to positions of authority and leadership. These and other important obligations and expectations may be held between people who share what are called "extended family relations"— those that exist beyond the nuclear family (parents and children), including grandparents and grandchildren, uncles, aunts, cousins, clan mates, lineage mates, godparents, and so forth. As such, children in tribal communities are usually born into a deep and intricate web of kin ties, where they are often cared for and raised as much by extended family as by their biological mother and father. It is by virtue of this care that they learn and practice the most fundamental elements of the ethics and morality that ground their tribe's culture, values, and law. Wilma Mankiller (Cherokee) explains, "My identity, my sense of who I am, is derived from my family and my community. My family and community shaped my ideas and caused me to get involved in things around me."[1]

Indeed, these relationships are so important that it is common in many tribal societies for a part of ceremonial and religious practices to include rituals that create kinship bonds between nonbiologically related members. In some tribes, men and women must agree to sponsor individuals seeking to be initiated into their ceremonial societies. When they agree to act as these sponsors, they become known as the ceremonial "fathers," "mothers," "aunts," or "uncles" of these individuals—now their "children"—who will subsequently have additional duties and obligations toward these people and their families. This is the case in many Pueblo communities. In other ceremonial systems and tribes, individuals have the opportunity to be initiated into ceremonial brotherhoods and sisterhoods, and it is to their ceremonial "siblings" that all members of these groups possess certain rights and expectations.

Even beyond this, it is common in many tribal communities to hear the use of kin terms as expressions of the honor and respect that is shared between members, whether or not these relations are biological or even ritually sanctioned. Referring to an older man as "father" or "grandfather," or a woman as "mother" or "grandmother," and hearing these people refer to others as "my child" or "grandchild" is the language of mutual respect between tribal members. This is true primarily because kinship and kin relations carry with them the implied sense of duty and obligation that is at the heart of most tribes' cultural and legal heritage.

Thus, along with marriage, these are the bonds that ideally work to most fully integrate an individual into the tribal social life that exists beyond their biological family. Indeed, it is often a fundamental feature of life in any tribe that interaction between tribal members (especially those who are at first unfamiliar with each other) involves the working out of the biological and ceremonial kin relationships they have with each other, and, by implication, the kinds of obligations and entitlements the two can expect to have between them. Moreover, dispute and conflict among tribal members is often expressed as a violation of the norms surrounding the rights and duties they owe each other as kin (biological or ceremonial). A man who steals from another, more elderly man from his community may find himself chastised for violating the duties of honor and respect he owes this "grandfather." Two women who physically assault each other might be brought to task for not treating each other as "sisters" should treat each other. Teenagers caught with drugs or alcohol might be described as failing to live up to the duties and obligations they owe to their parents, grandparents, and clan.

With regard to the unique legal heritage of any particular tribe, a discussion of the tribal laws of familial and domestic relations is really a consideration of the core elements of that heritage. This is dramatically different than the way in which family relations are idealized in the traditions of Anglo-Americans and the role those relations play in the broader scope of Anglo-American society. In that society, the nuclear family is a fairly isolated caregiving unit. While extended family such as grandparents, aunts, uncles, and cousins often play a part in the life of a child, their role is much less central than in most tribal familial relations. They are not usually treated as care-givers of the degree of importance equal to that of the child's biological parents. Furthermore, there is little recognition of any clan, lineage, or other familial institution beyond the nuclear unit. Though the role of "godparent" has a pur-pose in some Western traditions (such as in Catholicism), this, too, is much more of a symbolic relationship than the ceremonial kinship bonds often cre-ated in tribal communities.

The relationships that constitute the family unit in Anglo-American soci-ety are most often perceived as separated from the rest of society as a truly pri-vate realm. This private "nuclear family" realm is not one that is normally regulated by the government and its laws. In this sense, the world of law and society has always been kept relatively separate and distinct from the world of family and kinship in Anglo-American society. Since the mid-1800s, there has been a widely held belief that the development of children into U.S. citizens requires that they receive an education beyond what could be taught by their family. At that time, the integration of Anglo-American children into U.S. society was achieved through governmental actions and incentives that encour-aged sending them to schools. It is important to point out that these efforts were generally not extended to children of other ethnic groups—African Americans, Latino-Americans, Asian-Americans, even other European-Amer-ican children (Irish, Italian, Jewish)—until later. Ironically, such efforts were extended to Native American children, but they were sent to school often against their will and the will of their families and communities. This is the subject of the next chapter.

Generally speaking, children sent to school learned U.S. history and government; the basic skills of reading, writing, and arithmetic; and per-haps some manual or domestic trade. Becoming an adult in Anglo-Ameri-can society required a child to learn the skills and roles they would be expected to use outside their family relations. It was as individuals (not as members of a family or clan) that these children became American citizens. It was widely believed that only a standardized education could change chil-dren into individuals capable of productive contribution to U.S. democratic society.

In many tribal communities, the full integration of the child into larger tribal society means the extension—not the setting aside—of kin relations. Following are some examples of the nature of tribal kinship laws.

TIOSPAYES

Red Cloud Indian School, 1972[*]

Every Lakota person is born having many relatives. The *tiospaye* is the name given to indicate a person's relatives. There is more than just the father and mother of a child. The tiospaye includes grandparents, aunts, uncles, cousins, and all married and adopted relatives.

As the Lakota person grows up, his relatives will give him help. All the families of a tiospaye give attention to the young child growing up. Their interest in a growing person is their hope for a respectful, full-grown adult. Later in life, the young Lakota will be given responsibility to help his relatives when it is necessary.

During all of Lakota history, the tiospaye has been very important. Even though some families have left the Pine Ridge Indian Reservation, the tiospaye is as important as ever. Everyone should know their relatives. When a person is acquainted with his relatives, he knows where he comes from and who he is. This is why the tiospaye is so important.

The word in Lakota, *tiospaye*, can be broken into two meaningful small words:

- *Ti*—a short form of *Tipi*, meaning "house"
- *Ospaye*—A group of people separated from a larger or the main body of people

The tiospayes are small groups of persons who are related to each other. A long time ago, these small groups traveled separately when hunting. They claimed their own hunting territories and kept peace with each other. Each small group was a tiospaye.

---

[*] Red Cloud Indian School, *Tiospayes* (1972).

FAMILY AND CLAN STRUCTURE

Henry Old Coyote (Crow)[*]

Our people are divided into clans. Originally we had 13 clans, but now we're down to about 9, because some of the clans have been absorbed into others. In our clan system we automatically belong to the mother's clan and are identified with that clan. I happen to belong to what is known as the Whistling Water Clan and my wife belongs to the Greasy Mouths. The original name for my clan was Prairie Dog Do-Gooders, but someone in our clan married back into his own clan. So then there was a joke about it, that these people who married back into their own clan would go along the waterways whistling. That's why they gave us the name, "Whistling Waters." My wife's clan were noted for getting good game. They had greasy mouths all the time and because of it, got the name. . . .

Now the girl receives a certain amount of information from the mother and the female members of the mother's clan, such as how to make clothes and ornaments, how to prepare food, take care of a home and all that. They contribute to the more practical instruction of the girl. For instance, as the girls are making moccasins, they teach them that they should include good things in their thoughts, so that wherever the moccasins tread, they will lead to good things in life—good health and good days. The male members of the mother's clan look on the girl as their sister, so not much communication goes on between them. The things they speak of among themselves would never be repeated in front of the girl. The girl's actual brothers treat her the same way.

In the case of the boy, a certain amount of instruction comes from the male members of the mother's clan, such as how to go after game, how to handle horses, how to dress, how to conduct yourself and what to seek in life. They also teach the boy how to treat domestic animals. Even pets understand kindness, and the clan brothers use that as an example. For instance, if a dog is mistreated, it cringes every time anyone speaks in a loud voice or indicates an act of violence in its presence. But if the person is kind, he can go through any motion or action, and the animal—despite the fact that animals are considered to be dumb—recognizes that he is to be trusted. . . .

---

[*] Henry Old Coyote, *Family and Clan Structure,* in *Respect for Life: The Traditional Upbringing of American Indian Children* (Sylvester M. Morey & Olivia L. Gilliam, eds., 1974).

We have different degrees of respect for different people. While a certain amount of advice comes from the parents and grandparents, it's mostly from the male and female members of the father's clan. They are the group that both the boy and girl learn to respect from childhood on. They give spiritual guidance and advice; at the same time, they're the ones who present the boy and girl to the public and try to build up their reputation. They're more or less their public relations people and the ones who make wishes and offer prayers for them. In other words, if a father wants prayers for his child, he'll go to these people. So they are the ones we respect and we try not to disappoint them by our conduct. They are also the ones we have to watch out for. We aren't supposed to pass in front of the members of our father's clan, for example, no matter how humble they may be.

The offspring of the male members of the father's clan are called "Teasing Cousins." They are the ones who remind the girl or boy who they are—who they actually are. The members of the father's clan, the public relations people, can go out in public and say, "We have the best boy among the whole tribe because he's smart, he behaves well, he listens." The teasing cousins say, "Baloney!" If they catch the boy telling a lie, they ridicule him in public. By being ridiculed in public, he refrains from telling lies. The same way with the girl. The girl may be brought out and told that she's a good respectable girl and shows good judgment. But some little incident is picked up by the teasing cousins and they say, "Baloney! She has no brains!" So morals are passed on to both girl and boy, and they learn to live by them.

When the child is born, the aunts on the father's side are responsible for providing the cradle, the little moccasins and any other clothing or part of the cradle that go to the child. The wish that goes into the aunt's work as she makes those little moccasins is that the moccasins will be pointed toward good days, good luck, good health and well-being. If the child is in need of something, it's up to her to furnish it until that boy or girl reaches a certain age. It's also up [to] the aunt to provide something that's not common. For example, she usually preserves berries and things like that and probably uses them to make pudding or pemmican. Now it's up to her to give some of this to her niece or nephew. She puts in the best she has and offers it to the child. In so doing, the father of the child is obligated to give the aunt a gift, like a horse. The more he loves his child, the more valuable the gift. When he makes the gift, the aunt in turns makes a wish. She may have had a dream or vision of a certain season, so she makes a wish that the child will live to see that season.

FAMILY RULES: ADOPTIONS

Joan Ryan[*]

Upon the death of a parent, or in a case where a woman could not raise her child, the adoption process was clear. The mother's female relatives had the responsibility and privilege of raising babies and small children. If a mother with children old enough to help their father died, a male child of ten or older might stay with the father while the younger ones went to the mother's relatives, usually to sisters, but occasionally to her parents.

Agreements were verbal and binding. Once a child had been given to a relative to raise, she or he became that person's child and was treated no differently than natural children. Since the community was small, everyone knew a child's family history, and relationships between children and their birth parents were encouraged. For example, a man whose wife died might leave their children with her sister for several years, then later he would take his male children on the trap line with him. Such arrangements gave children an extended family and a sense of security. No limits were placed on relationships. So even if a mother's sister had raised her children, their natural fathers knew them, related to them, and some reclaimed them when they became youths. Children raised by relatives expressed no sense of being abandoned or unwanted by natural parents.

---

[*] Joan Ryan, *Doing Things the Right Way: Dene Traditional Justice in Lac La Martre, N.W.T.* (1995).

CONVERSATION WITH ATSENHAIENTON: RESPONSIBILITY

Taiaiake Alfred[*]

People always talk about how as a people we were warlike, and reacted emotionally, and how we were told by the Peacemaker that we had to put emotions aside and use reason and a good mind to co-exist. But there's

---

[*] Taiaiake Alfred, *Responsibility: A Conversation with Atsenhaienton,* in *Peace, Power, Righteousness: An Indigenous Manifesto* 102–3 (1999).

another important part of the story—the clan system. He brought the clan system to us, where all the wolves and the bears and the turtles were of the same family. The bears in the Mohawks were brother of the Oneida bears; there was a linkage. This is what broke down hostility and discouraged war; you would have to war against your brothers and sisters. Once all members of the same clan were brothers and sisters across the nations, it made it difficult to wage war against one another. People forget that is one of the reasons for the clan system. I think that the clan system breaks down nationalism; it's the nationalism that causes conflict—Mohawk versus Oneida, or Onondaga. If we all sat in our clans and discussed the issues, we would get away from the nationalism that divides us. Peace would be achievable, and leadership would take on a different focus. We would talk about the issues rather than posturing as a nation.

A tribal-centered consideration of family law (represented by the excerpts in this chapter) explores what is, for many tribal people, the most important and most emotionally and intellectually complex areas of contemporary tribal law and life. For example, we are primarily focusing our attention here on issues of child welfare. These issues are incredibly sensitive, ones that touch on some of the most basic concerns of all people, whether they are Native or non-Native. But equally important to tribal (as well as other) governments in ensuring the welfare of families is the effective enforcement of the criminal laws regarding domestic violence, the laws related to marriage and divorce, and the protection of elders from abuse and neglect. Such matters are considered in more depth in other volumes in this series, and we encourage you to explore them more there, and in other writings, as well as in open but respectful conversations within your own communities and families. We think it is not an overstatement to say that, for many Indian nations, the very idea of tribal sovereignty would be meaningless were they denied the power and authority to address and administer the welfare of tribal families in the manner they believe most fit.

Questions

1. How does the Anglo-American understanding of kinship differ from the philosophy of many Native cultures?
2. What is "legal" about kinship in Native cultures?
3. What is the difference between a tiospaye and a clan?
4. Can ceremonies be considered legal proceedings? Why or why not?

5. Is the application of kinship limited to domestic matters? Does Atsen-haienton's description of the purpose of the clan system extend to foreign relations?

In Your Community

1. Interview elders about the traditional kinship relations of your tribal community. Do any of the reported kinship relationships still exist? If so, describe how the kinship relationships involve legal or social obligations.
2. Is there a history of anyone in your community adopting a non-Indian, either as a child or an adult? Interview someone who has knowledge of this kind of adoption and find out what legal proceedings are involved.

Glossary

Clan: A group of related people.

Extended family relations: Family relations that extend beyond the nuclear family.

Nuclear family: Biological parents and children.

Sanctioned: Agreed; accepted.

Tiospaye: A group of related people.

Suggested Further Reading

Carole Goldberg-Ambrose, *Of Native Americans and Tribal Members: The Impact of Law and Indian Group Life*, 28 Law & Society Review 1123 (1994).

Note

1. Wilma Mankiller, *To Preserve as Tribal People*, 19 Native Americas 55 (2002).

CHAPTER 15

Boarding Schools and the Removal of Tribal Children

I T SHOULD COME as little surprise that nineteenth- and twentieth-century U.S. federal policies that called for the assimilation of Indian peoples and the "termination" of tribal nations attempted to accomplish these goals by undoing the kinship systems and familial relations that gave order to many tribal peoples. For example, the General Allotment Act (1887), which resulted in the division and distribution of the collective land holdings of tribal nations, was implemented during the same time period that the first federal Indian boarding schools opened. These institutions were filled with Indian children who were removed (often forcibly) from their families and tribal homelands. While the U.S. government had been encouraging and supporting the efforts of Christian missionary groups to run schools in Indian Country since the early 1800s, it was with the founding of off-reservation schools like the Carlisle Industrial Training School in Pennsylvania (1879), the Sherman Indian School in California (1902), and others that the most invasive actions to disrupt tribal life were undertaken.

There was an assumption that to achieve assimilation, Indian children must be taught to abandon their tribal ways and to adopt "civilized" ways. Thus, these schools were designed to limit and even prevent contact with the child's culture and tradition. Indian children from various tribes often remained in these schools for many years—sometimes thousands of miles from their homeland, with no contact from parents or other family members. Upon their arrival, the children were given English names, had their hair cut short, were placed in age groupings away from their siblings and relatives, and had their traditional clothes replaced with school uniforms. They were often prohibited from speaking their native language and would be punished severely for breaking that rule. Instead of the skills, ethics, and rules they would have learned from kin and tribal members at home, boarding school attendees were taught reading, writing, arithmetic, and trades that were the usual subject matter of Anglo-American education at the time.

The principle behind boarding schools as a tool of assimilation was described in "Survey of the Economic and Social Condition of the American Indians," commissioned by the secretary of the interior in 1926. In a 1928 report to the secretary of the interior entitled "The Problem of Indian Administration," Lewis Meriam wrote, "The theory was that the problem of race could be solved by educating the children, not to return to the reservation, but to be absorbed one by one into the white population." The report continues:

> The plan involved the permanent breaking of family ties, but provided for the children a substitute for their own family life by placing them in good homes of whites for vacations and sometimes longer, the so-called "outing system." The plan failed . . . largely by reason of its artificiality. Nevertheless, the worst of its features still persists, and many children have not seen their parents or brothers and sisters in years.[1]

Even those children who would eventually make it back to their homes after their tenure at boarding school would not necessarily find an easy reentry into tribal life. One Navajo mother is quoted in the Meriam report as saying, "I hated to send this boy to school. I knew I was saying goodbye. He would come back a stranger." Torn from the webs of responsibility and rights that continued to order their family and tribal relations back home, these children sometimes returned as unknown quantities, unsure of themselves and the role they should now play in their communities. Relatives were not sure if they could or should expect these children, now schooled in the Anglo-American ways, to assist with the labors that sustained the family, to participate in the dances and rituals they had been taught were "savage" and "false," and to otherwise adhere to the tribal norms, structures, and practices that the Anglo-American schools had tried to make them abandon.

The following excerpt, which describes the experience of a Taos Pueblo boy named Sun Elk, provides an example of how some children experienced the boarding schools.

HE IS NOT ONE OF US

Edwin R. Embree[*]

When I was about thirteen years old I went down to St. Michael's Catholic School. Other boys were joining the societies and spending their time in the kivas being purified and learning the secrets. But I wanted to learn the white man's secrets. I thought he had better magic than the Indian. . . . So I drifted a little away from the pueblo life. My father was sad but he was not angry. He wanted me to be a good Indian like all the other boys, but he was willing for me to go to school. He thought I would soon stop. There was plenty of time to go into the kiva.

Then at the first snow one winter . . . a white man—what you call an Indian Agent—came and took all of us who were in that school far off on a train to a new kind of village called Carlisle Indian School, and I stayed there seven years. . . .

Seven years I was there. I set little letters together in the printing shop and we printed papers. For the rest we had lessons. There were games, but I was too slight for foot and hand plays, and there were no horses to ride. I learned to talk English and to read. There was much arithmetic. It was lessons: how to add and take away, and much strange business like you have crossword puzzles only with numbers. The teachers were very solemn and made a great fuss if we did not get the puzzles right.

There was something called Greatest Common Denominator. I remember the name but I never knew it—what it meant. When the teachers asked me I would guess, but I always guessed wrong. We studied little things—fractions. I remember that word too. It is like one half of an apple. And there were immoral fractions. . . .

They told us that Indian ways were bad. They said we must get civilized. I remember that word too. It means "be like the white man." I am willing to be like the white man, but I did not believe Indian ways were wrong. But they kept teaching us for seven years. And the books told how bad the Indians had been to the white men—burning their towns and killing their women and children. But I had seen white men do that to Indians. We all wore white man's clothes and ate white man's food and went to white man's churches and spoke white man's talk. And so after awhile we

---

[*] Edwin R. Embree, *He Is Not One of Us*, in *Indians of the Americas* (1939) (1967).

also began to say Indians were bad. We laughed at our own people and their blankets and cooking pots and sacred societies and dances. I tried to learn the lessons—and after seven years I came home. . . .

It was a warm summer evening when I got off the train at Taos station. The first Indian I met, I asked him to run out to the pueblo and tell my family I was home. The Indian couldn't speak English, and I had forgotten all my Pueblo language. But after awhile he learned what I meant and started running to tell my father, "Tulto is back. . . ."

We chattered and cried, and I began to remember many Indian words, and they told me about an uncle, Tha-a-ba, who had just died, and how Turkano, my old friend, had finished his year's fast and was joining the Black-eyes to become a priest and a delight-maker.

Two little sisters and many little cousins had come along with the family to meet me. All these children liked me and kept running up and feeling my white man's clothes and then running away laughing. The children tried to repeat the English words I said, and everyone was busy teaching me Pueblo words again. We sat down on the grass and talked until it become very dark. . . .

I went home with my family. And next morning the governor of the pueblo and the two war chiefs and many of the priest chiefs came into my father's home. They did not talk to me; they did not even look at me. When they were all assembled they talked to my father.

The chiefs said to my father, "Your son who calls himself Rafael has lived with the white man. He has been far away from the pueblo. He has not lived in the kiva nor learned the things that Indian boys should learn. He has no hair. He has no blankets. He cannot even speak our language and he has a strange smell. He is not one of us."

The chiefs got up and walked out. My father was very sad. I wanted him to be angry, but he was only sad. So I would not be sad and was very angry instead.

And I walked out of my father's house and out of the pueblo. I did not speak. My mother was in the other room cooking. She stayed in the other room cooking. She stayed in the other room but she made much noise rattling her pots. Some children were on the plaza and they stared at me, keeping very still as I walked away.

I walked until I came to the white man's town, Fernandez de Taos. I found work setting type in a printing shop there. Later I went to Durango and lived in other towns in Wyoming and Colorado, printing and making a good living. But this indoor work was bad for me. It made me slight of health. So then I went outside to the fields. I worked in some blacksmith shops and on farms.

All this time I was a white man. I wore white man's clothes and kept my hair cut. I was not very happy. I made money and I kept a little of it and after many years I came back to Taos.

My father gave me some land from the pueblo fields. He could do this because now the land did not belong to all the people, as it did in the old days; the white man had cut it up and given it in little pieces to each family, so my father gave me a part of his, and I took my money and bought some more land and some cattle. I built a house just outside the pueblo. I would not live in the pueblo so I built outside a house bigger than the pueblo houses all for myself.

My father brought me a girl to marry. Her name was Roberta. Her Indian name was P'ah-tah-zhuli (Little Deer Bean). She was about fifteen years old and she had no father. But she was a good girl and she came to live with me in my new house outside the pueblo.

When we were married I became an Indian again. I let my hair grow. I put on blankets, and I cut the seat out of my pants.

Boarding school experiences were not identical across the United States. Many Indian children thrived even under these harsh circumstances, achieving notable degrees of success both in the school and afterward in mainstream American society more generally. But in much the same way we just read in Edwin Embree's story, the boarding school experience left many students with mixed feelings, for even as they lost ties to family, tribe, and tradition back home, many found and built new relations with their fellow Indian classmates, as well as their non-Indian teachers and neighbors, finding common experiences, ethics, and values across tribal lines.

As the first generations of Indian children forced to attend boarding schools began raising their own children, some resisted boarding-school education, while others felt that the experience would offer their children the best preparation for Anglo-American society and its ways of life. Even as the federal policy of forcing Indian children to go to boarding schools waned in the 1930s and 1940s, many Indian families continued to send their children to these schools. Indeed, many scholars and activists argue that it was these experiences that first planted the seeds of what is now known as the phenomenon of "pan-Indianism"—the emerging sense of shared identity among Indian people regardless of tribe—and the more visible rise in the 1960s and 1970s of such Indian activist groups as the American Indian Movement (AIM) and the National Indian Youth Council (NIYC).

Yet, despite the successes of many Indian individuals, it is undeniable that the boarding-school experience has worked dramatic changes on the ordering of family and kin relations within tribal communities and the broader heritage of tribal norms, practices, and structures that operated through those relations. Some survivors of boarding schools have filed lawsuits against the government and the churches that ran boarding schools. These individuals have indicated that they have continued to suffer the effects of forced assimilation and abuse for years.

BOARDING SCHOOL VICTIMS WANT REPARATION

*David Melmer**

WAGNER, S.D.—Sherwyn Zephier remembers how priests would come to the dormitory at night and call out names of students. The students would then be beaten with a two-by-four with the names of the board of education written on it; and if the students cried loud enough they would stop the beating and have the student sign the board.

He said he knew of no reason for the beatings in a recollection from a Catholic boarding school in South Dakota. Zephier recalls many incidents and they are recurring more frequently.

Zephier now teaches at the school he attended for 12 years, now the school is run by the Yankton Sioux Tribe and is called Marty Indian School instead of the St. Paul's Marty Mission. Zephier attended St. Paul's from 1963–75. The next year, the school was turned over to the tribe.

A lawsuit has been filed against the federal government in U.S. Court of Claims in Washington. The class action suit has yet to be certified but thousands of names of American Indians who suffered similar physical and sexual abuse in boarding schools are accumulating.

Six members of the Yankton Sioux tribe, who act as lead plaintiffs in the lawsuit, allege that treaty violations occurred when many American Indian children were removed from their homes and forced to reside and sometimes die at the boarding schools run by religious denominations sanctioned by the federal government.

The stories are numerous and familiar. American Indian people, seniors and adults talk about beatings at the hands of clergy of both sexes and

---

* David Melmer, *Boarding School Victims Want Reparation*, Indian Country Today (April 23, 2003).

by attendants at the schools—sometimes American Indian themselves. Beatings with wire coat hangers, punishment that nearly starved children and isolation to correct "non-acceptable behavior" were common.

All [was] performed in the name of teaching the American Indian how to be civil, and to "kill the Indian and save the child" as was put by Captain Richard Henry Pratt in 1878 when he advocated for the creation of Carlisle Indian School, the most famous of all boarding schools.

"All my life I've never wanted to think about these things, I pushed them as far back as I could," said Adele Zephier, Sherwyn's sister. She claims she was physically abused by nuns and sexually abused by a priest while attending St. Paul's Marty Mission School in Marty, S.D.

State Social Services and Indian Children

Another assault on the comprehensive extended family and kin relationships that existed in tribal communities was the evaluation of Indian child safety and well-being by state social service agencies. In addition to the removal of thousands of children to boarding schools, thousands of Indians were relocated to cities as a result of the federal relocation policy. It included an "incentive program" that provided for adults to receive transportation and temporary living subsidies if they would move to urban areas to learn trades and skills. Sometimes, the adults went alone; other times, both parents were enrolled in skills programs and took an elder or another extended family member with them to care for the children while in the city.

While the families may have continued to live as they would in their homelands, the non-Indian social services agency had a different standard for evaluating families and child safety and did not comprehend tribal life or social structure. Initially, the state social service agencies began to remove Indian children from their families in the city. Later, they would even take action on reservations and in tribal communities. By such acts, Indian children were removed, often permanently, from kin and tribes and usually placed into non-Indian families. In many situations, the child's extended family had no further contact and no opportunity to regain custody and care of the child.

As described earlier, healthy tribal families are not necessarily organized like the ideal Anglo-American family. Extended family members often take a much more central role in child rearing in tribal families. Moreover, it is sometimes the case that biologically closer relatives, such as the father, are not expected to play as important a part in the daily life of children as are the children's maternal grandparents, uncles, and aunts. But despite the vast differences in caregiving practices between Anglo-American and most tribal societies, these differences were not taken into account by state agencies responsible for reviewing child welfare matters.

Instead, state social workers with little appreciation or understanding of these cultural differences presumed that many Indian families were failing to provide the necessary care for their children. As a result, across the United States, Indian families that were often caring for their children in a culturally appropriate manner were being broken up at alarming rates. By the early 1970s, a survey cited by the U.S. Congress reported that in states with large Indian populations, "approximately 25–35 percent of all Indian children are separated from their families and placed in foster homes, adoptive homes, or institutions."[2] In some states, Indian children were being removed from their families at per capita rates five, ten, thirteen, and in some cases nineteen times greater than non-Indian children.[3] At the same time, state agencies were not concerned with placing the Indian children they removed into homes of other tribal members. In sixteen states surveyed in 1969, "approximately 85 percent of all Indian children in foster care were living in non-Indian homes."[4] The Association of American Indian Affairs carefully documented this phenomenon in a 1977 report, excerpted below.

THE PLACEMENT OF AMERICAN INDIAN CHILDREN: THE NEED FOR CHANGE

*Carl Mindell and Alan Gurwitt**

We would like to focus here on the fact that today American Indian children are regularly removed from their families and communities by government and voluntary agencies and some religious groups, ostensibly for reasons of dependency, abandonment or neglect.

The Association of American Indian Affairs asserts that these practices have resulted in wholesale, and often unwarranted, removal of Indian children from their homes, reservations and people. The figures are alarming. In the state of South Dakota, on a per capita basis, approximately 16 times as many Indian children as white children are living in foster homes. In Montana, the rate is 13 times the national foster home placement rate. In

---

* Carl Mindell & Alan Gurwitt, Association on American Indian Affairs, *The Placement of American Indian Children: The Need for Change*, in *The Destruction of American Indian Families* 62–67 (1977).

Minnesota, among the Indian children, the rate of foster home placement is five times greater than for non-Indian children.

In the United States, one in every 200 children lives outside of his home of origin. In North Dakota, South Dakota and Nebraska one in every nine Indian children is in a foster home, adoptive home, institution or boarding facility. Indian children in these states are withdrawn from their homes at a rate 20 times the national average. In Minnesota during 1971–1972, one in every seven Indian children was in placement outside of his own home (there were about 1,413 Indian children under eighteen in adoptive placement while there were 241 Indian children under eighteen in foster care). Non-Indian homes accounted for 91 percent of the adoptions. In a survey of 16 states, "approximately 85 per cent of all Indian children in foster care are placed in non-Indian homes."

There are, then, two trends which are both obvious and alarming: (1) American Indian children are being placed outside of their natural homes at an enormous rate, and (2) they are being given over to the care of non-Indians in very considerable numbers.

There is much clinical evidence to suggest that these Native American children placed in off-reservation, non-Indian homes are at risk in their later development. Often enough, they are cared for by devoted and well-intentioned foster or adoptive parents. Nonetheless, particularly in adolescence, they are subject to ethnic confusion and a pervasive sense of abandonment with its attendant multiple ramifications. Consequently, these problems combined with their untoward early childhood preplacement experiences adversely affect their young adulthood and their own potential capacities as parents.

The two trends noted above appear to be final common pathways reflecting:

1. The professed policy of the Bureau of Indian Affairs, state welfare agencies, and of voluntary and religious groups had been to admit Indian people into the mainstream of America. While this policy has changed at higher levels of the Bureau, the change is unevenly applied at the lower levels. It is not clear that the policy has changed among the other groups.

2. Alternatives to placement are either not available, not thought of, or are inaccessible for varied reasons. Families which have become disorganized or have had difficulties in providing for the needs of their children are usually well known to various agencies. The decision to place the child often assumes that other options have been tried and have failed. All too often, however, neither tribe, state nor federal agency

has made any real effort at early intervention and support for the child and his family. As a result, when things get bad enough, the only clear option appears to be placement.

3. The decision to remove a child from his parents is often made by federal and state agency personnel who are poorly trained and who have limited understanding of Indian culture, or by Indian personnel with little clinical and developmental training.

4. The parents may have no understanding of their rights, e.g., they may be induced to waive their parental rights voluntarily without understanding the implications. Furthermore, the child, and in most cases his parents, do not have an advocate in court to represent their respective interests even if there is a court proceeding.

5. The decision to place the child is often made by a state court. This procedure typically fails to utilize the rich information about potential support and care readily available from the child's extended family and neighboring community. (While there has been some growth of tribal courts with greater understanding of cultural and community resources, there have been procedural and jurisdictional problems.)

6. The standards used in non-Indian courts in making the placement reflect the majority culture's criteria for suitability (e.g., so many square feet of space available per foster child in the home) and do not take into sufficient account what may be characteristic of the child's socio-cultural milieu. Thus Indian families are discriminated against as potential foster families.

7. The tribes generally have been given little or no responsibility for controlling or monitoring the flow of monies available for child care and family welfare.

8. There is no systemic review of placement judgments to insure that the child's placement offers him the least detrimental alternative.

9. There is no person or agency charged with focusing on the needs of Indian children that would compile information and develop comprehensive planning models adaptable to different regions.

Recently, Indian communities have become actively involved with these threats to their survival. In some instances tribal councils have established welfare committees to become involved in decisions pertaining to child neglect and dependency, and have adopted more stringent tribal codes governing child-welfare matters. Depending on the local circumstances, such active participation on the part of tribal groups has led to a reduction of off-reservation placements. Indeed, there are some innovative efforts by Indian tribes to find and support foster homes, establish group homes and residential care centers for families, and provide for other child-care services. While there are some complex issues resulting from the various degrees of jurisdictional authority, the relationship with the BIA [Bureau of Indian Affairs], the availability or assistance from the Indian Health Service (a section of the U.S. Public Health Service), and the local or state welfare departments, coordinating working relationships are possible. The major point here is that the tribal groups have made an effort to assume parental, and in many ways, grandparental authority over the families and children in their community. Indeed this corresponds to the increasing activity on the part of Native Americans to gain control over their own lives.

Recommendations

1. The Bureau of Indian Affairs and state welfare agencies, which are the recipients of federal funds, should explicitly assert that a major goal of their work is to support the integrity of Indian families and communities. In the area of child placement, this policy would be implemented by recommendation No. 2.
2. Options other than placement should be sought out and made available to Indian communities. These options should be integrated into a continuum of services under the general direction of the tribal government. The options would be flexible, i.e., capable of responding to the changing needs of an individual family. Such options might include (a) in-home help, such as homemaker care and home-counselor-child-rearers able to work within a family for extended periods of time; and (b) out-of-home help, such as pre- and after-school care, day care, respite service, group homes, and residential treatment facilities. Both kinds of support should be provided by Indian people or by personnel familiar with Indian culture who are trained in the psychological aspects of child development.
3. When placement is considered, the child and his parents should each be represented by an advocate. This would help to insure that the interests of each are represented. It is important to keep in mind that these interests are not necessarily the same, and may be different from the state's interests.
4. Decisions about the custody or placement of Indian children should be made under the auspices of Indian tribal governments. Agency personnel and professionals should be available in an advisory capacity, but they should not be the decision-makers.
5. The standards that govern these decisions should be developed and monitored by appropriate groups under the auspices of the tribe. Thus

the fate of a child and his family would be determined by persons who share the child's and family's socio-cultural milieu.

6. Monies for the support and care of children should flow through the tribe, rather than through the BIA and state welfare agencies. Funds should be available for innovative responses to the needs for child care—e.g., the funding of foster families at a rate reflecting their training, their experience, and the magnitude of the child's needs; the development of group homes; the establishment of family centers; the improvement of housing to allow for better child care; arrangements for subsidized adoption, etc.

7. Judgments pertaining to child care and placement should be under systematic review. In every case the tribes should be the responsible agents for this ongoing process of evaluation. The goal of the progress would be to insure that the service is providing the child with the least detrimental alternative.

8. Within the BIA there are offices focusing on roads, business and economic development, relocation, etc. But there is no office, at any level, charged with focusing on the needs of Indian children. Since it seems unlikely that "children's rights cannot be secured until some particular institution has recognized them and assumed responsibility for enforcing them," this issue should be explored.

These recommendations can be legislated by Congress. Indeed, the Association on American Indian Affairs has made very specific legislative recommendations that would enable broad implementation of similar policies.

States, also, can respond to the spirit of these new approaches. This is evidenced by recent developments in Wisconsin. There the American Indian Child Welfare Service Agency, with an all-Indian policy board, has been established with broad responsibility for supervising all child-placement decisions.

Questions

1. Do you think that the removal of children from Native communities affected the ability of tribes to effectively govern themselves? How do you know?

2. Do you think that the federal government accomplished its goal of assimilating Indians into American society? Is it likely that a person's cultural background can be totally erased? What aspects of your own culture do you feel most connected to?

In Your Community

1. In your tribal history, were children removed from the community? Where were most children in your community sent for school?
2. If Indian children of your community were put into boarding schools, do you think they benefited or were harmed by the placement in the institutions or with non-Indian families? Were there any positive outcomes of the policy of sending Indian children to boarding school?
3. Did your tribal government and legal systems suffer because of the removal of children from the community? Explain why or why not.

Glossary

Assimilation: The social process of one cultural group being absorbed by another.

Auspices: Support and approval.

Kiva: A Pueblo Indian ceremonial building that is usually round and partly underground.

Milieu: Environment; setting.

Ostensibly: Apparently or visibly.

Pan-Indianism: A political and social movement that became popular in the 1960s and 1970s and called for the alliance of all Native Americans despite traditional tribal animosities.

Per capita: (Latin for "by head.") By the number of individual persons, each equally.

Termination: In federal Indian law, the era during which the United States stopped recognizing tribal governments.

Waive: To voluntarily give up a right.

Suggested Further Reading

David Wallace Adams, *Education for Extinction: American Indians and the Boarding School Experience, 1875–1928* (1995).

Robert Bensen, *Children of the Dragonfly: Native American Voices on Child Custody and Education* (2001).

Andrea A. Curcio, *Civil Claims for Uncivilized Acts: Filing Suit against the Government for American Indian Boarding School Abuses*, 4 Hastings Race & Poverty Law Journal 45 (2006).

Donald Fixico, *Termination and Relocation: Federal Indian Policy, 1945–1960* (1986).

Ann Murray Haag, *The Indian Boarding School Era and Its Continuing Impact on Tribal Families and the Provision of Government Services*, 43 Tulsa Law Review 149 (2006).

Linda Lacey, *The White Man's Law and the American Indian Family in the Assimilation Era*, 40 Arkansas Law Review 327 (1987).

Laura Tohe, *No Parole Today* (1999).

Notes

1. Lewis Meriam et al., *The Problem of Indian Administration* (1928) at www.alaskool.org/native_ed/research_reports/IndianAdmin/Indian_Admin_Problms.html.

2. Legislative History, P.L. 95-608, Indian Child Welfare Act of 1978, House Report No. 95-1386, p. 7531.

3. *Id.*

4. *Id.*

CHAPTER 16

The Indian Child Welfare Act of 1978

T RIBES HAVE long recognized the problems with removal of Indian children from their communities. As many of those children who were raised in boarding schools and non-Indian foster or adoptive homes matured into adults, the voice of these "lost" Indian children came to be heard around the country, and they began to describe their painful experiences and the other negative effects of being removed from their families and communities. Some national organizations concerned with Indian welfare began addressing this problem in the late 1960s and early 1970s. This chapter provides an overview of one of the major results of the national effort to reform the processes by which the welfare of Indian children is assessed and ensured: The Indian Child Welfare Act of 1978 (ICWA).

Documentation and testimony presented before Congress leading up to passage of ICWA compiled a painful and tragic history of the devastating effect governmental policies and actions toward Indian children were having, not just on the children themselves but also on the larger tribal communities from which they were taken. As a result of the policies and practices of state social service agencies as well as federal Indian boarding and mission schools, vast numbers of tribal children had been raised and educated by nonmembers and non-Indians. With so many children no longer living with their tribal families and kin, a real threat emerged that the very heart of many tribes' cultural heritage would be lost or forgotten.

If kin relations and the duties, obligations, and expectations that surround those relations constitute the fundamental ways in which tribal customs and traditions are expressed and exercised, what would happen if those kin relations were never learned or experienced by tribal children? There is a substantial risk that both the Indian children excluded from such ties and the larger tribal communities from which they come would suffer. This was precisely what was happening to children removed to boarding schools or non-Indian foster homes. Throughout tribal communities, there was a fear that these policies and practices of targeting Indian children and raising them outside of their cultural heritage would ultimately spell the death of many tribal societies, beliefs, languages, and communities.

Over a five-year period, tribes, their allies, and Indian child welfare organizations developed a comprehensive legislative package that would address the practices of states in removing Indian children and placing them in non-Indian homes. An extensive lobbying effort took place, and the legislation that eventually passed the U.S. Congress had broad bipartisan cosponsorship. In 1978, Congress approved the Indian Child Welfare Act as 25 U.S.C. 1901-1963, P.L. 95-608, 92 Stat. 3069.

In enacting this act, Congress found that "there is no resource that is more vital to the continued existence and integrity of Indian tribes than their children." Congress also determined that states "often failed to recognize the essential tribal relations of Indian people and the cultural and social standards prevailing in Indian communities and families." Congress declared:

> It is the policy of this nation to protect the best interest of Indian children and to promote the stability and security of Indian Tribes and families by the establishments of minimum federal standards for the removal of Indian children from their families and the placement of such children in foster or adoptive homes which will reflect the unique values of Indian culture.

The ICWA had two overall purposes:

1. To affirm existing tribal authority to handle child protection cases (including child abuse, child neglect, and adoption) involving Indian children and to establish a preference for exclusive tribal jurisdiction over these cases
2. To regulate and set minimum standards for the handling of those cases remaining in state court and in state child social services agencies

LEGISLATIVE HISTORY OF THE ICWA, PUBLIC LAW 95-608*

Standards

The Indian Child Welfare crisis will continue until the standards for defining child mistreatment are revised. Very few Indian children are removed from their families on the grounds of physical abuse. One study of a North Dakota reservation showed that these grounds were advanced in only 1 percent of the cases. Another study of a tribe in the Northwest showed the same incidence. The remaining 99 percent of the cases were argued on such vague grounds as "neglect" or "social deprivation" and on allegations of the emotional damage the children were subjected to by living with their parents. Indian communities are often shocked to learn that parents they regard as excellent caregivers have been judged unfit by non-Indian social workers.

In judging the fitness of a particular family, many social workers, ignorant of Indian cultural values and social norms, make decisions that are wholly inappropriate in the context of Indian family life and so they frequently discover neglect or abandonment where none exists.

For example, the dynamics of Indian extended families are largely misunderstood. An Indian child may have scores of, perhaps more than a hundred, relatives who are counted as close, responsible members of the family. Many social workers, untutored in the ways of Indian family life or assuming them to be socially irresponsible, consider leaving the child with persons outside the nuclear family as neglect and thus as grounds for terminating parental rights.

Because in some communities the social workers have, in a sense, become a part of the extended family, parents will sometimes turn to the welfare department for temporary care of their children, failing to realize that their action is perceived quite differently by non-Indians.

Indian child-rearing practices are also misinterpreted in evaluating a child's behavior and parental concern. It may appear that the child is running wild and that the parents do not care. What is labeled "permissiveness" may often, in fact, simply be a different but effective way of disciplining children. BIA boarding schools are full of children with such spurious "discipline problems."

---

* U.S. Congress, House Report No. 95-1386, *House Report, PL* 95-608 (1978).

One of the grounds most frequently advanced for taking Indian children from their parents is the abuse of alcohol. However, this standard is applied unequally. In areas where rates of problem drinking among Indians and non-Indians are the same, it is rarely applied against non-Indian parents. Once again cultural biases frequently affect decision-making. The late Dr. Edward P. Dozier of Santa Clara Pueblo and other observers have argued that there are important cultural differences in the use of alcohol. Yet, by and large non-Indian social workers draw conclusions about the meaning of acts or conduct in ignorance of these distinctions.

The courts tend to rely on the testimony of social workers who often lack the training and insights necessary to measure the emotional risk the child is running at home. . . . Rejecting the notion that poverty and cultural differences constitute social deprivation and psychological abuse, [states] must prove that there is actual physical and emotional harm resulting from the acts of the parents.

The abusive actions of social workers would largely be nullified if more judges were themselves knowledgeable about Indian life and required a sharper definition of the standards of child abuse and neglect.

Discriminatory standards have made it virtually impossible for most Indian couples to qualify as foster or adoptive parents, since they are based on middle-class values. Recognizing that in some instances it is necessary to remove children from their homes, community leaders argue that there are Indian families within the Tribe who could provide excellent care, although they are of modest means. While some progress is being made here and there, the figures cited above indicate that non-Indian parents continue to furnish almost all the foster and adoptive care for Indian children.

Due Process

The decision to take Indian children from their natural home is, in most cases, carried out without due process of law. For example, it is rare for either Indian children or their parents to be represented by counsel or to have the supporting testimony of an expert witness.

Many cases do not go through [a judicial] process at all, since the voluntary waiver of parental rights is a device widely employed by social workers to gain custody of children. Because of the availability of the waivers and because a great number of Indian parents depend on welfare payments for survival, they are exposed to the sometimes coercive arguments of welfare departments. In a recent South Dakota entrapment case, an Indian parent in a time of trouble was persuaded to sign a waiver granting temporary custody to the State, only to find that this is now being advanced as evidence of neglect and grounds for the permanent termination of parental rights. It is an unfortunate fact of life for many Indian parents that the primary service agency to which they must turn for financial help also exercises police powers over their family life and is, most frequently, the agency that initiates custody proceedings.

The conflict between Indian and non-Indian social systems operates to defeat due process. The extended family provides an example. By sharing the responsibility of child rearing, the extended family tends to strengthen the community's commitment to the child. At the same time, however, it diminishes the possibility that the nuclear family will be able to mobilize itself quickly enough when an outside agency acts to assume custody. Because it is not unusual for Indian children to spend considerable time away from other relatives, there is no immediate realization of what is happening—possibly not until the opportunity for due process has slipped away.

Critics of ICWA oppose the idea that a tribe should have jurisdiction over Indian child welfare proceedings when the parents do not want the tribe to have that power. This issue was tested in the Supreme Court case *Mississippi Band of Choctaw Indians v. Holyfield*, 109 S.Ct. 1597, 490 U.S. 30, 104 L.Ed.2d 29 (1989). In that case, the parents of two Indian children purposely left the reservation for the birth of their twins, and then voluntarily gave them up for adoption through a State court proceeding, to a non-Indian family. The Mississippi Band of Choctaw Indians challenged the adoption, claiming that under ICWA they had exclusive jurisdiction to hear the case. The parents argued that because the children were born off of the reservation, the children were not "domiciled" on tribal land. As such, they argued that the tribal court did not have exclusive jurisdiction over their children's case. Furthermore, the parents argued that because they were voluntarily giving up their child for adoption, the state court did not need to inform the tribe of the proceeding, and the tribe did not have the power to intervene or request transfer in the adoption proceeding.

The Supreme Court decided the case in favor of the tribe, finding that it did have exclusive jurisdiction over the case. The court ruled that Congress, in passing the ICWA, was concerned about protecting Indian tribes' interests in the welfare of Tribal children. The Court found that the goals of ICWA would be utterly defeated if the Indian parents in this case could so easily avoid the exclusive jurisdiction of the tribal court by leaving the reservation when it came time to give birth to their children. Thus, the Court held that in this case, the children born to these Indian parents—who at all times resided and were domiciled on the Choctaw reservation—were themselves domiciled on the reservation, even though they were not born there, and had not lived there since their birth. As a result, the Court reversed the adoption proceeding of the state court, finding that the tribal court had exclusive jurisdiction to hear and determine the child custody proceedings.

In this way, the Supreme Court has affirmed the idea that ICWA was passed to protect the significant interests that Indian tribes have in the welfare of tribal children, insofar as it is their children, and the manner in which they are raised, which best safeguards the future survival of their unique tribal heritage.

INDIAN CHILD WELFARE ACT (ICWA), 25 U.S.C. 1901 *ET SEQ.*

Sec. 1901.—Congressional Findings

Recognizing the special relationship between the United States and the Indian tribes and their members and the Federal responsibility to Indian people, the Congress finds—

1. that clause 3, section 8, article I of the United States Constitution provides that "The Congress shall have Power. . . . To regulate Commerce . . . with Indian tribes" and, through this and other constitutional authority, Congress has plenary power over Indian affairs;
2. that Congress, through statutes, treaties, and the general course of dealing with Indian tribes, has assumed the responsibility for the protection and preservation of Indian tribes and their resources;
3. that there is no resource that is more vital to the continued existence and integrity of Indian tribes than their children and that the United States has a direct interest, as trustee, in protecting Indian children who are members of or are eligible for membership in an Indian tribe;
4. that an alarmingly high percentage of Indian families are broken up by the removal, often unwarranted, of their children from them by nontribal public and private agencies and that an alarmingly high percentage of such children are placed in non-Indian foster and adoptive homes and institutions; and
5. that the States, exercising their recognized jurisdiction over Indian child custody proceedings through administrative and judicial bodies,

have often failed to recognize the essential tribal relations of Indian
people and the cultural and social standards prevailing in Indian communities and families.

Sec. 1902. Congressional Declaration of Policy

The Congress hereby declares that it is the policy of this Nation to protect
the best interests of Indian children and to promote the stability and security
of Indian tribes and families by the establishment of minimum Federal
standards for the removal of Indian children from their families and the
placement of such children in foster or adoptive homes which will reflect
the unique values of Indian culture, and by providing for assistance to
Indian tribes in the operation of child and family service programs.

Sec. 1903.——Definitions

For the purposes of this chapter, except as may be specifically provided otherwise, the term—

1. "child custody proceeding" shall mean and include—
   a. "foster care placement" which shall mean any action removing an
      Indian child from its parent or Indian custodian for temporary
      placement in a foster home or institution or the home of a guardian
      or conservator where the parent or Indian custodian cannot have
      the child returned upon demand, but where parental rights have
      not been terminated;
   b. "termination of parental rights" which shall mean any action result-
      ing in the termination of the parent-child relationship;
   c. "preadoptive placement" which shall mean the temporary place-
      ment of an Indian child in a foster home or institution after the ter-
      mination of parental rights, but prior to or in lieu of adoptive
      placement; and
   d. "adoptive placement" which shall mean the permanent placement
      of an Indian child for adoption, including any action resulting in a
      final decree of adoption.
   Such term or terms shall not include a placement based upon an act
   which, if committed by an adult, would be deemed a crime or upon an
   award, in a divorce proceeding, of custody to one of the parents.
2. "extended family member" shall be as defined by the law or custom of
   the Indian child's tribe or, in the absence of such law or custom, shall
   be a person who has reached the age of eighteen and who is the Indian

child's grandparent, aunt or uncle, brother or sister, brother-in-law or sister-in-law, niece or nephew, first or second cousin, or stepparent;

3. "Indian" means any person who is a member of an Indian tribe, or who is an Alaska Native and a member of a Regional Corporation as defined in 1606 of title 43;

4. "Indian child" means any unmarried person who is under age eighteen and is either
   a. a member of an Indian tribe or
   b. is eligible for membership in an Indian tribe and is the biological child of a member of an Indian tribe;

5. "Indian child's tribe" means
   a. the Indian tribe in which an Indian child is a member or eligible for membership or
   b. in the case of an Indian child who is a member of or eligible for membership in more than one tribe, the Indian tribe with which the Indian child has the more significant contacts;

6. "Indian custodian" means any Indian person who has legal custody of an Indian child under tribal law or custom or under State law or to whom temporary physical care, custody, and control has been transferred by the parent of such child;

7. "Indian organization" means any group, association, partnership, corporation, or other legal entity owned or controlled by Indians, or a majority of whose members are Indians;

8. "Indian tribe" means any Indian tribe, band, nation, or other organized group or community of Indians recognized as eligible for the services provided to Indians by the Secretary because of their status as Indians, including any Alaska Native village as defined in section 1602(c) of title 43;

9. "parent" means any biological parent or parents of an Indian child or any Indian person who has lawfully adopted an Indian child, including adoptions under tribal law or custom. It does not include the unwed father where paternity has not been acknowledged or established;

10. "reservation" means Indian country as defined in section 1151 of title 18 and any lands, not covered under such section, title to which is either held by the United States in trust for the benefit of any Indian tribe or individual or held by any Indian tribe or individual subject to a restriction by the United States against alienation;

11. "Secretary" means the Secretary of the Interior; and

12. "tribal court" means a court with jurisdiction over child custody proceedings and which is either a Court of Indian Offenses, a court established and operated under the code or custom of an Indian tribe, or any

other administrative body of a tribe which is vested with authority over child custody proceedings.

Subchapter 1—Child Custody Proceedings

Sec. 1911.—Indian Tribe Jurisdiction over Indian Child Custody Proceedings

a. *Exclusive jurisdiction.* An Indian tribe shall have jurisdiction exclusive as to any State over any child custody proceeding involving an Indian child who resides or is domiciled within the reservation of such tribe, except where such jurisdiction is otherwise vested in the State by existing Federal law. Where an Indian child is a ward of a tribal court, the Indian tribe shall retain exclusive jurisdiction, notwithstanding the residence or domicile of the child.

b. *Transfer of proceedings; declination by tribal court.* In any State court proceeding for the foster care placement of, or termination of parental rights to, an Indian child not domiciled or residing within the reservation of the Indian child's tribe, the court, in the absence of good cause to the contrary, shall transfer such proceeding to the jurisdiction of the tribe, absent objection by either parent, upon the petition of either parent or the Indian custodian or the Indian child's tribe: Provided, that such transfer shall be subject to declination by the tribal court of such tribe.

c. *State court proceedings; intervention.* In any State court proceeding for the foster care placement of, or termination of parental rights to, an Indian child, the Indian custodian of the child and the Indian child's tribe shall have a right to intervene at any point in the proceeding.

d. *Full faith and credit to public acts, records and judicial proceedings of Indian tribes.* The United States, every State, every territory or possession of the United States, and every Indian tribe shall give full faith and credit to the public acts, records, and judicial proceedings of any Indian tribe applicable to Indian child custody proceedings to the same extent that such entities give full faith and credit to the public acts, records, and judicial proceedings of any other entity.

Sec. 1912.—Pending Court Proceedings

[selections a, b, and c omitted]

d. *Remedial services and rehabilitative programs; preventive measures.* Any party seeking to effect a foster care placement of, or termination of parental rights to, an Indian child under State law shall satisfy the court that active efforts have been made to provide remedial services and rehabilitative programs designed to prevent the breakup of the Indian family and that these efforts have proved unsuccessful.

e. *Foster care placement orders; evidence; determination of damage to child.* No foster care placement may be ordered in such proceeding in the absence of a determination, supported by clear and convincing evidence, including testimony of qualified expert witnesses, that the continued custody of the child by the parent or Indian custodian is likely to result in serious emotional or physical damage to the child.

f. *Parental rights termination orders; evidence; determination of damage to child.* No termination of parental rights may be ordered in such proceeding in the absence of a determination, supported by evidence beyond a reasonable doubt, including testimony of qualified expert witnesses, that the continued custody of the child by the parent or Indian custodian is likely to result in serious emotional or physical damage to the child.

Sec. 1913.—Parental Rights; Voluntary Termination

a. *Consent; record; certification matters; invalid consents.* Where any parent or Indian custodian voluntarily consents to a foster care placement or to termination of parental rights, such consent shall not be valid unless executed in writing and recorded before a judge of a court of competent jurisdiction and accompanied by the presiding judge's certificate that the terms and consequences of the consent were fully explained in detail and were fully understood by the parent or Indian custodian. The court shall also certify that either the parent or Indian custodian fully understood the explanation in English or that it was interpreted into a language that the parent or Indian custodian understood. Any consent given prior to, or within ten days after, birth of the Indian child shall not be valid.

b. *Foster care placement; withdrawal of consent.* Any parent or Indian custodian may withdraw consent to a foster care placement under State law at any time and, upon such withdrawal, the child shall be returned to the parent or Indian custodian.

c. *Voluntary termination of parental rights or adoptive placement; withdrawal of consent; return of custody.* In any voluntary proceeding for termination of parental rights to, or adoptive placement of, an Indian child, the consent of the parent may be withdrawn for any reason at any time prior to the entry of a final decree of termination or adoption, as the case may be, and the child shall be returned to the parent.

d. *Collateral attack; vacation of decree and return of custody; limitations.* After the entry of a final decree of adoption of an Indian child in any State court, the parent may withdraw consent thereto upon the grounds that consent was obtained through fraud or duress and may petition the court to vacate such decree. Upon a finding that such consent was obtained through fraud or duress, the court shall vacate such decree and return the child to the parent. No adoption which has been effective for at least two years may be invalidated under the provisions of this subsection unless otherwise permitted under State law.

Sec. 1914.—Petition to Court of Competent Jurisdiction to Invalidate Action upon Showing of Certain Violations

Any Indian child who is the subject of any action for foster care placement or termination of parental rights under State law, any parent or Indian custodian from whose custody such child was removed, and the Indian child's tribe may petition any court of competent jurisdiction to invalidate such action upon a showing that such action violated any provision of sections 1911, 1912, and 1913 of this title.

Sec. 1915.—Placement of Indian Children

a. *Adoptive placements; preferences.* In any adoptive placement of an Indian child under State law, a preference shall be given, in the absence of good cause to the contrary, to a placement with

1. a member of the child's extended family;
2. other members of the Indian child's tribe; or
3. other Indian families.

b. *Foster care or preadoptive placements; criteria; preferences.* Any child accepted for foster care or preadoptive placement shall be placed in the least restrictive setting which most approximates a family and in which his special needs, if any, may be met. The child shall also be placed within reasonable proximity to his or her home, taking into account any special needs of the child. In any foster care or preadoptive placement, a preference shall be given, in the absence of good cause to the contrary, to a placement with—

1. a member of the Indian child's extended family;
2. a foster home licensed, approved, or specified by the Indian child's tribe;
3. an Indian foster home licensed or approved by an authorized non-Indian licensing authority; or

4. an institution for children approved by an Indian tribe or operated by an Indian organization which has a program suitable to meet the Indian child's needs.

c. *Tribal resolution for different order of preference; personal preference considered; anonymity in application of preferences.* In the case of a placement under subsection (a) or (b) of this section, if the Indian child's tribe shall establish a different order of preference by resolution, the agency or court effecting the placement shall follow such order so long as the placement is the least restrictive setting appropriate to the particular needs of the child, as provided in subsection (b) of this section. Where appropriate, the preference of the Indian child or parent shall be considered: Provided, that where a consenting parent evidences a desire for anonymity, the court or agency shall give weight to such desire in applying the preferences.

d. *Social and cultural standards applicable.* The standards to be applied in meeting the preference requirements of this section shall be the prevailing social and cultural standards of the Indian community in which the parent or extended family resides or with which the parent or extended family members maintain social and cultural ties.

e. *Record of placement; availability.* A record of each such placement, under State law, of an Indian child shall be maintained by the State in which the placement was made, evidencing the efforts to comply with the order of preference specified in this section. Such record shall be made available at any time upon the request of the Secretary or the Indian child's tribe.

Questions

1. What problems does the ICWA attempt to remedy?
2. In your opinion, should the tribe have equal standing with the parent in regard to placement of a tribal member's child?
3. Do you think the tribe should always intervene in a state court proceeding involving a Native child? Why or why not?
4. What might be some unintended consequences of the ICWA?

In Your Community

1. In your community, are there stories or cultural understandings of who the "protectors" of children are other than parents? Who is responsible for the care and upbringing of your tribal children?

2. Has your tribe ever intervened in a state court adoption proceeding? If so, was the case transferred to tribal court?

Glossary

Declination: A formal refusal.

Domicile: A person's permanent home, legal home, or main residence.

Nullified: No longer having any legal effect or validity.

Ward: A person, especially a child, placed by the court under the care of a guardian.

Suggested Further Reading

Jill E. Adams, *The Indian Child Welfare Act of 1978: Protecting Tribal Interests in a Land of Individual Rights*, 19 American Indian Law Review 301 (1995).
B. J. Jones, *The Indian Child Welfare Act Handbook: A Legal Guide to the Custody and Adoption of Native American Children* (2008).
Native American Rights Fund, *A Practical Guide to the Indian Child Welfare Act* (2007).

CHAPTER 17

Tribal Court Custody Proceedings

ODAY, THE tribal laws of family and domestic relations reflect both the centrality that kin relations have always played in tribal life and the history of colonization and domination of tribes by Anglo-American forces. While the Indian Child Welfare Act of 1978 (ICWA) addresses issues like child protection, termination of parental rights, and adoption, family law covers a broader range of concerns. Thus, the kinds of conflicts and disputes handled by tribal courts today that are categorized as "family law disputes" primarily center around matters of marriage, divorce, and child custody. This is quite different from the historical role that family law played in many tribal societies, where, as we saw earlier, matters of kinship and the norms, structures, and practices surrounding those relations were at the center of a tribe's entire legal and cultural heritage. At least on its surface, family law in most tribes today looks much more like Anglo-American family law: a special body of norms, structures, and practices separate from other areas of law such as criminal law, contract law, and personal injury law.

At the same time, however, the conflicts and disputes involving matters of family and domestic relations often raise the most important issues of any tribe's cultural and legal heritage. In his analysis of 359 written opinions from fifty-six different tribal courts, Russel L. Barsh discovered that the judges relied on principles of custom and tradition in cases of family law and property inheritance more than any other kinds of cases.[1] Thus, despite the fact that what is today considered a matter of tribal family law has considerably narrowed in scope from historical times, it is still the case that the matters of family, kinship, and marriage strike at the very heart of tribal life.

This chapter will review how different tribal courts are addressing issues of child custody proceedings today. Particular attention will be paid to the ways in which tribal judges are turning to their own customs, traditions, and other aspects of their cultural and legal heritage to resolve these disputes.

TRIBAL CHILD WELFARE LEGISLATION AND COURT DECISIONS: SOME EXAMPLES

*Barbara Ann Atwood**

Tribal courts vary in their approach to custody and visitation disputes involving extended family members, but one often finds an explicit appreciation for the cultural role of a child's relatives and a marked willingness among tribal judges to protect that role. Some tribes have enacted specific grandparent visitation provisions as part of their tribal code. The Rosebud Sioux Tribe, for example, has given its tribal court the power to grant reasonable rights of visitation to grandparents with or without a petition from the grandparents, so long as the court finds that visitation is in the best interests of the children. In other tribes, the tribal courts have ordered visitation with extended family members even though no code provision authorizes it. For example, in *In re C.D.S.*, the Court of Indian Offenses for the Delaware Tribe of Western Oklahoma took judicial notice of "the unique relationship that exists between Indian grandparents and grandchildren, and the need for maintenance of these contacts, despite the fact there is no written tribal law on the subject." The court further observed that grandparents are crucial vehicles for passing on knowledge of tribal tradition:

> Since this is an Indian family, where grandparents often times provide the necessary guidance in traditional tribal customs, history, and culture, and function as the central part of the family, the court would find it difficult to completely ignore the need to maintain and foster such important relationships. The fact that the children in this case

---

* Barbara Ann Atwood, *Tribal Jurisprudence and Cultural Meanings of the Family*, 79 Nebraska Law Review 577 (2000).

have lived with the petitioner for a significant period of their child-hood, is a weighty factor in reaching this conclusion.

Although the court referred to the increasing recognition of grandparent visitation rights in state courts, its decision was based primarily on its view of the unique role of Indian grandparents:

> [I]t is common knowledge in Indian Country that both the maternal and paternal grandmothers traditionally play a very significant role in the Indian family. . . . Based upon traditional tribal custom, the court concludes that a grandparent may, in appropriate instances, have the right to visitation especially where the children have lived with the grandparent for a significant period of time and continued contact would not be detrimental to them.

The court's approach to the question of grandparent visitation contrasts with the posture of most state courts. The absence of a tribal code provision authorizing grandparent visitation did not preclude the court from granting such visitation, since it relied instead on unwritten tribal custom. In addition, the court's explanation suggests that a grandparent who has had a significant caretaking role, vis-à-vis the children in question, acquires a presumptive right of contact that the court will honor unless there is a showing of detriment to the child. That receptivity to grandparent contact rests in part on recognition of the vital role that the grandparent will have in fostering the child's sense of tribal identity and knowledge about the tribe's customs and traditions. State laws, in contrast, typically require the grandparent to prove that visitation would be in the child's best interests. . . .

State law, moreover, is generally silent as to any role the grandparent might have in helping the child maintain a sense of cultural heritage.

The Native respect for extended family members sometimes has extended beyond visitation to an outright award of physical custody to the relative over the objections of parents. In one case, the tribal court for the Sac and Fox Nations cited the continuing acrimony between the parents as a reason for awarding temporary custody to the child's paternal grandmother. In a similar vein, the Rosebud Sioux Tribal Court of Appeals pointedly suggested such a solution to the trial court after expressing disapproval of the parents' excessively negative evidence. An extended discussion of tribal tradition with respect to the role of relatives as potential custodians appears in *Deer v. Okpik*. There a Quebec court considered a custody dispute over the young son of a Mohawk father and Inuit mother. Although not a tribal court itself, the Quebec court's reasoning has been expressly endorsed by the

Navajo judiciary. The facts showed that the child had been living with his maternal grandparents so that his mother could pursue work as a translator. The Quebec court found that although an "adoption" by the grandparents had taken place in accordance with Inuit custom, that did not signify an abandonment by the mother. In considering the welfare of the child, the court noted that he was integrated into Inuit culture and would suffer were he to be uprooted. The court also pointed out that any resolution of the dispute should be in harmony with Inuit custom and tradition. In its order, the court decreed that the child should continue to live with the grandparents but awarded legal custody to the mother with visitation rights to the father.

The Navajo district court in *Goldtooth* described *Deer* at some length and expressed approval of its reasoning. The Navajo court stated in part:

> While recognizing the natural law rights of the parents, the [*Deer*] court held, in reasoning adopted by this court, that the dominant principle to guide the court is always that the interests of the child are the principal factor to be considered. . . . To look at an award to either natural parent would be to disrupt the child's integration into the Inuit culture. While the court concluded that the parents could not be blamed for their conduct, it found that the best interests of the child required that he remain with his Inuit grandparents.

In *Deer*, the court awarded physical custody to the child's grandparents over the objection of his legal parents, even though no misconduct by the parents was established. In addition to the finding that a change of physical custody would be detrimental to the child, the customary role of grandparents in Inuit tradition informed the court's thinking. The strong endorsement of the *Deer* court's reasoning in *Goldtooth* suggests that the Navajo judge would be equally receptive to grandparent custody under similar circumstances. . . .

In sum, visitation and custody requests by nonparents in tribal courts are construed through a distinct cultural lens. A tribal tradition of involving extended family members in child rearing may strongly influence any judicial response to an intra-familial dispute and may lead to the tribal court's use of a presumption favoring the extended family member. In state courts, on the other hand, [case law] has reaffirmed the dominant culture's protection of the nuclear family and, more specifically, the autonomy of parents. While tribal laws likewise respect parents' rights . . . tribal courts applying tribal custom and tradition can sometimes override parental authority in order to give effect to a culturally-grounded role for grandparents or other relatives.

CHILDREN'S CODE

*Little River Band of Ottawa Indians**

Section 1. Short Title and Purpose

1.01. *Short Title*. This ordinance shall be entitled "The Children's Protection Code."

1.02. *Purpose*. The Children's Protection Code shall be liberally interpreted and construed to fulfill the following expressed purposes:

a. To provide for the welfare, care and protection of the Indian children and families of the Little River Band of Ottawa Indians;
b. To provide for the safety of tribal children and preserve family unity;
c. To provide procedures for intervention in state court proceedings regarding Indian Children;
d. To provide procedures for the transfer of jurisdiction over Indian Children from state and other Tribal Courts to this Tribal Court;
e. To provide for the exercise of the Tribe's rights and responsibilities under the Indian Child Welfare Act 1978.

Section 1a. Philosophy and Goals

a. To take such actions that will best serve the spiritual, emotional, mental and physical welfare of the child and the best interest of the Tribe to prevent the abuse, neglect and abandonment of children;
b. To provide a continuum of services for children and their families with emphasis whenever possible on prevention, early intervention and community-based alternatives;
c. To protect the rights of and ensure fairness to the children, parents, guardians, custodians and other parties who come before Tribal Court, the state courts, or other Tribal courts;
d. To recognize, acknowledge, and respect the many diverse and important Anishnaabek customs, traditions and ways in the Indian community;
e. To preserve and strengthen the child's cultural and ethnic identity whenever possible.

---

* Little River Band of Ottawa Indians, Ordinance No. 98-900-01 (June 6, 2001), www.lrboi.com/council/docs/ordinances/Title%20900-01.pdf.

Section 3. Jurisdiction of the Court

3.07. *Substantive and Procedural Law Applicable in Court.*

(a) *Tribal Law Controlling.* Because of the vital interest of the Tribe in its children and those children who may become members of the Tribe, this Code, other ordinances, regulations, public policies, recognized customs and common law of the Tribe shall control in any proceeding involving a child who is a member of the Tribe.

(b) *Use of State Substantive and Procedural Law in the Absence of Applicable Tribal Law.* The substantive law and procedures for the state courts shall not be binding upon the Court except where specifically provided for in this Code. In the absence of promulgated rules of procedure, procedural rules of the State of Michigan may be utilized as a guide. Michigan case law may serve as a guide for the Court but shall not be binding. Any matters not covered by the substantive laws, regulations, customs or common law of the Little River Band of Ottawa Indians, or by applicable federal laws or regulations, may be decided by the Court according to the laws of the State of Michigan.

3.08. *Transfer of Jurisdiction to Other Courts.* In any proceedings arising under the Children's Protection Code, the Court may transfer the proceedings to an appropriate state court or another Tribal Court where the state or the other Indian Tribe has a significant interest in the child and the transfer would be in the best interests of the child.

3.09. *Transfer of Jurisdiction from State Courts to Tribal Court In Accordance With the Indian Child Welfare Act.*

(a) *Receipt of Notice.* The Tribal Presenting Officer (Prosecutor) shall be the agent for service of notice of state court child custody proceedings. The Presenting Officer shall provide copies of the notice to the Binojeeuk Commission and the Family Services Department within three (3) days after receipt of certification of eligibility by the Enrollment Department.

(b) *Intervention.* The Presenting Officer shall file a Notice of Intervention with the state court within five days of receipt of notice upon certification by the Little River Band membership office that the child is a member or is eligible for membership in the Little River Band of Ottawa Indians. The Presenting Officer shall provide copies of the Intervention and other pleadings in his possession to the Binojeeuk Commission and the Director of Family Services within three (3) days after filing of said Notice of Intervention.

(c) *Investigation and Pre-transfer Report.* The Tribal family services department shall conduct an investigation in collaboration with the state social services agency and shall file a written report, comporting with tribal regulations, with the Presenting Officer and the Binojeeuk Commission no later than forty-eight (48) hours before the next regularly scheduled Binojeeuk Commission meeting. If an emergency meeting is required, an oral report with appropriate documentation may be submitted. However, the written report shall be filed no later than forty-eight (48) hours after the emergency meeting. Such written report shall include the following:

(i)   The best interests of the child;
(ii) The best interests of the Tribe;
(iii) Availability of services for the child and the family;
(iv) Prospects for permanent placement for the child; and
(v)   Conservation of Tribal resources.

(d) *Decision to Request Transfer*. The Binojeeuk Commission shall make written recommendations to the Presenting Officer on whether or not the Tribe should petition for transfer from the state court. The Binojeeuk Commission shall consider these factors:

(i)   The best interests of the child;
(ii) The best interests of the Tribe;
(iii) Availability of services for the child and the family;
(iv) Prospects for permanent placement for the child; and
(v)   Conservation of Tribal resources.

(e) *Petition for Transfer*. The Tribal petition for transfer shall be filed in the state court by the Tribal Prosecutor within five days of receipt of the Binojeeuk Commission's recommendation for transfer. If either parent or the Indian custodian objects to the transfer to Tribal Court, the matter must remain in state court under the terms of the Indian Child Welfare Act.

(f) *Hearings upon Grant of Transfer Request by State Court*. Upon receipt of transfer jurisdiction from state court, the Tribal Court shall hold appropriate hearings in accordance with this code.

Section 5. Binojeeuk Commission

5.01. *Creation of the Binojeeuk Commission*. The Binojeeuk Commission is created for the purpose of protecting the best interests of the child and promoting the stability and security of Indian families by fully exercising the Tribe's rights and responsibilities under the Indian Child Welfare Act of 1978 and this Code.

5.02. *Membership*. The Binojeeuk Commission shall consist of five (5) adult members of the Tribe who are age 21 or older, appointed by the Tribal Ogema and ratified by the Tribal Council. The term of office for Commission members shall be four (4) years. Commissioners' character must be determined to be in compliance with 25 U.S.C. §3207 which provides that no individual shall be appointed to a position, the duties and responsibilities of which involve regular contact with, or control over, Indian children if such person has been found guilty of, or entered a plea of nolo contendere or guilty to, any felonious offense, or any of two or more misdemeanor offenses, under Federal, State, or Tribal law involving crimes of violence; sexual assault, molestation, exploitation, contact or prostitution; crimes against persons; or offenses committed against children.

5.03. *Duties*. The Binojeeuk Commission shall act under the authority expressly delegated to it by the Tribal Council, in this Code or in other enactments by the Tribal Council. The Binojeeuk Commission shall have the following duties:

a. Advise the Tribal Council and the Tribal Court on child welfare matters and recommend policies and procedures for implementing federal and Tribal child welfare law.
b. Monitor child welfare proceedings involving Tribal members in the state or Tribal Courts.
c. Make recommendations regarding intervention in such proceedings and transfer of jurisdiction from state court to the Tribal Court as provided in the Indian Child Welfare Act.
d. Conduct informal conferences with a child and the child's parent(s), guardian or custodian to discuss alternatives to formal Court jurisdiction for resolving concerns about the proper care and supervision of a child.
e. Make recommendations to authorize the filing of child-in-need-of-care petitions in the Tribal Court pursuant to this Code.
f. Make recommendations to the Tribal family services workers, placement agency workers and the Tribal Prosecutor regarding the care, custody and supervision of Tribal children under Court jurisdiction, including recommendations as to case plan, guardianship and termination of parental rights.
g. License and monitor group, shelter, foster and adoptive homes and child placing agencies.
h. Engage in further activities as to protect and improve the welfare of the children of the Little River Band of Ottawa Indians.

Section 11. Filing Child Protection Petition

11.01. *Authorization to File Petition.*

(a) Upon the request by the Binojeeuk Commission, a child protective services worker or the Indian Child Welfare worker, the Presenting Officer shall conduct a preliminary inquiry to determine if formal child protection proceedings should be initiated by filing a child protection petition on behalf of the Tribe and in the best interests of the child.

(b) Any person may file a complaint with the Binojeeuk Commission, Indian Child Welfare Worker, a protective services worker, Presenting Officer, law enforcement or the Court alleging that a child is in need of care.

(c) After completion of the preliminary inquiry on a petition, the Binojeeuk Commission or the Presenting Officer shall either authorize the filing of a petition or decline to authorize the filing of a petition.

(d) If a child has been removed and placed in detention or custody, and filing the petition is not authorized by either the Binojeeuk Commission or the Presenting Officer, the petition shall be dismissed and the child immediately released to his/her parent, custodian or guardian.

(e) Only the Presenting Officer may file a petition alleging that a child is in need of care. The Presenting Officer shall file any petition that is authorized by the Binojeeuk Commission.

(f) Nothing in this section shall preclude law enforcement or protective services personnel from taking emergency actions authorized under Section 10 of this Code.

11.02. *Time Limitations.* If a child has been removed from the home, then a child protection petition shall be filed with the Court within forty-eight (48) hours, excluding Saturdays, Sundays and legal holidays, or the child must be returned to his/her home.

11.03. *Contents of Petition.* The child protection petition shall set forth the following with specificity:

a. The name, birth date, sex, residence and Tribal affiliation of the child;
b. The basis for the Court's jurisdiction;
c. The specific allegations which cause the child to be a child-in-need-of-care;
d. A plain and concise statement of the facts upon which the allegations of child-in-need-of-care are based, including the date, time and location at which the alleged facts occurred;
e. The names, residence and Tribal affiliation of the child's parents, guardians or custodians, if known;

f. The names, relationships and residences of all known members of the child's extended family and all former caregivers, if known. If the identity, residence or location of any parent, guardian, or custodian is unknown, the name, relationship and address of any known adult relative(s) residing in the same city or county as the child;

g. If the child is placed outside of the home, where the child is placed, the facts necessitating the placement and the date and time of the placement, unless the Presenting Officer determines that disclosure of the child's location will expose the child to a substantial risk of emotional or physical harm;

h. The name of the Presenting Officer presenting the petition and the date and time presented;

i. If any matters required to be set forth by the section are not known, a statement that they are not known should be made; and

j. The type of relief requested, including whether temporary or permanent custody is sought.

11.04. *Filing and Dismissal of Petition.*

(a) The petition shall be filed with the Clerk of the Court.

(b) A petition alleging that a child is in need of care or supervision shall be dismissed with prejudice if a preliminary hearing is not held within:

1. Seventy-two (72) hours, excluding Saturdays, Sundays and legal holidays, from the date of the petition is filed when a child is taken into custody; or

2. Twenty (20) days from the date the petition is filed when a child is not in custody or has been released to his/her parent, custodian or guardian.

(c) Notwithstanding the time limitations specified in paragraph (b), above, the time for holding the preliminary hearing may be continued upon motion of the Presenting Officer if the custodial parent, guardian or custodian or other material evidence and/or witnesses are unavailable. The motion must include information regarding the nature of the material evidence presently unavailable and/or the names and addresses of unavailable persons or other witnesses. A continuance will be granted only upon a showing by the Presenting Officer that he/she has exercised due diligence in his/her attempt to secure the evidence and/or attendance of witnesses. If a proper showing of due diligence is not made, and the preliminary hearing is not held within the time period required in paragraph (b), the petition must be dismissed with prejudice, unless the parties have agreed to an Informal Adjustment Conference. If a continuance is granted, the preliminary hearing must be held within ten (10) days from the date the petition was filed, if the child was taken into custody, or within twenty (20) days, if a child is not in custody.

SPOTTED TAIL V. SPOTTED TAIL

Rosebud Tribe Court of Appeals*

Before Pommersheim, Amiotte and Roubideaux, Justices

Background

On May 4, 1988, plaintiff/appellee, Dennis Spotted Tail, filed an action for divorce against the defendant/appellant, Brenda Dubray Spotted Tail, in the Rosebud Sioux Tribal Court. On September 20, 1988, the maternal grandmother, Pauline Big Crow, filed a motion to intervene. The trial was held on October 13, 1988, in which both parties were represented by counsel. As part of the trial, the maternal grandmother's motion to intervene was denied. At the conclusion of the trial, the court granted the parties a divorce based on irreconcilable differences and reserved a ruling on the custody of the children.

On November 18, 1988, the court entered its findings of fact and conclusion of law and its decree of divorce. That order granted legal custody of the parties' three minor children, [J.S.T.], date of birth, February 19, 1982, [S.S.T.], date of birth, December 2, 1983, and [S.S.T.], date of birth, July 22, 1986, to the plaintiff/appellee, Dennis Spotted Tail. A notice of appeal was filed on December 1, 1988.

Analysis

The sole issues raised on appeal relate the sufficiency of the evidence and whether the award of custody of the three minor children to the appellee was in the best interests of the children. It is beyond dispute that the applicable tribal court standard for the determination of the custody of a minor child is the best interest of the child. . . .

---

* Rosebud Tribe Court of Appeals, *Spotted Tail v. Spotted Tail*, 19 Indian Law Reporter 6032 (1989).

In awarding custody of minors, the trial court must be guided by what appears from all the facts and circumstances to be the best interest of the child's temporal, mental, and moral welfare. . . . Although the trial court is accorded broad discretionary powers in awarding custody of the minor children, that discretion is not uncontrolled, it must have a sound and substantial basis in the testimony. . . .

In the present case, the record is essentially devoid of evidence relating to what is in the best interests of the children, but is, instead, replete with evidence and accusations concerning the alcohol problems and other alleged "immoral" conduct of the respective parties. Such an inquiry in which the parties concentrate on demeaning each other's actions misses the critical point, namely that it is the trial court's job to determine what is truly in the best interests of the children. . . . The court's primary consideration when awarding custody is the best interest of the children and not the shortcomings of the parents. . . . Given the misdirected inquiry at the trial court, there is necessarily insufficient evidence to support its award of custody.

Therefore the decision of the trial court is reversed and remanded and the trial court is directed to hold an evidentiary hearing and to develop a record that supports an award of custody that comports with the standard of the best interests of the children. In order to insure this result, the court notes the following as reasonable to frame and to guide the trial court's considerations:

1. The trial court, on its own order if necessary, must insure that testimony and evidence is presented from professional and disinterested persons such as teachers, counselors, or social workers (including, for example, a potential home study conducted by the Tribal Department of Social Services).
2. The trial court should also authorize the receipt of testimony from neighbors and members of the extended family, particularly, Ms. Pauline Big Crow, the maternal grandmother. It is also noted that it is well within the framework of Lakota tradition and custom that placement be made, if appropriate, with a member of the extended family, particularly when that individual has provided substantial care and nurture to any of the children.

These guidelines are meant to be suggestive rather than exhaustive, as the court has full confidence in the expertise of the trial court to solicit and to obtain all the necessary and pertinent evidence.

It is so ordered.

ROBERT BOOZER V. DARLENE WILDER ET AL.

Confederated Tribes of the Colville Reservation Court of Appeals[*]

Before Dupris, Chief Justice; Nelson and Pascal, Justices

The Appellees, maternal grandparents of K.W.B. (Minor), a minor, filed a Guardianship Petition for Minor on June 4, 2003 upon the untimely death of Minor's mother, Mawe We-Ta-Lo Wilder-Boozer (Wilder-Boozer). At the time of her death, Wilder-Boozer and Appellant Robert Boozer (Appellant) had a pending dissolution proceeding before the tribal court, including custody issues regarding Minor. Minor is, as was her mother, a member of the Colville Tribes. Appellant is a non-Indian resident of the State of Georgia.

Between June 2003, when Appellees filed their Guardianship Petition, and March 2006, when the trial court issued its final order, several hearings were held regarding the custody of Minor. Appellant, at one point, filed a Habeas Corpus proceeding in federal district court seeking the return of Minor. The trial court entered its final order March 31, 2006, which is the subject of this appeal.

In its final Order the trial court found that Mr. Boozer, the father of Minor, was a fit parent and granted him custody, and dismissed the guardianship petition. In the same order the trial judge entered orders, *inter alia*, restricting Appellant's ability to remove Minor from the Colville Reservation; granting grandparent visitation to Appellees; and directing Appellant to raise Minor as Catholic. At the Initial Hearing, Appellant stipulated to all the findings of fact. He appeals these last three (3) orders, asserting the trial court lacked personal and subject matter jurisdiction to enter the orders, and violated Appellant's due process rights.

The Colville Tribes, through its legal counsel, Office of Reservation Attorneys, moved to be allowed to file an amicus brief; the motion was granted. In its Brief of Amicus Curiae the Tribes take the position that the trial judge applied the guardianship laws erroneously; the Tribes also take the position the visitation orders regarding the grandparents/Appellees should be upheld. Appellant objects to those portions of the amicus brief addressing visitation rights of Appellees. Appellees assert, through analogy,

---

[*] Confederated Tribes of the Colville Reservation Court of Appeals, *Robert Boozer v. Darlene Wilder et al.*, 34 Indian Law Reporter 6023 (2007).

that the intents and purposes of the Indian Child Welfare Act apply to this case, and to prevent manifest injustice, the trial court orders challenged should stand.

We find that the trial court, having proper jurisdiction over the parties, did exceed its subject matter jurisdiction. Based on the reasoning below we reverse those portions of the trial court's orders which exceed its jurisdiction, and remand for an order consistent with our rulings. . . .

Issue: Did the trial court, after finding Appellant a fit parent and dismissing the Guardianship Petition of Appellees, have jurisdiction under the Indian Child Welfare Act to enter the orders regarding grandparent visitation, placement and how the child should be reared? . . .

Discussion: The biggest problem underlying the trial court's actions in this case are caused by the trial judge not having a thorough understanding of what type of proceeding was before her throughout the term of the case. It started out as a dissolution and custody between the parents. Personal and subject matter jurisdiction existed with the trial court for this action. Once the mother passed away, there was no legal basis for the dissolution and custody action.

At the mother's death, the maternal grandparents filed a Petition for Guardianship and sought a temporary order restricting the father from taking Minor into his custody. The temporary order was granted. . . .

Appellant asserts after the trial court found him to be a fit parent and dismissed the guardianship petition it lost jurisdiction over him. He is not a Colville member, and he resides off the Colville Reservation. Appellees assert ICWA protects the best interests of the child, and therefore, its standards should apply herein, including continuing jurisdiction to enter the orders appealed in this case.

A review of the laws and facts support the trial court's finding of subject matter jurisdiction over the guardianship herein. The subject of the guardianship, Minor, is a member of the Tribes, and is a minor. The Guardianship Code is not clear regarding when one can seek a guardianship over a minor when there is a parent available. The Tribes maintains the Guardianship Code is "primarily designed to accommodate who have no parents available, either through unfitness, or other inability to care for the child, or through the death of the natural parents. The record shows the trial judge reviewed the evidence for fitness of the remaining parent, Appellant herein.

Guardianships are third-party actions affecting custody over a minor. The ICWA provides for exclusive jurisdiction to the Tribes in third-party custody actions over Indian children. As the federal court recognizes, our Courts have jurisdiction over this matter as long as there is a question of the "fitness" of Appellant as a parent, even when he is not a tribal member, nor a resident of the Reservation. This is the extent to which the ICWA applies to this case. . . .

It is important for the trial court to consider only those matters properly before it. In this case, the maternal grandparents stepped in after their daughter's death and sought guardianship of their granddaughter. The Guardianship Code directs the trial court to consider whether, in this case, Appellant was not a fit parent/guardian. It does not allow for grandparent visitation if the parent is found fit, which Appellees could have filed a Petition for, but did not. It does not provide for a continuing jurisdiction over the way the fit parent raises his child, including what religious instruction must be given, or where the child can live.

We understand the cultural ramifications of our findings here. There is no question it can take Minor away from her Reservation and remaining Indian family. In our Courts we walk a fine line, however. It is not the role of the Judges or Justices to enter a judgment solely to protect a child's "Indianness." Minor has two parents, one Indian and one not. Nothing in our traditions and customs would support that one culture is better for a child than the other. She is a child of both. Nothing precludes Appellant from raising Minor to know of both her heritages. It is the role of a parent to make that decision, not the Court systems. It appears from the record that the trial judge used "culture" as a super-factor in her analysis as the one factor that trumped a fit parent's right to child. . . .

It is so ordered that the orders of the trial court imposing grandparent visitation, restricting Appellant from removing Minor from the Reservation area, and requiring Appellant to raise Minor in the Catholic faith are reversed, and this matter is remanded to the trial court for Orders consistent with this Opinion.

Questions

1. Describe the Binojeeuk Commission as provided for in the Little River Band Tribal Code. Do you think this is a good model for providing culturally appropriate responses to child welfare cases?

2. What should happen in cases in which a parent is unable to care for a child? Should a tribal court grant custody to grandparents? What if the parent later is able to care for the child again?

3. In *Spotted Tail v. Spotted Tail*, why did the Rosebud Sioux Tribal Court of Appeals return the case to the trial court? Do you agree with the decision?
4. What do you think "best interests of the child" means? How do you think a tribal court judge should decide custody cases?
5. In *Boozer v. Wilder*, the Colville appellate court found that the non-Indian father's rights took precedent over the Indian grandparent's rights. Is this consistent with ICWA? Does ICWA necessarily apply in tribal courts? Does it apply when there is a biological parent able to care for the child?

In Your Community

1. Review the current child custody laws in your community. Does your tribal code include recognition of the role of extended family members in a child's life?
2. In your community, what role do grandparents and other extended family members play in the life of a child? Do you think it is important for these relationships to be acknowledged by tribal laws?

Glossary

Acrimony: Harsh words, manner, or disposition.

Amicus Curiae: (Latin for "Friend of the Court.") A third party (not directly involved in the lawsuit) providing information to a court to assist the court in reaching a conclusion.

Habeas Corpus: (Latin for "You shall have the body.") A legal action filed to protect a person from unlawful detention.

Presumptive: May be inferred.

Suggested Further Reading

Carole E. Goldberg-Ambrose, *Heeding the "Voice" of Tribal Law in Indian Child Welfare Proceedings*, 7 Law & Anthropology 1–26 (1994).
Patrice H. Kunesh, *Borders beyond Borders: Protecting Essential Tribal Relations off Reservation under the Indian Child Welfare Act*, 42 New England Law Review 15 (2007).
C. L. M. Lujan et al., *Profile of Abused and Neglected American Indian Children in the Southwest*, Child Abuse and Neglect 13 (1989).
Kelly Stoner & Richard A. Orona, *Full Faith and Credit, Comity, or Federal Mandate? A Path That Leads to Recognition and Enforcement of Tribal Court Orders, Tribal Protection Orders, and Tribal Court Custody Orders*, 34 New Mexico Law Review 381 (2004).
Michelle Zehnder, *Who Should Protect the Native American Child? A Philosophical Debate*

between the Rights of the Individual versus the Rights of the Indian Tribe, 22 William Mitchell Law Review 903 (1996).

Note

1. Russel Lawrence Barsh, *Putting the Tribe in Tribal Courts: Possible? Desirable?* 8 Kansas Journal of Law & Public Policy 74 (1999).

CHAPTER 18

Introducing Indian Civil Rights

W HEN MOST citizens of the United States think of the U.S. Constitution today, what probably first comes to their minds are some of the protections listed in the first ten amendments, known as the Bill of Rights, as well as other important amendments such as the Thirteenth, Fourteenth, and Fifteenth. The freedoms of speech, assembly, and religious expression and the rights to equal treatment under the law, to a fair trial, and to vote are often the civil rights that U.S. citizens will tell you they are either exercising or fighting for when they are participating in political activities, protesting the actions of elected officials, or appealing the judicial decisions of federal or state courts. At the time of their writing, these amendments constituted some of the most unique principles of government and limitations of governmental power ever seen. It is no surprise, then, that the Bill of Rights and Thirteenth, Fourteenth, and Fifteenth Amendments stand as some of the defining characteristics of government in the United States as distinct from other political systems, both past and present. Indeed, as we discussed in chapter 1, they stand for some of the defining characteristics of the American social identity as well.

It is this same distinctiveness that leads members of many American Indian tribal nations today to have mixed feelings about the Bill of Rights. Tribes have their own political histories and traditions that predate the arrival of Europeans in North America, their colonial rule over tribes, and the passage of the U.S. Constitution and its amendments. Tribal sovereignty existed

242

prior to the creation of the United States, and Indian tribes never agreed to the terms of the Constitution and Bill of Rights. These facts lead some tribal members to the conclusion that to accept those documents as controlling their political activities would be to allow the imposition of foreign principles of government and limitations on their sovereign power.

Furthermore, some scholars and tribal members argue that imposing the U.S. Bill of Rights on tribal governments poses an even more fundamental threat to tribal sovereignty than the curtailing of contemporary tribal jurisdiction. They fear that such an application would strike a blow to the very heart of tribal life and law.

What is it they fear? Consider the amount of time spent in this text discussing the centrality of kinship to the expression and exercise of legal norms, structures, and practices for most tribal nations. We have described how inherent to the biological and ceremonial relations among tribal members the variety of duties and obligations that relatives owe each other is. The prominence that these relations and their duties and obligations have in the lives of most tribal nations has led many scholars to describe tribal life as fundamentally *communitarian*. Communitarian societies are those communities where social relations and the duties people owe to each other define group life and where individuals are understood primarily in terms of the roles they play in those relations.

These societies are contrasted to *individualistic* societies, where group life is defined in terms of the rights and expectations individuals have independent of their biological or ceremonial connections to others. Thus, in individualistic societies, social relations are understood either as the product of private choices made by these individuals or as necessary (but minimal) limitations placed on the rights and expectations of these individuals by that society. Anglo-American society and its laws—especially the Bill of Rights—are considered the prime example of an individualistic social group and its rules. Mohawk scholar Taiaiake Alfred explains:

> The concept of "rights," especially in the common Western sense, leads nowhere for indigenous peoples because it alienates the individual from the group. By contrast, the tension between individual and collective rights is a mainstay of discussions about justice in Western societies, which conceive of rights only in the contest of a sovereign political authority because the law that defines and protects them depends on the existence of a single sovereign. There can indeed be acknowledgement of diversity, and even concessions to real difference, but to gain access to this tolerance it is necessary to be part of the community ruled by the sovereign state.[1]

Many legal scholars and tribal members have emphasized not only the difference between the individualism of U.S. society (and its rights-based laws) and the communalism of tribal nations, but also that the two systems are incompatible. For them, the norms of tribal life that dictate that a person has a duty (because of the family or clan in which they were born) to share certain resources, take care of certain property and people, and occupy certain political positions conflict fundamentally with the Anglo-American norms that hold that individuals have the right to choose with whom they will share, whom they will care for, and what they will make of their lives.

Other tribal members and scholars of tribal law suggest that contrasting tribal communalism to Anglo-American individualism may not give an entirely accurate depiction of tribal life and legal systems. It is undoubtedly true that kinship is much more at the center of the norms, structures, and practices of the tribal nation than it is to U.S. social structure and organization. It is also true that the ways in which individualism is expressed and emphasized in Anglo-American society may not be matched in the beliefs and practices of many tribal nations. But is it fair to say that tribal nations generally place little or no value on the rights of individuals? Oren R. Lyons (Onondaga) asserts that free speech has always been a necessary component of traditional governance: "It was always noted that Indians generally (and the Haudenosaunee were no exception) enjoyed free speech. Indeed, Indian decision-making processes at the local level required the free input of information and advice for these processes to work at all."[2]

We have cautioned before about making statements that generalize too much about tribal nations. A generalization about the lack of individualism in tribes is no exception to this rule. In fact, there are examples of legal principles and practices from tribal nations all across Indian Country that recognize the specialness of the individual and provide measures for their support and protection from unfair group pressure. These more individualistic legal norms, structures, and practices emerge both from the legal heritages of many of these tribes as well as from more contemporary changes to tribal societies and governance, resulting from Anglo-American sociocultural influence and colonial imposition.

For example, among Pueblo groups like the Hopi and Zuni, there is a strong belief that adult individuals are ultimately free to act as they see fit and are not to be judged by other humans for their actions. Thus, even though the obligations and duties toward one's kin are emphasized as necessary for the proper order of Hopi or Zuni society, at the same time it is often said that individuals cannot be forced into following these norms. Rather, there are spiritual forces at work in the world that will work on the individual to fix their improper behavior. In Hopi, this respect for individual freedom is expressed by the phrase "*Pi um pi*"—"Really, it's [up to] you." This is sometimes said by a person advising another to change his behavior because he had been acting contrary to their duties and obligations to others.

Other tribal nations, like the Coast Salish communities of the Puget Sound, place a strong emphasis on the private, sacred relationship that every individual has with a spiritual guardian. This relationship bestows special talents and "gifts" on the individual—talents that are necessary for their success in the world and, as such, should be respected and encouraged. At the same time, extended family relations exert a strong influence on tribal life and law. People recognize that they are expected to share with, care for, and protect the interests of their kin.

Furthermore, as described throughout this text, tribal communities have not remained unaffected or uninfluenced by the Anglo-American social and governmental norms, structures, and practices imposed on them. After years of federal efforts at forced assimilation, many members of tribal communities have adopted Anglo-American notions of individual rights and come to expect protections of those rights from their tribal governments. Though these rights often go hand in hand with tribal notions of individual respect, at other times the demand made by tribal members for such rights has pitted tribal members against each other. The basic principle of Anglo-American individualism—that all people should be treated equally by their government—has, on occasion, come into direct conflict with tribal communitarian values that recognize that, while individuals should all be respected, people often fulfill different roles in society in a manner that prohibits their equal treatment. These situations have led to bitter disputes, in which some tribal members accuse tribal leaders of abuse of office, corruption, and discrimination, while those leaders respond that they are merely following their traditional and customary duties.

For example, it was precisely these issues that were at the heart of one of the more controversial Supreme Court cases concerning federal Indian law in recent years, *Santa Clara Pueblo v. Martinez*, 436 U.S. 49 (1978). We will read more about the *Martinez* case later, but basically it involved a dispute between a tribal member who applied to enroll her child (whose father was a nonmember) in the tribe, but was rejected because tribal enrollment restrictions required that only children whose fathers were tribal members could be enrolled. The woman claimed that the rule was a form of gender discrimination that violated her equal rights. The tribe claimed that the rule followed an important part of their tribal traditions and was central to their sovereign powers. How this case was ultimately decided (in favor of the tribe), and why, has been a controversial topic among not only tribal legal scholars but also scholars of feminism, race relations, and the law.

Consequently, the degree to which these and many other tribal nations place a value in respecting both individuals and their rights, along with the duties and obligations among kin groups, suggests that a simple opposition cannot be drawn between Anglo-American and tribal legal systems.

This is not to say, however, that the peoples who recognize the role that individualism plays in tribal life are any less opposed to the application of the U.S. Bill of Rights to their tribal operations. For many tribal members, respecting individuals' rights involves important principles already recognized in the operation of their tribal laws in a manner sensitive to their unique cultural contexts. For people who think this way, there is no need to be held subject to the Bill of Rights, and the oversight of U.S. federal review that would come with it would unnecessarily intrude on a tribal legal system that already works well enough for its members.

Talton v. Mayes and the Application of the Bill of Rights to Indian Tribes

The history of U.S. federal application of the Bill of Rights and its principles to Indian tribes prior to 1968 was generally consistent with the belief that, because tribal sovereignty predates the Constitution, the Bill of Rights did not impose limitations on tribal government practices. This is most clearly embodied in the Supreme Court's decision in *Talton v. Mayes*, 163 U.S. 376 (1895), which you will recall from chapter 6. The Court in this case held that the limits on government expressed in the Constitution do *not* apply to tribal governments and their court systems. This decision did not mean that tribes had no limitations—only that they could not be required to follow the same requirements in the Constitution that the U.S. government or state governments have to follow.

The U.S. Supreme Court held that Indian tribes are "distinct, independent political communities." As such, they are not like states, and they are not arms of the federal government. "The powers of local self-government enjoyed by the Cherokee Nation existed prior to the Constitution," the Court held, and therefore these powers are not subject to the limitations on government contained in the Fifth Amendment. Talton was eventually executed pursuant to a lawful order of the Cherokee Nation Court.

The *Talton v. Mayes* decision had an impact on the legal relationship between Indian tribes and the state and federal governments. The case held that those provisions of the U.S. Constitution that were designed to protect individual liberties and property rights generally did not apply to actions of Indian governments. It confirmed that Indian tribes are recognized governmental institutions that stand apart from the political divisions of the federal and state governments.

More than sixty years after the *Talton* decision, a federal court of appeals heard *Native American Church v. Navajo Tribal Council*, 272 F.2d 131 (10th Cir. 1959), which concerned the criminalization of peyote by the Navajo Nation. The Native American Church claimed that the action of the Navajo Nation violated the right to free exercise of religion as guaranteed in the U.S. Constitution. In upholding the power of the Navajo government to take such action, the federal court stated that the U.S. Constitution "is binding upon Indian nations only where it expressly binds them, or is made binding by treaty or some act of Congress."

The *Talton v. Mayes* decision was consistent with the general principle of federal Indian law and policy that, unless limited by congressional action (for example, by a treaty or other legislation, such as the Major Crimes Act), tribes retained their sovereignty over internal affairs and activities conducted on their tribal lands and/or involving tribal members. The understanding that the Bill of Rights did not apply to tribes continued up through the 1960s, as can be seen in many federal court decisions such as *Toledo v. Pueblo De Jemez*, 119 F.Supp. 429 (D.N.M. 1954) and *Barta v. Oglala Sioux Tribe*, 259 F.2d 553 (8th Cir. 1958).

In the next few chapters, we will explore the application of civil rights laws in tribal courts. Below, you will find the U.S. Constitution's amendments that define the civil rights recognized in American courts.

AMENDMENTS TO THE U.S. CONSTITUTION

First Amendment

Congress shall make no law respecting an establishment of religion, or prohibiting the free exercise thereof, or abridging the freedom of speech, or of the press; or the right of the people peaceably to assemble, and to petition the Government for a redress of grievances.

Second Amendment

A well-regulated Militia, being necessary to the security of a free State, the right of the people to keep and bear Arms, shall not be infringed.

Third Amendment

No Soldier shall, in time of peace be quartered in any house, without the consent of the Owner, nor in time of war, but in a manner prescribed by law.

Fourth Amendment

The right of the people to be secure in their persons, houses, papers, and effects against unreasonable searches and seizures, shall not be violated, and no Warrants shall issue, but upon probable cause supported by Oath or affirmation, and particularly describing the place to be searched, and the persons or things to be seized.

Fifth Amendment

No person shall be held to answer for a capital, or otherwise infamous crime, unless on a presentment or indictment of a Grand Jury, except in cases arising in the land or naval forces, or in the Militia, when in actual service in time of War or public danger; nor shall any person be subject for the same offense to be twice put in Jeopardy of life or limb; nor shall be compelled in any criminal case to be a witness against himself, nor be deprived of life, liberty, or property, without due process of law; nor shall private property be taken for public use, without just compensation.

Sixth Amendment

In all criminal prosecutions, the accused shall enjoy the right to a speedy and public trial, by an impartial jury of the State and district wherein the crime shall have been committed, which district shall have been previously ascertained by law, and to be informed of the nature and cause of the accusation; to have compulsory process for obtaining witnesses in his favor, and to have the Assistance of Counsel for his defense.

Seventh Amendment

In Suits at common law, where the value in controversy shall exceed twenty dollars, the right of trial by jury shall be preserved, and no fact tried by a jury, shall be otherwise re-examined in any Court of the United States, than according to the rules of common law.

Eighth Amendment

Excessive bail shall not be required, nor excessive fines imposed, nor cruel and unusual punishments inflicted.

Thirteenth Amendment

Section 1.

Neither slavery nor involuntary servitude, except as a punishment for crime whereof the party shall have been duly convicted, shall exist within the United States, or any place subject to their jurisdiction.

Section 2.

Congress shall have power to enforce this article by appropriate legislation.

Fourteenth Amendment

Section 1.

All persons born or naturalized in the United States, and subject to the jurisdiction thereof, are citizens of the United States and of the State wherein they reside. No State shall make or enforce any law which shall abridge the privileges or immunities of citizens of the United States; nor shall any State deprive any person of life, liberty, or property, without due process of law; nor deny to any person within its jurisdiction the equal protection of the laws.

Section 2.

Representatives shall be apportioned among the several States according to their respective numbers, counting the whole number of persons in each State, excluding Indians not taxed. But when the right to vote at any election for the choice of President and Vice-president of the United States, Representatives in Congress, the Executive and Judicial officers of a State, or the members of the Legislature thereof, is denied to any of the male inhabitants of such State, being twenty-one years of age, and citizens of the United States, or in any way abridged, except for participation in rebellion, or another crime, the basis of representation therein shall be reduced in the proportion which the number of such male citizens shall bear to the whole number of male citizens twenty-one years of age in such State.

Fifteenth Amendment

Section 1.

The right of citizens of the United States to vote shall not be denied or abridged by the United States or by any State on the account of race, color, or previous condition of servitude.

Section 2.

The Congress shall have the power to enforce this article by appropriate legislation.

Nineteenth Amendment

The right of citizens of the United States to vote shall not be denied or abridged by the United States or by any state on account of sex. Congress shall have power to enforce this article by appropriate legislation.

Questions

1. Do you think tribal governments should be required to follow the legal principles in the U.S. Constitution's Bill of Rights?
2. Imagine a tribal council passes a resolution saying that tribal members will be thrown out of public council meetings (or disenrolled) if they say anything bad about the council. Should these members be able to fight this law in tribal court saying it violates their First Amendment right to freedom of speech? Is this argument necessary?
3. Now suppose a tribal council made up of elders passes a law saying that tribal members will be thrown out if they say anything negative about the council during their sacred ceremonies—for example (depending on the tribe), during events held in a sweat lodge or a kiva. If some tribal members enter the sweat lodge or kiva during one of these ceremonies and begin to complain that the council is not handling tribal money properly and are thrown out, should these members be able to fight this action in tribal court as a violation of their First Amendment right to freedom of speech? Does someone have a free speech right to interrupt a church service?
4. Is there another way you see to fight the Navajo government's decision to outlaw the Native American Church's ceremonies on the reservation without basing your argument on the Navajo government being subject

to the Bill of Rights and the Constitution? What about the possibility of using the tribe's customs and traditions to find this kind of protection?

In Your Community

1. Do your tribal traditions recognize any values similar to the individual rights protected in the Indian Civil Rights Act or the U.S. Bill of Rights? Does your tribe have a Tribal Bill of Rights, or some similar legislation?
2. Do you think that your tribal government should be required to follow the legal principles in the Bill of Rights? If not, how should the rights of tribal members be protected?

Glossary

Communitarian: Of or relating to social organization in small cooperative, partially collectivist communities.

Discrimination: The act of exposing or discerning differences among individuals, usually used in a negative sense.

Egalitarian: Promoting a belief in human equality with respect to social, political, and economic rights and privileges.

Individualistic: Relating to the character of persons as individuals rather than as members of a community.

Militia: A part of the organized armed forces of a country, liable to call-up only in an emergency.

Petition for habeas corpus: A request to the court for a judicial order requiring someone who is holding a person to bring that person to court.

Transgress: To violate a law, command, or duty.

Suggested Further Reading

Carole Goldberg, *Individual Rights and Tribal Revitalization*, 35 Arizona State Law Journal 889 (2003).

Donald Grinde Jr. & Bruce E. Johansen, eds., *Exemplar of Liberty: Native America and the Evolution of Democracy* (1991).

Bruce E. Johansen, *Forgotten Founders: How the American Indian Helped Shape Democracy* (1982).

Bruce Miller, *The Individual, the Collective, and Tribal Codes*, 21 American Indian Culture & Research Journal 107 (1997).

John R. Wunder, *"Retained by the People": A History of American Indians and the Bill of Rights* (1994).

Notes

1. Taiaiake Alfred, *Peace Power Righteousness: An Indigenous Manifesto* 140 (1999).

2. Oren R. Lyons, *American Indian in the Past*, in *Exiled in the Land of the Free: Democracy, Indian Nations, and the U.S. Constitution* 32 (1992).

CHAPTER 19

The Indian Civil Rights Act of 1968

D URING THE 1960s, U.S. governmental officials began to express concerns with what they saw as a lack of tribal legal protections for individual rights. The result of this concern was the Indian Civil Rights Act (ICRA) of 1968, 25 U.S.C. 1301–3.

Rising concerns about abuses of rights and lack of equal treatment of American minority groups gripped the political consciousness of non-Indians in the United States throughout the 1960s. By the mid-1960s, these concerns began to influence politics in Indian communities as well. The influences came from different sources, some Indian and some non-Indian. The different motivations behind them suggest that the mixed feelings tribal members had toward the application of federal civil rights legislation to tribal governments were well founded.

The earliest American Indian expressions of civil rights concerns were targeted not at tribal governments but at ongoing abuses by federal and state non-Indian entities. Groups like the National Indian Youth Council (NIYC) and the American Indian Movement (AIM) emerged to challenge the treatment of Indian communities and Indian individuals by federal agencies such as the Bureau of Indian Affairs, as well as more localized problems like police brutality against Indians living in Minneapolis. Even later on, when AIM and other groups would take stands against tribal government corruption, including the events leading up to the Wounded Knee Incident in 1973, they would see the fight as one with tribal leaderships that were actually just puppets of federal authorities. In this respect, the civil rights struggle in which many Indians were engaged was mainly one concerning abuses of Indian rights by non-Indian powers in the United States. It was many of these same issues that Indians brought before Congress when the question of their civil rights was first raised in the Senate in the mid-1960s.

The Indian rights concerns that many federal lawmakers had, however, were of a different sort. For them, the question was much more about the lack of civil rights protections against abuses by tribal rather than federal and state governments. Members of Congress expressed concern that tribal governments were not bound by the Bill of Rights and that they could limit the rights and freedoms of people under tribal jurisdiction without any remedy. They were especially concerned that criminal defendants could be held in tribal jails indefinitely without any promise of a speedy and fair trial by a jury—rights promised to all American citizens in state and federal court.

It was these issues, and not the Indian concerns of rights violations by federal and state authorities, that were addressed in the Indian Civil Rights Act of 1968. It is not entirely surprising, then, that in the congressional hearings leading up to the passage of the ICRA, many Indians representing tribes across Indian Country objected to the terms of the ICRA and its application to their tribal governments. The basic complaint was that the ICRA was another intrusion on tribal sovereignty. Even those who recognized the value of protecting individuals' civil rights from abuse by tribal governments nonetheless felt that tribal governments already had those protections in place and did not need more federal law telling them how they should run their own society.

Lawmakers in Congress did not entirely ignore the tribal sovereignty concerns of the tribal members who testified before them. Thus, the ICRA does not incorporate all of the limitations included in the U.S. Bill of Rights. For example, the clause in the First Amendment that prohibits U.S. federal and state governments from passing any laws about religion (commonly known as the "Establishment Clause") was not included in the ICRA out of respect for the religious-based governments of the Pueblo tribes of the southwest. These and other such modifications were made before the Act's final passage.

THE INDIAN CIVIL RIGHTS ACT OF 1968, 25 U.S.C. 1301–3

1301. Definitions

For purposes of this subchapter, the term

1. "Indian tribe" means any tribe, band, or other group of Indians subject to the jurisdiction of the United States and recognized as possessing powers of self-government;
2. "powers of self-government" means and includes all governmental powers possessed by an Indian tribe, executive, legislative, and judicial, and all offices, bodies, and tribunals by and through which they are executed, including courts of Indian offenses; and means the inherent power of Indian tribes, hereby recognized and affirmed, to exercise criminal jurisdiction over all Indians;
3. "Indian court" means any Indian tribal court or court of Indian offense; and
4. "Indian" means any person who would be subject to the jurisdiction of the United States as an Indian under section 1153, title 19, United States Code, if that person were to commit an offense listed in that section in Indian country to which that section applies.

1302. Constitutional Rights

No Indian tribe in exercising powers of self-government shall

1. make or enforce any law prohibiting the free exercise of religion, or abridging the freedom of speech, or of the press, or the right of the people peaceably to assemble and to petition for a redress of grievances;
2. violate the right of the people to be secure in their persons, houses, papers, and effects against unreasonable search and seizures, nor issue warrants, but upon probable cause, supported by oath or affirmation, and particularly describing the place to be searched and the person or thing to be seized;
3. subject any person for the same offense to be twice put in jeopardy;
4. compel any person in any criminal case to be a witness against himself;
5. take any property for a public use without just compensation;

6. deny to any person in a criminal proceeding the right to a speedy and public trial, to be informed of the nature and cause of the accusation, to be confronted with the witnesses against him, to have compulsory process for obtaining witnesses in his favor, and at his own expense to have the assistance of counsel for his defense;

7. require excessive bail, impose excessive fines, inflict cruel and unusual punishments, and in no event impose for conviction of any one offense any penalty or punishment greater than imprisonment for a term of one year or a fine of $5,000 or both;

8. deny to any person within its jurisdiction the equal protection of its laws or deprive any person of liberty or property without due process of law;

9. pass any bill of attainder or ex post facto law; or

10. deny to any person accused of an offense punishable by imprisonment the right, upon request, to a trial by jury of not less than six persons.

1303. Habeas Corpus

The privilege of the writ of habeas corpus shall be available to any person, in a court of the United States, to test the legality of his detention by order of an Indian tribe.

Since its enactment in 1968, the ICRA has been amended twice. It was first amended in 1986 to increase the sentencing limitations in section 1302(7). This provision originally limited tribes' ability to impose sentences for a single offense to no greater than six months' imprisonment or a fine of $500 or both. In 1986, this provision was amended (as part of a federal drug and alcohol prevention act) to the current limits of one year's imprisonment, a fine of $5,000, or both.

The ICRA was amended again in 1991 in order to overturn the U.S. Supreme Court decision in *Duro v. Reina*, 495 U.S. 676 (1990). The *Duro* decision held that tribal courts did not have criminal jurisdiction over nonmember Indians. The U.S. Congress overturned the *Duro* decision (in the so-called Congressional *Duro*-Fix) by adding "and means the inherent power of Indian tribes, hereby recognized and affirmed, to exercise criminal jurisdiction over all Indians" to the definition of "powers of self-government." This Congressional *Duro*-Fix restored tribal court criminal jurisdiction over all Indians (members and nonmembers), and was upheld by the U.S. Supreme Court in *United States v. Lara* in 2004, as explained in chapter 12.

Questions

1. Do you agree that the ICRA was needed in 1968? Do you think that tribal governments were able to protect civil rights without federal intrusion?
2. How do the provisions of the ICRA differ from the provisions of the Bill of Rights? Do you think that the ICRA provisions are different enough from the Bill of Rights to allow tribal governments to maintain sovereignty?

In Your Community

1. In your opinion, do the norms, structures, and practices embodied in your tribe's customs and traditions protect people's "civil rights"? Are there some customs and traditions of your tribe or nation that conflict with the "civil rights" outlined in the ICRA? Explain your answer and give examples, if possible.
2. Imagine you have a friend who is a reporter for the tribal newspaper. Suppose your friend has recently written an article that criticizes the tribal chairman for agreeing to allow non-Indian logging on the reservation. Now imagine that your friend has recently been fired from his job and kicked off the reservation by the tribal council because of the article he wrote.
   a. What ICRA provision would provide your friend with a way to challenge his exclusion from the reservation?
   b. Can you think how the norms or practices of your tribe's customs and traditions might also give your friend a way to challenge his exclusion from the reservation?
   c. Are there customs and traditions in your tribe that the tribal chairman could use to explain and justify his decision to exclude the reporter?

Glossary

Bill of attainder: A legislative act pronouncing a person guilty without a trial and sentencing the person to death.

Ex post facto: (Latin for "After the fact.") An ex post facto law attempts to make an action a crime even though it was not against the law at the time it was committed.

Habeas corpus: A judicial order to someone holding a person to bring that person to court.

Suggested Further Reading

Donald Burnett, *An Historical Analysis of the 1968 Indian Civil Rights Act*, 9 Harvard Journal on Legislation 557 (1972).

Casey Douma, *Fortieth Anniversary of the Indian Civil Rights Act: Finding a Way Back to Indigenous Justice*, 55 Federal Lawyer 34 (2008).

Joseph de Raismes, *The Indian Civil Rights Act of 1968 and the Pursuit of Responsible Tribal Self-Government*, 20 South Dakota Law Review 59 (1973).

CHAPTER 20

Affirming Tribal Authority
Santa Clara Pueblo v. Martinez

OR SEVERAL years after its passage, the perception was that the Indian Civil Rights Act (ICRA) gave the federal courts broad powers to hear and decide claims of civil rights violations by tribal governments. This changed dramatically, however, in 1978 with the U.S. Supreme Court decision in *Santa Clara Pueblo v. Martinez*, 439 U.S. 49 (1978).

During the ten-year period from the date of the passage of the ICRA in 1968 to the *Martinez* decision in 1978, federal courts heard approximately eighty cases involving the application of the Act. These cases covered many subjects, including tribal election disputes, reapportionment of voting districts on Indian reservations (evaluating whether tribes were abiding by rules announced in the ICRA that guaranteed an equal right to vote for every member of the tribe—sometimes called "one man, one vote" rule), tribal government employee rights, land-use regulations and condemnation procedures, criminal and civil proceedings in tribal courts, tribal membership and voting, tribal police activities, conduct of tribal council members and council meetings, and standards for enforcing due process of law and equal protection of the law in tribal settings.

Indeed, it was so taken for granted that the ICRA gave federal courts jurisdiction to hear claims of civil rights violations by tribes that the federal courts actually announced rules for interpreting the Act that they expected to be followed in the future. For example, among the rules devised by the courts were the following:

1. While the ICRA is generally patterned after the Bill of Rights, the same language does not necessarily have to be interpreted in the same way.
2. The ICRA does not require that Indians and non-Indians always have to be treated identically by tribal governments; that is, different treatment is permitted and justified in certain circumstances (for example, tribal membership requirements).
3. Tribal customs, traditions, and culture must be considered in interpreting and applying the ICRA.
4. Tribal remedies must first be exhausted before a dispute can be heard in federal court.

It is important to mention that during this same ten-year period, no ICRA cases reached the Supreme Court. As a result, the federal courts were acting in something of a legal vacuum, not knowing if the rules they were devising for interpreting the ICRA would be supported as the authoritative statement of law by the United States' highest court. Indeed, the judges deciding these ICRA cases during this period didn't really know if the Supreme Court would even interpret the ICRA as giving jurisdiction to the federal courts over civil rights claims against tribal governments, though they operated on the presumption that it did. Thus when the Supreme Court did finally decide to hear an ICRA case in 1978—one arising from a claim by a woman who was a member of Santa Clara Pueblo—and when the pueblo raised questions about whether the ICRA did in fact grant jurisdiction to the federal courts over such civil rights claims against tribal courts, many interested parties anxiously awaited the Court's opinion. What follows is a brief discussion of the background facts in the case; an excerpt from the Court's majority opinion, written by Justice Thurgood Marshall; and some analysis we provide of the opinion.

Santa Clara Pueblo v. Martinez, 439 U.S. 49 (1978)

Santa Clara Pueblo is a Tewa-speaking tribal nation located in northern New Mexico. It has about 1,200 members living in it, along with about 150 to 200 non-members. In 1939, the tribal council of the pueblo adopted an ordinance that extended tribal membership to the children of male members who married nonmembers, but denied membership to children of female members who married nonmembers. The tribal nation justified the ordinance on the basis of its patriarchal traditions, along with the economic need to restrict tribal enrollment.

Julia Martinez, a full-blooded member of the Pueblo, married a Navajo. Even though their children were raised in the pueblo, spoke the Tewa language, and continued to live there, they were denied membership in the tribal nation because of the 1939 ordinance. After unsuccessfully attempting to get the pueblo to change the ordinance, Martinez sued the tribal nation and its governor in federal court. She claimed that the ordinance denied her and her children equal protection of the tribal laws as guaranteed by the ICRA.

Among the arguments made by the tribe was that the ICRA did not grant federal courts jurisdiction over tribes with regard to such matters as tribal membership. Though the District Court of New Mexico did find that the ICRA granted the federal courts jurisdiction, it did not find that the pueblo's laws violated the equal protection clause of the ICRA. Martinez appealed, and while once again the Tenth Circuit found that the ICRA granted the federal courts jurisdiction, it held that the pueblo's membership laws *did* violate the ICRA's equal protection clause, and thus found for Martinez.

Notice the fact that both the district and circuit courts, like many federal courts before them, found that the ICRA gave them jurisdiction over civil rights claims against tribal nations. When Santa Clara Pueblo appealed this decision to the U.S. Supreme Court, it was this issue that was at the heart of Justice Marshall's majority opinion and the Court's decision to reverse the holding of the Tenth Circuit.

SANTA CLARA PUEBLO V. MARTINEZ, 436 U.S. 49 (1978)

United States Supreme Court

This case requires us to decide whether a federal court may pass on the validity of an Indian tribe's ordinance denying membership to the children of certain female tribal members.

Petitioner Santa Clara Pueblo is an Indian tribe that has been in existence for over 600 years. Respondents, a female member of the tribe and her daughter, brought suit in federal court against the tribe and its Governor, petitioner Lucario Padilla, seeking declaratory and injunctive relief against enforcement of a tribal ordinance denying membership in the tribe to children of female members who marry outside the tribe, while extending membership to children of male members who marry outside the tribe. Respondents claimed that this rule discriminates on the basis of both sex and ancestry in violation of Title 1 of the Indian Civil Rights Act of 1968 (ICRA), 25 U.S.C.A. 1301–1303 (1970), which provides in relevant part that "[n]o Indian tribe in exercising powers of self-government shall . . . deny to any person within its jurisdiction the equal protection of its laws." Ibid., 1302(8).

Title I of the ICRA does not expressly authorize the bringing of civil actions for declaratory or injunctive relief to enforce its substantive provisions. The threshold issue in this case is thus whether the Act may be interpreted to impliedly authorize such actions, against a tribe or its officers, in the federal courts. For the reasons set forth below, we hold that the Act cannot be so read.

I

Respondent Julia Martinez is a full blooded member of the Santa Clara Pueblo, and resides on the Santa Clara reservation in Northern New Mexico. In 1941 she married a Navajo Indian with whom she has since had several children, including respondent Audrey Martinez. Two years before this marriage, the Pueblo passed the membership ordinance here at issue, which bars the admission of the Martinez children to the tribe because their father is not a Santa Claran. Although the children were raised on the reservation and continue to reside there now that they are adults, as a result of their exclusion from membership they may not vote in tribal elections or hold secular office in the tribe; moreover, they have no right to remain on the reservation in the event of their mother's death, or to inherit their mother's home or her possessory interests in the communal lands. . . .
[Sections 2 and 3 omitted.]

IV

[In analyzing congressional intent behind passage of the ICRA, the Court referred to the general policy of "self-determination" and to other titles of the ICRA that were designed to strengthen tribal courts and tribal government.]

This commitment to the goal of tribal self-determination is demonstrated by the provisions in Title I [of the ICRA] itself. Section 1302, rather than providing in wholesale fashion for the extension of constitutional requirements to tribal governments, as had been initially proposed, selectively incorporated and in some instances modified the safeguards of the Bill of Rights to fit the unique political, cultural, and economic needs of tribal governments. Thus, for example, the statute does not prohibit the establishment of religion, nor does it require jury trials in civil cases, or appointment of counsel for indigents in criminal cases. . . .

Moreover . . . implication of a federal remedy in addition to habeas corpus is not plainly required to give effect to Congress' objective of extending constitutional norms to tribal self-government. Tribal forums are available to vindicate rights created by the ICRA, and 1302 has the substantial and intended effect of changing the law which these forums are obliged to apply. Tribal courts have repeatedly been recognized as appropriate forums for the exclusive adjudication of disputes affecting important personal and property interests of both Indians and non-Indians. See, e.g., *Fisher v. District Court*, 424 U.S. 382 (1976); *Williams v. Lee*, 358 U.S. 217 (1959). See also *Ex parte Crow Dog*, 109 U.S. 556 (1883). Non-judicial tribal institutions have also been recognized as competent law-applying bodies. See *United States v. Mazurie*, 419 U.S. 544 (1975). Under these circumstances, we are reluctant to disturb the balance between the dual statutory objectives which Congress apparently struck in providing only for habeas corpus relief. . . .

Our reluctance is strongly reinforced by the specific legislative history underlying 25 U.S.C.A. 1303. This history, extending over more than three years, indicates that Congress' provision for habeas corpus relief, and nothing more, reflected a considered accommodation of the competing goals of "preventing injustices perpetrated by tribal governments, on the one hand, and, on the other, avoiding undue or precipitous interference in the affairs of the Indian people. . . ."

After considering numerous alternatives for review of tribal convictions, Congress apparently decided that review by way of habeas corpus would adequately protect the individual interests at stake while avoiding unnecessary intrusions on tribal governments. . . .

|G|iven Congress' desire not to intrude needlessly on tribal self-government, it is not surprising that Congress chose at this stage to provide for federal review only in habeas corpus proceedings.

By not exposing tribal officials to the full array of federal remedies available to redress actions of federal and state officials, Congress may also have considered that resolution of statutory issues under 1302, and particularly those issues likely to arise in a civil context, will frequently depend on questions of tribal tradition and custom which tribal forums may be in a better position to evaluate than federal courts. . . .

|E|fforts by the federal judiciary to apply the statutory prohibitions of 1302 in a civil context may substantially interfere with a tribes ability to maintain itself as a culturally and politically distinct entity.

As we have repeatedly emphasized, Congress' authority over Indian matters is extraordinarily broad, and the role of courts in adjusting relations between and among tribes and their members correspondingly restrained. See *Lone Wolf v. Hitchcock*, 187 U.S. 553, 565 (1903). Congress retains authority expressly to authorize civil actions for injunctive or other relief to redress violations of 1302, in the event that the tribes themselves prove deficient in applying and enforcing its substantive provisions. But unless and until Congress makes clear its intention to permit the additional intrusions on tribal sovereignty that adjudication of such actions in a federal forum would represent, we are constrained to find that 1302 does not impliedly authorize actions for declaratory or injunctive relief against either the tribe or its officers.

The judgment of the Court of Appeals is, accordingly,
Reversed.

The critical issue was whether the ICRA prohibits an Indian tribe from setting membership criteria that discriminate against women. For some people, this membership law violated the concept of equal rights for women. Upon closer examination, however, the lawsuit represented a larger question of cultural norms and legal values. The Supreme Court in *Martinez* never actually decided the merits of the case (whether gender discrimination was legal under tribal law). It disposed of the case on a jurisdictional basis—that is, that the ICRA does not give federal courts broad jurisdiction to review tribal government actions in Indian Country. Thus, Martinez's challenge to the tribal ordinance could not go forward in federal court. In reaching this conclusion, the Court noted that Congress had two purposes in mind in enacting the ICRA:

1. Protection of individual civil rights in Indian Country, which it did by prohibiting tribal governments from taking actions that might interfere with individual freedoms; and
2. Encouragement of tribal self-government, which it did by implicitly recognizing the importance of tribal governments on reservations, reaffirming the idea of sovereign immunity as applied to Indian tribes, and giving tribal institutions the principal responsibility for resolving disputes over civil rights.

Recall that the only section of the ICRA that actually mentions a "court of the United States" is section 1303, which gives people held in custody by an Indian tribe a right to go to federal court to challenge that detention. In *Santa Clara Pueblo v. Martinez*, the Supreme Court interpreted the ICRA as not giving the federal court any power to review any complaints of ICRA violations by a tribal government *except* those arising under section 1303 as writ of habeas corpus actions—complaints of unlawful detention raised by individuals being held in tribal custody. The decision held that violations of all the other rights guaranteed under the ICRA, including freedom of speech and equal protection rights, fell under tribal jurisdiction and thus could be brought only in tribal court. The Court ruled that Julia Martinez could not bring her complaint for ICRA violations to federal court because she was not being detained (jailed) by the Pueblo.

This decision is usually seen as a victory for tribal sovereignty and self-determination. However, the facts of the *Santa Clara Pueblo* case raise difficult questions about the equal rights of men and women in this tribe. In this case, a woman wanted her child to be enrolled as a member of her tribe. The tribe, though, allowed children of only male members to enroll, and the child's father was from another tribe.

In 2004, another Santa Clara mother, Ruth Swentzell, expressed her response to the 1978 decision, excerpted below.

TESTIMONY OF A SANTA CLARA WOMAN

*Ruth Swentzell**

I thought long and hard about the *Martinez* case. I wanted my children to be members of Santa Clara, although I had married a non-Indian who I met in college. If the case favored the Martinez family, who I assumed had been encouraged by non-Native people to initiate the lawsuit, I felt that Santa Clara would lose any remnants of itself as a vital, self-determining community. I was relieved to hear the decision. Santa Clara was to retain the ongoing conversation about who is a recognized member of the community. But, more importantly, the Western world was acknowledging a way of life which traditionally honored nurturing and feminine qualities. . . .

When American lawyers became involved with the writing of the 1936 Santa Clara Constitution, which was written mostly by non-pueblo people, a different mentality and approach to life came into the forefront. Opposites in the American world are adversarial. It is one or the other, not both. It is a cultural approach that also acknowledges that the world is in tension, but in the Western world, only one side wins.

---

* Ruth Swentzell, *Testimony of a Santa Clara Woman*, 14 Kansas Journal of Law and Public Policy 97 (2004).

As I have talked with all three of my daughters (34 to 42 years old) and three granddaughters (17, 19 and 20 years old) who are affected by the *Martinez* decision, I hear their pain of being excluded—to some point. My middle daughter, mentioned above, built her house at Santa Clara, participates in Pueblo activities and is honored by the Winter group to which she belongs and at this point, even more than my son who is a full member. She moves through the hills and Pueblo as if she belongs. She assumes that the Pueblo is home and that if there are problems about her being there, they will most certainly come from one member of our extended family who claims the family allotment of land on which she lives. But, this has nothing to do with the tribe. In fact, the rest of the family knows that if the issue goes to Tribal Council, the Council would protect my daughter's right to stay in her house. Yet, she cannot ever "own" the house in a legal sense, but then, nobody else can either. Private ownership of property is still a murky issue, because property is not altogether viewed as commodity. It cannot be sold on the open market because it is legally United States Government Trust Property. The land "belongs" to the tribe but is assigned or passed down through family—male or female line—for use. It does not define personal worth. Therefore, ownership of property remains a vague notion in everyday Pueblo life. As long as an individual, family, or extended family uses the land, it is theirs, but there is an implicit understanding that land can revert back to the tribe if not used after some time.

As I talk to this middle daughter who lives at Santa Clara about the *Martinez* case issues, she prefers to have decision-making about tribal membership stay within the community. She was on the tribal membership committee when an amendment to base membership on other than gender was proposed some eight years ago. She recalls that the amendment was tabled not because of disagreement over issues but because of an interpersonal conflict between a councilperson and an angry female. The conversation has been quieted but awaits an impetus to awaken and continue, she says. She feels that the pain of non-acceptance and inequality is still held in the hearts of those affected and will surface again when the time is right. . . .

In summary, as our myths, stories, and songs tell us, there are tensions and struggles in life. Our traditional beliefs tell us that we are all relations, that we are all children of the community, which is part of the universe, which daily harmonizes opposites. It also tells us that it is an inclusive, not exclusive, world that we share and cooperation, not competition, is ideal behavior. That world also knows that "things come around"—that things will change.

What has been introduced by outside thinking is that we have to choose between uncompromising opposites, between male and female dominance, between individual rights or community wellbeing. We cannot have both. In this either/or world, those who are included must be better than those who are excluded. We are even tempted to think that American law can bring equality by written mandates, making us forget that we are capable of remembering a system in which focus on relationships might lead us to different solutions. We then begin to find personal security in property ownership and legal acknowledgement. We begin to be less spiritually oriented and worry about looking "right" in skin color, because the outside world expects us to look like Indians. We move more and more from living respectfully and acknowledging our interdependency with other beings, including the land, the place. Insecurity and fear, rather than trust that we are capable of loving inclusive actions, comes with giving ourselves to the idea of individual rights not mediated by community welfare. Deep harmony, which comes from our efforts to balance universal tensions, such as between male and female, becomes scattered and forgotten.

In 2003, the University of Kansas School of Law hosted an event during which the case of *Santa Clara Pueblo v. Martinez* was reargued, as part of an academic exercise, in front of a "Supreme Court" made up entirely of Native women law professors, lawyers, and judges. While the decision is not binding in any jurisdiction, the analysis used by this "Court" differs sharply from the basis of the U.S. Supreme Court. Nonetheless, the Kansas court reached the same ultimate result. Consider how this decision (based in a tribal-centered view) differs from that of the U.S. Supreme Court.

SANTA CLARA PUEBLO V. MARTINEZ (REARGUMENT, 2003)

Supreme Court of the American Indian Nations[*]

Before turning to the question presented, it is first necessary to review the decision rendered in this case by the Supreme Court of the United States in 1978, and the arguments now presented by counsel urging reversal and affirmance of the decision.

---

[*] Supreme Court of the American Indian Nations, *Santa Clara Pueblo v. Martinez (Reargument, 2003)*, 14 Kansas Journal of Law and Public Policy 91 (2004).

The initial line of inquiry of the Supreme Court of the United States was whether a federal court may pass on the validity of a tribal law. Because federal courts are courts of limited jurisdiction, a federal statute must provide the basis for federal jurisdiction.

In the present case, the Defendant at the District Court level was an Indian tribe, immune from suit under the well-established doctrine of sovereign immunity. Therefore, the Supreme Court examined the ICRA to determine whether Congress had expressly abrogated tribal sovereign immunity. Although we agree with the ultimate conclusion of the Supreme Court, we disagree with this rationale.

The Supreme Court failed to question the source of congressional authority to pass the ICRA in the first instance. Further the Supreme Court failed to question how Congress derives the power to waive a tribe's sovereign immunity to suit in any court.

The Supreme Court correctly noted that "Indian tribes are 'distinct, independent political communities, retaining their natural rights' in matters of local self-government."

The Supreme Court correctly characterized the power of tribal self-government when it noted that tribes "have power to make their own substantive law in internal matters . . . and to enforce that law in their own forums."

Tribes preexisted the United States and have been regarded as unconstrained by the United States Constitution. The Supreme Court incorrectly assumed in this case, and countless others, that the Congress of the United States "has plenary authority to limit, modify or eliminate the powers of local self-government which the tribes otherwise possess." In this instance, the Supreme Court reviewed the ICRA to find a waiver of sovereign immunity, with the assumption that Congress possesses the authority to waive a tribe's immunity. . . .

We noted that it is a well-established principle of American law that any Congressional enactment must be based on the enumerated powers in the Constitution. A review of the Supreme Court's decision below indicates that Congress's power to enact this statute was and continues to be presumed as a matter of fact. This has been the norm of Supreme Court precedent since *Kagama*. In *Kagama*, the Supreme Court noted that neither the Indian Commerce Clause nor the "Indians not taxed" provisions provide Congress with the authority to broadly enact legislation in Indian country. Nonetheless in *Kagama*, and the cases that followed through to *United States v. Lara*, the Supreme Court permits

Congress full discretion to legislate in Indian affairs under the highly suspect doctrine of plenary power. The plenary power doctrine is a colonial myth rooted in imperialist history of the late nineteenth century policies of the United States with respect to Indian and foreign relations that should be, for that reason, rejected and abandoned. In the Supreme Court's decision below, the federal courts lacked jurisdiction on the sole basis of statutory interpretation. Because the Supreme Court interpreted the ICRA as providing only habeas review of tribal governmental actions, the case below was dismissed. The Supreme Court's approach to this case continues a long pattern of the federal courts ignoring the sovereignty of indigenous nations.

In passing the ICRA, Congress is purporting to "extend" certain civil rights to individuals who come within the power of tribal governmental action. Congress ignores in the passage of the ICRA that tribal governments operate under their own laws, many of which include civil and community rights guarantees. In reviewing the legality of the ICRA and interpreting whether ICRA extends jurisdiction to federal courts, the Supreme Court should have addressed the impact of congressional action and subsequent federal review in light of tribal self-determination. At a base level, the ICRA's interference with tribal self-governance is yet another reason Congress lacked authority in this matter.

We do agree with the Supreme Court's emphasis, in dicta, on the importance of ensuring that determinations of tribal citizenship are retained exclusively in the tribal government. The Supreme Court rightly noted that "a tribe's right to define its own membership for tribal purposes has long been recognized as central to its existence as an independent political community."

IV. Conclusion

The U.S. Supreme Court reached a conclusion in this case that this Court affirms: the federal courts lack jurisdiction to review tribal governmental actions. We depart significantly from the U.S. Supreme Court on the reasons for this conclusion. The foremost factor for consideration in this instance is the self-determination of the Santa Clara Pueblo. Any federal review of tribal decisions is an unlawful intrusion on the sovereignty of indigenous nations. Only indigenous nations possess the authority to consent to suit.

The Impact of the *Martinez* Decision

Enforcement of Civil Rights after the *Martinez* Case: Habeas Corpus

The *Martinez* decision held that there is only one exception to the general rule that the ICRA does not grant federal courts jurisdiction to hear alleged violations of the ICRA: namely, habeas corpus actions. A petition for habeas corpus is available when someone who is being detained by a tribal court, police officer, or other tribal official would like to challenge the legality of that detention (see section 1303 of the ICRA). These petitions are often filed in criminal matters when the defendant being detained feels that his or her rights have been violated through such actions as the denial of bail, denial of a speedy trial or jury trial, denial of the right to counsel, illegal arrest, conviction by illegal confession, and cruel and unusual punishment. In noncriminal matters, habeas corpus can be used for such reasons as a person being detained in a hospital or mental institution involuntarily, a questionable child custody case, or someone being illegally restrained or detained by a tribe. For tribal cases, federal courts can decide only if the detainment is legal and, if not, can release the individual from tribal custody.

Only a few habeas corpus cases have reached the federal courts under the ICRA. Subsequently, the decisions have required tribes to do the following:

■ Permit professional attorneys to represent criminal defendants in tribal courts;
■ Grant a jury trial upon request of the defendant in a criminal case;
■ Not impose unfair or cruel sentences on criminal defendants;
■ Define crimes specifically and without vagueness or ambiguity; and
■ Have a prosecutor in criminal proceedings.

Other Civil Rights

The major impact of the *Martinez* decision, then, is that it no longer gives federal courts the jurisdiction over tribal civil rights disputes in Indian Country, except when an individual challenges the legality of their detention. However, it is important to point out that simply because the federal government lacks the power to review most ICRA complaints against tribes does not mean that tribal members are entirely without protections from abuses of tribal government. To that end, while some tribes have adopted the terms of the ICRA, others have enacted their own legislation protecting individual civil rights. In either situation, the best efforts by tribes to pass civil rights legislation seem to do so in ways that remain sensitive to and reflect the tribe's unique legal heritage.

Another important way tribes protect the civil rights of tribal members from abuses by tribal government is through their tribal courts and what is called the "power of judicial review." Indeed, in *Martinez*, the Supreme Court acknowledges that tribal courts bear the primary responsibility for enforcing the civil rights protections set forth in the ICRA, which they will do through their power of judicial review.

Judicial review is the power of the judicial branch of government to consider the rules, regulations, and official actions of the other branches of government (legislative and executive) and determine whether those activities violate the civil rights provisions expressed in the ICRA or tribal law. If the judicial branch does find a violation, it can strike down those rules and actions as illegal and require the other branches of the government to stop using them. To help explain judicial review, consider the following two examples.

- *Example 1:* The Fall River Tribal Council enacts an ordinance that provides that the children of male members of the tribe who marry nonmembers can enroll in the tribe, but that the children of female members of the tribe who marry nonmembers cannot enroll (essentially the facts of the *Martinez* case). A female member of the tribe who married a nonmember challenges the denial of membership to her children based on due process and equal protection under both the Indian Civil Rights Act and tribal law. Does the court have the authority to set aside this ordinance? If so, then the court has the power of judicial review.
- *Example 2:* The Fall River Tribal Council enacts an ordinance that provides that criminal defendants in the Fall River Tribal Court shall no longer be entitled to jury trials since jury trials are so expensive. Does the Fall River Tribal Court have the authority to set aside the ordinance if the court finds that it violates the ICRA or tribal law? If the court does have this authority, then it has the power of judicial review.

Tribal Sovereign Immunity

There remains a significant hurdle to ensuring the civil rights protections of tribal members against abuses by tribal government. This obstacle exists even if the tribe has an effective tribal court with effective court decisions supporting judicial review, tribal legislation protecting civil rights, and even a tribal constitution with such protections. The hurdle has to do with the question of whether or not the tribal government has immunity from being sued in court, whether for this or any other kind of legal claim made against it.

Because tribal governments are the governments of sovereign entities (tribes), just like federal and state governments are the governments of sovereign entities (the U.S. and the several states), they are recognized as generally possessing immunity from lawsuits. The logic behind this "sovereign immunity" is that if individuals were allowed to sue governments every time they feel they were wronged, such suits would quickly deplete the government's funds, diverting them from public purposes to compensate for private wrongs.

There are, however, special circumstances under which a sovereign government can waive its immunity to be subject to lawsuits for certain purposes. For example, the federal government, by legislation, waived its immunity for personal injuries caused by federal employees in 1946. Since that time, individuals suffering personal injuries caused by the actions of employees of the U.S. government have been able to sue the U.S. government for damages, and the federal courts have jurisdiction to hear those cases, where before 1946 they did not.

In the same way, tribes can waive their own immunity for specific purposes, opening themselves up for lawsuits in tribal courts. They could do this for civil rights claims. Indeed, some tribes have done so. Some tribal courts have even found that when a tribe passes legislation ensuring civil rights protections, it has also waived its sovereign immunity and opened itself up to civil rights lawsuits brought in tribal court.

Indeed, because of the decision in the *Martinez* case, the only place to enforce most ICRA protections (again, except for habeas corpus petitions) has been in tribal courts. Thus if principles of tribal sovereign immunity would prohibit a tribe from being sued in tribal court, including ICRA suits, then there is no judicial forum to enforce the ICRA. Tribal members and others would have no place to go if they ever felt that a tribal government had violated their civil rights. To avoid this situation, many tribal courts have in fact made decisions that held that sovereign immunity does not bar ICRA actions, even if the tribe has not made any explicit waiver of sovereign immunity in the area of civil rights protections.

There remains some concern that tribal courts cannot act alone to assert jurisdiction over tribal governments in ICRA matters. Some tribal leaders and scholars of tribal law argue that tribal governments need to do more to show that they respect civil rights of their tribal members, including passing legislation that explicitly waives their sovereign immunity from suit under the ICRA and other kinds of tribal civil rights laws. Indeed, some fear that unless tribal governments take more action to correct this situation in their tribal legislation, the U.S. Congress may very well amend the ICRA and perhaps nullify the flexibility that *Martinez* permits tribal governments in addressing their own

civil rights matters. This, of course, would be a serious erosion of tribal jurisdiction and a real limit on tribal sovereignty.

Conclusion

The Supreme Court's decision in *Santa Clara Pueblo v. Martinez* meant that
claims of ICRA violations could be brought only in tribal court. Many scholars
of tribal and federal Indian law saw this as a clear victory for the recognition of
tribal sovereignty, at least in light of the long history of U.S. efforts to diminish
that sovereignty, often through laws and political actions that, like the ICRA,
were claimed to be for the benefit of Indian peoples. At the same time, the
Indian Civil Rights Act is legislation that announces and calls for the protection of individual rights against intrusions by tribal governments—rights that
many tribal members both believe they already have and believe should be protected from being abused by governments, whether tribal or nontribal.

As a result, at first glance, the decision in *Santa Clara Pueblo* might seem
to suggest that the rights of tribal sovereignty, and the protection of tribal traditions and legal heritages, are at direct odds with laws, like the ICRA, that
would protect individual civil rights. And this perspective would seem to be
supported by tribal governments which claim that their rights as sovereigns
mean that they cannot be sued in court for their governing activities, even
when those activities violate the civil rights of tribal members. One might read
Justice Marshall's opinion in this case to mean precisely this.

But it is important to point out that in the *Martinez* case, Santa Clara
Pueblo argued only that U.S. federal courts were not granted jurisdiction by
the ICRA to hear civil rights claims brought against tribes by their members.
This does not mean that the Santa Clara Pueblo's tribal legal forum couldn't
hear this claim. The opinion in *Martinez* makes no mention of that.

Of course, a tribe sued in its own tribal court on the grounds that its governmental actions violated the ICRA might well argue that the tribe hadn't
waived its sovereign immunity to allow lawsuits against it on those matters,
even in its own courts. It is certainly the case that some tribal governments
have claimed that they are immune from such lawsuits. As you might well
imagine, it can sometimes be difficult to get members of a tribal (or really any)
government to agree to limit their own power and be subject to lawsuits and
court review. This means tribal members could have a hard time challenging
tribal laws that they felt were discriminatory.

On the other hand, a good argument has been made that many tribes
have, in their unique legal heritage, a central commitment to acknowledging,
respecting, and protecting the rights of individuals. In this sense, one might
even say that at the heart of real and lasting tribal sovereignty is, among other

things, a commitment to individual rights, such that the two can't really be
seen as oppositional at all. As a result, a government from such a tribe that was
acting in a way that discriminated against the rights of individuals, according
to its own unique legal heritage, might be said not to be acting like a sovereign
at all and, as such, not to have the immunity from lawsuits afforded to such
sovereigns.

Questions

1. Do you agree or disagree with the decision of the Supreme Court in the
   Martinez case?
2. What is the difference between the U.S. Supreme Court's decision and the
   decision reached by the American Indian Supreme Court at the University of Kansas Law School?
3. What is the purpose of sovereign immunity? Do you think that individuals should be able to sue governments when they feel those governments
   have acted improperly? Imagine a woman who wants to challenge her
   tribe's law that allows only men to apply and obtain permits to graze cattle on tribal land. If her tribe has not waived its sovereign immunity in
   tribal court to be sued for violations of the ICRA, does she have a case?
4. What are some of the advantages and disadvantages for tribal governments if they waive their sovereign immunity in tribal courts?

In Your Community

1. Has your tribal government waived any of its sovereign immunity?
2. Are there people living in your tribal community who are not members
   of your tribe and who do not have the right to vote for or hold positions
   in your tribal government? Do you think this is a fair arrangement? Do
   you think they have enough civil rights protections from actions of the
   tribal government?
3. If you could change any provisions of the ICRA or the sovereign immunity provisions of your tribe, what would those changes be? If you would-
   n't make any changes, explain why you are satisfied with these provisions
   the way they are.

Glossary

Judicial review: A court's power to declare a law unconstitutional and to interpret state laws. The term also refers to an appeal from an administrative
agency.

Merits: Reward or punishment due; the intrinsic rights and wrongs of a legal case as determined by substance rather than form.

Sovereign immunity: A government's freedom from being sued.

Waive: To give up a privilege, right, or benefit with full knowledge of what you are doing.

Suggested Further Reading

Robert Laurence, Martinez, Oliphant *and Federal Court Review of Tribal Activity under the Indian Civil Rights Act*, 10 Campbell Law Review 411 (1988).

Judith Royster, *Stature and Scrutiny: Post-Exhaustion Review of Tribal Court Decisions*, 46 Kansas Law Review 241 (1998).

Tiane L. Sommer, *Exhaustion of Tribal Remedies Required for Habeas Corpus Review under the Indian Civil Rights Act*, 11 American Indian Law Review 57 (1985).

Alvin Ziontz, *After* Martinez: *Indian Civil Rights under Tribal Government*, 12 University of California-Davis Law Review 1 (1979).

CHAPTER 21

Contemporary Civil Rights Issues

W E WILL conclude our discussion of tribal civil rights by looking at the different ways in which contemporary tribal governments have themselves addressed the rights of individuals within their communities and their jurisdiction. First, we will read some excerpts from some tribal civil rights codes and an academic article about those codes to reveal how these tribes have worked to incorporate notions of individual rights into their contemporary governance norms, structures, and practices. As you read these code provisions, consider whether their terms appear to come from the tribes' own legal heritage or are more informed by notions of Anglo-American-style civil rights, or both. Also consider whether any effort is made to incorporate provisions of the Indian Civil Rights Act itself.

Then we will turn to an article that reviews the ways in which civil rights have been addressed in the actions of tribal courts in the thirty years following the passage of the ICRA. Again, consider how tribal courts have afforded protections to individual rights by turning either to their own legal heritage, to Anglo-American notions of civil rights, or to the ICRA itself.

We will then read the findings and recommendations from the June 1991 U.S. Commission on Civil Rights report on the enforcement of the ICRA in Indian Country. It remarks on the success that tribal courts have had in protecting individual rights even though they have had little support from the federal government in doing so. The report finds that tribal courts are drastically underfunded nationally and that their efforts at protecting individual rights and promoting justice in tribal communities generally would be improved if increased funding were set aside for their use.

Finally, we will review an example of a recent tribal civil rights controversy— namely, the question of whether gay and lesbian tribal members have a right to be recognized as a married couple under tribal law.

As you read, think about the kinds of difficult questions that tribal leaders everywhere have to ask themselves regarding individual rights and their protection in tribal communities. Consider how civil rights provisions included in tribal codes provide protections of people's individual rights. Tribal governments must often balance traditional legal concepts that might conflict with individual rights in contexts such as kin relations, clan authorities, and religious responsibilities. It is also important to consider the expectations and values of contemporary tribal members. People in almost every tribal community today make different life choices regarding how they balance their cultural practices and values while getting an education, holding a job, and raising a family, whether those differences reflect the influences of nontribal society, different interpretations of the same tribal cultural heritage, or a mix of both.

Civil Rights Provisions in Tribal Codes

NAVAJO NATION BILL OF RIGHTS, 1 N.N.C. §§ 1–9

1. Other Rights Not Impaired; Deletion or Abridgment Only by Public Referendum

The enumeration herein of certain rights, shall not be construed to deny or disparage others retained by the people. No provision of this Chapter, the Navajo Nation Bill of Rights, shall be abridged or deleted by amendment or otherwise, except by referendum vote of the Navajo electorate, in accordance with applicable provisions of the laws of the Navajo Nation.

2. Equality of Rights Not Abridged by Entitlements, Benefits or Privileges; nor by Affirmative Action Necessary to Support Rights of the Navajo People to Economic Opportunity

Recognition, enactment, lawful implementation and enforcement of provisions for specific entitlements, benefits, and privileges based upon membership in the Navajo Nation or in other recognized Tribes of Indians and affirmative action in support of Navajo or other Indian preference in employment and business contracting or otherwise necessary to protect and support the rights of Navajo People to economic opportunity within the jurisdiction of the Navajo Nation, shall not be abridged by any provision herein nor otherwise be denied.

3. Denial or Abridgment of Rights on Basis of Sex; Equal Protection and Due Process of Navajo Nation Law

Life, liberty, and the pursuit of happiness are recognized as fundamental individual rights of all human beings. Equality of rights under the law shall not be denied or abridged by the Navajo Nation on account of sex nor shall any person within its jurisdiction be denied equal protection in accordance with the laws of the Navajo Nation, nor be deprived of life, liberty or property, without due process of law. Nor shall such rights be deprived by any bill of attainder or ex post facto law.

4. Freedom of Religion, Speech, Press, and the Right of Assembly and Petition

The Navajo Nation Council shall make no law respecting an establishment of religion, or prohibiting the free exercise thereof; or abridging the freedom of speech, or of the press; or the right of people peaceably to assemble, and to petition the Navajo Nation government for a redress of grievances.

5. Searches and Seizures

The right of the people to be secure in their persons, houses, papers, and effects, against unreasonable searches and seizures, shall not be violated, and no warrants shall issue, but upon probable cause, supported by oath, or affirmation, and particularly describing the place to be searched, and the persons or things to be seized.

6. Right to Keep and Bear Arms

The right of the people to keep and bear arms for peaceful purposes, and in a manner which does not breach or threaten the peace or unlawfully damage or destroy or otherwise infringe upon the property rights of others, shall not be infringed.

7. Rights of Accused; Trial by Jury; Right to Counsel

In all criminal prosecutions, the accused shall enjoy the right to a speedy and public trial, and shall be informed of the nature and cause of the accusation; shall be confronted with the witnesses against him or her; and shall have compulsory process for obtaining witnesses in their favor. No person accused of an offense punishable by imprisonment and no party to a civil action at law, as provided under 7 N.N.C. § 651 shall be denied the right, upon request, to a trial by jury of not less than six persons; nor shall any person be denied the right to have the assistance of counsel, at their own expense, and to have defense counsel appointed in accordance with the rules of the courts of the Navajo Nation upon satisfactory proof to the court of their inability to provide for their own counsel for the defense of any punishable offense under the laws of the Navajo Nation.

8. Double Jeopardy; Self-incrimination; Deprivation of Property

No person shall be subject for the same offense to be twice put in jeopardy of liberty, or property; nor be compelled in any criminal case to be a witness against themselves; nor shall private property be taken nor its lawful private use be impaired for public or governmental purposes or use, without just compensation.

9. Cruel and Unusual Punishment; Excessive Bail and Fines

Excessive bail shall not be required, nor excessive fines imposed, nor cruel and unusual punishment inflicted.

FORT MOJAVE CONSTITUTION, ARTICLE V, SEC. 2

Members shall continue undisturbed in their customs, culture, and their religious beliefs, including, but not limited to, the customs of cremation, ceremonial dancing and singing, and no one shall interfere with these practices, recognizing that we have been a people and shall continue to be a people whose way of life has been different.

COLVILLE TRIBAL CIVIL RIGHTS ACT

1-5-1 Title

This Chapter shall be known as the Civil Rights Act of the Confederated Tribes of the Colville Reservation.

1-5-2 Civil Rights of Persons within Tribal Jurisdiction

The Confederated Tribes of the Colville Reservation in exercising powers of self-government shall not:

a. Make or enforce any law prohibiting the free exercise of religion, or abridging the freedom of speech, or of the press, or the right of the people peaceably to assemble and to petition for a redress of grievances;
b. Violate the right of people within its jurisdiction to be secure in their persons, houses, papers, and effects against unreasonable search and seizures, nor issue warrants, but upon probable cause, supported by oath or affirmation, and particularly describing the place to be searched and the person or thing to be seized;
c. Subject any person for the same Tribal offense to be twice put in jeopardy;
d. Compel any person in any criminal case to be a witness against himself;
e. Take any private property for a public use without just compensation;
f. Deny to any person in a criminal proceeding the right to a speedy and public trial, to be informed of the nature and cause of the accusation, to be confronted with the witnesses against him, to have compulsory process for obtaining witnesses in his favor, and at his own expense to have the assistance of counsel for his defense;
g. Require excessive bail, impose excessive fines, inflict cruel and unusual punishments;
h. Deny to any person within its jurisdiction the equal protection of its laws or deprive any person of liberty or property without due process of law;
i. Pass any bill of attainder or ex post facto law; or
j. Deny to any person accused of an offense punishable by imprisonment the right, upon request, to a Tribal jury of not less than six persons.

1-5-3 Right of Action

Any person may bring an action for declaratory and/or injunctive relief only, against any executive officer or employee of the Confederated Tribes, or any employee or officer of any governmental agency acting within the jurisdiction of the Colville Tribal Court, to protect the rights set out in CTC §1-5-2 of this Chapter.

1-5-4 Colville Tribal Court

Actions brought under CTC §1-5-3 shall be brought only in the Courts of the Confederated Tribes of the Colville Reservation; notwithstanding the fact that a court of another jurisdiction may have concurrent jurisdiction.

1-5-5 Sovereign Immunity

When suit is brought in the Colville Tribal Court under CTC §1-5-4 to protect rights set out in CTC §1-5-2, the sovereign immunity of the Colville Tribes is hereby waived in the Courts or the Tribes for the limited purpose of providing declaratory and injunctive relief, where appropriate under the law and facts asserted to protect those rights; provided, the immunity of the Tribes is not waived with regard to damages, court costs, or attorneys' fees.

1-5-6 Other Law Unaffected

The laws of the Confederated Tribes, insofar as they do not violate the rights set out in CTC §1-5-2 of this Chapter, shall be unaffected by this Chapter. The Tribal Rules of Civil Procedure, the Tribal Statutes of Limitations, and all other rules of practice and procedure shall apply to suits brought under this Chapter.

1-5-7 Custom and Tradition to Be Respected

In construing this Chapter, the Tribal Court shall consider, when properly presented to the Court, the history, customs, and traditions of the tribes and bands which make up the Confederated Tribes.

TRIBAL LAW: A SURVEY OF CIVIL RIGHTS PROVISIONS IN TRIBAL CONSTITUTIONS

*Elmer Rusco**

Guarantees of Equality

After first amendment rights, guarantees of equality are most common in tribal constitutions. A total of seventy-three constitutions contain some guarantee of equality, usually more detailed than the equal protection clause of the ICRA and the fifth and fourteenth amendments to the United States Constitution. A guarantee of "equal protection of the laws" does occur in eleven constitutions; however, in one of these, that of the Menonimee Indian Tribe of Wisconsin, the clause is qualified by the provision that "this clause shall not be interpreted to grant to non-tribal members those rights and benefits to which the tribal members are entitled by virtue of their membership in the Tribe."

Twenty-seven constitutions contain a provision for equality of economic participation in tribal activities, of which the constitution of the Blackfeet Tribe is typical: "All members of the tribe shall be accorded equal opportunities to participate in the economic resources and activities of the reservation." A very similar statement, but including "political rights," is found in eleven constitutions. An example of this approach is the constitution of the Cocopah Tribe, which reads: "All members of the tribe shall be accorded equal political rights and equal opportunities to participate in the economic resources and activities of the tribe." Still another very similar provision is found in six constitutions, of which the constitution of the Ely Indian Colony is an example: "All members of the Ely Indian Colony shall have equal rights, equal protection, and equal opportunity to participate in the economic resources, tribal assets, and activities of the Colony." Still another form of such a constitutional provision guarantees life, liberty or pursuit of happiness to members; three constitutions contain such provisions.

Twelve constitutions contain a provision essentially like the section of the constitution of the Absentee-Shawnee Tribe of Indians of Oklahoma which states: "All members of . . . the Tribe . . . shall be accorded equal rights pursuant to tribal law."

* Elmer Rusco, *Tribal Law: A Survey of Civil Rights Provisions in Tribal Constitutions*, 14 American Indian Law Review 269, 280–82 (1990).

Finally, several other constitutions contain pledges of economic equality more specific than any of those cited above. For example, the governing document of the Cheyenne-Arapaho Tribes of Oklahoma states, "All enrolled members of the tribes shall be eligible for all rights, privileges, and benefits given by this constitution and by-laws, such as claims, credits, acquisition of land, all educational grants, and any other future benefits." The constitution of the Pueblo of Santa Clara states that "all lands of the pueblo . . . shall forever remain in the pueblo itself and not in the individual members thereof," but that "all the members of the pueblo are declared to have an equal right to make beneficial use, in accordance with ordinances of the council, of any land of the pueblo which is not heretofore or hereafter assigned to individual members."

A related provision of the bylaws of the Salt River Pima-Maricopa Indian Community reads: "No law granting irrevocably any privilege, franchise, or immunity shall be enacted."

A number of the equality provisions allow for exceptions specified in the constitution. For instance, the constitution of the Lovelock Tribe guarantees "equal rights, equal protection and equal [economic] opportunity" except for assignment of lands; another provision states that in tribal assignment of lands, "preference shall be given first to members of the . . . Tribe who are heads of a household."

The Application of Civil Rights in Tribal Courts

CIVIL RIGHTS IN TRIBAL COURTS

*Robert J. McCarthy**

Separation of Powers

A classic case of separation of powers was decided under the ICRA when the Ute Tribal Court ruled that the Tribal Business Committee lacked authority to withdraw jurisdiction from the court and vest jurisdiction in

* Robert J. McCarthy, *Civil Rights in Tribal Courts: The Indian Bill of Rights at Thirty Years*, 34 Idaho Law Review 465, 492–97 (1998). (The views expressed are those of Mr. McCarthy and do not necessarily represent the opinion of the United States Department of the Interior.)

the Business Committee itself where the Business Committee was a party to the litigation. The tribal court and appellate court previously had ordered the Business Committee to enroll the plaintiffs' children as tribal members. Despite a permanent injunction and writ of mandamus from the tribal court, the Business Committee refused to enroll the children. The court noted the Business Committee would have authority to establish an alternative forum for addressing future grievances related to enrollment, but that such a forum would need to ensure a fair, impartial, and independent hearing pursuant to the ICRA.

The Southern Ute Tribal Court ruled that it had jurisdiction to hear a claim that the tribal election board violated the ICRA and tribal law although the tribal constitution, without any reference to the tribal court, made the election board the final authority on election disputes. The court held that, although courts have no inherent authority to hear election disputes, tribal courts are the proper forum to present ICRA claims. The ICRA's guaranty of equal protection makes it impermissible for tribes to intentionally interfere with a member's right to vote as granted by the tribe. Judicial review of actions by tribal agencies and boards is necessary to provide a remedy for an injured party. "Where a tribe has not adopted a form of tribal government providing for distinct separation of powers, allowing court review for purposes of insuring compliance with constitutional provisions, statutory requirements and the Indian Civil Rights Act becomes a critical component in insuring a remedy exists to adequately protect guaranteed rights."

Tribal constitutions may provide independent bases for civil rights enforcement. The 1991 Report of the U.S. Commission on Civil Rights noted that most tribes with constitutions had followed a model prepared by the BIA [Bureau of Indian Affairs]. The model did not include a separation of tribal government powers into executive, legislative, and judicial branches, but instead placed judicial power with the tribal councils. A survey of 220 tribal constitutions in effect in 1981 in all states except Alaska and Hawaii found that over half were written under the authority of the Indian Reorganization Act. Twenty-two of the governing documents incorporate the ICRA. Fifty-nine constitutions reference state or federal constitutional rights which are not to be abridged by tribal law. Eighty-nine of the documents list First Amendment rights, protecting free speech and religion, although several limit free speech against abuse. Seventy-three constitutions guaranty equality, with twenty-seven of these specifying equality of economic participation in tribal activities. Due process of law and property rights are protected in thirty-five constitutions, but only one constitution prohibits discrimination on the basis of sex, and that constitution confines the right to holding tribal office. Only a handful of constitutions mention the rights of persons accused of crime.

"Constitutional decision making in tribal courts provides a unique opportunity for the tribes, in the framework of actual cases, to develop a body of indigenous constitutional law." Although most have their origins in a federal model, tribal constitutions nevertheless represent a set of core values affirmatively adopted by the governed, rather than being imposed, like the ICRA, by another sovereign power. Tribal court opinions interpreting tribal constitutions seem imbued with a higher authority than many ICRA decisions.

Several appellate opinions have found tribal constitutional rights to equal or exceed the requirements imposed by the ICRA. For example, the Hoh Tribal Court of Appeals reinstated a complaint for wrongful termination from tribal employment, finding the Hoh Constitution guaranteed tribal members the right to petition for redress of grievances, which the court construed as a waiver of the Tribe's sovereign immunity. Looking solely to the Navajo Nation Bill of Rights, the Navajo Supreme Court rejected a claim by attorneys appointed to represent an indigent defendant in a criminal proceeding that their appointment constituted a taking of private property—their services—for public use without just compensation.

Tribal Tradition and Custom

As tribal judicial systems have evolved over the course of the past two centuries, some tribes have attempted to retain or to re-establish traditional forums for dispute resolution. Perhaps the best known of these is the Navajo Nation's Peacemaker Court, which allows parties to choose a culturally-based type of mediation as an alternative to adversarial litigation. Much more common are efforts among tribal courts to incorporate Indian custom as tribal common law. One scholar criticizes reliance on Anglo-American law by tribal courts as being based in non-Indian values and causing tribes to lose their own unique world views, and urges litigants and judges to identify and apply customary law whenever possible.

Prior to *Martinez*, federal courts had held the ICRA should be construed with due regard for tribal tradition and custom, and that the ICRA was not coextensive with the U.S. Constitution's Bill of Rights. A few decisions, however, have found specific ICRA requirements to be identical to the Bill of Rights.

Many tribal courts have held that tribes have greater flexibility in applying principles of due process as found in the ICRA than do state and federal courts in applying principles of due process found in state and federal constitutions. The northwestern tribal appellate courts have generally recognized that the ICRA is not intended to interfere with tribal traditions and institutions. Even as they have recognized that the ICRA grants to tribal members rights comparable to those contained in the Bill of Rights, the courts routinely have ruled that the meaning and application of the ICRA is not determined by Anglo-American constitutional interpretations.

Traditional methods may be the only way to effectively resolve certain disputes. After issuing some initial orders which led to potentially violent confrontations between the parties and tribal police, the District Court of the Cheyenne Arapaho Tribes declined to exercise jurisdiction to decide the rightful possession of sacred ceremonial items. The court held that civil rights must be interpreted in the light of centuries of customs and traditions, in ordering that the right of possession be decided by Cheyenne tribal members, chiefs, and headsmen in traditional dispute resolution procedures.

Attempts to balance traditional law and Anglo common law are not always successful. The Nisqually Tribal Court of Appeals held that a provision of the Tribal Code which permitted the tribal court to apply state law where not in conflict with Tribal law was impermissibly vague. As a result, the appellate court reversed the conviction of a tribal member for negligent driving, where the charge had been brought under a Washington statute. A dissenting opinion stridently castigated the majority for its application of the Anglo doctrine of vagueness to invalidate a prosecution based on "the central role of traditional mores in the tribal community."

REPORT ON THE INDIAN CIVIL RIGHTS ACT

U.S. Commission on Civil Rights*

Findings

Finding 1.

The Commission on Civil Rights finds that the United States Government has established a government-to-government relationship with our Nation's tribal governments; that these tribal governments have retained the powers of self-government; and that for many of these governments, the powers of

---

* U.S. Commission on Civil Rights, *The Indian Civil Rights Act: A Report of the United States Commission on Civil Rights* (1991).

self-government are exercised through passage and enforcement of their own laws, the latter often being by means of their own tribal court systems.

Finding 2.

The Commission finds that in passing the Indian Civil Rights Act of 1968 the United States Congress did not fully take into account the practical application of many of the ICRA's provisions to a broad and diverse spectrum of tribal governments, and that it required these procedural protections of tribal governments without providing the means and resources for their implementation.

Finding 3.

With the exception of habeas corpus actions, enforcement of the Indian Civil Rights Act today takes place solely in tribal forums. Neither the Federal courts nor any Federal agency enforces or oversees enforcement of the ICRA.

Finding 3(a).

The Interior Department's ICRA role is limited almost exclusively to providing funding and marginal levels of training to tribal court personnel on the ICRA's requirements.

Finding 3(b).

The Interior Department does not today provide the possible relief suggested by the Supreme Court in its reference in footnote 22 of the *Martinez* decision, specifically, that persons who are aggrieved by tribal laws requiring Secretarial approval may have recourse with the Department of Interior.

Finding 3(c).

At least since 1978, the Department of Interior's use of its statutory authority under 25 U.S.C. 450m to rescind a contract with a tribe whenever the "Secretary determines that the tribal organization's performance under such contract or grant agreement involves . . . the violations of the rights or endangerment of the health, safety or welfare of any persons . . ." has not been exercised because of ICRA violations and the Department does not believe that Congress intended for it to do so.

Finding 4.

The adjudication of civil ICRA suits in tribal forums can be problematic due to the form of government imposed on some tribes through the Indian Reorganization Act of 1934, as well as the later imposition of the Indian Civil Rights Act of 1968 without adequate resources for its implementation.

Finding 5.

The failure of the United States Government to provide proper funding for the operation of tribal judicial systems, particularly in light of the imposed requirements of the Indian Civil Rights Act of 1968, has continued for more than 20 years. Funding for tribal judicial systems may be further hampered in some instances by the pressures of competing priorities within a tribe.

Finding 6.

The vindication of rights guaranteed by the Indian Civil Rights Act within tribal forums is contingent upon the extent to which the tribal government has waived its immunity from suit; concern about the potential effects of law suits, even for declaratory or injunctive relief, on the viability of tribal government has made some tribes reluctant to waive sovereign immunity to any extent, with the result that plaintiffs' efforts to adjudicate ICRA claims are frustrated.

Finding 7.

Public recognition and respect for tribal court authority is hindered by assaults on their jurisdiction by litigants as well as jurisdictional disputes with neighboring courts and authorities.

Recommendations

The Commission is encouraged by the recent Congressional focus on tribal court funding and the strengthening of tribal forums, and strongly encourages the Congress to go forward in this area. If the United States Government is to live up to its trust obligations, it must assist tribal governments in their development, and must continue to promote the recognition of this authority, as the Congress has previously done by means of the Indian Child Welfare Act.

The Commission strongly supports the pending and proposed Congressional initiatives to authorize funding of tribal courts in an amount equal to that of an equivalent State court. The Commission is hopeful that this increased funding will allow for much needed increases in salaries for judges, the retention of law clerks for tribal judges, the funding of public defenders/defense counsel, and increased access to legal authorities.

The Commission also supports the pending and proposed Congressional initiatives to provide a more equitable distribution of funding for tribal forums, such as a system based on caseloads, population, etc., independent of the Indian Priority System; to provide for an annual survey and report to Congress regarding the funding needs of tribal courts; and to provide funding in a manner that allows for flexibility among tribal forums.

The Commission believes that Federal support for reciprocal recognition of State and tribal court judgments will result in greater public respect for tribal court authority, and encourages the Congress to reflect such support in tribal court legislation.

The Commission supports the Congressional reversal of the effects of the Duro decision through legislation which recognizes the authority of the tribes to exercise criminal jurisdiction over nonmember Indians.

The Commission recommends to Congress that special attention be placed not only on the needs of tribal judicial personnel for training, but on the need to train the council members also. If the ICRA is to be fully implemented, all members of the tribal government must be trained in its requirements and the need for an impartial forum for resolution of disputes under the ICRA.

The Commission recommends that the Congress establish a mechanism and provide sufficient means for each tribal government to report at least biennially as to (1) the amount and adequacy of funding allocated to resolution of disputes; (2) the forum(s) within each tribal government with authority to resolve ICRA claims, and the extent of that authority, including the types of relief the respective forum is authorized to render under the ICRA; (3) the number of written ICRA complaints, both civil and criminal, filed with each tribal government, the forum within the tribal government in which they were filed, the violation alleged, and their final disposition; (4) the method of selecting and retaining tribal court judges; judicial personnel, and others whose duties pertain to the resolution of ICRA claims; (5) whether an appeal process exists and was exercised; and for these reports to be compiled and the data analyzed by a designated agency in a manner that will enable the Congress to monitor the success or shortcomings of the Indian judicial systems.

The Commission recommends that funds be authorized and appropriated for the establishment of several pilot projects to assist tribal governments in an exploration of the extent to which they might enact statutory waivers of sovereign immunity to allow for civil rights suits against the tribe, without jeopardizing the tribal government's viability.

Although the Commission received testimony from several witnesses who supported Federal court review of ICRA claims, most of them indicated that amending the statute to provide for such review should be a means of last resort. The Commission believes that respect for tribal sovereignty requires that, prior to considering such an imposition, Congress should afford tribal forums the opportunity to operate with adequate resources, training, funding, and guidance, something which they have lacked since the inception of the ICRA.

With a renewed commitment by Congress to provide adequate funding, training, and resources to tribal governments such that their judicial systems might achieve the respect that is due them, as well as Congressional support for the recognition of tribal court judgments by State courts and authorities, the Commission is hopeful that the current trend towards the narrowing of tribal jurisdiction will be reversed, and that instead the future will be one of promise and greater respect for tribal sovereignty and authority.

RELATIONSHIPS, TWO-SPIRIT PEOPLE, AND THE MARRIAGE DEBATE

*N. Bruce Duthu**

The national debates on the right of same-sex couples to marry have spilled over into Indian Country as gay and lesbian tribal members demand that tribes recognize their rights to marry as expressions of individual autonomy and traditional tribal cultural values.

In September 2003, an Oklahoma hospital refused Dawn McKinley's request to be with her partner, Kathy Reynolds, who was hospitalized and treated for a serious back injury. McKinley was not considered a family member under state law. To avoid a recurrence of this problem, the two women, enrolled members of the Cherokee Nation in Oklahoma, obtained a marriage application from their tribe and were married in May 2004 by a tribally sanctioned religious official. At the time, Cherokee marriage law

---

* N. Bruce Duthu, *Relationships, Two-Spirit People, and the Marriage Debate*, in *American Indians and the Law* 147–49 (2008).

defined marriage as a union between a "provider" and a "companion." In June 2004, the Cherokee Tribal Council voted unanimously to amend the tribe's marriage act to expressly prohibit marriage between persons of the same sex. The minutes of that council meeting reflect that several members objected to same-sex marriage as being contrary to Christian values and teachings. At the same time, one council member viewed the proposed legislation as overly intrusive of individual rights but ultimately voted in favor of it based on feedback from his constituents.

Lawsuits filed against the couple in tribal courts have thus far prevented them from registering their marriage certificate with the Cherokee Nation, the final step in validating their marriage. On two occasions, the Cherokee Nation's highest court, the Judicial Appeals Tribunal (JAT—now called the Supreme Court), dismissed the suits on grounds that the individuals filing the actions lacked "standing," or in other words, a sufficiently strong legal interest in the matter to bring the claim. The Cherokee Nation requires persons to demonstrate a specific particularized harm or actual injury in order to bring claims in Cherokee courts. The latest suit, filed by several members of the Cherokee Tribal Council, was thrown out in December 2005. The JAT ruled that the council members' concern from the reputation of the Cherokee Nation and their assertion that same-sex marriages were inconsistent with Cherokee culture were insufficient grounds to support standing. The court did not have occasion to rule on the substantive questions regarding same-sex marriage as a matter of tribal law, though it did receive a detailed affidavit from anthropologist Brian J. Gilley, who maintained that Cherokee culture and traditional law recognized marriages involving "two-spirit" people. . . .

In the Cherokee setting, it is unclear whether Reynolds and McKinley will ever be allowed to finalize their marriage. . . . Likewise it is uncertain whether the Cherokee Supreme Court would uphold the amendment to the Cherokee marriage act if it were challenged on constitutional grounds. The recently amended Cherokee Constitution guarantees all persons that "equal protection shall be afforded under the laws of the Cherokee Nation."

Questions

1. How do contemporary tribal codes address civil rights?
2. What does the Civil Rights Commission report suggest about the legitimacy of federal concerns for the protection of civil rights in Indian Country?
3. What role does the lack of resources and training play in the enforcement of ICRA provisions?

In Your Community

1. Does your tribal constitution or code provide a Bill of Rights or similar articulation of tribal civil rights? Does it use language similar to ICRA?
2. Have you ever felt that the actions of your tribal government violated people's civil rights? What were these situations?
3. Has anyone brought a lawsuit against your tribal government for violating the ICRA?

Glossary

Castigate: To subject to severe punishment or criticism.

Strident: Commanding by a harsh or obtrusive quality.

Writ of mandamus: (Latin *mandamus*, "We command.") A judge's order requiring a public official or government department to do something.

Suggested Further Reading

Jennifer S. Byram, *Civil Rights on Reservations: The Indian Civil Rights Act and Tribal Sovereignty*, 25 Oklahoma City University Law Review 491 (2000).

Kristen A. Carpenter, *Considering Individual Religious Freedoms under Tribal Constitutional Law*, 14 Kansas Journal of Law and Public Policy 561 (2005).

Christian Freitag, *Putting* Martinez *to the Test: Tribal Court Disposition of Due Process*, 72 Indiana Law Journal 831 (1997).

Patrick M. Garry et al., *Tribal Incorporation of First Amendment Norms*, 53 South Dakota Law Review 335 (2008).

Vincent C. Milani, *The Right to Counsel in Native American Tribal Courts: Tribal Sovereignty and Congressional Control*, 31 American Criminal Law Review 1279 (1994).

Robert D. Probasco, *Indian Tribes, Civil Rights, and Federal Courts*, 7 Texas Wesleyan Law Review 119 (2001).

CHAPTER 22

Sources of Law

THE PRECEDING chapters have shown how the study of tribal legal systems must balance traditional law and Anglo-American law. This is true whether one is interested in studying the historical development of a specific tribal legal system or in describing the character of its law today. Any such study cannot consider the influences of law from tribal and Anglo-American sources in isolation, but must explore how they interact with each other in shaping the unique quality of each tribe's legal system.

Understanding this interaction is not important only for those who study tribal law. It is equally (if not more) significant for those who actually *practice* tribal law. Tribal legislators, judges, and lawyers constantly think about how to strike this balance between tribal and Anglo-American law, whether they are drafting legislation, judicial opinions, or legal complaints. The very question of the law's legitimacy—whether or not people inside and outside the tribe view the law as valid and something they feel rightfully required to follow—and the broader interest in promoting tribal sovereignty hangs on how tribal legal actors strike this balance.

Often, tribal legal legitimacy and promoting tribal sovereignty go hand in hand. It is easy to see how problems of legal legitimacy can cause problems for tribal sovereignty. For example, imagine a tribal probate code provision that follows Anglo-American legal norms, by which a woman's property, upon her death, is distributed equally to her surviving spouse and children. Now suppose that the tribe's own legal heritage, followed by tribal members, is informed by matrilineal customs and traditions which hold that property should pass from women to their daughters only. This new law would so

293

completely go against the tribe's norms, structures, and practices that one could expect many tribal members to refuse to follow it. One could imagine these people seeing this law as an illegitimate piece of legislation because it fails to reflect what they value as the proper way of dealing with inheritance of property.

Furthermore, consider how creating a law like this could cause confusion in the tribe, as certain individuals who never had rights in their mother's property might suddenly believe they have a legal (if not moral) claim that they can get enforced in tribal court. When these individuals take this claim to court, the tribal judge would be in the impossible position of having to choose between tribal custom and this contemporary tribal law.

Think back to our discussion about the centrality of kinship to the whole of tribal life, and we begin to see how this kind of confusion about inheritance rights could affect not just the narrow area of property law but also many other areas of tribal life—including political, economic, cultural, and even spiritual matters. Such confusion, coupled with the fact that the legislation itself promotes Anglo-American legal norms foreign to the legal heritage of the tribe, would severely undermine the vitality of the tribe as a living community, including its capacity to govern itself according to its own norms, structures, and practices.

Now imagine the opposite situation. Imagine a tribal council that is seeking to preserve aspects of the nation's unique legal heritage and therefore passes a tribal probate law that follows a principle of matrilineal inheritance of property that is an important part of the nation's history. Suppose, however, that the majority of people in the tribal community no longer follow this practice and that women today are more accustomed to passing their homes and other property equally among their surviving spouses and children. In this situation, the law that attempts to revive an aspect of the tribe's unique legal heritage but ignores the people's contemporary norms, structures, and practices would also cause a great deal of confusion. It, too, could lead to difficult conflicts in tribal court and generally threaten the legitimacy of the tribe's law.

The Complexities of Tribal Legal Heritages

Tribal citizens sometimes disagree about the nature of a tribe's legal heritage. The customs and traditions of property inheritance may have changed over the years due to the contemporary circumstances of tribal life. Because of these changes, even people who call themselves "traditional" may have very different ideas about how their tribal probate code should be written to reflect their values and practices. These different ideas add another layer of complexity for tribal lawmakers trying to ensure the legitimacy of their laws.

In the above examples, the tribal probate codes in question would neither be legitimate in the eyes of all the tribal members nor promote a true sovereign expression of the tribe's unique legal heritage. A tribal probate code that is responsive to the norms, structures, and practices of contemporary tribal members would stand a better chance of being respected by them as a legitimate law. Such a probate code more effectively promotes the sovereignty of the tribe.

There are other circumstances, as well, where the questions of legal legitimacy and tribal sovereignty appear to be at odds with each other. This is particularly true in areas such as criminal law, where the federal government already treads heavily on the capacity of tribal nations to govern themselves. Another example is tribal civil rights laws. If a tribal judge were to uphold the sentencing of a criminal defendant to jail time, even though the sentence was originally passed without a jury verdict, a federal court following the Indian Civil Rights Act might find this an illegitimate legal action and immediately order the criminal defendant released. In this situation, failure by the tribal judge to follow the Anglo-American legal principles expressed in the ICRA when ordering the incarceration of a tribal prisoner might result in a weakening of the power of the tribal court to enforce its own laws. This would be true even if nothing like the practice of holding a jury trial can be found in the legal customs of the tribe. In fact, in more than one tribal nation, it is difficult to hold a jury trial because many claim that being a juror violates tribal traditions and values which hold that members should not believe themselves so superior to criminal defendants that they can judge the moral quality of their behavior.

In this example, questions concerning the legitimacy of the tribal law come from two different sides, with the tribal judge caught in the middle. On one side, they come from a federal court empowered by Congress to see that tribal governments and courts do not wrongfully imprison criminal defendants. On the other side, they come from a tribal membership that evaluates the decisions of tribal judges to see if they follow local norms, structures, and practices. Promoting tribal sovereignty under these circumstances can often mean violating the legitimacy concerns of one or the other side. Unfortunately, given the broad power of Congress to erase tribal self-rule, it is often the case that promoting tribal sovereignty means following a law whose source is in U.S. federal powers and undermining the principles embodied in tribal law and society.

There are many areas of tribal governance today where legal actors for the tribe can and do promote reliance on their own legal heritage as the primary source of tribal law. This is true even when the final outcome of the work by a tribal legislator, judge, or lawyer ends up looking a lot like something that comes from Anglo-American law. For example, when a tribal judge finds that a written contract between two tribal members is valid, although there is no tradition or custom of written contracts, he or she may still be promoting the tribe's unique legal heritage if that decision is based on a recognition that the tribe's customs and traditions have certain requirements of fairness when promises—whether oral or written—are made between tribal members. Although on the surface they seem to be adopting nontribal principles and practices, even these kinds of tribal legal activities can still be understood as advancing a legal legitimacy that is sensitive to the values and institutions of tribal members, thereby promoting tribal sovereignty.

Often there are real differences among members of a tribal nation in the degree to which they live by the traditions and customs of their tribe. In many tribes, you will hear people describe themselves and others as more or less "traditional." This is often an expression of the values they hold, the kinds of work they do, how they keep their home, and how they relate to family and other tribal members. This description is in contrast to tribal members who are described as living more "Anglo" or "white" lifestyles. These are people who may work in nearby cities, have homes that look more like Anglo-style structures, and relate to family in ways that are different than traditional kinship organizations.

These are not hard-and-fast distinctions, and members of many tribal nations would likely describe themselves as following some aspects of a traditional way of life (such as their kin relations or ceremonial obligations), while also engaging in some activities that are more like Anglo ways (such as working at an office job).

Because of these differences, tribal members may often disagree with each other about whether tribal laws should derive from custom and tradition or from Anglo-American principles of law. For example, take a tribe that has a custom and tradition of having only men serve in positions of political leadership, while women customarily assert their influence in the home and on family members. Now imagine that today this tribe has a tribal council and a tribal court—two forms of tribal leadership that were not historically part of the tribe's legal and cultural heritage. Some members of the tribe might say that, by custom and tradition, women should not hold positions as council members or tribal judges. These people might move to pass a law to this effect. Others might disagree and suggest that, because these are nontraditional governmental institutions, traditional norms and practices preventing women from holding leadership offices do not apply. These people might move to pass a law to ensure that both men and women can be council members or tribal judges.

Would the law proposed by either side in this hypothetical debate be considered legitimate in the eyes of tribal members? It depends on whom you ask. What is clear is that debates over the use of traditional or nontraditional principles in tribal law, when they arise between members of a single tribal nation, are fundamentally different than when forces outside the nation try to impose nontraditional principles into tribal law.

Internal debates like these are not contrary to tribal sovereignty. A tribal nation can choose to adopt a nontraditional legal principle as part of its tribal law (perhaps because it most closely matches the ways in which at least some members live their lives), and this does not necessarily violate its sovereign authority. In fact, it is the very essence of the sovereignty of any nation to choose what legal principles—traditional or nontraditional—it wishes to incorporate into its law. If, at a later time, members of the tribe that have a more traditional outlook come to power, they might change the law to reflect that interest. This, too, would just be another expression of the same sovereignty. Traditions themselves are not necessarily static; they evolve and change over time.

Given that customs and traditions in any contemporary tribal legal system must share space with laws that have their origins in U.S. federal and state jurisdictions, tribal legal actors constantly have to think about how that space is going to be shared. Many tribes have set out procedures in either legislation or case law dictating the manner in which this must be accomplished. Such procedures might tell lawyers and judges that they have to use tribal custom and tradition as a source of law before turning to U.S. federal or state law when attempting to resolve a dispute. Other procedures might explain how and when tribal elders are brought into legal matters, either as consultants knowledgeable about tribal custom and tradition or as ultimate authorities responsible for actually resolving disputes.

Common Law Principles in Tribal Law

One important way in which many tribes are integrating tribal customs and traditions with structures and practices adopted from nontribal legal systems is in the development of their tribal common law. The term *common law* comes from the Anglo-American legal system. It refers to the fact that, in Anglo-American legal practice and history, most of the substantive norms have their source in the customs and traditions of the communities where the people in dispute live. The Anglo-American system is known as a common law system, because the law is made up of legal principles, set down in legal opinions written by judges when they decide a case, that express norms derived from the customs and practices common to the citizens of each state in the United States. This practice has its origins in the old English legal system, where the local judges were charged with resolving disputes by relying on a common law whose source was the customs of the common people living on and working for the different feudal estates and the lords who controlled territories across the English countryside.

Today, every state in the United States is understood as having its own common law, made up of the decisions that judges give in cases by interpreting and applying laws based on the norms of that state's citizenry. Generally speaking, the laws of states (including their common law) regulate activities in the state unless the U.S. Congress passes legislation (for example, in the area of employment discrimination), the U.S. Supreme Court finds that a certain activity violates the U.S. Constitution (such as racial segregation in schools), or the state legislature passes statutes that supersede the common law. This is true because it is a fundamental element of the Anglo-American common law system that legitimate law is based on the practices and principles of the people who live under it.

Many tribal legal actors are finding this kind of common law principle useful for integrating their tribe's customs and traditions into their contemporary legal system. Some tribes, and especially their legislators, judges, and lawyers, are developing procedures for dealing with tribal customs, traditions, and culture so these can be used as sources of law in the decisions made by tribal judges. The legal norms, structures, and practices invoked in the judge's legal opinion become elements of the tribe's common law, and then become available as part of the tribe's body of legal principles that can be applied in future cases for arguing and resolving disputes.

Whether developing their own common law, creating procedures for consulting tribal elders, or passing legislation about the preference for tribal over U.S. state and federal law in resolving tribal disputes, many tribal nations are thoroughly involved in figuring out how to strike the proper balance in their legal practices with regard to their reliance on tribal versus nontribal sources of law. As should be expected, different tribes have developed their own procedures for determining which source of law should be used and when. Nonetheless, they all generally share a similar commitment to promoting—whenever possible and when consistent with values and practices of tribal members—the use of the tribe's own legal heritage as their guiding source of law. In this respect, most tribal legal actors seem to be in agreement that promoting true tribal sovereignty today requires development of contemporary tribal legal systems whose legitimacy is measured primarily by those tribal members subject to it. As such, tribal common law must adequately reflect the norms, structures, and practices that govern the ways in which tribal members live their lives.

The following excerpt is from one of the leading articles on these topics and is written by Professor Valencia-Weber of the University of New Mexico law school. It provides a good introduction to some of the issues regarding the use of tribal customs and traditions in contemporary legal systems. It also gives some interesting examples of the ways in which the courts of different tribal communities have been turning to their unique legal heritage in the resolution of their disputes. This reading is followed by an excerpt from another article, written by a legal scholar who takes a more skeptical view of the ways in which custom and tradition are being used by tribal judges when writing their legal opinions. Whose arguments do you find more persuasive?

TRIBAL COURTS: CUSTOM AND INNOVATIVE LAW

*Gloria Valencia-Weber**

Custom and Indian Law

The legal principles derived from American Indian custom distinguish the tribal nations' judicial system from non-Indian American jurisprudence. The development process of converting custom into common law should not seem alien to non-Indians; a similar process occurred in Anglo-American common law. For tribal courts, the customary underlying beliefs and conduct provide a contemporary foundation, not just an inescapable past. The difference between the Anglo-American courts and the indigenous nation's judicial systems must be more than the ethnic identity of the people who operate the courts, the geographical location, or the physical arrangement of the forum. External sources, other governments and their citizens, require from tribal courts a justification beyond cultural and idiosyncratic elements. There must be guiding principles which promote integrity. Likewise, tribal courts cannot be measured or justified solely by the degree to which they imitate state and federal courts.

The tribal courts creatively use indigenous customs and usages that survived the five-hundred-year encounter and struggle with Euro-American cultures. Despite the repeated efforts to destroy the cultural foundation of American Indian tribes, important customary principles persisted. Custom and usage identify different parts of the cultural system. Custom is the belief component. Usage identifies the conduct or behavior in conformance to specific customary beliefs.

---

* Gloria Valencia-Weber, *Tribal Courts: Custom and Innovative Law*, 24 New Mexico Law Review 225, 244–56 (1994).

When custom and usage underlie the tribal codified and common law, the created tribal jurisprudence is appropriate for the indigenous people governed by it. It is . . . integral to the idea of a custom that the past practice of conformity is conceived as providing at least part of the reason why the practice is thought to be proper and the right thing to do. Clearly the common law is an institution that is in part customary in this sense.

Custom as a concept must be separated from other cultural elements that imply nonformalized ideas and codes of conduct. To become "enforceable as common law a custom had to be: (1) legal, (2) notorious, (3) ancient or immemorial and continuous, (4) reasonable, (5) certain, (6) universal and obligatory . . . a creature of its history." Custom is distinctively a pattern of thought or way of perceiving and feeling about the elements of life. When conduct is affected by this thought process, then usage occurs through the practice or regularity of behavior.

For judges in the tribal courts, the thought and conduct must be "known, accepted, and used by" the people of the present day. The tribal litigators and judges must decide when custom and usage, which do evolve and change in some degree, should be determinative in decisions. This process is similar to the Anglo-American experience, which may be serendipitous. This writer proposes only that the similarity should facilitate the understanding and acceptance of tribal common law. The legitimacy of the tribal common law, however, is not dependent upon a shared process with Anglo-American common law.

In common law, "the starting-point is in customs, not the customs of individuals but the customs of courts governing communities." Those courts, in England essentially community meetings, had to make all kinds of decisions. As Milsom describes these community meetings, they made decisions about the legal future concerning allocation of resources and the settlement of disputes. The common law, as described by Blackstone, consisted of customs, used throughout a country, or of customs specific to a geographically identified people. "The materials of the common law, therefore, were the customs of true communities whose geographical boundaries had in some cases divided peoples and cultures, and not just areas of governmental authority." As Milsom describes the development of common law, it arose from different governmental authorities or jurisdictions using varied customary foundations.

The descriptions of Anglo-American common law do not present a generative community different in capacity from that found in tribal common law. The variance is among the over 500 tribal nation-communities and differences with the non-Indian common law. Time and generational distance from earlier Anglo-American customs, as well as skepticism, may prompt those who question the similar use of custom by American Indian courts. Yet, indigenous jurisprudence, like its Anglo-American counterpart, is capable of producing cognizable fairness and justice.

Federal Indian law recognizes Indian customs as decisional principles. Besides the tribes' inherent sovereignty, federal policy aims to promote tribal self-determination; under both sources tribal nations authorize their courts to use custom. The CIO/CFR [Courts of Indian Offenses/Code of Federal Regulations] courts are also permitted to apply tribal customs in civil cases. One process to establish the existence of custom is addressed in the code for the CIO/CFR courts, "where any doubt arises as to the customs and usages of the tribe the court may request the advice of counselors familiar with these customs and usages." Tribal courts use similar directives. A significant legitimizing of custom occurs in the federal and state court decisions that recognize and affirm tribal custom in decisions.

Tribal courts and commentators point out that custom does not necessarily mean unwritten, irregular, or inconsistent rules of law. Customary principles may be codified or established when the court takes judicial notice of custom, uses it for the decision, and then publishes the opinion. Increasingly, the need to codify, document, and publish is recognized because the development of a law system provides the benefits of precedent, predictability, and notice to those subject to the law. Codification and publication are largely noncustomary parts of Indian law that require tribes to appreciate this practice of Anglo-American law.

Achieving regularity through publication and codification of custom helps legitimate the tribal courts and allay the fears of nonmembers about tribal courts. In Kafkaesque nightmare scenarios, Indian and non-Indian members envision a capricious, unfair, and unjust system subject to political abuse. A brief review of how custom functions in tribal court decisions demonstrates the uniqueness, the legitimacy, and fairness of custom-based rules of law.

Custom in Indian Law Decisions: Selected Tribal Court Decisions

A selective review of tribal court decisions illustrates how custom can be explicitly recognized and used in substantive law. The use of custom and the associated reasoning reveal the integrative task facing tribal courts. Initially, the tribal courts must determine what is validated custom. The question is whether the indigenous people acknowledge, accept, and conform their conduct in accordance with a stated concept. Additionally, the court may look to state and federal law for culturally appropriate models and guidance. Both of these law-seeking tasks call for the skills and sensitivities found among able legal-warriors.

The limits of each type of law become evident when the human situation does not fit within the existing notions of tribal, federal, or state law. In some areas, such as environmental law, the tribal government is subject to the provisions of federal statutes and regulations. Whether by choice or federal requirement, the tribal courts look at federal and state law for principles and rules of law. Whatever is used should make sense for a culture with traditional values to be accommodated in a contemporary tribal society.

The selected tribal court decisions also show how customary alternatives to the adversarial forum can function in contemporary tribal judicial systems. The adversarial win-lose paradigm is not appropriate in customary alternatives. Indigenous custom and law can offer useful models for the majority culture. The adoption of alternative dispute resolution methods in Anglo-American law affirms the usefulness of methods long established in the indigenous nations.

The results of using custom are not necessarily uniform across the different tribal nations holding a commonly stated value. It is possible to hold a deep regard for land, the elderly, or children as the critical future resource of a society and reach similar and dissimilar decisions. The legal reasoning based on custom can also result in outcomes facially indistinguishable from those based on federal or state law. One must distinguish external form from internal substance to appreciate how the outwardly similar is not so. This approach is critical in jurisprudence and other ways of studying human phenomena, including how indigenous people perceive, organize, and explain their world. One must avoid stereotypical expectations to appreciate how customary reasoning works. These specific cases are illustrative and instructional.

A prototypic situation in tribal courts is a generational dispute involving child custody or visitation rights. In one case from a CIO/CFR court, the grandchildren were raised during a substantial period by the grandmother. She desired a visitation right when her daughter became able to perform her parental role. In both the Delaware and Kiowa tribal ordinances governing the respective parties, the court was unable to find codified law. The court recognized a mainly orally transmitted custom and stated: "The court does not hesitate in taking judicial notice of the unique relationship that exists between Indian grandparents and grandchildren, despite the fact there is no written tribal law on the subject." Moving beyond the indigenous custom, the court then looked to external models.

While the Anglo-American common law historically did not recognize a grandparent's legal right to visit, the CIO/CFR court noted this principle had changed. The court considered the state court cases creating such a right and found that over forty states have enacted statutes providing a grandparent visitation right. Based on its inquiry, the court recognized and granted the grandmother a visitation right. The court rendered a decision in accord with acknowledged custom that valued the grandparent-grandchild relationship, as well as the wisdom found in the majority of the states' policy. This decision exemplifies the productive use of knowledge of Indian custom and Anglo-American law by legal-warriors who serve as judges.

A similar child-related dispute in the Rosebud Sioux Tribal Court points out the misfit between Anglo-American law and the underlying dispute that arises from a cultural or custom-based conflict. Here a grandmother charged that her daughter failed to pay the grandmother for taking care of the grandchildren. Though pled as a financial dispute, the underlying offense or "cultural wrong" was the disrespectful removal of the children from the grandmother's care without obtaining her proper consent. As Pommersheim points out, this case cries out for a nonlegal or "culturally consonant way to mediate the conflict." This type of dispute is what alternative dispute resolution traditionally dealt with and can continue to resolve.

Disputes involving cultural beliefs and a failure to comply with custom are the subject matter for bodies such as the Peacemaker Court in the Navajo and Seneca Nations, the Court of Elders in the Sitka Community Association and the Northwest Intertribal Court System. Domestic disputes and interpersonal conflicts are appropriate subject matter even when personal and property damage occurs. Judgments and verdicts must be based on concepts accepted by the constituent community. The traditional retained models of adjudication and alternative dispute resolution focus upon restitution, not punishment. The models of Anglo-American law focus on determining the guilt of the offender and imposing a punishment. The concepts of guilt and punishment fail to make amends to all the affected parties or entities in some tribal situations.

In contrast, nonlegal models provide flexibility to the parties and to the judicial system. The indigenous preference for restitution can be accommodated in the remedies and penalties, without restrictions based on the civil or criminal prosecution dichotomy. The Navajo Peacemaker Court is part of the judicial system; when parties consent to or seek its resolution process, the dispute is converted from a criminal matter into a civil case. Even if the matter remains a criminal action, under Navajo law the court can order punishment for the offender and compensation for the victim. The criminal code continues the Navajo custom that required the offender to compensate the victim and the clan of the victim.

The Sitka Community Association code and the tribal court rules provide that "at the discretion of the Tribal Court, questions of tribal custom may be certified to the Court of Elders." This certification process follows from other code provisions providing that, absent the prescription by the code . . . any suitable process or mode of proceeding may be adopted by the Court which appears most consistent with the spirit of tribal law. Where the Court deems appropriate it may determine and apply the customary law of the Tribe. The Court may refer to other sources of law for guidance, including the law of other tribes, federal, state or international.

The Sitka Code and rules manifest the importance of the custom of this sovereign.

Sitka tribal law is a practical approach for a modern tribal court that integratively uses the sources of law serving an indigenous people. Here the code specifies that the duty of judges is to reach for knowledge within and without the tribe. Expansive and integrative reach requires the knowledge which legal-warriors possess.

The integrative approach can use similar procedures and reach results similar to Anglo-American courts, yet the legal reasoning justifying the result may differ. The legal knowledge and skill of attorneys is important in determining what is disingenuously distinguished and what will be adapted from external sources into the tribal common law. For instance, marital privilege as an evidentiary rule and procedure has endured in state and federal courts. Some tribal courts have similar evidentiary rules.

When the Navajo Supreme Court considered the marital privilege rule, it acknowledged borrowing the rule from the federal system. However, the court rejected one of the historical principles for the marital rule: that the wife had no separate legal existence from her husband because a marital unit was one legal party and "the husband was the one." This justification has no support in custom, which the court called "Navajo tradition and culture." The Navajo world is a matrilineal and matrilocal society in which the woman's role is revered. Important matters in Navajo society, including individual status, identity, and some rights to property and productive sheep herds, derive from the mother and her clan. The Navajo Supreme Court then found cultural accord with the Anglo-American principle to preserve the harmony and sanctity of the marriage relationship and denied the marital privilege in this case.

Sometimes customary tribal law will produce results different from an Anglo-American court's determination because the substantive law arises from a fundamentally different view on the matter at issue. In the use of tribal trust lands and in probate distribution of property there is an important difference. The Anglo-American concept of property as individualized ownership and exploitation is not germane. The American Indian custom of stewardship and practice of common ownership and benefits prevail over individualistic entitlements.

For instance, for agricultural permits and land, Navajo law uses the customary trust. This is "a unique Navajo innovation which requires the appointment of a trustee to hold the productive property for the benefit of the family unit." Custom and the Navajo policy of avoiding unproductive fragmenting of agricultural land on the tribal lands determined the outcome. The customary usage interest in the Navajo nation's land was awarded to the heir in "the best position to make proper and beneficial use of the land." This decision also involved the critical American Indian belief that communal lands cannot be owned. The Navajos and other tribes, through custom and express law, have established possessory interests that are recognized and inherited.

In the Navajo probate system, fairness among the heirs is achieved through custom. In the customary interest case, the heirs were denied an equal portion of the possessory land interest at issue and received other property from the estate. In another probate case, the Navajo Supreme Court relied on the custom that parents should "view" each of their children equally. Each of the children was treated equally in accordance with the common benefit custom which regards family and clan members as one economic unit. The family and clan "camp" keeps the productive goods while the unproductive goods are distributed among the decedent's immediate family and relatives.

A critical difference that distinguishes the custom underlying tribal law from Anglo-American law is the definition of the immediate family and the role of extended family. Issues arising in the context of tribal domestic relations, child custody, and probate cases, include definitions of family and role broader than the definitions in Anglo-American law. Tribal cases uniformly recognize that the extended family is a customary definition with legal consequences for those within the expansive unit of a family or clan. Customary definitions are also evident in law created outside the tribal court.

Federal Indian Law and Custom

Federal Indian law already accommodates customary concepts based on indigenous belief and preference for restitution. Different legal standards and burdens upon the litigants accompany the legal definitions in Indian law. For instance, recognition of the substantive difference exists in the tort law standards in the CIO/CFR regulations. While binding on these courts, the tort standard has also been adopted by some tribally authorized courts. The standard for the defendant's conduct is "carelessness" rather than negligence. The standard allows the judge and jury to decide whether the defendant's conduct appeared careless under the circumstances without requiring a focused determination of elements such as duty and the standard of care the defendant owes.

The carelessness standard rule allows the judge and jury to use the expansive viewpoint that is common among American Indians. The intent of the [governmental body that issues] the tort regulation is not clear, but the usage is culturally compatible for American Indians. The parties, their environment when the charged misconduct occurred, and other cultural elements come into the consideration of the defendant's conduct. Some tribally authorized courts expressly use custom which precludes Anglo-American tort concepts and defenses such as contributory or comparative negligence. Precluding these defenses allows a broader view of what occurred and who was injured in the particular instance. A broader view is generally not permitted in Anglo-American law because the tort elements are restrictively defined. However, this expanded universe of the parties or persons with interests at stake befits the shared viewpoint of life held by many native peoples, that humans are in relationships with the earth and all living forms, not just human beings. The permissibility of the American Indian expansive view is confirmed in the federal tort regulation's provision for liability when injury is deliberately inflicted. When such liability is determined, "the judgment shall impose an additional penalty upon the defendant, which additional penalty may run either in favor of the injured party or in favor of the tribe." The remedies in the tort regulation free the tribal courts to consider community standards of the tribe in the determination of the penalty.

Judicial freedom in the use of customary law provides the advantages of invention. The tribal courts can be accountable to the community and its customs in a way that is not available in Anglo-American law. The creation of law based on indigenous custom and appropriate Anglo-American law sources ultimately distinguishes the tribal courts of the third sovereign.

THE PROBLEM OF CUSTOMARY LAW

Elizabeth E. Joh[*]

The ability of Indian tribal courts to use custom rests on their reconstitution as institutions run by, and for, Indian governments. In 1883, the Bureau of Indian Affairs (BIA) established the Courts of Indian Offenses, the first formal Western-style courts on Indian land. Indian involvement in these CFR courts (a reference to the Code of Federal Regulations used), was nominal or nonexistent. Although many traditional practices, including indigenous methods of adjudication, were suppressed or extinguished by external regulatory practices like the CFR courts, the assimilation goals of the federal government were nonetheless considered a failure by the 1930s. Consequently, the Indian Reorganization Act (IRA) of 1934 reflected a shift in federal policy to encourage the development of tribal self-government. Under the IRA, tribes could establish their own court systems, draft their own constitutions, and enact their own legislation. CFR courts also continued to exist, although in a modified form aimed at encouraging tribal government. In the past thirty years, Indian tribes have increasingly focused their attentions on the development of tribal government, including tribal courts. A recent BIA report noted that there are now 254 tribal courts of both types, with CFR courts in the definite minority. Although their jurisdictional powers have been severely curtailed, particularly with regard to criminal cases, tribal courts are now the primary forum for adjudication in Indian country on nearly 260 federal reservations.

Tribal courts are authorized to use custom as a source of law when applicable. Not only is custom an approved source of law, but for many commentators the use of custom is an essential element of self-determination. Put another way, greater reliance on customary law represents, both instrumentally and expressively, a "return" to indigenous sovereignty. However, this emphasis on customary law assumes two propositions: that customs can be ascertained, and that these customs can be applied in a satisfactory manner.

Invariably, the search for an applicable customary legal principle raises questions of authenticity, legitimacy, and essentialism. Where does

---

[*] Elizabeth E. Joh, *Custom, Tribal Court Practice, and Popular Justice*, 25 American Indian Law Review 117, 119–22, 125 (2001).

one find custom? Many tribal courts have established procedures for proving the existence of a custom, by reference to an elder's advice, or to sociological studies. The less onerous method of judicial notice may also be sufficient. All three methods are vulnerable to competing claims of legitimacy. Not everyone may agree with a particular elder's interpretation of an asserted custom. Many prominent sociological or anthropological studies of Indian culture have been conducted by non-Indian outsiders, whose assessment of Indian customs may be colored by prejudice or mistake. The use of judicial notice may imply that Indian tribal judges, by virtue of being Indian (and not all of them are), are able to discern and legitimate customary laws. Advocates of traditional law compound the problem by evaluating the successful use of custom with the fundamental fairness and "natural wisdom" of tribal judges. Some normative claims about how judges "find" custom appear no different than descriptions of how any judge, Indian or otherwise, draws upon his own cultural values. Is the influence of culture on personal decision making so remarkable? Alternatively, is there something to the status of being Indian which confers a knowledge of custom? Such claims of inherent knowledge sound suspiciously essentialist.

When a tribal judge does claim to find applicable custom, is it enough—as some opinions suggest—that the custom is generally "Indian"? In a typical case, *In re C.D.C. and C.M.H.*, the tribal judge for the Delaware Tribe of Western Oklahoma based a child custody decision on the following custom: "[I]t is common knowledge in Indian country that both the maternal and paternal grandmothers traditionally play a very significant role in the Indian family." This invocation of custom suggests that "Indian" here is meant to be a contrast to non-Indian, or Western values: a rather indeterminate category. Surely the many Indian tribes of North America, originally distributed over a vast geographic range, differ to some extent in their cultural practices. Yet the use of "custom" at this general level can be found in many instances. "Indian" traditions in these decisions represent a number of broad values—community, family, reconciliation, healing, and harmony—which suggest as much a nostalgia for "small-town" norms as they do for Indian ones.

Furthermore, the applicability of customary law in contemporary Indian life is far from obvious. In many kinds of law, such as complex commercial litigation, no one suggests that custom ought to play a dominant role. On the other hand, in areas of law in which custom is most frequently invoked, such as family law and hunting rights, the use of custom presents a number of difficulties. Members of Indian tribes are not uniformly allied in a "re-traditionalization movement"; some find the use of custom outdated or undesirable. The influence of modernization and Western culture on American Indians has resulted in reorganization of the very order, consensus, and internal social controls on which the customary law model relies. For instance, while "positive" influences like the American feminist movement may have mobilized Indian women around causes like domestic violence, such influences may rattle traditional views on gender relations in customary law. No less disruptive is the influence of modern Western social pathologies—e.g., gang violence and substance abuse—for which custom may provide a meager anodyne. The legitimacy of tribal courts depends in large part on the extent to which Indians can identify with the values the courts promote. . . .

These several complications suggest an alternative interpretation to the justification for custom in tribal courts. Given the ambiguity of its definition, the values it attempts to vindicate, the uncertainty of its application, and the timing of its popularity, custom in tribal court practice appears to be not so much a literal recapture of historically accurate practices but rather a mode of resistance to all that Western legal culture represents. Defined in this way, the support of custom in tribal court practices shares many attributes of other legal movements which seek their vindication in opposition to conventional formal law.

Questions

1. Do you think tribal traditions should be incorporated into contemporary court systems? Why or why not?
2. Valencia-Weber states that she believes tribes should appreciate codification and publication practices of Anglo-American law. Do you agree? Are there ever tribal laws that should not be codified or published?
3. Joh asserts that using custom in tribal court proceedings is more about displaying resistance to Anglo-American society and legal systems than it is about accurately reflecting historical tribal practice. Do you agree?
4. What do you think are some ways in which tribal courts can develop legitimacy?

In Your Community

1. Are there any laws for your tribe that do not reflect your community's norms, structures, and practices? If so, how were those laws passed in the first place? Is it possible that the laws were written by people unfamiliar with your tribal beliefs and customs?

2. Are your tribal judges, prosecutors, and other legal actors members of your tribe? If not, how do these people learn about the unique legal traditions of your tribe?
3. In your tribe, is tribal custom ever codified or published, as Valencia-Weber recommends? If not, do you think it should be?

Glossary

Capricious: Not based on fact, law, or reason.

Cognizable: Knowable or perceivable.

Common law: Judge-made law.

Constituent: A citizen in a government who is represented by an official.

Dichotomy: A division or the process of dividing into two mutually exclusive or contradictory groups.

Essentialism: The practice of categorizing a group based on an artificial social construction that imparts an "essence" of that group, which suggests that all members are the same and ignores individuality and difference.

Evidentiary: Related to or constituting evidence.

Generative: Having the ability to produce or generate.

Heir: A person who inherits property.

Idiosyncratic: A structural or behavioral characteristic peculiar to an individual or group.

Integrative: Tending to combine diverse elements into a whole.

Judicial notice: The act of a judge in recognizing the truth of certain facts.

Legitimacy: Credibility.

Liability: Legal obligation, responsibility, or debt.

Notorious: Generally known and talked of by the public.

Prototype: An original or model.

Serendipitous: Being lucky in finding things one was not looking for.

Stewardship: The careful and responsible management of something entrusted to one's care.

Tort: A civil (as opposed to criminal) wrong other than a breach of contract.

Suggested Further Reading

Pat Sekaquaptewa, *Evolving the Hopi Common Law*, 9 Kansas Journal of Law and Public Policy 761 (2000).

Pat Sekaquaptewa, *Key Concepts in the Finding, Definition, and Consideration of Custom Law in Tribal Lawmaking*, 32 American Indian Law Review 319 (2007).

CHAPTER 23

Common Law in Contemporary Legal Systems

MANY TRIBES have incorporated tribal custom and common law into their written laws and court opinions. This chapter provides several examples of ways in which traditions are given respect and authority in contemporary legal systems.

Many tribal governments have a statute that authorizes tribal court judges to refer to common law and tradition whenever making decisions. For example, the San Ildefonso Pueblo Code contains the following section:

> *Sec. 1.3—Interpretation of this Code.*
> This Code shall be interpreted pursuant to the traditions and customs of the San Ildefonso Tribe. Where any doubt arises as to these traditions and customs, the Court may request the advice of elders as counselors who are familiar with these traditions and customs. If none such exists, then the Court may use applicable federal and state case law and statutory law, adopting those principles and procedures not in conflict with the laws, customs and traditions of the Pueblo of San Ildefonso.[1]

Tribal court opinions often reflect an effort by a tribal court judge to evaluate the norms, structures, and practices of the tribal community. These opinions stand as examples of how common law can develop out of a combination of tribal and nontribal legal principles. As you read these case excerpts, consider what elements of tribal legal customs and traditions—substantive or procedural norms, practices, and/or structures—are being discussed and used in the legal decision.

Incorporating a Trickster Tale in a Tribal Court Opinion

CHAMPAGNE V. PEOPLE OF LITTLE RIVER BAND OF OTTAWA INDIANS

*Little River Band of Ottawa Indians Tribal Court of Appeals**

Before Edmondson, Fletcher, and Kraus, Justices

There are many trickster tales told by the Anishinaabek involving the god-like character Nanabozho. One story relevant to the present matter is a story that is sometimes referred to as "The Duck Dinner." There are many, many versions of this story, but in most versions, Nanabozho is hungry, as usual. After a series of failures in convincing (tricking) the woodpecker and muskrat spirits into being meals, Nanabozho convinced (tricks) several ducks and kills them by decapitating them. He eats his fill, saves the rest for later, and takes a nap. He orders his buttocks to wake him if anyone comes along threatening to steal the rest of his duck dinner. During the night, men approach. Nanabozho's buttocks warn him twice: "Wake up, Nanabozho. Men are coming." Nanabozho ignores his buttocks and continues to sleep. When he awakens to find the remainder of his food stolen, he is angry. But he does not blame himself. Instead, he builds up his fire and burns his buttocks as punishment for their failure to warn him. To some extent, the trick has come back to Nanabozho—and in the end, with his short-sightedness, he burns his own body.

The relevance of this timeless story to the present matter is apparent. The trial court, per Judge Brenda Jones Quick, tried and convicted the defendant and appellant, Hon. Ryan L. Champagne, a tribal member, an appellate justice, and a member of this Court, of the crime of attempted fraud. Justice Champagne's primary job during the relevant period in this case was with the Little River Band of Ottawa Indians. Part of his job

---

* Little River Band of Ottawa Indians, Tribal Court of Appeals, *Champagne v. People of Little River Band of Ottawa Indians*, 35 Indian Law Reporter 6004 (2007).

responsibilities included leaving the tribal place of business in his personal vehicle to visit clients. While on one of those trips, Justice Champagne took a personal detour and was involved in an accident. The Band and later the trial judge concluded that his claim for reimbursement from the Band was fraudulent. Judge Quick found that Judge Champagne "attempted to obtain money by seeking reimbursement from the Tribe for the loss of his vehicle by intentionally making a false assertion that he was on his way to a client's home at the time of the accident." Justice Champagne was neither heading toward the tribal offices nor toward a client's home.

Like Nanabozho, Justice Champagne perpetrated a trick upon the Little River Ottawa community—a trick that has come back to haunt him. It would seem to be a small thing involving a relatively small sum of money, but because the Little River Ottawa people have designated this particular "trick" a criminal act, Justice Champagne has burned himself.

When Written Law Conflicts with Tribal Customs

IN RE THE MARRIAGE OF NAPYER

Yakima Nation Tribal Court*

Before Pinkham, Judge

Amended Court Order

This matter has come before the court on Helen Napyer's motion for summary judgment. The court is being requested to find the 1959 Indian custom marriage of Helen Napyer and Louis Napyer, Sr., valid despite conflicting provisions in the Yakima Indian Nation 1953 Law and Order Code, now the court makes the following findings of fact and conclusions based on the testimony of witnesses regarding traditional Yakima wedding trades.

---

* Yakima Nation Tribal Court, *In Re the Marriage of Napyer*, 19 Indian Law Reporter 6078 (1992).

Findings of Fact

1. Helen Sohappy Napyer, the petitioner, and Louis Napyer, Sr., partici-pated in a wedding trade at the Indian community at Horn Dam at West Richland, Washington, on June 9 of 1959. The family of Tumi Buck (Helen Napyer's aunt) traded for Helen Sohappy Napyer, and the family of Ambrose Whitefoot traded for Louis Napyer, Sr. (Mrs. Minnie Whitefoot was Louis Napyer's aunt.)

2. Ambrose and Minnie Whitefoot gave Tumi Buck six or seven *Suptukay* (Indian suitcases) and a blanket full of clothing including a wing dress and Tumi Buck fed them and then gave them all of the dishes and root baskets and other items from the meal.

3. About a week later Tumi Buck took six or seven large *P'satanawas* (root bags) full of all kinds of roots and some men's clothing to Ambrose and Minnie Whitefoot's house. Minnie and Ambrose Whitefoot fed Tumi Buck and gave Tumi Buck the dishes and root baskets and other items from the meal.

4. Helen Jim, whom the court recognizes as a traditional elder with broad knowledge of the traditions and customs of the Yakima Nation, testi-fied as to the nature of the traditional Yakima wedding trade: "Old people get married, Indian way, not go to white men, they trade each other."

5. The court finds that Helen and Louis Napyer's 1959 wedding trade was in accordance with Yakima traditions.

6. Helen Sohappy Napyer was previously married to Clayton Queah-pama in a 1941 Indian custom marriage. That both parties were tradi-tional people. That their marriage was dissolved by Indian custom in 1956 or 1957 by mutual agreement and permanent separation of the parties. That Yakima custom recognizes mutual agreement as one grounds for custom divorce.

7. Louis Napyer, Sr. had been previously married to Florence Eli, who died in 1951, and to Elaine Frank, from whom he was divorced in a tribal court action on August 4, 1958.

Conclusions of Law

The above evidence establishes that Helen Sohappy Napyer and Louis Napyer, Sr., were married in accordance with the Indian way and the Washat religion, which is very strong, and also in accordance with the customs of the Yakima Nation, by engaging in a traditional wedding trade between repre-sentatives of the families on both sides, the man's and the woman's.

That Helen Sohappy Napyer's prior marriage to Clayton Queahpama was dissolved by tribal custom divorce as recognized under Yakima tribal customs.

That Louis Napyer's prior marriages were terminated before his wedding trade with Helen Sohappy Napyer.

That under RYS Sec. 2.02.07(2)(F) this court may recognize Yakima tribal customs and traditions when deciding cases and applicable law and under that authority this court finds as a matter of law that chapter 3, section 5 of 1953 Law and Order Code of the Yakima Indian Nation can be, and is, not considered in the present case as it conflicts with Yakima tribal custom in regard to marriage and divorce. Although the court does not in this decision invalidate the above 1953 code provisions, the court notes that chapter 3, section 5 is inconsistent with the 1968 Indian Civil Rights Act, the 1978 American Indian Religious Freedom Act, and the 1977 Yakima Nation Codes, which each protect the practice of Indian tradition, customs, and religion.

What Is a Traditional Navajo Will?

IN THE MATTER OF THE ESTATE OF CHISNEY BENALLY

Court of Appeals of the Navajo Nation[*]

Before Neswood, Acting Chief Justice, Bluehouse and Walters, Associate Justices.

The opinion of the court was delivered by: Neswood, Acting Chief Justice.

I.

Prior to his death on October 12, 1972, Chisney Benally held a grazing permit for District 12 with a carrying capacity of thirty (30) sheep units.

---

[*] Court of Appeals of the Navajo Nation, *In the Matter of the Estate of Chisney Benally*, 1 Navajo Reporter 219 (1978).

Shortly before his death, the decedent orally devised his grazing permit to his wife, Christine Benally. This was done in the presence of his wife and his four (4) children by her, Stella J. Benally, Casey Benally, Clarence P. Benally and Marilyn Dawes. The decedent's children by his first marriage, Florence Warner, Esther Joe, Ruth Charley, and May Jean Benally, were not present at the time the decedent devised the permit.

The appellees filed a petition for probate of the estate in the Shiprock District Court on October 18, 1976, alleging that the only item within the estate was the grazing permit, which was community property. The petition named only the four (4) children of the second marriage.

Three of the decedent's children of his first marriage then filed a motion to intervene and maintained they were entitled to a portion of the estate.

On January 20, 1977, the Appellee filed an amended petition naming the children from both marriages. The petition alleged that the decedent had orally devised the grazing permit to the Appellee in the presence of his immediate family.

On February 7, 1977, appellants filed a "Claim Against The Estate" alleging that the permit was given to Ruth Charley by the decedent.

The Shiprock District Court found that the decedent made an oral will in the presence of his immediate family and therefore assigned the permit to the Appellee.

From the probate decree of the Shiprock District Court, Ruth Charley appeals.

II.

The appeal in this matter raises four issues:

1. What is the definition of the "immediate family" for the purpose of an oral will?
2. Did the decedent satisfy all the requirements in making an oral will?
3. Are decedent's widow and children competent to testify as to the oral will?
4. May a grazing permit be devised through a valid oral will?

III.

In the case of *In Re Estate of Lee* (1971), the Court of Appeals stated:

It is a well established custom that a Navajo may orally state who shall have his property after his death when all of his immediate family are present and agree and that such a division will be honored after his death. We know of no other custom in this respect. We hold, therefore, that unless all of the members of his immediate family are present and agree a Navajo cannot make an oral will. Since the wife and children were not present when the deceased made the alleged oral will to the petitioner, we hold that it was invalid.

The appellant maintains that the decedent's children by his first marriage are members of the immediate family. Since these children were not present when the decedent devised the grazing permit, the appellant claims that the requirement of *In Re Estate of Lee* was not met and that there was no oral will.

This Court has examined the definitions of "immediate family" by other courts. These courts have all held that mere blood relationship does not make a person a member of the immediate family.

In *Lewandowski v. Preferred Risk Mutual Insurance*, 33 Wis.2d 69, 146 N.W.2d 505, the Wisconsin Supreme Court stated: "'immediate family' means person related by blood, adoption or marriage and living together in the same household, and immediate relative is not necessarily a member of the immediate family."

In *Cincinnati, N. & C. Railway Company v. Peluso*, 293 S.W.2d 556, 558, the Court of Appeals of Kentucky stated: "the 'immediate family' are those members of the same household who are bound together by ties of relationship."

We adopt the rule that the children of the decedent's first marriage, who were not living with the decedent when he died, are not members of the immediate family for the purpose of an oral will.

We are limiting this rule on the immediate family to cases involving oral wills because the Court is mindful of the Navajo concept of the extended family. This rule is adopted because it would work too great a hardship on the Navajo People to require the presence of all who might be considered immediate family by the Navajo extended family concept. Since many Navajo cannot write, cannot afford to have an attorney write a will and do not understand the concept of a written will, it is important that there be some alternate method by which a person may devise his property.

IV.

Since the children of the first marriage are not members of the decedent's family, we look to see if the remaining requirements of an oral will were met.

The will was made in the presence of the decedent's wife and children of that marriage. No evidence was produced at the trial to show any disagreement among the members of the immediate family. We therefore conclude that there was a valid oral will.

[Section V omitted.]

VI.

Appellant's final argument is that a grazing permit can only be devised by a written will. For this proposition, appellant cites 3 N.T.C 355(a) which states:

> a. Permittees and licensees may execute a will designating the person or person(s) to receive the permit or license, which must be approved by the Court of the Navajo Tribe after the death of permittee or licensee.

In the absence of such an instrument approved by the Court, and unless stipulated to the contrary under agreement of the potential heirs approved by the Court, the Court is hereby authorized to distribute such permits or licenses in accordance with moral and legal rights as determined by the said Court.

As we stated earlier in this opinion, it would create a great hardship for the Navajo People if they were required to make written wills in every instance in order to devise their property. Therefore, the law must be interpreted liberally to allow oral wills if the statute can be so construed without changing its intent or meaning. *Black's Law Dictionary* defines "execute" as to complete; to make; to perform; to do. The definition does not require that the execution be in writing.

We believe that 3 N.T.C. 355(a) should be read in this manner. Nothing in the Navajo Tribal Code leads us to believe that the Tribal Council intended to require a written document.

The judgment of the District Court is Affirmed.

Bluehouse, Associate Justice and Walters, Associate Justice, concur.

What Is Traditional Adoption?

DUMARCE V. HEMINGER

Northern Plains Intertribal Court of Appeals[*]

Before Zendejas, Johnson, and Foughty, Justices

Summary

This appeal comes from the C.F.R. Court of the Sisseton Wahpeton Tribe of the Lake Traverse Indian Reservation.

Anita DuMarce, the appellant and natural mother of [B] [The child in question is referred to as B in this opinion.], has appealed asking that this court reverse the decision of the trial court which has granted a traditional adoption or *ecagwaya* adoption of said minor child to the appellees, Gerald and Rosella Heminger.

This court is persuaded that pursuant to SWST Code 38-03-24 the requirements of a traditional adoption were not complied with and the decision of the trial court is reversed and orders that the order for traditional adoption be vacated.

The natural father, Keith DuMarce, has not participated in the proceedings nor participated in the appeal.

Facts

[B] was born to Keith and Anita DuMarce on February 25, 1989. Keith and Anita DuMarce were legally married. They are parents of five children, all of them under the age of 10 years. At the time of [B]'s birth, Keith and Anita resided near Sisseton, South Dakota, within the boundaries of the Lake Traverse Indian Reservation. [B], his parents, and siblings are all members of, or eligible for membership in, the Sisseton Wahpeton Sioux Tribe.

On May 2, 1989, the Child Protection Program (hereinafter CPP) for the tribe received a referral on the DuMarce's home with allegations that

---

[*] Northern Plains Intertribal Court of Appeals, *DuMarce v. Heminger*, 20 Indian Law Reporter 6077 (1992).

the DuMarce children were home alone. Upon investigation by tribal police and CPP workers, the allegations were confirmed. All five of the DuMarce children were placed into foster homes. The DuMarce's male children were placed with the Hemingers in foster care. Anita and Keith were summoned into C.F.R. court on petition of the tribe for emergency placement of their children. Anita responded and appeared in court on May 11, 1989, and requested additional time to seek legal counsel. The hearing was continued, and Anita retained her present counsel, who filed a notice of appearance dated June 1, 1989.

Both Keith and Anita were abusers of alcohol, and Keith was also a frequent spouse abuser.

Anita admitted herself into the Sioux San Hospital in Rapid City, South Dakota, on May 28, 1989, through June 1989, for alcohol evaluation and counseling, as well as counseling for domestic violence.

Anita attended her next court hearing with legal counsel on July 14, 1989. At that time the court ordered legal custody of the DuMarce children remain with CPP. Anita was given physical custody of the four older children and [B] remained in foster care. Following this court hearing and prior to future review hearings, CPP workers returned all five DuMarce children to their home. The four older children have remained in the home with DuMarce since that time.

A few weeks after the children were returned to Keith and Anita DuMarce the Hemingers asked to have [B] stay with them during the weekend. After allowing the Hemingers to take [B] for the weekend, Anita and Keith decided that it would be in the best interest of [B] and the rest of the family if the Hemingers retained [B] on an extended basis, until such time as they were able to adequately care for [B].

It had been determined that [B] suffers from fetal alcohol syndrome and he was an unhealthy child in other respects. [B]'s health problems along with Anita's own poor physical health brought on in part by the birth of [B] caused extreme stress on Anita. In addition to these stress factors Keith continued to abuse alcohol and abuse her, creating further tensions. The next oldest child to [B] was 10 months old at the time of [B]'s birth.

After the Hemingers were given physical custody of [B] a meeting to discuss a more long-term arrangement was made. This meeting was cancelled because of Keith's absence. In September of 1989 a meeting took place between the Hemingers, Keith, Anita and two CPP workers. The parties agreed at that meeting that the Hemingers would retain [B] in their physical care for an indefinite period of time.

In November of 1989 and February 1990 the court held review hearings. Anita attended the hearings without counsel. She agreed at both hearings to the retention of [B] by the Hemingers, which arrangement was reduced in writing in the form of court orders granting CPP legal custody of [B], to be placed in foster care at the discretion of CPP.

In the spring of 1990 Anita left Sisseton and enrolled in United Tribes Technical College in Bismarck, North Dakota to begin classes, with the goal of becoming a licensed practical nurse. Her classes were to begin in August of 1990.

In the summer of 1990 Anita had determined that she had resolved many of her difficulties which had prompted her to place [B] with the Hemingers. She approached the Hemingers to seek the return of [B], but they declined to return [B] without a court order.

Anita continued with her plans and moved to Bismarck for school. [B] was left in the Hemingers' home pursuant to the earlier referred to orders. Partially due to her indigency Anita was unable to visit [B] or her family from August 1990 to early 1991. Prior to that period of time, Anita had maintained contact with [B]. In September, 1989, visits were arranged through CPP case workers and others were accomplished without assistance. Since early 1991 Anita has returned to Sisseton for court hearings, other personal matters and has routinely sought and received visitation with [B] on such occasions.

Since March 13, 1991, Anita has been separated from her husband. An action for divorce which was filed in the summer of 1991 is still pending in Wahpeton Sioux C.F.R. Court because of difficulty with service on Keith.

A C.F.R. court-ordered home study of Anita by North Dakota Social Service in Bismarck concluded that the living environment was adequate and that Anita was capable and willing to care for [B].

On August 13, 1991 Gerald and Rosella Heminger filed a petition for adoption of [B]. Said petitioners prayed that the parental rights of the child's parents be terminated and that the Hemingers be allowed to adopt [B] under the "Anglo" adoption law (Sisseton Wahpeton Sioux Tribal Code, ch. 39 and 43). In the alternative the Hemingers asked the court to grant an adoption pursuant to a traditional adoption SWST Code 38-03-24 "Ecagwaya or traditional adoption."

Gerald Heminger is 66 years of age and Rosella is 58. They have resided on the Lake Traverse Indian Reservation for many years. They have been the primary caretakers of [B] since May of 1989 when he was brought to them by representatives from CPP of the Sisseton Wahpeton Sioux Tribe. They have received many children into their home over a period of many years as licensed foster parents for CPP and its predecessor agencies.

The "Anglo" adoption which is governed by chapter 39 "Parental Termination" and chapter 43 "Adoption" of the Tribal Code is in summary a two-step process of first terminating parental rights on the grounds of aban-donment or neglect and then granting adoption for the orphan child if it is found in the best interest of the child. In this case the tribal court found that the petitioners failed to prove abandonment. As a consequence that prayer of the petition asking for an "Anglo" adoption was denied.

Analysis of Law and Fact

There are three issues the appellant raises:

1. The trial court erred as a matter of law in deciding that the standard of proof for an Indian adoption under tribal law is clear and convincing evidence rather than beyond a reasonable doubt.
2. The Hemingers did not present sufficient evidence to prove a tradi-tional adoption.
3. The Hemingers did not satisfy the technical requirements of the adop-tion ordinance.

This court is of the opinion that the appellees [Hemingers] have failed to fulfill the technical requirements of a traditional adoption and as that relates to evidence, there is insufficient evidence to prove up the case for a traditional adoption. This court will not address the standard of proof issue.

The section of law at issue is: SWST Code 39-03-24

Ecagwaya or "Traditional Adoption"—means according to Tribal Custom, the placement of a child by his/her natural parent(s) with another family but without any Court involvement. After a period of two (2) years in the care of another family, the Court, upon petition of the adoptive parents, will recognize that the adoptive parents, in a custom or traditional adoption have certain rights over a child even though parental rights of the natural parents have never been termi-nated. Traditional adoption must be attested to by two (2) reliable wit-nesses. The Court, in its discretion, on a case-by-case basis, shall resolve any questions that arise over the respective rights of the natu-ral parent(s) in the custom adoption. The decision of the Court shall be based on the best interests of the child and on recognition of where the child's sense of family is. Ecagwaya is to raise or to take in as if the child is a biological child. The Court shall take "Judicial Notice" after proper due process proceedings, that, indeed, Ecagwaya is a custom and tradition of the tribe.

Under Anglo law, before an adoption can take place, parental rights must be terminated. If the termination is contested there must be a showing of abandonment or deprivation. Under Anglo law parents have a fundamental right to their children which is of a constitutional dimension. Because of this constitutional protection parental rights may not be terminated unless such care falls below a minimum community standard of care. *In Interest of L.J.*, 436 N.W.2d 558 (N.D. 1989) at 561. Because natural parents are only required to meet a minimum standard of care in rearing their birth child the best interest of the child is of little concern to the court when rights of a psychological parent and child are raised vis-à-vis the natural parents' right.

Ecagwaya adoption is a legal and traditional recognition of a child's relationship to his natural parents and a legal effort to act in the best interest of the child.

A *psychological parent* is one who on a continuing basis through interaction and companionship and interplay fulfills the child's psychological needs as well as the child's physical needs. Certainly a natural parent can fill that role and in most cases does, but such role is not limited to the natural parent.

Ecagwaya adoption is a legal acknowledgement that when a natural parent is unable or unwilling to care for a child that it is a community's obligation to care for such a child. And when members of a community take on the obligation of a psychological parent they will hold the same legal status as a natural parent with regard to custody of such child when the natural parent wishes to take back custody of said child. Before an ecagwaya adoption can take place certain things must take place without court involvement before the adoption is recognized by the court at a later date. For an ecagwaya adoption to take place there must be placement of a child by a natural parent with another family without any court involvement. After a period of two (2) years in the care of another family the court will recognize that the caretakers have certain rights over a child even though the natural parents' rights have not been terminated. . . .

The appellees [Hemingers] in this action argue that there was no court involvement in the placement of [B] with the Hemingers when [Anita] returned him to the Hemingers in August or September of 1989 and that the Hemingers have had physical custody of [B] for two years and as such are entitled to a status of adoptive parents pursuant to an ecagwaya adoption.

This court disagrees with this analysis. On May 3, 1989 [B] was made a ward of the trial court and put into custody of CPP and placed with the Hemingers as foster parents. On July 14, 1989, the court issued a continuing order making [B] a ward of the court and custody remaining with CPP.

When Anita returned |B| to the Hemingers later that summer she could only do so with acquiescence of CPP since they had legal custody. And CPP would have been unable to acquiesce to an ecagwaya adoption, as only the natural parents have authority to initiate such an adoption and CPP was under court order to make reasonable efforts to return |B| to his home. . . .

This court concludes that there have been continuing adversary court proceedings in this case since May 1989 and have continued through the decree of ecagwaya adoption on February 14, 1992. This court finds that an ecagwaya adoption cannot take place because of such court involvement.

For the reasons set out in this opinion the trial court's decision to grant such adoption is reversed and the adoption is vacated.

Questions

1. In the four court opinion excerpts, how were the principles of tribal custom used in relationship to other forms of tribal and nontribal law? Do you agree with the justices that legal principles from tribal custom and tradition were the proper principles to apply?
2. Do you think custom and tradition change when they are incorporated into cases like these?
3. What purpose does the trickster tale serve in the *Champagne v. People of Little River Band of Ottawa Indians* opinion?
4. In the Yakima case *In Re the Marriage of Napyer*, the court overruled the written tribal law on marriage in order to find the Napyer marriage valid. Do you think tribal judges should be able to override written law in cases like this? Why or why not?
5. In the Navajo case *In Re Estate of Benally*, the court looked at state case law to help define "immediate family." Do you agree with the way the court handled this question?
6. In *DuMarce v. Heminger*, why do you think that the trial court found that the petitioners failed to prove abandonment? How long would Anita have had to go without seeing her son in order for the court to find abandonment?
7. Describe the difference between "Anglo" adoption and ecagwaya adoption as explained by the court in *DuMarce v. Heminger*.

In Your Community

1. Does your tribal code acknowledge that custom and tradition can be used by a tribal judge?

2. Are there any cases in your tribal nation in which a tribal court used custom to decide a case? If so, do you agree with the outcome(s)?

Glossary

Acquiesce: To agree; accept; go along with something.

Competent: Properly qualified; adequate.

Decedent: A dead person.

Decree: A judgment of a court that announces the legal consequences of the facts found in a case.

Devise: A gift by will, especially of land or things on land.

Indigency: A level of poverty with real hardship and deprivation.

Instrument: A formal or legal document.

Intervene: To voluntarily enter into a lawsuit between other persons.

Prayer: In law, a request in a legal pleading.

Predecessor: Someone or something that goes before.

Stipulate: Specify as a condition or requirement in a contract or agreement.

Vacate: Annul; set aside; take back.

Suggested Further Reading

Matthew L. M. Fletcher, *Rethinking Customary Law in Tribal Court Jurisprudence*, 13 Michigan Journal of Race and Law 57 (2007).

Note

1. San Ildefonso Pueblo Code, Title 1 § 1.3 (1996).

CHAPTER 24

Traditional Dispute Resolution

I N ADDITION TO the different tribal legal procedures and principles already addressed, there are other approaches to contemporary tribal law that an increasing number of tribes have been adding to their existing legal systems. These approaches, which include peacemaking movements and other forms of contemporary traditional dispute resolution systems, come from a recognition that some disputes between tribal members are not well suited to being handled by Anglo-American-style legal procedures.

Disputes between members of the same family or community involving divorce, child custody, or property constitute some of the most emotionally charged conflicts in any tribe. These disputes are often only the visible surface conflicts of much deeper relationship problems that involve entire families and communities. Thus, it is not enough to simply solve the immediate dispute existing between two individuals when there are probably many more people involved—people who, for the benefit of the community or tribe, will have to continue to live, work, and relate to each other as members of the same household, clan, band, or village. It is not an accident that these kinds of issues also arise in those areas of tribal life in which aspects of their unique cultural and legal heritage are most strongly felt and followed.

To compel tribal members to take these kinds of matters to tribal court, where they may be required to argue against one another, is often considered an unsatisfactory way of redressing these conflicts. Furthermore, where such legal procedures require the tribal judge to find that one side wins and the

other loses, there is often a real sense that such procedures do not promote lasting health for tribal communities. James Sa'ke'j Youngblood Henderson and
Wanda D. McCaslin explain:

> Our vision of justice as healing recognizes that when an appropriate heal-
> ing process is clear but is not followed, expressions of abhorrence at the
> wrong and demands for justice are often subtle ways of tolerating
> wrongs. When we look for visions of justice, we should look at the best
> in our traditions of raising children, rather than consult Eurocentric
> books on justice. While we should be willing to dialogue about grant sys-
> tematic European theories of justice in modern society, we should also
> clarify their failures and how they [are] different from our visions.[1]

Consequently, tribal jurists are finding that ensuring the legitimacy of
the tribal legal system requires heeding the customary and traditional procedural norms that call for nonadversarial forms of conflict management.
Peacemaking and other contemporary traditional dispute resolution systems
are approaches that address these needs by creating forums for handling these
conflicts that are alternatives to the adversarial systems of most tribal courts.
These alternative systems work by using tribal traditions and customs of dispute resolution. Their emphasis on communal, consensual conflict management gives the disputants and their relatives an opportunity to work through
their conflict, guided by knowledgeable and respected members of the tribal
community. Through nonlitigation structures and practices, people in conflict address their problems according to their own cultural values and in light
of their own unique circumstances. In these ways, these systems are based on
the belief that those who best know the people and circumstances involved in
the conflict are also the ones who can best assist them to come to a workable,
lasting resolution.

Incorporating traditional dispute resolution has not been without its challenges. As discussed earlier, people in tribal communities often disagree about
the extent to which traditional norms, structures, and practices represent their
contemporary beliefs and way of life. They can also have these disagreements
when considering the handling of disputes. Some tribal members may feel that
the resolution they seek to their conflict can be best handled through the adversarial proceedings of tribal court. Perhaps they feel that the people presiding
over the traditional dispute resolution proceeding are prejudiced against them.
Many tribal members may feel that they better understand the adversarial
process and that they have a better chance of winning there. Perhaps some
members simply no longer feel connected to the tribal community in ways that
require deeper resolution to the conflict.

An excerpt below from an article by Ada Pecos Melton provides a valuable description of some of the fundamental differences between principles of law and justice shared among Indians and those principles of law and justice expressed in Anglo-American legal norms, structures, and practices. She gives a broad overview of the different kinds of traditional dispute resolution forums that currently operate in tribal communities across Indian Country, as well as the importance of continuing to rely on and preserve these forums in today's tribal legal systems. Following that, we excerpt a section of an article by law professor Elizabeth Joh, who describes some of the critiques that tribal members and non-Native legal professionals and scholars have with the use of traditional dispute resolution forums.

INDIGENOUS JUSTICE SYSTEMS AND TRIBAL SOCIETY

*Ada Pecos Melton**

In many contemporary tribal communities, dual justice systems exist. One is based on what can be called an American paradigm of justice, and the other is based on what can be called an indigenous paradigm.

The American paradigm has its roots in the worldview of Europeans and is based on a retributive philosophy that is hierarchical, adversarial, punitive, and guided by codified laws and written rules, procedures, and guidelines. The vertical power structure is upward, with decision making limited to a few. The retributive philosophy holds that because the victim has suffered, the criminal should suffer as well. It is premised on the notion that criminals are wicked people who are responsible for their actions and deserve to be punished. Punishment is used to appease the victim, to satisfy society's desire for revenge, and to reconcile the offender to the community by paying a debt to society. It does not offer a reduction in future crime or reparation to victims.

In the American paradigm, the law is applied through an adversarial system that places two differing parties in the courtroom to determine a defendant's guilt or innocence, or to declare the winner or loser in a civil case. It focuses on one aspect of a problem, the act involved, which is discussed

---

* Ada Pecos Melton, *Indigenous Justice Systems and Tribal Society*, 79:3 Judicature (1995).

through adversarial fact finding. The court provides the forum for testing the evidence presented from the differing perspectives and objectives of the parties. Interaction between parties is minimized and remains hostile throughout. In criminal cases, punitive sanctions limit accountability of the offender to the state, instead of to those he or she has harmed or to the community.

The indigenous justice paradigm is based on a holistic philosophy and the worldview of the aboriginal inhabitants of North America. These systems are guided by the unwritten customary laws, traditions, and practices that are learned primarily by example and through the oral teachings of tribal elders. The holistic philosophy is a circle of justice that connects everyone involved with a problem or conflict on a continuum, with everyone focused on the same center. The center of the circle represents the underlying issues that need to be resolved to attain peace and harmony for the individuals and the community. The continuum represents the entire process, from disclosure of problems, to discussion and resolution, to making amends and restoring relationships. The methods used are based on concepts of restorative and reparative justice and the principles of healing and living in harmony with all beings and with nature.

Restorative principles refer to the mending process for renewal of damaged personal and communal relationships. The victim is the focal point, and the goal is to heal and renew the victim's physical, emotional, mental, and spiritual well-being. It also involves deliberate acts by the offender to regain dignity and trust, and to return to a healthy physical, emotional, mental, and spiritual state. These are necessary for the offender and victim to save face and to restore personal and communal harmony.

Reparative principles refer to the process of making things right for oneself and those affected by the offender's behavior. To repair relationships, it is essential for the offender to make amends through apology, asking forgiveness, making restitution, and engaging in acts that demonstrate a sincerity to make things right. The communal aspect allows for crime to be viewed as a natural human error that requires corrective intervention by families and elders or tribal leaders. Thus, offenders remain an integral part of the community because of their important role in defining the boundaries of appropriate and inappropriate behavior and the consequences associated with misconduct.

In the American justice paradigm, separation of powers and separation of church and state are essential doctrines to ensure that justice occurs uncontaminated by politics and religion. For many tribes, law and justice are part of a whole that prescribes a way of life. Invoking the spiritual realm through prayer is essential throughout the indigenous process. Restoring spirituality and cleansing one's soul are essential to the healing process for everyone involved in a conflict. Therefore, separation doctrines are difficult for tribes to embrace; many find it impossible to make such distinctions. Whether this is good or bad is not the point. It is, however, an example of the resistance of indigenous people to accept doctrines or paradigms that contradict their holistic philosophy of life.

Law as a Way of Life

The concept of law as a way of life makes law a living concept that one comes to know and understand through experience. Law, as life, is linked to the elaborate relationships in many tribal communities. In some tribes it is exemplified by tribal divisions that represent legal systems prescribing the individual and kin relationships of members and the responsibilities individual and group members have to one another and to the community. For example, in several Pueblo tribes, one is born into one of two moieties, or tribal divisions, decided by patrilineal lines. A woman can change membership only through marriage, when she joins her husband's moiety. Males generally cannot change their moiety, unless it is done during childhood through adoption or if their mother remarries into the opposite moiety. This illustrates how tribal law becomes a way of life that is set in motion at birth, and continues through an individual's life and death.

The indigenous approach requires problems to be handled in their entirety. Conflicts are not fragmented, nor is the process compartmentalized into pre-adjudication, pretrial, adjudication, and sentencing stages. These hinder the resolution process for victims and offenders and delay the restoration of relationships and communal harmony. All contributing factors are examined to address the underlying issues that precipitated the problem, and everyone affected by a problem participates in the process. This distributive aspect generalizes individual misconduct or criminal behavior to the offender's wider kin group, hence there is a wider sharing of blame and guilt. The offender, along with his or her kinsmen, is held accountable and responsible for correcting behavior and repairing relationships.

Indigenous Systems Today

The status of tribes as sovereign nations are both preconstitutional and extra-constitutional. Tribes continue to possess four key characteristics of their sovereign status: a distinctive permanent population, a defined territory with identifiable borders, a government exercising authority over territory and population, and the capacity to enter into government-to-government relationships with other nation-states.

Table 24.1. Differences in Justice Paradigms

American Justice Paradigm	Indigenous Justice Paradigm
Vertical	Holistic
Communication is rehearsed	Communication is fluid
English language is used	Native language is used
Written statutory law derived from rules and procedure, written record	Oral customary law learned as a way of life by example
Separation of powers	Law and justice are part of a whole
Separation of church and state	The spiritual realm is invoked in ceremonies and prayer
Adversarial and conflict oriented	Builds trusting relationships to promote resolution and healing
Argumentative	Talk and discussion is essential
Isolated behavior, freeze-frame acts	Reviews problem in entirety, contributing factors are examined
Fragmented approach to process and solutions	Comprehensive problem solving
Time-oriented process	No time limits on the process, long silences and patience are valued
Limits participation in the process and solutions	Inclusive of all affected individuals in the process and solving problem
Represented by strangers	Representation by extended family members
Focus on individual rights	Focus on victim and communal rights
Punitive and removes offender	Corrective, offenders are accountable and responsible for change
Prescribes penalties by and for the state	Customary sanctions used to restore victim-offender relationship
Right of accused, especially against self-incrimination	Obligation of accused to verbalize accountability
Vindication to society	Reparative obligation to victims and community, apology and forgiveness

The administration of justice, law, and order is a function of government retained by the tribes as sovereign nations. It is within this realm that indigenous justice systems exist. Although there have been many efforts to limit the jurisdiction of tribal justice systems, tribes retain the authority to determine the legal structure and forums to use in administering justice and to determine the relationship of the legal structure with other governing bodies. Tribes have personal jurisdiction over their members and non-member Indians, territorial jurisdiction over their lands, and subject-matter jurisdiction over such areas as criminal, juvenile, and civil matters. While limited by the Indian Civil Rights Act in sentencing, tribes have concurrent jurisdiction over the felony crimes enumerated under the Major Crimes Act.

The forums for handling disputes differ for each tribe, which may use varying combinations of family and community forums, traditional courts, quasi-modern courts, and modern tribal courts.

Family forums, such as family gatherings and talking circles, are facilitated by family elders or community leaders. Matters usually involve family problems, marital conflicts, juvenile misconduct, violent or abusive behavior, parental misconduct, or property disputes. Customary laws, sanctions, and practices are used. Individuals are summoned to these gatherings following traditional protocols initiated by the chosen elder. For example, in Pueblo communities the gathering is convened by the aggrieved person's family, which must personally notify the accused and his or her family of the time and place of the gathering.

Generally, elders are selected as spokespersons responsible for opening and closing the meetings with prayers. During the meeting, each side has an opportunity to speak. The victim may speak on his or her own behalf, and the family may assist in conveying the victim's issues. Extended family members often serve as spokespersons if the victim is very young or vulnerable. Similarly, a spokesperson may be designated to speak on behalf of the accused, especially if the accused is a juvenile or if other circumstances prevent the accused from speaking. When the family forum cannot resolve a conflict, the matter may be pursued elsewhere. Offender compliance is obligatory and monitored by the families involved. It is discretionary for decisions and agreements to be recorded by the family.

Community forums require more formal protocols than family forums, but draw on the families' willingness to discuss the issues, events, or accusations. These are mediated by tribal officials or representatives. Some tribes have citizen boards that serve as peacemakers or facilitators. Customary laws, sanctions, and practices are used. Personal notice is made by tribal representatives to the individuals and families involved. Usually, this is all that is necessary to compel individuals to meet in both the family and community forums. When necessary, a personal escort to the gathering place may be provided by tribal officials. In some tribal communities notice may be by mail.

In the community forum, the tribal representative acts as facilitator and participates in the resolution process along with the offender and victim and their families. As with the family forum, prayers are said at the beginning and at closure. An unresolved matter may be taken to the next level, however, but tribes may or may not offer an appeal process for the community forum. In the Navajo peacemaker system, formal charges in the Navajo district court may be filed. In some Pueblo communities, matters may be pursued through the traditional court. Offender compliance is obligatory and monitored by the families involved and tribal officials.

Traditional courts incorporate some modern judicial practices to handle criminal, civil, traffic, and juvenile matters, but the process is similar to community forums. These courts exist in tribal communities that have retained an indigenous government structure, such as the Southwest Pueblos. Matters are initiated through written criminal or civil complaints or petitions. Defendants are often accompanied by relatives to the hearings. Generally, anyone with a legitimate interest in the case is allowed to participate from arraignment through sentencing. Heads of tribal government preside and are guided by customary laws and sanctions. In some cases written criminal codes with prescribed sanctions may be used. Offender compliance is mandated and monitored by the tribal officials with assistance from the families. Noncompliance by offenders may result in more punitive sanctions such as arrest and confinement.

Defendants are notified in writing. Although rare, matters may be appealed to the tribal council. In some tribes where a dual system exists, interaction between the modern American court and traditional court are prohibited. That is, one may not pursue a matter in both lower-level courts. However, an appeal from either court may be heard by the tribal council, which serves as the appellate court. Generally, these courts record proceedings and issue written judgment orders.

Quasi-modern tribal courts are based on the Anglo-American legal model. These courts handle criminal, civil, traffic, domestic relations, and juvenile matters. Written codes, rules, procedures, and guidelines are used, and lay judges preside. Some tribes limit the types of cases handled by these courts. For instance, land disputes are handled in several Pueblo communities by family and community forums. Like traditional courts, noncompliance by offenders may result in more punitive sanctions such as arrest and confinement. These are courts of record, and appellate systems are in place.

Modern tribal courts mirror American courts. They handle criminal, civil, traffic, domestic relations, and juvenile matters and are guided by written codes, rules, procedures, and guidelines. They are presided over by law-trained judges and often exist in tribal communities that have a con-stitutional government. Like traditional courts and quasi-modern tribal courts, noncompliance by offenders may result in more punitive sanctions such as arrest and confinement. Like quasi-modern tribal courts, these are courts of record, and appellate systems are in place.

Some of the quasi-modern and modern courts incorporate indigenous justice methods as an alternative resolution process for juvenile delinquency, child custody, victim–offender cases, and civil matters. The trend of tribal courts is to use the family and community forums for matters that are highly interpersonal, either as a diversion alternative, as part of sentencing, or for victim–offender mediation. Some are court-annexed programs such as the Alternatives For First Time Youth Offenders Program sponsored by the Laguna Pueblo tribal court in New Mexico. Under this program, juve-nile offenders are referred to the village officers, who convene a commu-nity forum. Recommendations for resolving the matter may be court-ordered, or the resolution may be handled informally by the village officers. This joint effort by the court and village officers allows them to address the problem at the local village level and to intervene early to pre-vent further delinquency.

THE PROBLEM OF CUSTOMARY LAW

Elizabeth E. Joh[*]

No less problematic is the structure of Indian court practice, which is often defended on the grounds that it is more amenable to, or resembles, tradi-tional procedures. Most Indian judges are not law school graduates, nor do they receive any systematic legal training. Many tribal courts do not have prosecutors. Although Indian defendants are given a qualified right to an attorney in criminal cases, most cannot afford them. The majority of dis-putants represent themselves, or are represented by a lay advocate, a fellow reservation member who may only have a high school education. While at first glance these appear to be institutional shortcomings, a number of tribal

[*] Elizabeth E. Joh, *Custom, Tribal Court Practice, and Popular Justice*, 25 American Indian Law Review 117, 123–24 (2001).

court supporters insist that this situation enhances a customary approach to justice. For instance, Deloria and Lytle contend that:

> [I]f attorneys were to take over the systems of tribal justice, it would not be too long before Indian customs and traditions, the studied informality of the tribal courts, and the particular attention that tribal judges pay to family situations and responsibilities would be replaced by a variety of model codes written by and for the convenience of the attorneys.[2]

In this view, custom is invoked to justify the relaxation, or virtual elimination, of Anglo-American procedural rules in many tribal justice systems. Advocates of the current system point to instances where tribal judges take the disputing parties aside, away from the courtroom, and suggest informal resolutions to disputes. Thus, the tribal court judge is recast in the role of tribal mediator, the traditional elder whose aim is to restore harmony to the group.

The invocation of custom here, however, masks causal explanations for the differences in structure between a tribal court and a state or federal court. A variety of factors contribute to the absence of practicing attorneys in tribal courts: the lack of access to professional schools for Indians; the reluctance of the few Indian lawyers to practice in tribal courts; and the dismally underfunded tribal courts themselves, in a profession where prestige is often tied to salary. In theory the withdrawal from formal procedures and principles may not affect proceedings that focus on "talking out" the resolution of disputes. On the surface of things, it may appear that a tribal court proceeding vindicates customary practices; the judge may know the parties or be related to them, many "legalistic" practices are tossed aside, and all parties are relatively free to speak their minds. Studies of tribal court practice, however, suggest that in a large number of cases, individuals in tribal courts receive neither a Western-style adjudication nor a customary one. Criminal defendants may be convicted or pressured into pleading guilty on the basis of virtually no evidence: a phenomenon [Samuel J.] Brakel deplores as "summary justice." And, unlike the use of customary law, tribal court practices are not a choice among alternatives in individual cases. The absence of formality and "legalese" is not necessarily identical to the practice of customary law.

Questions

1. Do you agree with the comparisons and contrasts made by Melton between traditional forms of tribal law and Anglo-American forms of law and dispute resolution? Do you think these stark contrasts still hold true today? Explain your answer.
2. Should people in these situations be forced to address their problems through traditional dispute resolution systems? When the two sides disagree about the best way to handle their dispute, how should the proper procedure be selected?
3. Consider the validity of Joh's criticisms of tribal court procedure. Why does she think it is important that many tribal judges have not attended law school?

In Your Community

1. Do you think that a traditional dispute resolution process is appropriate for your community? Which of the models of traditional dispute resolution described by Melton would work best for your people?
2. Using the table provided by Melton, review each statement in the left or right column and explain which one best describes your tribe's unique legal norms, structures, and practices. Make your own table, listing aspects of your tribe's legal system, and explain how they compare with Anglo-American legal principles.

Glossary

Hierarchical: Classified according to certain criteria into successive levels.

Mediation: Outside help in settling a dispute.

Moiety: Either of two kinship groups based on unilateral descent that together make up a tribe or society.

Paradigm: Outstanding clear or typical example; in social science, the way a theory and its parts are coherent.

Reparative: That which repairs.

Restorative: That which serves to restore, correct, or heal.

Retributive: Relating to or marked by reward or punishment.

Suggested Further Reading

Fredric Brandfon, *Tradition and Judicial Review in the American Indian Tribal Court System*, 38 UCLA Law Review 991 (1991).

S. R. Weber, *Native Americans before the Bench: The Nature of Contrast and Conflict in Native American Law Ways and Western Legal Systems*, 19 Sociology Journal 47 (1982).

James Zion, *The Navajo Peacemaker Court: Deference to the Old and Accommodation to the New*, 11 American Indian Law Review 89 (1983).

Notes

1. James Sa'ke'j Youngblood Henderson & Wanda D. McCaslin, *Introduction*, in *Justice as Healing: Indigenous Ways* (Wanda D. McCaslin, ed., 2005).

2. Vine Deloria Jr. & Clifford M. Lytle, *American Indians, American Justice* 122 (1983).

CHAPTER 25

Introduction to Peacemaking

P EACEMAKING as a way of handling disputes has captured the imagination and attention of tribal communities and their leaders across Indian Country as a valuable alternative to tribal courts. This suggests that peacemaking addresses certain fundamental principles of law, justice, and the handling of community conflict that tribal peoples share, despite the vast differences in their cultures and histories. While we must be careful not to overemphasize the similarities among tribes and thereby ignore the uniqueness of each tribe's cultural and legal heritage, it is important to account for the popularity of peacemaking models in Indian Country. This will help us understand some of the dissatisfaction that tribal members everywhere express about tribal court systems that rely primarily on adversarial systems of dispute resolution.

The modern peacemaking movement is generally considered to have its origins with the creation of the Navajo Hozhooji Naat'aanii, or Peacemaker Court. Rules for the Peacemaker Court were adopted in 1982 by the judges of the Navajo Nation to create another avenue for dispute resolution that was recognized officially by contemporary Navajo law but would manage conflicts without the formal, adversarial procedures used by the Navajo Tribal Court. This was a response precisely to the need for a Navajo tribal forum that could resolve disputes not suited for the Anglo-style tribal court by relying on the traditional Navajo practice of selecting a *naat'aanii*, a respected community leader, who would help parties solve their problems. The Peacemaker Court continues to be a strong and active part of the Navajo legal system today.

In the following passage, Philmer Bluehouse explains how he worked to develop the peacemaking process for the Navajo Nation.

IS IT "PEACEMAKERS TEACHING" OR IS IT "TEACHING PEACEMAKERS"?

Philmer Bluehouse[*]

I knew that the actual process of peacemaking had to be cultural and traditional. Among other matters of developing the internal mechanisms of administration and management, I would take the time to go to a secluded place in nature to pray and discover. This was not too unusual for me at the time, because it was part of the events unfolding within the responsibility I was made a part of.

For two weeks, I went to a place I chose, behind the rocks at Window Rock. There I scribed, in my mind's eye, and at a real place, an area about ten feet square. Here I prayed, and I saw things that could not have been ordinarily visible, things I had not actively sought out until then in a real way. It was interesting to rely on things I cannot explain, but it happened.

Some matters I received guidance from were the way the things of nature interacted. The wind (air) interacting with the puddles of water, the pollen soup in the water, the thirty or more varieties of plants in that area, the sand and minerals, their colors and how they sparkled or were dull, the heat and cold, the creation that was there without my influence, it was nature! My relatives there humbled me; there was peace. It was here where I remembered the Mother Earth and Father Universe sand painting that I observed in my childhood.

It was my Auntie Jones who was the patient. I remember the medicine man describing the contents, and allowing myself and my cousins to participate in the drawing. The necessity for peace and planning between man and woman, the importance of peace and healing among all of creation. It was very clear then, and it became clearer in the spring of 1992. It represented the traditional law codified by the painting. It was by a man and his assistants who had no formal Western education, but who obviously had an abundance of traditional education.

I decided this was the path embodied in that sand painting. I remember I had no computer assigned to me at my new office. I brought it from home, my Radio Shack-Tandy 1000 with the dot matrix printer, which printed only in black. I went to the Tandy and drew the painting from

[*] Philmer Bluehouse, *Is It "Peacemakers Teaching" or Is It "Teaching Peacemakers"?* 20:4 Conflict Resolution Quarterly (2003).

memory the way it was presented to me, that day, behind the rocks. It was awesome. . . . This is the paradigm I have used from that point on, as the foundation for peacemaking.

I knew that peacemaking was a natural phenomenon, as was the phenomenon of warrioring; it is the balance represented in the sand painting. It is this awesomeness of realizing and the humility that guided me, and it still guides me. There is value in that thing otherwise considered to be "uneducated." Traditional values and their education, the knowledge they contain, cannot be placed with a monetary value. This has a value of life itself, it is beyond just what is in the books, and it is esoteric and organic at the same time as it exists.

There are other alternatives to tribal court that relate to tribal customs and traditions of conflict management. In fact, given the uniqueness of each tribe's customs and traditions, even those tribes that are using peacemaking and Peacemaker Courts usually have created a system that is different than the one being used by the Navajo Nation. For example, some contemporary traditional dispute resolution systems working today rely on leaders from families or clans rather than communities or villages to assist in the resolution of their relatives' disputes. These leaders were seen as the traditional bearers of dispute resolution responsibilities. Still other systems rely on the use of a panel of leaders, rather than just one or two, to guide the resolution of their members' disputes.

The conflict management systems that tribes have in place are as varied as the cultures and practices of the communities they serve. Thus, it is important that when any tribe considers developing a dispute resolution system based on its customs and traditions, it takes the time to thoroughly investigate its own culture and practices of conflict management and to tailor its emerging contemporary approach of dispute resolution to its own unique legal concerns. For these reasons, the processes necessary for developing peacemaker or traditional dispute resolution systems in tribes today are closely tied to the processes of developing tribal common law discussed earlier. Both require approaching tribal customs and traditions as primary sources of law, and then determining how the principles and practices derived from traditional sources can be used in contemporary tribal legal contexts, in ways that are sensitive to the current values and ways of life of tribal members.

When one tribe or nation adopts the peacemaking systems of another tribe without first considering its own unique legal heritage of dispute resolution, it may face threats to its own legal legitimacy and tribal sovereignty. Favoring any kind of law from "outside" the tribe may fail to respect and value the norms, structures, and practices that constitute that tribal community's law and ways of life. Such a failure can be especially problematic because traditional dispute resolution is supposed to return to the legal traditions of each community.

The development of both tribal common law and traditional dispute resolution systems is grounded in using the norms, structures, and practices of the tribal community as the basis for tribal law and legal practices. At the same time, both have to deal with the fact that there are Anglo-American-style legal systems in place on and off the reservation that affect the use of custom and tradition as sources of substantive and procedural tribal law.

The essay below by the Honorable Robert Yazzie, chief justice of the Navajo Nation, considers some of these same distinctions as they apply in a comparison between Navajo and Anglo-American concepts of law and legal practice. In this comparison, he distinguishes between the "vertical justice" of the adversarial system, with its organization around the power to enforce win/lose punitive decisions to resolve disputes, and the "horizontal justice" of Navajo legal concepts, which are concerned with consensus-based conflict management by which people in dispute determine for themselves the best forms of restitution to return the community to a healthy working state.

"LIFE COMES FROM IT": NAVAJO JUSTICE CONCEPTS

Robert Yazzie[*]

The Navajo System: "Horizontal" Justice

Navajo justice is a sophisticated system of egalitarian relationships where group solidarity takes the place of force and coercion. In it, humans are not in ranks or status classifications from top to bottom. Instead, all humans are equals and make decisions as a group. The process—which we call "peacemaking" in English—is a system of relationships where there is no need for force, coercion or control. There are no plaintiffs or defendants, no "good guy" or "bad guy." These labels are irrelevant. "Equal justice" and "equality before the law" mean precisely what they say. As Navajos, we do not think of equality as treating people before the law; they are equal in it. Again, our Navajo language points this out in practical terms.

---

[*] Robert Yazzie, *"Life Comes from It": Navajo Justice Concepts*, 24 New Mexico Law Review 175, 181–89 (1994).

Under the vertical justice system, when a Navajo is charged with a crime, the judge asks (in English): "Are you guilty or not guilty?" A Navajo cannot respond because there is no precise term for "guilty" in the Navajo language. The word *guilt* implies a moral fault which commands retribution. It is a nonsense word in Navajo law due to the focus on healing, integration with the group, and the end goal of nourishing ongoing relationships with the immediate and extended family, relatives, neighbors and community.

Clanship—*dooneeike'*—is part of the Navajo legal system. There are approximately 210 Navajo clans. The clan institution establishes relationships among individual Navajos by tracing them to a common mother; some clans are related to each other the same way. The clan is a method of establishing relationships, expressed by the individual calling other clan members "my relative." Within a clan, every person is equal because rank, status, and power have no place among relatives.

The clan system fosters deep, learned emotional feelings which we call *k'e*. The term means a wide range of deeply-felt emotions which create solidarity of the individual with his or her clan. When Navajos meet, they introduce themselves to each other by clan: "I am one of the (name) clan, born for the (name) clan, and my grandparents' clans are (name)." The Navajo encounter ritual is in fact a legal ceremony, where those who meet can establish their relationships and obligations to each other. The Navajo language reinforces those bonds by maxims which require duties and mutual (or reciprocal) relationships. Obviously, one must treat his or her relatives well, and we say: "Always treat people as if they were your relative." That is also k'e.

Navajo justice uses k'e to achieve restorative justice. When there is a dispute the procedure, which we call "talking things out," works like this: Every person concerned with or affected by the dispute or problem receives notice of a gathering to talk things out. At the gathering everyone has the opportunity to be heard. In the vertical legal system the "zone of dispute" is defined as being only between the people who are directly involved in the problem. On the other hand, as a Navajo, if my relative is hurt, that concerns me; if my relative hurts another, I am responsible to the injured person. In addition, if something happens in my community, I am also affected. I am entitled to know what happened, and I have the right to participate in discussions of what to do about it. I am within the zone of a dispute involving a relative. In the horizontal system the zone is wider because problems between people also affect their relatives.

The parties and their relatives come together in a relaxed atmosphere to resolve the dispute. There are no fixed rules of procedure or evidence to limit or control the process. Formal rules are unnecessary. Free communication without rules encourages people to talk with each other to reach a consensus. Truth is largely irrelevant because the focus of the gathering is to discuss a problem. Anyone present at the gathering may speak freely about his or her feelings or offer solutions to the problem. Because of the relationship and obligation that clan members have with each other, relatives of the parties are involved in the process. They can speak for, or speak in support of, relatives who are more directly involved in the dispute.

The involvement of relatives assures that the weak will not be abused and that silent or passive participants will be protected. An abused victim may be afraid to speak; his or her relatives will assert and protect that person's interests. The process also deals with the phenomenon of denial where people refuse to face their own behavior. For instance, a perpetrator may feel shame for an act done, and therefore hesitant to speak. Relatives may speak to show mitigation for the act and to try to make the situation right. For example, Judge Irene Toledo of the Navajo Nation Ramah Judicial District has recounted a story in which the family helped a man confront the results of his actions.

The actions of this particular man commenced as an adversarial paternity proceeding familiar to today's child support enforcement efforts. The alleged father denied paternity while the mother asserted it. Judge Toledo sent the case to the district's Navajo Peacemaker Court for resolution. The parents of the couple were present for talking things out in peacemaking. It is difficult for a man and a woman to have a relationship in a small community without people knowing what is going on. The couple's family and everyone else who was present at the peacemaking were well aware of the activities of the couple. In light of the presence of family, the man admitted that he was the father of the child, and the parties negotiated paternity and child support as a group. The participation of a wider circle of relations is an effective means to address denial and get directly to a resolution of a problem rather than get sidetracked in a search for "the truth."

The absence of coercion or punishment is an important Navajo justice concept because there are differences in the way people are treated when force is a consideration. If, as in the vertical system, a decision will lead to coercion or punishment, there are procedural controls to prevent unfair decisions and state power. These safeguards include burdens of proof on the state, a high degree of certainty (e.g., "proof beyond a reasonable doubt"), the right of the accused to remain silent, and many other procedural limitations. If, however, the focus of a decision is problem-solving and not punishment, then parties are free to discuss problems.

Thus, another dynamic which we may see in Judge Toledo's example is that if we choose to deal with a dispute as a problem to be solved through discussion, rather than an act which deserves punishment, the parties are more likely to openly address their dispute.

Traditional Navajo civil procedure uses language and ceremony to promote the process of talking things out. Navajo values are expressed in prayers and teachings—using the powerful connotative force of our language—to bring people back to community in solidarity. Navajo values convey the positive forces of *hozhooji*, which aims toward a perfect state. The focus is on doing things in a "good way," and to avoid *hashkeeji naat'aah*, "the bad or evil way of speaking."

The process has been described as a ceremony. Outside the Navajo perspective, a "ceremony" is seen as a gathering of people to use ritual to promote human activity. To Navajos, a ceremony is a means of invoking supernatural assistance in the large community of reality. People gather in a circle to resolve problems but include supernatural forces within the circle's membership. Ceremonies use knowledge which is fundamental and which none of us can deny. Traditional Navajo procedure invokes that which Navajos respect (i.e., the teachings of the Holy People or tradition) and touches their souls. Put in a more secular way, it reaches out to their basic feelings.

For example, traditional Navajo tort law is based on *nalyeeh*, which is a demand by a victim to be made whole for an injury. In the law of nalyeeh, one who is hurt is not concerned with intent, causation, fault, or negligence. If I am hurt, all I know is that I hurt; that makes me feel bad and makes those around me feel bad too. I want the hurt to stop, and I want others to acknowledge that I am in pain. The maxim for nalyeeh is that there must be compensation so there will be no hard feelings. This is restorative justice. Returning people to good relations with each other in a community is an important focus. Before good relations can be restored, the community must arrive at a consensus about the problem.

Consensus makes the process work. It helps people heal and abandon hurt in favor of plans of action to restore relationships. The dispute process brings people together to talk out a problem, then plan ways to deal with it. The nature of the dispute becomes secondary (as does "truth") when the process leads to a plan framed by consensus. Consensus requires participants to deal with feelings, and the ceremonial aspect of the justice gathering directly addresses those feelings. If, for any reason, consensus is not reached (due to the human weaknesses of trickery, withholding information or coercion), it will present a final decision from being reached or void one which stronger speakers may force on others.

There is another Navajo justice concept which we must understand for a better comprehension of Navajo justice, and that is distributive justice.

Navajo case outcomes are often a kind of absolute liability where helping a victim is more important than determining fault. Distributive justice is concerned with the well-being of everyone in a community. For instance, if I see a hungry person, it does not matter whether I am responsible for the hunger. If someone is injured, it is irrelevant that I did not hurt that person. I have a responsibility, as a Navajo, to treat everyone as if he or she were my relative and therefore to help that hungry person. I am responsible for all my relatives. This value which translates itself into law under the Navajo system of justice is that everyone is part of a community, and the resources of the community must be shared with all. Distributive justice abandons fault and adequate compensation (a fetish of personal injury lawyers) in favor of assuring well-being for everyone. This affects the legal norms surrounding wrongdoing and elevates restoration over punishment.

Another aspect of distributive justice is that in determining compensation, the victim's feelings and the perpetrator's ability to pay are more important than damages determined using a precise measure of actual losses. In addition, relatives of the party causing the injury are responsible for compensating the injured party, and relatives of the injured party are entitled to the benefit of the compensation.

These are the factors that Navajo justice planners have used in the development of a modern Navajo legal institution—the Navajo Peacemaker Court. Before the development of the Peacemaker Court, Navajos experienced the vertical system of justice in the Navajo Court of Indian Offenses (1892–1959) and the Courts of the Navajo Nation (1959–present). Over that one-hundred-year period, Navajos either adapted the vertical system to their own ways or expressed their dissatisfaction with a system that made no sense.

In 1982, however, the Judicial Conference of the Navajo Nation created the Navajo Peacemaker Court. This court is a modern legal institution which ties traditional community dispute resolution to a court based on the vertical justice model. It is a means of reconciling horizontal (or circle) justice to vertical justice by using traditional Navajo legal values, such as those described above.

The Navajo Peacemaker Court makes it possible for judges to avoid adjudication and avoid the discontent adjudication causes by referring cases to local communities to be resolved by talking things out. Once a decision is reached, it may (if necessary) be capped with a formal court judgment for future use.

The Navajo Peacemaker Court takes advantage of the talents of a naat'aanii (or "peacemaker"). A naat'aanii is a traditional Navajo civil leader whose authority comes from his or her selection by the community.

The naat'aanii is chosen due to his or her demonstrated abilities, wisdom, integrity, good character, and respect by the community. The civil authority of a naat'aanii is not coercive or commanding; he or she is a leader in the truest sense of the word. A peacemaker is a person who thinks well, who speaks well, who shows a strong reverence for the basic teachings of life and who has respect for himself and others in personal conduct.

A naat'aanii acts as a guide, and in a peacemaker's eyes everyone—rich or poor, high or low, educated or not—is treated as an equal. The vertical system also attempts to treat everyone as an equal before the law, but judges in that system must single out someone for punishment. The act of judgment denies equality, and in that sense, "equality" means something different than the Navajo concept. The Navajo justice system does not impose a judgment, thereby allowing everyone the chance to participate in the final judgment, which everyone agrees to and which benefits all.

Finally, the naat'aanii is chosen for knowledge, and knowledge is power which creates the ability to persuade others. There is a form of distributive justice in the sharing of knowledge by a naat'aanii. He or she offers it to the disputants so they can use it to achieve consensus.

Today's consumers of justice in the Navajo system have a choice of using the peacemaking process or the Navajo Nation version of the adversarial system. The Navajo justice system, similar to contemporary trends in American law, seeks alternatives to adjudication in adversarial litigation. The Navajo Nation alternative is to go "back to the future" by using traditional law.

Navajo Justice Thinking

The contract between vertical and horizontal (or circle) justice is only one approach or model to see how Navajos have been developing law and justice. We, as Navajo judges, have only recently begun to articulate what we think and do on paper and in English. Navajo concepts of justice are simple, but our traditional teachings which we use to make peace, may sound complicated. Peacemaking—Navajo justice—incorporates traditional Navajo concepts, or Navajo common law, into modern legal institutions. Navajo common law is not about rules which are enforced by authority; it deals with correcting self to restore life to solidarity. Navajo justice is a product of the Navajo way of thinking. Peacemakers use the Navajo thought and traditional teachings. They apply the values of spiritual teachings to bond disputants together and restore them to good relations.

This paper uses English ways of saying things and English language concepts. It uses "paper knowledge" to try to teach you some of the things that go on in a Navajo judge's mind. To give a flavor of Navajo language thinking consider the following:

Never let the sun catch you sleeping. Rise before the sun comes up. Why? You must not be dependent. You must do things with energy and do things for yourself. You must be diligent or poverty will destroy you.

Watch your words. Watch what you say. Remember, words are very powerful. The Holy People gave them to us, and they created you to communicate. That is why you must think and speak in a positive way. Be gentle with your words. Do not gossip. Gossip has a name. It has a mind, eyes and a voice. It can cause as much trouble as you make by calling it, so do not call it to you. It causes disharmony and creates conflict among people. It is a living monster because it gets in the way of a successful life. So, as we and our young Anglo friends say, "What goes around comes around." Remember that there are consequences to everything you say and do.

Know your clan. Do not commit incest. You cannot court or marry within your own clan. If you do, you will destroy yourself; you will jump in the fire. Incest is something so evil that it will make you crazy and destroy you.

You have duties and responsibilities to your spouse and children. If you are capable and perform them, you will keep your spouse and children in a good way. If not, you will leave them scattered behind. You will not be a worthy man or woman. If you act as if you have no relatives, that may come to you.

The Holy People created human beings. Due to that fact, each must respect others. One cannot harm another. If so, harm will come back on you. There are always consequences from wrongful acts, just as good comes from good. Like begets like, so harm must be repaired through restitution (nalyeeh), so there will be no hard feelings and victims will be whole again.

These teachings, and many others, are spoken from the beginning of childhood. Navajo judges are beginning to look at familiar childhood experiences as legal events. For example, when a baby first becomes aware of surroundings and shows that in a laugh, there is a ceremony—the "Baby's First Laugh Ceremony." Family and relatives gather around the baby, sharing food and kinship, to celebrate with it. What better way can we use to initiate babies into a world of good relationships and teach them the legal institution that is the clan?

These learned values serve as a guide in later years. As a child grows, he or she will act according to the teachings. Elderly Navajos tell us that we must always talk to our children so they can learn these Navajo values and beliefs. If we do not there will be disorder in the family and among relatives. The children will not listen, and they will have no responsibility to live by. We have youth violence because parents failed to talk to their children.

Conclusion

Traditional peacemaking is being revived in the Navajo Nation with the goal of nourishing local justice in local communities. The reason is obvious: life comes from it. Communities can resolve their own legal problems using the resources they have. Local decisions are the traditional Navajo way, in place of central control. Everyone must have access to justice that is inexpensive, readily available and does not require expensive legal representation. Peacemaking does not need police, prosecutors, judges, defenders, social workers or the other agents of adversarial adjudication. Peacemaking is people making their own decisions, not others forcing decisions upon them. There are 110 chapters or local governmental units in the Navajo nation. As of this writing, there are 210 peacemakers in 89 chapters, and we will extend the Navajo Peacemaker Court to every community.

This revival assures that Navajo justice will remain Navajo justice, and not be an imported or imposed system.

Concerns Raised by Victims

Many advocates for victims of violent crime have raised significant concerns about the application of peacemaking in cases of domestic violence, child sexual abuse, and rape. Because of the inherent power differences between a perpetrator and victim, the normal standards of "horizontal" justice may prove more difficult to apply. Moreover, victim advocates have reported that victims may feel coerced, pressured, or shamed into participating in a "restorative" process with the perpetrator. Worse, some victims have reportedly been subject to increased threats and violence even after participating in peacemaking. This application remains an area of controversy.

Professor Donna Coker was one of the first scholars to publish some formal critiques of the Navajo peacemaking system, in 1999. As a non-Navajo legal scholar, she focused her observations on some of the weaknesses of peacemaking as applied in domestic violence cases. Seven years later, Coker revisited the issue. Consider whether concerns about safety, coercion, and justice could be resolved through changes in the substantive or procedural guidelines.

RESTORATIVE JUSTICE, NAVAJO PEACEMAKING, AND DOMESTIC VIOLENCE

*Donna Coker**

Limitations of Peacemaking

None of the battered women's advocates in the Navajo Nation that I spoke with in 1997 supported Peacemaking, as it was then constituted, for domestic violence cases. . . . Some advocates believed that with appropriate safeguards and training, Peacemaking might be appropriate for some women, while others believed that either because of changes in Navajo culture or the inherent power imbalance between batterer and victim, Peacemaking could not be reformed to meet the needs of battered women. To some extent, their concerns echoed those of others who are critical of mediation and [restorative justice] processes in these cases. The concerns are that women would be coerced into agreements, the seriousness of the violence would be minimized and the process would place undue emphasis on an abuser's apology without emphasizing a change in behaviour; what I call a "cheap justice" problem. The advocates also raised concerns that were unique to Peacemaking: the Peacemakers held an anti-divorce bias; there was misplaced reliance on traditional Navajo stories and concepts when many Navajo had little or no understanding of, nor respect for, traditional stories and values; and there were inadequate mechanisms for enforcement.

Coercion and Safety

Coercion was a particular problem for the self-referred cases initiated by abusive men. Peacemaker liaisons told me that in self-referred cases they first contact the parties; if a woman claimed abuse, they would try to persuade her to attend, but they would not compel her attendance. In contrast, domestic violence advocates told me that battered women receive subpoenas ordering them to attend, that the subpoena offers no information regarding one's ability to resist the subpoena and Peacemakers repeatedly call shelters urging women to attend. Thus, advocates were concerned that abusive men used Peacemaking to "flush women out of hiding." (One

---

* Donna Coker, *Restorative Justice, Navajo Peacemaking, and Domestic Violence*, 10 Theoretical Criminology 67 (2006).

instance of this problem was a woman who was attacked by her husband in the parking lot after a Peacemaking session.) The ability to self-petition appealed to the significant number of battered women who initiated the process, but the lack of safeguards for battered women who were respondents created serious risks for others.

Domestication

Cobb describes the manner in which stories of abuse are domesticated as mere "disputes" in the discourse within civil court mediation sessions. I found clear evidence of domestication in one Peacemaking file, where the Peacemaker referred to severe battering as a mere 'dispute' and failed to contradict an abuser's statement equating his violence with his partner's questioning his whereabouts. I did not find other examples of domestication, but some Navajo Nation battered women's advocates believed it occurred more often.

Cheap Justice

An over-emphasis on the importance of an offender's apology creates two kinds of cheap justice problems. First, too much attention is given to the offender's rehabilitation at the expense of expressions of moral solidarity with the victim. This may ignore the victim's needs and coerce the victim to forgive the offender. Second, a sincere apology or reconciliation between the offender and the victim may fail to address the victim's primary needs for material assistance. Barbara Wall (2001) provides an example of the first concern. She describes a Peacemaking session initiated by a mother with her adult son, due to his alcoholism. Wall describes their reconciliation and the son's agreement to seek help for his alcohol addiction. Nearly lost in Wall's account is a brief mention of the son's abuse of his wife. The wife's need for protection and the son's need to seek assistance with stopping his violence thus received little attention.

Questions

1. How sensitive to tribal custom and tradition can a dispute resolution system be if it relies on the dispute resolution practices of some other, historically unrelated tribe?
2. Tribal peoples today live in circumstances where the social, economic, and political forces influencing their lives are vastly different than in the past. In light of these changes, do you think there is a place in today's tribal

communities for legal norms, practices, and structures that are based on principles of Anglo-American justice?
3. Should peacemaking be limited to cases that do not involve physical violence? Why or why not?

In Your Community

1. Does the "horizontal" justice model described by Chief Justice Yazzie also describe the model of justice in your tribe?
2. Does your tribe have customs and traditions of conflict management that differ greatly from the adversarial procedures seen in Anglo-American legal practices and the tribal courts that borrow from them?
3. Who are the traditional leaders in your community who were historically seen as the people responsible for assisting in the resolution of disputes? How did they undertake that responsibility? Did they hold private or public meetings in which entire families or entire communities were allowed to come and speak their minds? Did the people in dispute come to a resolution for their own conflict, or did the leaders decide for them? Were these decisions binding?
4. In developing a traditional dispute resolution system today, what kinds of adjustments need to be made so that this system addresses the non-Indian influences on your tribe's contemporary ways of life and law? Will these adjustments strike a balance between your tribe's unique legal heritage and Anglo-American law that promotes the legal legitimacy and tribal sovereignty of your tribe? How?

Glossary

Egalitarian: A belief in human equality with respect to social, political, and economic rights.

Fetish: An excessive or irrational devotion to an activity.

Punitive: Inflicting or aiming to inflict punishment.

Restitution: Giving something back; making good for something.

Suggested Further Reading

William C. Bradford, *Reclaiming Indigenous Legal Autonomy on the Path to Peaceful Coexistence: The Theory, Practice, and Limitations of Tribal Peacemaking in Indian Dispute Resolution*, 76 North Dakota Law Review 551 (2000).
Marianne O. Nielsen & James W. Zion, eds., *Navajo Nation Peacemaking: Living Traditional Justice* (2005).

CHAPTER 26

Models of Peacemaking

NAVAJO NATION Chief Justice Yazzie's article in the last chapter introduced some of the philosophies and practices behind the Navajo Peacemaker Court. We will now turn to a consideration of some of the peacemaking approaches being developed by other tribes. The first excerpt is from an article by Robert Odawi Porter, a citizen of the Seneca Nation and a professor at Syracuse Law School. His article offers a review of some of the peacemaking traditions of the Seneca People as part of their participation in the Haudenosaunee or Six Nations Iroquois Confederacy. This excerpt provides a discussion of the unique traditions of peacemaking as a form of both governance and traditional dispute resolution. As should be expected, the unique legal heritage described by Porter differs from the heritage that informs the Navajo peacemaking processes. There are, however, some interesting similarities. Consider how the Seneca might be able to use these principles in developing a peacemaker dispute resolution system today.

After this reading, we will turn our attention to the peacemaking system of the Little River Band of Ottawa Indians, called the Gda Dwendaagnananik. This is an excerpt of the tribe's *Peacemaking Guidelines*, a legal document that lists various rules and procedures for running and participating in the Gda Dwendaagnananik. Parts of this code are given in detail so that you might get a sense of some of the complex issues that have to be addressed when developing and running a contemporary system of traditional dispute resolution. We have included a discussion of, among other things, the criteria for selecting who can participate in a peacemaking session, how cases get referred to the peacemaking process, who can be a peacemaker and what the responsibilities entail, and a list of the steps of the Gda Dwendaagnananik session itself. When reading these guidelines, consider whether you agree or disagree with the kinds of cases that can be handled through peacemaking, the kinds of people who can go through the peacemaking process, and who can be a peacemaker, and decide whether the process itself is a good one.

The final reading reviews the process by which one Indian community, the Tlingit village of Kake, Alaska, learned about and then implemented its own contemporary traditional dispute resolution system. Its system, based on a model called "circle sentencing," was introduced to the community by Native and non-Native peoples from Canada and Alaska. However, the people of Kake tailored the system to their own unique legal and cultural heritage.

TRADITIONAL AND CONTEMPORARY SENECA DISPUTE RESOLUTION

*Robert Porter**

The Tradition of Seneca Peacemaking

The Seneca People have a peacemaking tradition that is hundreds of years old and coincides with the establishment of the Six Nations Iroquois Confederacy, or Haudenosaunee, under the Great Law of Peace. For the Haudenosaunee, peace was not simply the absence of war, it "was the law" and an affirmative government objective. So dominant was this philosophy that its pursuit affected the entire range of international, domestic, clan, and interpersonal relationships of the Haudenosaunee.

According to Haudenosaunee history, the Great Law was a gift from the Creator that had the purpose of saving the people of the Six Nations from destroying themselves. Against the grisly backdrop of cannibalism and civil war, a young man, born of mysterious circumstances and known outside of Iroquois ceremonies only as the "Peacemaker," brought a powerful message to the survivors of this tribal warfare: "all peoples shall love one another and live together in peace."

---

* Robert Porter, *Strengthening Tribal Sovereignty through Peacemaking: How the Anglo-American Legal Tradition Destroys Indigenous Societies*, 28 Columbia Human Rights Law Review 235, 239–55 (1997).

In addition to his substantive message, the Peacemaker also proposed a governmental structure through which his message could be brought into practice. The longhouse, or the traditional Haudenosaunee dwelling, had many fires, but was designed to ensure that those residing within it could "live together as one household in peace." This structure reflected a philosophy designed to ensure that the Haudenosaunee would "have one mind and live under one law" and was based upon the ideal that "thinking shall replace killing, and (that) there shall be one commonwealth."

As might be expected, given the times, the Peacemaker's message was not universally or quickly accepted. It took years for there to be an appreciable acceptance of his message of peace. While the process was slow and time-consuming, the Peacemaker eventually was able to bring together the leadership of what was to become the Mohawk, Oneida, Onondaga, Cayuga, and Seneca nations. Solely on the basis of his teachings, these five nations formed a great alliance that was dedicated to perpetuating the message of peace through unity and strength.

Pursuing peace was relevant not just to the establishment of the Haudenosaunee, but also to its perpetuation. Foremost, the Great Law was a tool of government and frequently has been referred to as the Iroquois Constitution. As such, it set forth a variety of mechanical rules governing the process by which the member nations addressed confederate affairs, including the management of diplomatic and military relations with the other continental powers, trade relations with governmental and private interests, and colonial relationships with client tribes.

The manner in which the Haudenosaunee arrived at decisions is evidence of their commitment to peace. Unlike the system of majority-rule utilized by the Anglo-Europeans, the Haudenosaunee relied upon a governing process that was both dependent upon and designed to achieve consensus. Actions could not be taken unless there was unanimity and its leaders of "one mind."

In order to facilitate consensus, the longhouse, the location at which Grand Council meetings were held, was structured so that all debate took place "across the fire." Discussion on a particular subject would be carried through three separate and elaborate stages until consensus was reached. As might be expected, there was often disagreement which impeded the discussions. Depending upon the stage at which the discussion broke down, the matter would be referred back to the point at which the process ceased. If, however, it was not possible to achieve unanimity, the matter was laid aside until a later time. Unreasonableness in this process was not tolerated and any "sachem" so acting would have "influences . . . brought to bear on him which he could not well resist."

The Haudenosaunee decision-making process ensured that the official positions it took would carry the full support of all the member nations. Ultimately, when decisions were reached, they had been extremely well discussed, with each of the nations fully informed of the competing considerations. This deliberative process facilitated the compromises and accommodations necessary to achieving "one mind" regarding any planned actions.

Because it was not possible for the Haudenosaunee to act without all nations being in agreement, there was no risk that a decision could be perceived by a political minority as being illegitimate. Commensurately, the fact that minority positions had veto power ensured that power was exercised wisely and deliberately. This consensus-oriented decision-making process allowed for such a concentration of political strength that the Haudenosaunee was the dominant military presence in the eastern portion of the North American continent for over 300 years.

This dominance often confused outsiders into thinking that the Haudenosaunee were strong solely as the result of their use of force. The reality, however, was that the Haudenosaunee made peace their objective and relied heavily upon diplomacy to achieve it, utilizing force only when necessary to enforce their law.

This philosophy characterized the Haudenosaunee approach to international relations. According to the Great Law, an invitation was held out to any nation, including the hostile ones, to join the Haudenosaunee upon acceptance of the Great Law. If a hostile nation refused an offer of peace, it would be met with a declaration of war and conquest, which occurred occasionally.

Because of its foundational belief that all human beings have the power of rational thought and that all significant decisions must be achieved through consensus, Seneca society was afflicted with little interpersonal conflict and transgressions of community norms. Individual behavior was governed by a strong unwritten social code that relied upon social and psychological sanctions, such as ridicule and embarrassment, as the primary methods of enforcement.

Behavior was governed not by published laws enforced by police, courts, and jails, but by oral tradition supported by a sense of duty, a fear of gossip, and a dread fear of retaliatory witchcraft.

Public opinion, therefore, proved an effective deterrent because it related directly to the central problem facing the community—the weakness of the criminal. These types of corrective sanctions, however, did not generally escalate to complete ostracism.

Most disputes in Seneca society were resolved by mutual consent. Instances of extreme violence, such as murder or the practice of witchcraft, were punishable by death or by restitution to the victim's family. If the wrongdoer repented, he could offer goods and services, and the matter would be resolved. Liquor usually was the primary source of social discord.

Major disputes in Seneca society were resolved with the assistance of a peacemaker. The peacemakers, who might be the chiefs, elders, or other respected persons, relied upon their position, as well as precedent (for example, legends and stories from the community) to move the parties toward reconciliation. For example, if a husband and wife were unable to resolve matters between them, the mothers of the married pair would intercede to facilitate a reconciliation. Throughout the dispute resolution process, the restoration of peace—amongst the disputing individuals and within the community as a whole—was paramount.

Despite the fact that pursuing peace was the foundation of Seneca and Haudenosaunee strength, it was also its weakness. With the coming of the Revolutionary War, the Haudenosaunee was torn apart because of the tension between its long-standing relationship with Great Britain and the earnestness of the American struggle for freedom. Unable to maintain a unified diplomatic position, within 25 years after the War the Haudenosaunee had lost almost all of its land holdings and its membership was scattered throughout small reservations in upstate New York and Canada.

As a tool of governance, the Great Law required a total commitment to peace and a commensurate commitment to achieving peace through reason. For the Senecas, it facilitated the establishment of a society that made disputes rare, and when they did occur, readily resolvable by peacemaking and social pressures. This effective dispute resolution was undoubtedly a key to internal, and thus external, strength. As a result, the Senecas were able to govern themselves with considerable success for over 300 years.

Peacemaking and Other Traditional Native Dispute Resolution Mechanisms

The Elements of Peacemaking

Peacemaking is the primary method of dispute resolution traditionally found in indigenous communities. Peacemaking is the process of resolving disputes by involving respected third parties who induce disputing parties to find common ground and restore their underlying relationship by utilizing a variety of social, spiritual, psychological, and generational pressures. There are a number of characteristics that define peacemaking and distinguish it from litigation.

First, peacemaking is concerned with justice as it relates to the benefit of the community, and not just for the benefit of individual members.

Accordingly, the dispute resolution system assumes a role directly related to the protection of tribal norms and values for the benefit of the group and not for the primary benefit of the individual. Viewed this way, one's clan, kinship, and family identities are part of one's personal identity, and one's rights and responsibilities exist only within the framework of such familial, social, and tribal networks. Since one of the most important values for native people is the ability to be integrated within the community, peacemaking requires emphasis on the perpetuation of the disputing parties' relationships. The focus on relationship takes on increased significance as the size of the native community decreases.

Second, peacemaking is not an adversarial process but is instead a mediation process in which a peacemaker works actively with the parties to help them find a mutually beneficial solution. The process revolves around an appreciation of and sensitivity to the interests of both parties against the backdrop of respect for community norms. As a result, there is no "winner" or "loser." Instead, successful peacemaking benefits the tribe as the parties come to an understanding that will allow them to carry on without the risk of further disruptions.

Third, peacemaking does not involve lawyers or representatives but requires the parties to the dispute to engage in the dispute resolution process directly. This requirement ensures that parties are directly involved in the process and not insulated from the give-and-take that is characteristic of a peacemaking session. This dynamic is critical because subtle behavior altering mechanisms such as shame, embarrassment, anger, and satisfaction play an important part in the process of finding compromise. The absence of lawyers facilitates the ability of the parties to modify previously assumed negotiating positions.

Fourth, peacemaking involves an interested mediator and not a disinterested decision maker. Usually the peacemaker is a political or spiritual leader, or elder relative, from the community who knows and is known by the disputing parties. The existence of a prior relationship, involving respect for the peacemaker, allows the peacemaker to rely upon his or her own personal moral power to urge the parties toward resolution. Thus, scoldings and lectures, rather than any type of more obvious physical coercion, assists in restoring the relationship between the disputing parties.

Fifth, while peacemaking relies upon the use of substantive norms, these norms are transmitted orally rather than through written edicts. The effect of this formal difference is that the "law" can be utilized by the parties as more of a guide to achieving substantial justice, rather than as an additional source of rigidity that might prevent the parties from adjusting their positions towards a point of compromise. Emphasis is not on guilt or innocence, but rather on redress of the problem and the restoration of the disputing parties' relationship. This equitable approach, while it may seem to minimize the importance of the norms, in fact suggests greater respect for them because the parties are able to effectuate their own solution to accommodate the norm. The peacemaker thus assumes a critical role ensuring that the parties' solution is consistent with that of the community.

Finally, peacemaking relies upon a different method of enforcement than does litigation. In a tribal community, coercive pressure arises through response mechanisms such as ridicule, ostracism, and banishment. Unlike the American enforcement mechanism, which is based on physical coercion at the hands of the state, the subtle forms of native psychological sanction utilize societal pressure to play upon the wayward member's need to remain in good stead within the community. As a result, remedies avoid coercive governmental pressure and the perception of illegitimacy often associated with it. Thus, peacemaking avoids the need for government legitimacy because it is not the government that has the enforcement function.

In sum, peacemaking is a process in which respected community members assist disputing parties, who participate without legal representation, to find a compromise to their dispute. The restoration of relationship is the primary concern and is effectuated by disregarding fault and blame and instead ensuring that the community norms are respected. Successful dispute resolution by peacemaking maintains the wholeness of the individuals involved and ensures strength and unity within the tribal community.

The Utilization of Peacemaking and Other Traditional Native Dispute Resolution Processes

Indigenous people of North America maintained order within their communities in a significantly different manner than the European settlers who later colonized their aboriginal territory. So foreign were their justice systems—due to the absence of easily observable and written institutions and procedures—that the colonists concluded that they were without law or justice. The reality, however, was that the Indians did value law and justice and relied upon a variety of methods and systems in order to ensure that those objectives were satisfied.

The key to understanding traditional native justice systems lies in the closed nature of tribal communities and the obligations of individual tribal members to perpetuate established norms. Only then can ridicule, ostracism, banishment, punishment, and peacemaking—all processes utilized by indigenous people to ensure that individual misconduct was corrected and the community norms respected and perpetuated—make sense.

Each of these sanctions was integrally related to an overall process of keeping the peace and ensuring that internal disputes were minimized and the functioning of the community undisturbed. Simply put, maintaining good relationships between tribal members was the embodiment of traditional native dispute resolution.

In aboriginal times, peacemaking was a non-deliberative process that the people instinctively understood as members of the community. Through the traditional educational system—parents, family, and community—the peacemaking system perpetuated itself. It was not that there were not norms or mechanisms to redress misconduct, it was simply that precedent—that is, oral tradition—was conveyed to all members through the social network.

How, exactly, did peacemaking work? Because of the absence of courts, lawyers, judges, and written laws, it was easy for Anglo-Americans to conclude that traditional native systems lacked formal institutions. The reality, however, was that the norms governing individual behavior and the methods utilized to ensure that those norms were perpetuated were very much institutionalized within a particular tribe. The indigenous "legal system" was more difficult to comprehend than the Anglo-American system precisely because there was no written record—success was dependent upon the ability of tribal leaders to call upon their memory of how problems within the community had been previously addressed.

Comfort with the system, or more precisely, total understanding and acceptance of the system was an integral component to why peacemaking worked to resolve internal disputes. Peacemaking, by its very nature, served to reaffirm, and perhaps even redefine, the norms that were critical for tribal survival.

Prior to contact with the European colonists, indigenous people had little choice but to accept and live by the norms established by their communities. The primary reason was that effective dispute resolution was critical for individual and group survival. Excessive acrimony in such close-knit societies was disastrous to the effective functioning of the family and clan. The ripple effect of interpersonal conflict could easily result in other families and extended family members being drawn into a matter originally concerning only a few people. Thus, unsettled acrimony led to dysfunction, which threatened the basic ability of the tribe to engage in its fundamental activities of survival, such as hunting, farming, and diplomacy. In a very real sense, the failure of disputing parties to respect tribal norms contributed to the weakening of the tribe and jeopardized their lives and the lives of other tribal members.

Because of reliance on oral tradition, our knowledge of traditional peacemaking systems is limited to what the descendants of the native people remember and may still practice, and what the anthropologists and other colonists may have recorded. It is clear, however, that a variety of different Indian nations addressed intratribal conflict through peacemaking.

PEACEMAKING GUIDELINES

Little River Band of Ottawa Indians

Section 1. Establishment of Gda Dwendaagnananik ("All Our Relations")

1.01. The Tribal Government of the Little River Band of Ottawa Indians has established a Peacemaking System to be used in cooperation with the present court system for cases involving youth and children. Cases can be referred to Peacemaking through tribal courts, state courts, any federally recognized tribe, any state historic tribe or any Anishnabek of the Three Fires (Native people indigenous to this area) who would like to voluntarily access Peacemaking.

Section 2. Vision Statement

2.01. The vision of Gda Dwendaagnananik is to provide a traditional conflict resolution process to children, youth and families. Through this process our hope is to give resolution and healing to the parties involved which will promote healthier life-styles and relationships.

Section 3. Philosophy

3.01. The Peacemaking setting is much different from state court proceedings. Unlike the state court system which is divisive by its nature and involves a judge or jury making the decisions for others, Peacemaking encourages people to solve their own problems. Peacemaking sessions are conducted by two Peacemakers: one male and one female to create balance. Peacemaking involves: (1) discussing issues in a respectful manner; (2) assisting individuals with understanding and accepting responsibility for his/her wrongdoings; (3) promoting healthy relationships; and (4) working with participants to plan and make group decisions about future actions. Planning, respect and consensus in Peacemaking sessions replace imposed decisions which use punishment to correct behavior. Rather than judge people, Peacemaking addresses bad decisions and their consequences and substitutes healing in place of force.

Section 4. Purposes of Peacemaking

4.01. Little River Band of Ottawa Indians Peacemaking System encourages people to solve their own problems in a safe environment. In Peacemaking, decisions are reached through discussing the wrongdoing of the child, and any underlying issues involving the family. In a Peacemaking session, the Peacemakers will use their own knowledge and draw from the customs and traditions of the Anishnabek of the Three Fires. The Peacemakers will strive to achieve a setting which will (1) allow active participation from parents and families whose children are in trouble; (2) provide an environment for the wrong-doer to take responsibility for his/her wrongful behavior; (3) provide an environment that is safe for victims and wrong-doers to work out problems and begin the healing process; and (4) assist in locating traditional practices and teachings and community based services to children, youth, family members and others.

Section 5. Goals of Peacemaking

5.01. One major goal of Peacemaking is to help children, youth, families, and other interested persons help themselves within the community. Through Peacemaking people within the immediate and extended family, as well as persons in the community, will gather with the Peacemakers to address problems, acknowledge them and solve them in ways which will promote healthy relationships. The Peacemaking process will focus on strengthening families, responsible thinking and developing community based solutions to handle these conflicts. The Peacemakers will work:

a. To improve family relations for Little River Band members and their children in the Tribe's nine-county services area where they reside. These counties include: Manistee, Mason, Lake, Wexford, Oceana, Kent, Ottawa, Newaygo, and Muskegon.
b. To provide access to a traditional way of resolving disputes.
c. To provide a safe environment to handle cases involving children, youth and families.
d. To provide education within non-Native communities about Peacemaking and the Native American culture.

e. To find community based alternatives to keep children and youth within the Tribal community.

f. To assist in the treatment and rehabilitation of child and youth offenders.

g. To encourage parents, children and youth to work together in a good way.

h. To provide, at all times possible, alternatives to child and youth incarceration.

[Sections 6 and 7 omitted]

Section 8. Peacemaking Cases

8.01. *Steps in Peacemaking Sessions.* The following is a guideline to conduct a Peacemaking session. These guidelines may be altered if the participants request with the exception of the confidentiality clause.

a. *Smudging.* The Peacemakers will begin the session by smudging. Some or all of the participants may decide that they do not want to smudge and their decision shall be respected.

b. *Prayer.* The session will open with a prayer which is appropriate for the participants and the occasion. A Peacemaker may lead the prayer or designate any person to open with the prayer.

c. Preparatory Instructions:

  1. *Introductions.* All of the participants will introduce themselves and the Peacemakers will explain the following ground rules:

  2. *History.* Provide participants with information about Peacemaking, its history, philosophy and purpose.

  3. *Rules.* Describe the ground rules that all participants must follow during the Peacemaking session.

     i.   No cussing or name calling.

     ii. No interruptions.

     iii. Emphasize that everyone will have an opportunity to talk and help each other problem solve.

     iv. Explanation that Peacemaking is voluntary.

     v.   Judges and lawyers have no direct role in the Peacemaking session.

     vi. Describe the procedures and steps of Peacemaking.

     vii. Describe what the participants must do when the Peacemaking session does not work for them.

     viii. Describe how a Court may help Peacemaking and the participants with enforcement through a court order when the participants have failed to comply with the Peacemaking agreement.

  4. *Confidentiality.* Explain *confidentiality* and its importance. This information must be explained to each person and each participant must

agree to it. Aside from the agreement reached and signed by the parties, the work product and case file of a Peacemaker are confidential and not subject to disclosure in a judicial or administrative proceeding. Communications relating to the subject matter of the resolution made during the resolution process by a party, Peacemaker, or other person shall be a confidential communication. *The only exception* the Peacemakers will make to this confidentiality policy is in cases of suspected child abuse. Peacemakers are required to report to the proper authorities cases where there is reasonable cause to suspect child abuse. See attached Confidentiality Agreement form.

5. *Record Keeping.* Describe the records keeping function and its importance and purpose.

8.02. *Question/Investigation.* Each participant is encouraged to discuss the problems openly. The Peacemakers will help facilitate this discussion and ensure that there is balance, freedom to speak and concern for those who may be fearful of others or intimidated by the process.

a. The objectives are to reveal the problem, to make it clear so everyone sees it, understands it and begins to deal with it.
b. Reiterate the purpose of Peacemaking so as to remind one another about the objectives.
c. Use as much traditional information as possible in the form of narratives and story telling to clarify and avoid direct shame and hostility. Also use it to reframe issues and to form specific strategies or tactics to be included in the formation of an agreement.
d. Be specific about time, date, function and assignment of what each person is going to do to satisfy an agreement.
e. Use active listening, encourage it to be used by everyone. Allow elders to give advice.

8.03. *Decisions/Recommendation.* The Peacemakers will decide and provide recommendations with input from all parties as to the "Agreement" for the youth and family. The group must understand their "Agreement" is a legally binding contract.

8.04. *Sign Commitment Contract.* The agreement must be completed and signed. See Sample Agreement Form in attached Appendices.

8.05. Close with prayer and good blessing.

KAKE CIRCLE PEACEMAKING*

In 1999, in an effort to curb youth alcohol abuse, tribal members of the Organized Village of Kake (federally recognized Tribe of Kake, Alaska) established the Healing Heart Council and Circle Peacemaking, a reconciliation and sentencing process embedded in Tlingit traditions. Working in seamless conjunction with Alaska's state court system, Circle Peacemaking intervenes in the pernicious cycle by which underage drinking becomes an entrenched pattern of adult alcoholism. Today, the program not only enforces underage drinking sentences in an environment where such accountability had been rare, but also restores the Tlingit culture and heals the Kake community.

For generations, the Tlingit people of Kake, Alaska, have witnessed their youth population's descent into patterns of underage drinking and substance abuse. Over time, these illegal behaviors have grown more damaging prodded onward by intensifying patterns of "self-medication" for depression, anxiety, and other stresses associated with poverty. The result was an emerging adult population mired in alcoholism.

Alcohol abuse is not only a chronic problem in Kake, but also throughout Alaskan tribal villages and Indian Country, where it contributes to numerous social ills. A 1998 report of the National Institute on Alcohol Abuse and Alcoholism linked alcohol abuse to "child abuse, accidental death, assaults, rape, and suicide" and ranked Alaska among the five states that had the "highest annual rates" of these ills. The report also observed that approximately 67 percent of Alaska Native deaths between 1990 and 1993 were alcohol related. More generally, alcohol abuse has been identified as a factor in half of the top ten leading causes of death among American Indians and Alaska Natives.

The Organized Village of Kake had long recognized the devastating toll of rampant alcoholism. Unfortunately, one of the means of combating the problem, the justice system, appeared unavailable to Kake's Native citizens. The Alaska State justice system had not successfully addressed these issues in Alaska Native communities for decades. A primary problem was that its resources were stretched thin. The juvenile probation officer assigned to Kake lived on another island that was accessible only by ferryboat or plane. Responding to felony offenses consumed most of his time; therefore, he could pay only limited attention to the seemingly less serious

---

* *Kake Circle Peacemaking*, www.innovations.harvard.edu/awards.html?id=6164.

misdemeanors of Kake's youth. Unfortunately, without the consequences that good probation monitoring could provide, the minor infractions of village youth tended to grow into entrenched adult behavior.

By the late 1990s, Kake residents realized that without breaking this cycle, the Village's future looked bleak. Despite the confined jurisdictional space in which they operated (the state of Alaska has authority over most aspects of criminal justice in Native Alaska), they also realized that they could craft a solution that relied on local human and cultural resources. Looking to the philosophy of peacemaking and the process of "circle sentencing," Kake village volunteers organized the Healing Heart Council and Circle Peacemaking in 1999. This reconciliation and sentencing process is embedded in Tlingit tradition and works in conjunction with the Alaska State court system.

Circle Peacemaking begins when a Kake juvenile enters a guilty plea with the state court. Then, the state judge, with the concurrence of the prosecutor, the public defender, and the offender, may turn the juvenile's case over to the Healing Heart Council for sentencing. The Council initiates Circle Peacemaking by bringing together a group of village volunteers to formally sentence the young offender(s). Through the close attention, encouragement, and admonishment of this circle of volunteer justices, the juvenile's misdemeanors have a lower probability of leading to more serious adult substance abuse and crime. Circle Peacemaking heals the offender by addressing the underlying causes of the offending behavior and restores the rupture in community life by repairing the relationship between the offender and victim.

More specifically, Circle Peacemaking involves the participation of individuals and groups who rarely come together under western systems of justice: the offender, the victim, families, friends, church representatives, police, substance abuse counselors, and concerned or affected community members. Participants, who may number from six to sixty, sit in a circle while a Keeper of the Circle facilitates the discussion. Discussions always begin and end with a prayer, and negative comments are strictly forbidden. Circle discussions are kept entirely confidential, and the Keeper encourages participants to speak from their hearts. The meetings typically last two to four hours, but they can only end when forgiveness and healing are apparent and consensus is reached about the offender's sentence. This sentence then becomes public.

But Circle Peacemaking does not conclude with sentencing. The circle participants are themselves responsible for ensuring that offenders adhere to their sentences. A typical sentence for underage alcohol consumption might include a curfew, community service, or a formal apology.

It might also require that the offender meet with elders or others who have worked through comparable experiences. Frequently, a sentence requires the offender's participation in other support circles. Importantly, the circle participants play a key role in assessing whether the offenders compliance is satisfactory. It is not uncommon for them to call for additional circles. Non-compliant offenders must return to the Alaska State court for sentencing.

Since its inception, the dedication of volunteers and judicious use of its minimal annual budget, a few thousand dollars in most years, have enabled Circle Peacemaking to expand its jurisdiction from underage alcohol consumption cases to include broader community needs. Today, the Healing Heart Council offers not only sentencing circles for juvenile offenders, but also sentencing circles for adult offenders who request Circle Peacemaking, healing circles for victims, intervention circles for individuals who seem to be losing control of their lives, celebration circles for offenders who have completed their sentencing requirements, and critical incident circles for individuals involved in an accident or crime who require immediate counseling. Additionally, the Healing Heart Council offers annual Circle Peacemaking Workshops that attracts an average of 24 participants from Kake and other villages who are interested in learning how the Alaska State court system and Circle Peacemaking complement each other.

This interest is itself evidence of Circle Peacemaking's success in Kake. Only two offenders out of the eighty sentenced during the program's first four years rejected a circle's outcome and returned to state court for sentencing. All of the twenty-four juveniles who were assigned to circle sentencing for underage drinking successfully completed the terms of their sentences. Circle Peacemaking also reports very low levels of recidivism. Sixty-eight adults participated in circles without repeating their offenses or violating other laws during their probation periods. At the time of writing, approximately thirty village residents are enrolled in substance abuse recovery programs. Circle Peacemaking veterans are moving on with their lives in other ways as well. Several have gone on to trade schools to complete their education; several are enrolled in universities. One adult veteran of a circle is now a juvenile justice associate and working on an alcohol abuse counseling certificate. These successes are reflected in a positive trend in the circles themselves. Over four years, the number of mandated sentencing circles decreased and the number of volunteer support circles increased initiated by individuals who have not yet committed offenses and are determined to avoid doing so. Unsurprisingly, Kake now sponsors well-attended sobriety marches, and Village residents have begun to comment on the perceptible difference in their community. It is a community in which the intergenerational pattern of substance abuse is being broken, and where youth and adults alike face brighter, healthier futures.

Significantly, Kake Circle Peacemaking's successes are occurring where the Alaska State court system repeatedly failed. Over four years, Circle Peacemaking has experienced a 97.5 percent success rate in sentences fulfillment compared to the Alaskan court system's 22 percent success rate. The State of Alaska's Judicial Board recognized Kake Circle Peacemaking for its effectiveness as a judicial process and selected it from among 250 applications to win the Spirit of United Youth Courts of Alaska. The Chief Justice of Alaska visited Kake to investigate Circle Peacemaking. Impressed with the Healing Heart Council's achievements, he mentioned Circle Peacemaking in his State of the Judiciary address. Kake has also sent representatives of Circle Peacemaking to communities throughout Alaska. Haines, Sitka, and the Juvenile Justice Center in Anchorage are now using Circle Peacemaking to address juvenile crime with positive results.

The success of the Healing Heart Council and Circle Peacemaking in curbing underage drinking is only the beginning of a number of remarkable successes. Three of these deserve special mention. First, Circle Peacemaking offers healing for both the offender for whom the circle is called and for the entire community. In large part, this is because community-mindedness is the foundation for Circle Peacemaking. Even though the state court process tends to be impersonal, involve few reciprocal commitments, offer limited oversight, and provide a small amount of opportunities for rehabilitation, the circle process complements it by fulfilling the specific judicial needs of Kake. Community members personally commit to the offender and, through these multiple, ongoing relationships, gradually rebuild the offender's commitment to the community. By placing offenders within a circle of caring individuals who have committed themselves to offer only constructive commentary, peacemaking circles break patterns of retributive justice that distances the offender from the community. Participants regularly remark that the process affects every member of the circle. This has been particularly apparent during sentencing circles for underage drinkers, in which both youth and their parents found the encouragement and support to end their substance abuse.

Second, as it succeeds in healing the community, Circle Peacemaking promotes the health of Kake's Tlingit culture. As noted, the Healing Heart Council and Circle Peacemaking have strong traditional roots. The Council practices a form of community justice reminiscent of the Deer People, an almost-forgotten group of traditional Tlingit peacemakers who healed, restored, and prevented escalating harms within their villages by consulting with all who were affected by the actions of an offender. Contact and colonialism eroded these practices that the Healing Heart Council's founders, once they determined a course of action, were eager to revive. To do so, they invited Canada's Yukon Territory Tlingit Circle Peacemaking facilitators to Kake to study the peacemaking circles of the Carcross Tlingits. Now, Circle Peacemaking perpetuates Tlingit culture in Kake. In the circle, participants pass a diamond willow talking stick to order the discussion. The willow's brown, diamond-shaped marks represent the eyes of elders who watch to see if their community members aid one another through their comments. Circle participants are particularly encouraged to share traditional stories and pass on the knowledge borne of their own experiences. The Healing Heart Council reports that youth who have participated in Circle Peacemaking feel a renewed interest in their culture. Kake Circle Peacemaking grooms the future leaders of its community by discouraging the illicit use of alcohol and drugs among its youth. In demonstrating the power of Tlingit cultural practices to address modern problems, Circle Peacemaking ensures that those leaders will lead in accordance with Tlingit cultural values.

Third, it is significant to note that Kake Circle Peacemaking is succeeding because of, and not in spite of, all of its cultural realities. Skeptics of Circle Peacemaking challenged the ability of an isolated, small, and socially interconnected village to establish a successful sentencing process. In Circle Peacemaking, however, these realities lie at the heart of the circles' successes. Circle Peacemaking is not an impersonal, but a deeply personal justice system that depends upon and promotes the interconnectedness of a compact and culturally whole village. The successes of Kake Circle Peacemaking rely on the village's determination to understand and utilize its most salient characteristics as strengths.

This has, of course, been especially significant considering the neglect and even outright hostility that the Alaska state government so frequently displays toward Alaskan tribes. It should be noted, in conclusion, that notwithstanding targeted state efforts to reduce tribal decision-making power, Kake has instituted a system of justice that increases tribal sovereignty. It has done so in a manner that commands the respect of the state judicial system while honoring its own community traditions. Although peacemaking courts are spreading throughout Indian Country, their influence in Alaska has been limited. Other than Kake, the Metlakatla Tribe is the only tribe in Alaska that takes on criminal cases beyond its Indian Child Welfare load. In Alaska, the barriers to constructing tribal courts capable of entering into full faith and comity agreements with the state courts or of raising sentencing controversies to the level of federal court review, as tribal peacemaker courts have done elsewhere, are significant. Still, Kake Circle

Peacemaking has, to the great benefit of its village, expertly assumed a state court function that was otherwise executed ineffectively. The Organized Village of Kake intends to make Circle Peacemaking a permanent fixture of self-governance by enshrining it in their constitution. Circle Peacemaking's success and the village's determination to ensure its perpetuation stand as significant triumphs in the development of a robust tribal judicial system. These are remarkable and desperately needed achievements in Alaska.

Lessons:

- Indian nations that supplement state and federal court systems (which may be largely ineffective) with traditional tribal processes realize justice in their communities. Kake, for example, found that its peacemaking efforts both increase compliance with sentencing and reduce recidivism.
- When systems of justice reflect communal and cultural norms, they strengthen those communities and cultures. As perpetrators and victims join with relatives and friends to make amends through peacemaking, they reaffirm their membership in, and responsibility for, their community and reawaken interest in cultural practices.
- Indian nations that cannot create or sustain a tribal court may still embrace traditional tribal processes. Peacemaking is a low cost solution ideally suited for communities whose size, isolation, or social interconnectedness might make the establishment of a tribal court difficult or impractical.

Questions

1. How does Seneca dispute resolution differ from other forms of peacemaking, such as the Navajo Nation's system?
2. The Little River Ottawa Band limits its peacemaking process to cases involving juveniles and children. Why do you think they do this? Do you think their system would work well for adult offenders as well?
3. How does the Village of Kake balance legal traditions from outside its own heritage and those from within?

In Your Community

1. Does your tribe have a traditional system of dispute resolution? Is it officially recognized by your tribal government today? If so, how is this system similar to or different from the peacemaking models described in

your readings? If you could change any aspect of that system, what would you change and why?

2. If your tribe has no officially recognized system of traditional dispute resolution, how would you go about developing one? What kind of system would you develop? Would you want to borrow aspects of the three systems you read about here, or would your system be entirely different?

3. Would you have struck a similar balance or a different one if you were helping to develop a "circle sentencing" system for your tribe?

Glossary

Homogeneous: All of the same or similar kind or nature.

Perpetuate: To cause to continue indefinitely; make perpetual.

Recidivism: Habitual relapse into crime.

Reintegrative: Restoring to a condition of integration or unity.

Sachem: A chief of some Native American tribes or confederations.

Transgression: Violation of a law, command, or duty.

Unanimity: The condition of being unanimous; complete agreement within a group.

Suggested Further Reading

Emily Mansfield, *Balance and Harmony: Peacemaking in Coast Salish Tribes of the Pacific Northwest*, 10 Mediation Quarterly 4 (1993).

CHAPTER 27

Separation of Powers

O NE OF THE challenges facing contemporary tribal judiciaries is the issue of judicial independence. Tension between government leaders is not a new phenomenon, nor is it unique to tribal cultures. Political power, no matter what culture or worldview, can be dangerous if used in the wrong way. Effective governance necessarily requires consideration of a variety of perspectives. The U.S. Constitution's structure is often held up as the "gold standard" of balancing powers so that no single branch of government exerts too much control over the whole nation. In the American structure, the legislative branch writes laws, the executive branch enforces those laws, and the judicial branch interprets the laws (see figure 27-1).

The notion of balancing (or decentralizing) powers is not foreign to indigenous worldviews either. While much of the language used in this chapter concerning judicial independence and "checks and balances" originates from Anglo-American conceptions of liberty, the concepts and principles are not uniquely Anglo-American. Many tribal governments have an impressive history of balancing powers between large centralized bureaucracies (largely

FIGURE 27.1. Checks and Balances

Executive Branch	Legislative Branch	Judicial Branch
• President/Governors • Enforces laws	• Congress/Legislatures • Writes laws	• Courts • Applies laws

for military purposes) and local domestic powers. For example, the Creek Confederacy (originally formed in the eighteenth century) developed entire communities that had separate duties related to the management of their society. The "Red Chiefs" were primarily concerned with military (foreign) matters, and the "White Chiefs" with domestic matters. Tribal citizens were split into two categories, and every person knew what his or her responsibilities were in relationship to that category. Manley A. Begay Jr., Stephen Cornell, Miriam Jorgensen, and Joseph P. Kalt provide some additional descriptions of the "separation of powers" doctrine in traditional tribal governments below.

DEVELOPMENT, GOVERNANCE, AND CULTURE

Manley A. Begay Jr., Stephen Cornell, Miriam Jorgensen, and Joseph P. Kalt[*]

Lakota government, for example, prior to colonization, made use of such checks and balances and separations of powers. Executive functions, from negotiating with foreign powers to managing the hunt, were vested in multiple executive[s] selected and directed parliamentary-style by a council, itself selected by family-centered *tiyospayes*. With lawmaking in the hands of the tiyospaye-derived council, judicial functions of maintaining law and order were located in the *akicita*, or warrior societies. This separation of powers served as a check on individuals and groups who might try to gather too much control in their own hands, something that was evidently of concern to Lakota people.

Some similar effects are achieved very differently today at Cochiti Pueblo, using a system with deep roots in Cochiti history and culture. There the cacique, the senior spiritual leader of the pueblo, each year appoints new officers to oversee pueblo affairs. They include the war captain, who is responsible for ceremonial matters, the governor, who is responsible for secular affairs including relations with other governments, and others. But this is the cacique's only secular role in pueblo life, and these leadership selections alternate each year between the Turquoise and Pumpkin kivas. These aspects of Cochiti governance constitute a form of separation of powers and checks and balances designed, by the pueblo's own account, to prevent any one "side" of the pueblo from accumulating too much power.

---

[*] Manley A. Begay Jr. et al., *Development, Governance, and Culture,* in *Rebuilding Native Nations: Strategies for Governance and Development* 43 (Miriam Jorgensen, ed., 2007).

This chapter focuses specifically on the issue of tribal judicial independence, although this is only one facet of the checks-and-balances issue. In contemporary times, tribal governments have come under increasing scrutiny to ensure that political factions remain balanced and that no particular political group or family has control over the entire community.

Judicial Independence: Challenges for Tribal Governments

The "boilerplate" constitutions that were developed to comply with the Indian Reorganization Act of 1934 (IRA) did not contain a specific separation-of-powers construct like the U.S. Constitution. Turtle Mountain Chippewa professor Duane Champagne explains their problems this way:

> IRA constitutions suffered from significant structural flaws, even by the standards of the U.S. government and mainstream Western political theory. Some of the main difficulties include the absence of checks and balances and the relative absence of separation of powers among executive, legislative, and judicial branches. Many IRA governments did not develop courts, and those that did often subordinated them to the tribal council.[1]

The following opinion from the Lac du Flambeau Tribal Appellate Court provides one example of problems associated with a weak judiciary. Consider how the "structural flaws" described by Champagne become apparent in the following opinion.

LAC DU FLAMBEAU BAND OF LAKE SUPERIOR INDIANS V. ONE 200–250 FOOT SMALL MESH GILLNET ET AL.

*Lac du Flambeau Tribal Appellate Court**

Summary

Reviewing the governance documents of the Lac du Flambeau Band of Lake Superior Chippewas, the Lac du Flambeau Tribal Court holds that it

---

* Lac du Flambeau Tribal Appellate Court, *Lac du Flambeau Band of Lake Superior Indians v. One 200–250 Foot Small Mesh Gillnet et al.*, 16 Indian Law Reporter 6095 (1989).

does not possess the power to review any legislative actions by the governing power of the tribe.

Before Smart, Chief Judge, Soulier and Peters, Judges

3. Does the Tribal Court Have the Authority to Question Tribal Codes and Regulations?

The issue facing the appellate court is whether the Lac du Flambeau Tribal
Court has been empowered to review legislative action of the tribal governing body which has resulted in the creation and implementation of the 1985
Conservation Code that is intended to regulate the hunting and fishing
activities of the Lac du Flambeau tribal members using reservation natural
resources.

To determine the issue, it was necessary for the appellate court to
examine the evidence provided to find out: (1) if there is a declaration stating the fact that the Lac du Flambeau Tribal Court is empowered to review
the legislative actions of the tribal governing body, or (2) [if] there exists an
inference that the Lac du Flambeau Tribal Court has the power of review.

After examining the evidence, the following facts were presented.

1. A declaration granting the Lac du Flambeau Tribal Court the power
    to review legislative actions of the tribal governing body does not exist
    in the tribal constitution or in the tribal court code nor is it mentioned
    in the duly adopted legislation creating the 1985 Conservation Code.
2. The passages that the respondent uses to support his position as writ-
    ten in the 1975 court code are not applicable to this issue because the
    1985 Conservation Code deleted chapter IV of the court code and
    replaced it with chapter IX.

Based on these facts, it becomes apparent that the power to review by the
Lac du Flambeau Tribal Court must come from an alternate source if it
exists within the tribal judicial system.

The most common source mentioned is the said to be inherent powers that are present whenever a judicial system is created; the most common example used to support this position is the United States system,
where the lack of any declaratory statements in the constructionary [*sic*]
documents was interpreted to infer the power of review upon the Supreme
Court.

But unlike the Anglo system, the Lac du Flambeau Tribe lacks the
environment to support an undeclared power of review grant.

The court based this opinion on the following points:

1. There doesn't exist any separation of powers which exists by a creation of the (3) distinct branches of government that is needed to make the power of review by the judicial system viable in a governmental setting.
2. As state[d] in the Lac du Flambeau Tribal Constitution the tribal council has the authority to establish a tribal court and define its powers and duties. Given this authority, the tribal council would have to grant the tribal court the power to review if it wanted the court to have it.

In summary, it is our opinion that the tribal court does not possess the power to review any legislative actions by the governing body of the tribe and must limit its activities to whatever the tribal council defines them to be.

Working Toward Solutions

In Professor Champagne's view, judicial independence needs to be strengthened in tribal governments:

> Courts, when considered as part of a system of checks, will need to have buil[t]-in constitutional powers to ensure autonomy from executive and legislative powers. Courts need powers to interpret the constitution and to operate as referees between executive and legislative branches in regard to constitutional and legal issues. In most tribal governments, judiciary branches are often subordinated to tribal council powers. Tribal courts need greater financial and organizational support and assurances in their role as interpreters of the law and the constitution.[2]

In their chapter "Native Nation Courts," Joseph Thomas Flies-Away (Hualapai), Carrie Garrow (St. Regis Mohawk), and Miriam Jorgensen offer one possible strategy for assessing a tribe's judicial system. Consider whether these (and related) questions might be useful in your community.

NATIVE NATION COURTS: KEY PLAYERS IN NATION REBUILDING

*Joseph Flies-Away, Carrie Garrow, and Miriam Jorgensen**

Does the nation's constitution—written or otherwise—mandate a clear separation of powers between the tribal leaders and other branches of government? If not, are disputes being resolved impartially or are they being resolved politically?

> If the nation does not have a constitutional separation of powers or a set of institutions and processes that promote independent dispute resolution outside of the written constitution, it probably ought to pursue judicial independence through constitutional reform. In addition to constitutional provisions that explicitly acknowledge the judiciary as an independent branch (not program) of the government, Native nations may also opt to extend the jurisdiction and powers of their courts through various other measures, including increasing the number of judges, expanding funding, developing specialized courts, and making appropriate provisions for appeals.

Do the nation's judicial institutions serve as a check on certain powers of other branches of government?

> This question raises the bar on judicial independence: does the nation's court have the authority not only to make decisions in disputes between citizens and in cases concerning citizen misbehavior, but also to make determinations about the appropriateness of the legislature's or executive branch's actions? Can citizens use the courts to protect themselves against illegal or inappropriate governmental actions? If not, the judiciary is ultimately subservient to other branches of tribal government, and action should be taken to change that. Again, a Native nation can use explicit constitutional provisions and codes and ordinances to vest its judiciary with the power to review the legality of tribal legislation and certain actions of tribal officials.

---

* Joseph Flies-Away et al., *Native Nation Courts: Key Players in Nation Rebuilding,* in Jorgensen, *supra.*, 137–39.

In the past few years, more tribal nations are engaging in constitutional reform activities, which often include discussion and a popular vote on separation of powers. On November 4, 2008, Oglala Sioux Tribe members voted to separate judiciary powers from the tribal council and executive committee. This means tribal judges will no longer be subject to appointment or removal by the tribal council. A similar provision was enacted by the White Earth Tribal Nation in April 2009. The Apsaalooke (Crow) Tribe explains the significance of the separation of powers change below.

EFFECTS OF CONSTITUTIONAL CHANGES ON THE CROW TRIBAL GOVERNMENT

Apsaalooke (Crow) Tribe*

The Crow Tribe of Indians repealed its 1948 Constitution and By-Laws in July 2001, replacing it with a Constitution designed to provide a stable and professional tribal government and provide due process and equal protection rights to the tribal membership. The Crow Constitution and By-Laws of 2001 establish three branches of government, the Executive, Legislative, and Judicial branches, for the governance of the Crow Tribe. The new Constitution provides for a separation of powers to allow for a balance of power between branches and an independent Tribal Court. The powers of the Executive and Legislative branches are expressly enumerated in an attempt to provide orderly governance. Further, the terms of office for members of the Executive and Legislative branches have been lengthened to four years from the previous two year terms to achieve consistency in leadership. The Removal provisions for elected members of the Executive and Legislative branches have been revised to require cause and a higher voting quorum to further achieve stability and consistency of leadership.

The Crow Constitution, in Article X, provides for a separate and distinct Judicial Branch of Government that shall be specifically governed by the Crow Tribal Law and Order Code. The Crow Tribal Court, prior to the passage of the new Constitution, existed as an entity under the authority of the Crow Tribal Council. Without a separation of powers doctrine,

---

* Apsaalooke (Crow) Tribe, *Effects of Constitutional Changes on the Crow Tribal Government*, at www.crowtribe.com/govt.htm.

the Tribal Council had final order authority over the Crow Tribal Court. The Tribal Council had the authority to review Tribal Court actions, which created a concern of political interference with the disposition of legal disputes. Although numerous rulings from the Crow Tribal Court recognizing the sovereignty of the Crow Tribe have been upheld by the federal court system, the opportunity for political interference with the Court caused a lack of confidence that the Court was a fair and just forum for dispute resolution, particularly for non-Indian parties.

Further, a lack of confidence in the Crow Tribal Court among potential litigants did not facilitate a business-friendly environment.

After recent revisions to the Crow Law and Order Code, passed by the Legislative Branch and approved by the Executive Branch, the Tribal Judges must possess either a juris doctorate degree or must have 5 years experience in a judicial system after passage of the Crow Tribal Bar Exam.

After selection of a qualified candidate for a judgeship by the Executive, the Legislature will confirm the appointment after hearing to a life term. However, the judge may be removed for causes that are expressly stated in the Law and Order Code.

The development of a Tribal Court structure that brings professionalism to the judiciary and that stands independent of oversight by the Tribal Council will create an effective legal dispute resolution forum that, in turn, will facilitate a business-friendly environment. Such an environment should encourage economic development, effective law enforcement, and a heightened protection of the individual rights of tribal members.

Questions

1. Are the conceptions of "separation of powers" and "judicial independence" consistent with indigenous theories of governing?
2. Why do you think that many tribal courts have been subordinated to tribal councils? What role has colonization played in this so-called structural flaw?
3. What is the difference between judicial independence and judicial review?

In Your Community

1. Does your tribal constitution require an independent judiciary? If not, has this presented problems for the tribal court's integrity?
2. If enhancing judicial independence is a priority for your tribe, identify and describe specific steps to address the need.

Glossary

Parliamentary: Pertaining to a supreme legislative body of cabinet members selected by and responsive to the legislature.

Secular: Not directly connected with religion or spirituality.

Suggested Further Reading

Fredric Brandfon, *Tradition and Judicial Review in the American Indian Tribal Court System*, 38 UCLA Law Review 991 (1991).

Notes

1. Duane Champagne, *Remaking Tribal Constitutions: Meeting the Challenges of Tradition, Colonialism, and Globalization*, in *American Indian Constitutional Reform and the Rebuilding of Native Nations* 20 (Eric D. Lemont, ed., 2006).

2. Champagne, *supra.*, 28

CHAPTER 28

Ethics for Tribal Judges

C HALLENGES concerning judicial ethics are often very closely related to the separation-of-powers issues described in the last chapter. For many of the same reasons that judicial independence is important for credibility and legitimacy, it is very important that tribal judicial officers be respected individuals. The members of a tribe must feel that their tribal court is hearing each case fairly and will work toward a just solution. Thus, the manner in which a tribal judge and court personnel decide the ethical issues that arise before them will help determine if the community perceives the court as being fair. And if the court is seen as fair, tribal members may place more trust in the court and its ability to address their problems, thereby helping to ensure its growth and efficiency. On the other hand, if the court is seen as unfair, it can lead to distrust and disrespect.

If it appears as if a particular tribal judge is deciding cases based on some bias, favoritism, or allegiance to something other than the tribal constitution and rules, then the credibility and authority of the court will suffer. If the community members question the integrity of the court, they might take their disputes elsewhere or try to handle their problems on their own, in ways that could threaten the peace, security, and order of tribal society. Furthermore, it could pose a threat to tribal sovereignty. To avoid such threats, then, tribal court personnel must recognize that they and their legal system owe a duty to their community to provide just resolutions that reflect not only the laws of that tribe but also the norms, structures, and practices of the tribal community generally.

Judicial Ethics

Judges in any court system face many potential ethical dilemmas—and tribal judges are no exception. The following sections look at two of the most common situations tribal judges may face: conflicts of interest/recusal, and concerns with conduct outside the courtroom. After exploring the nature of the ethical issue, we will then look at the sample tribal code of judicial conduct developed by the National Tribal Judicial Center (NTJC) in 2007, as well as examples of existing tribal judicial ethics codes. The NTJC Judicial Rules were designed as a template that can serve as a starting point for developing a tribe-specific set of rules and guidelines. The entire Sample Tribal Code is quite lengthy and is highly recommended for a thorough approach. We provide here short excerpts concerning conflict of interest and extrajudicial activities. As you read through these judicial rules, consider whether these standards provide sufficient guidelines to ensure the integrity of tribal courts.

Conflict of Interest and Recusal

One common ethical issue faced by judges is a "conflict of interest" with the case before her or him. A conflict of interest occurs when a judge, for whatever reason, has an interest—financial, political, or personal—in the outcome of the decision and can't impartially hear and/or decide the case. If the tribal judge were to continue to hear and/or decide the case, then the outcome could well be unfair due to the judge's bias for or against one of the parties. Sometimes even the mere appearance of a conflict of interest is enough for parties to think the judge is biased and cannot rule fairly in the case. Typically, tribal codes or constitutions determine which situations qualify as a conflict of interest.

When a tribal judge knows that she or he has a conflict of interest—or (sometimes) just the appearance of one—with the present case, the judge should remove herself or himself from hearing the case. This removal is known as a *recusal*. As mentioned above, judges may recuse themselves voluntarily. If a judge fails to seek a recusal (and the parties have not knowingly waived the conflict of interest) and it is later determined that a conflict of interest exists, then another tribal body (for example, a legislative body or ethics committee) may recuse the judge from the case. For example, according to the constitution of the Ho-Chunk Nation, "Any Justice or Judge with a direct personal or financial interest in any matter before the Judiciary shall recuse; failure to recuse constitutes cause for removal [from the bench]." This rule means it is always preferable for a judge to recuse himself or herself if the judge knows that there is a conflict of interest.

SAMPLE TRIBAL CODE OF JUDICIAL CONDUCT

National Tribal Judicial Center[*]

Canon 2 (Judicial Rule 2)

A judge shall avoid impropriety and the appearance of impropriety in all of the judge's activities.

a. A judge shall respect and comply with the law and shall act at all times in a manner that promotes public confidence in the integrity and impartiality of the judiciary.

b. A judge shall not allow his/her family, social, political or other relationships to influence the judge's judicial conduct or judgment. A judge shall not lend the prestige of judicial office to advance the private interests of the judge or others; nor shall a judge convey or permit others to convey the impression that they are in a special position to influence the judge. A judge shall not testify voluntarily as a character witness.

c. A judge shall not hold membership in any organization that practices invidious discrimination on the basis of race, sex, religion, or national origin.

---

[*] National Tribal Judicial Center, *Sample Tribal Code of Judicial Conduct* (2007) at www.judges.org/ntjc.html.

Conduct Outside the Courtroom

In addition to their ethical obligations within the courtroom, tribal judges also owe a duty to maintain high ethical standards outside the courtroom. As stated previously, community respect is essential to a tribal court. The respect a tribal judge gives and receives within the courtroom is built not only on his or her decisions within the courtroom but also on the respect the community feels for the judge's everyday decisions. If a tribal judge behaves in a way that reflects a sense of being "above the law," then the community may quickly lose respect for the judge and her or his court. Obviously, a tribal judge is a person and, like any person, can sometimes make mistakes. This is understood. However, by taking on the role of tribal judge, that person has accepted a leadership role within the tribe that demands a higher ethical standard. A tribal judge must be a role model for the whole tribe in honoring the laws and values of the tribe.

Consequently, ethical standards require that tribal judges avoid membership in organizations that promote views that are contrary to, or would conflict with, the duties of the court. For example, a tribal judge should avoid organizations that espouse hatred of other groups. Not only would an affiliation with this organization call into question his or her impartiality, but it would also be grounds for appeals, calling into question any decision that judge has made concerning a party that is the organization's object of hate.

In addition, a tribal judge must be careful with the information he or she receives in court. Tribal judges cannot use information from cases for their own benefit. Nor should family and friends benefit from a tribal judge's knowledge. Again, all parties must feel that the judge is favoring neither side and that no conflict of interest exists. If a tribal judge were to use the information to her or his benefit, then a conflict of interest would instantly arise.

Alcohol and drug abuse affect all sorts of individuals, even tribal court judges. Many tribal judicial ethics codes forbid a judge from presiding over cases while under the influence of alcohol or other drugs. However, even if a tribal judge keeps his or her alcohol or drug problem from entering the courtroom, the community may still be aware of the abuse and could lose respect for the judge and tribal court. It is therefore imperative that a tribal judge with an alcohol and/or drug abuse problem seek help for that addiction. By reaching out to the community for help, a tribal judge reiterates the need for the community to work together. This creates a stronger community and a stronger tribal court.

SAMPLE TRIBAL CODE OF JUDICIAL CONDUCT

National Tribal Judicial Center

Canon 4 (Judicial Rule 4)

A judge shall so conduct the judge's extrajudicial activities as to minimize the risk of conflict with judicial obligations.

A. Disqualification

(1) A judge shall disqualify himself or herself in a proceeding in which the judge's impartiality might reasonabl[y] be questioned, including but not limited to instances where:

    a. The judge has a personal bias or prejudice concerning a party or a party's lawyer (advocate), or (has) personal (first-hand) knowledge of disputed evidentiary facts concerning the proceeding;

    b. The judge served as a lawyer in a matter in the controversy, or a lawyer with whom the judge previously practiced law served during such association as a lawyer concerning the matter, or the judge has been a material witness concerning it;

    c. The judge knows that he or she, individually or as a fiduciary, or the judge's spouse, parent or child wherever residing, or any other member of the judge's family residing in the judge's household, has an economic interest in the subject matter in controversy or in a party to the proceeding or has any other more than *de minimis* (minimal) interest that could be substantially affected by the proceeding;

    d. The judge or the judge's spouse, or a person within the third degree of relationship to either of them, or the spouse of such a person:

        i. Is a party to the proceeding, or an officer, director, or trustee of a party;

        ii. Is acting as a lawyer in the proceeding;

        iii. Is known by the judge to have more than de minimis interest that could be substantially affected by the proceeding; or

        iv. Is to the judge's knowledge, likely to be a material witness in the proceeding;

    e. The judge knows or learns by means of a timely motion that a party or a party's lawyer has within the previous |insert number| year|s| made aggregate contributions to the judge's campaign in an amount that is greater than $|insert amount| for an individual or $|insert amount| for an entity an|d| said amount is reasonable and appropriate for an individual or an entity.

    f. The judge, while a judge or a candidate for judicial office, has made a public statement that commits, or appears to commit, the judge with respect to

        i. An issue in the proceeding; or

        ii. The controversy in the proceeding.

(2) A judge shall keep informed about the judge's personal and fiduciary economic interests, and make a reasonable effort to keep informed about the personal economic interest of the judge's spouse and minor children residing in the judge's household.

Traditional Judicial Ethics:
The Navajo Nation Example

In 1991, the Navajo Nation Supreme Court approved the following Judicial Code of Conduct, which incorporates Navajo-specific values. Consider how this code differs from the codes of judicial conduct of mainstream legal systems.

NAVAJO NATION CODE OF JUDICIAL CONDUCT*

Canon 1

A Navajo Nation judge shall promote Navajo justice.

Principle

A Navajo judge should decide and rule between the Four Sacred Mountains. That means that judges, as Navajos, should apply Navajo concepts and procedures of justice, including the principles of maintaining harmony, establishing order, respecting freedom, and talking things out in free discussion.

Considerations

1. *Harmony:* Injustice, in the sense of evil or wrongdoing, is the result of disharmony. One of the goals of justice is to return people and their community to harmony in the resolution of a dispute. The judge must promote harmony between litigants, achieve harmony through assuring reasonable restitution to victims, and foster harmony by providing the means for offenders or wrongdoers to return to their communities. That is achieved through free discussion, conciliation, consensus, and guidance from the judge.
2. *Order:* Navajo justice is concerned with order, which is related to the principle of harmony. Court procedures and judicial decisions should be keyed to an orderly resolution of disputes.

---

* Navajo Nation Supreme Court, *Navajo Nation Code of Judicial Conduct* (1991) at www.navajocourts.org/Policies/CodeJudicialConduct.htm#ONE.

3. *Judicial Attitudes:* A judge should behave to everybody as if they were his or her relatives. This value requires judges, as *Hózhóji Naat'ááh* (leaders), to treat everyone equally and fairly. Navajos believe in equality and horizontal, person-to-person relationships as a part of their concept of justice. Obligations toward relatives extend to everyone, because that is a means of not only stressing personal equality, but creating solidarity.

4. *Coercion:* Given the Navajo value of fundamental equality, it is wrong to use coercion against another. While judges have the duty of making decisions for others, that should be done with patience, courtesy, and without aggression. A judge should patiently listen to all proper and relevant evidence, as well as the reasonable and well presented arguments of parties or their counsel.

5. *Humility:* Navajo judges are successors of the traditional Hózhóji Naat'ááh (peace chief), because they are chosen for their individual qualities. As such, they are only slightly higher than the others, and respect for their decisions depends upon their personal integrity. Humility is the personal value which prompts people to respect judges for their decisions, and not their position.

6. *Fair Play:* The procedure of Navajo justice is people talking out their problems for a consensual resolution of them. A judge should encourage free discussion of the problem before the court, within the limits of reasonable rules of procedure and evidence. A judge should not encourage or permit aggressive behavior, including the badgering of witnesses, rudeness, the infliction of intentional humiliation or embarrassment, or any other conduct which obstructs the right to a full and fair hearing.

7. *Leadership and Guidance:* Navajo leadership stresses obligations to others, and creates high duties to consider the overall good of the community. The honor and respect given to leaders is based upon an acceptance of their leadership qualities, and a duty to respect those who guide. While often judges are called upon to use the adjudication process to declare a winner and a loser, or inflict punishment upon an individual, Navajo common law encourages problem-solving and discussion to achieve harmony and order. Therefore, the judge should encourage discussion by the parties, settlement, and resolving underlying problems. The judge should have wisdom and knowledge to recommend plans, solutions, and resolutions to the parties before the court.

A judge shall always act with dignity and impartiality, to assure that parties have their day in court and an orderly and fair proceeding.

A judge should exercise patience, and use the authority of the court to decide cases in an atmosphere of reason, rather than contention. The court should immediately intervene to control inappropriate behavior, aggressive tactics, or any conduct which takes away from a fair hearing of the full case, and takes away from the respect due another human being.

8. *Restitution:* The Navajo common law of wrongs and crimes was primarily concerned with restitution (*nályééh*) not punishment. A judge should provide full restitution or reparation to injured parties, particularly in criminal cases. In addition, a judge should encourage appropriate apologies to those who have been wronged, and urge forgiveness for wrongdoers who admit fault and promise good behavior in the future.

Personal and Professional Standards

Judge Abby Abinanti (Yurok) drafted some specific standards for ethical behavior of tribal judges, both inside and outside the courtroom. Consider how this draft code differs from the codes of judicial conduct of mainstream legal systems.

DRAFT TRIBAL COURT CODE OF ETHICS

Abby Abinanti, 1990

Guideline 2: *Judges shall strive to attain and maintain a moral character which is consistent with their community responsibility.*

Judges will have the responsibility in their daily conduct for acting so as to be as free as possible from actions which wrongfully harm others, which lack true compassion for others or which are motivated by reasons not in the community interest. This is not meant to encourage Judges to be judgmental of the conduct of other members of the community. Rather it is to remind them that their responsibility is for their behavior, for it is by the Judge's behavior on the bench and in the community that the Court will be judged by the community.

Guideline 3: *Judges while acting in their normal capacity will endeavor to remember and reflect in their conduct that though they may strive for perfection they are not perfect.*

Judges shall in their conduct be mindful of their responsibility to be fair, courteous and respectful to all who appear before them. They will endeavor to avoid developing an arrogant attitude because of the power with which they have been entrusted. Judges will remember that though they have the responsibility for making decisions, and, must make decisions, a respectful approach to this responsibility will work toward issuing decisions that are correct both in the law and for the community. . . .

Guideline 5: *Judges shall refrain from public criticism of their peers, except as set out in this guideline as their responsibility.*

Judges shall not engage in discussions of their peers, judicial temperament, conduct or decisions except as to explain purpose of actions to inquiring community members. They will not discredit a peer personally or professionally in the community. However, in the confines of judicial conferences Judges should constructively comment in a kind manner to each other so as to improve the performance of the Judge receiving such criticism.

Review of Judicial Misconduct by Tribal Appellate Courts

A tribal appellate court often resolves cases involving allegations of judicial misconduct. Many times, the question of whether a judge should have recused herself or himself from a particular case is tied to other highly volatile or political issues within the tribal government. A number of judicial ethics cases involve election disputes or questions about legitimate tribal leadership. Therefore, these cases can have a significant impact on the sovereignty and integrity of the entire tribal government. The following case illustrates how important careful analysis can be in resolving questions of judicial ethics.

Pyatskowit v. Delabreau involves a dispute between a Menominee tribal prosecutor and a Menominee tribal judge. The prosecutor alleged that the judge engaged in *ex parte* communications regarding a case and that these communications resulted in prejudice against the prosecutor.

PYATSKOWIT V. DELABREAU

Menominee Tribal Supreme Court*

Before Kittecon, Chief Justice, and Skubitz, Associate Justice

Appellate Andrew J. Pyatskowit, tribal prosecutor, petitions this court for supervisory jurisdiction, pursuant to Menominee Rule of Appellate Procedure 104.17(1), over contempt proceedings initiated against the appellant by respondent, the Honorable Joan Delabreau of the Menominee Tribal Courts.

Background

Much of this dispute has its basis in the final hearing of an alcohol commitment proceeding which occurred on May 14, 1992, when respondent [Judge Delabreau] accepted a stipulated disposition for the committed party. In an earlier proceeding regarding the same matter, Judge Delabreau ordered the tribe to pay for the committed party's transportation to a doctor's appointment. While the tribe does not usually pay for transportation in voluntary commitments, Judge Delabreau stated that she was motivated by the committed party's heart condition, and that specific provisions acknowledging the committed party's condition had been contained in the commitment disposition (transcript, show cause hearing, Oct. 6, 1992).

For whatever reason, the committed party was not transported to his medical appointment. Before the May 14 hearing, Judge Delabreau learned of this in a conversation with the committed party's wife and, concerned that her order had not been carried out, she apparently remarked to the wife that appellant [Tribal Prosecutor Pyatskowit] could be held in contempt of court. Appellant's affidavit of prejudice (appellant's exhibit B) alleges that this ex parte conversation was initiated by respondent. . . .

[T]he Menominee Judicial Code . . . contains points of guidance:

> 7. A Judge's decision should be free from bias. An honest, impartial attitude shall be the rule toward each case presented. . . .

---

* Menominee Tribal Supreme Court, *Pyatskowit v. Delabreau*, 20 Indian Law Reporter 6069 (1993).

11. A Judge . . . shall not engage in ex parte interviews, arguments or other communications which may appear to influence his
judicial decision. . . .

Further, the ABA |American Bar Association| Code of Judicial Con-
duct contains three provisions which may be relevant to the case at hand:

Canon 2
    A. A judge . . . should conduct himself at all times in a manner
that promotes public confidence in the integrity and impartiality of
the judiciary. . . .
Canon 3 . . .
    |A.| 4. A judge should . . . neither initiate nor consider ex parte
or other communications concerning a pending or impending proceeding. . . .
    6. A judge should abstain from public comment about a pend-
ing or impending proceeding in any court.

Appellant's Affidavit

Judge Delabreau's Ex Parte Conversation with the Committed Party's Wife

In point 3 of his affidavit, appellant alleges that prior to the May 14 final hear-
ing in the commitment proceeding, detailed above, respondent |Delabreau|
initiated an ex parte conversation with the committed party's wife. The purpose of the conversation was apparently to ascertain whether the respondent's
order as to transportation of the committed party had been carried out.
    An ex parte communication occurs where a judge solicits or receives
information concerning a current or impending proceeding from an interested party outside the presence and often without the knowledge of the other
party. It is counter to the spirit of an adversarial judicial system as well as
expectations of fairness, because it does not afford the excluded party an opportunity to either hear or to counter the other side's information or allegations.
    Both Principle 11 of the Menominee Judicial Code and Canon 3(A)(4)
of the ABA Code, cited above, forbid such communications, and this allegation is the most substantial contained in appellant's affidavit. By receiving
information from the committed party's wife—who was herself a party to
the commitment—respondent created an impression of partiality. Appellant was not confronted with the information until later and was thus unpre-
pared to explain his position. This denial of the opportunity to respond to

information in a meaningful way is exactly the evil which prohibitions against ex parte conversations are designed to address, even when a proceeding, as here, may not have been a full-blown adversarial proceeding. . . .

Even assuming that respondent's ex parte conversation was motivated solely by concerns for the welfare of the committed party, respondent should have afforded appellant some notice of the information she received prior to the hearing, so that appellant would have a meaningful opportunity to respond. Additionally, respondent should have refrained from making public comments of a legally conclusory nature, that is, that appellant's conduct bordered on contempt. . . .

While both sides sought to exercise professional restraint, it is clear from the transcript that both felt that not only the authority of their respective offices, but also their personal dignity had been offended. Given the nature of the dispute, a reasonable person could assume that on the issue of contempt, both parties would have difficulty confining themselves to the merits.

Aside from allegations of past prejudice, a reasonable person could have the impression that conflict between the parties to this action might reasonably have affected the ultimate resolution of the action below. Thus, even if bias or prejudice did not in fact exist, the appearance of bias or prejudice did, in conflict with both the spirit and letter of the Menominee Judicial Code and the ABA Code of Judicial Conduct. . . .

While the affidavit may or may not have been conclusive proof of bias or prejudice against the appellant, portions of it were sufficient to support at least an appearance of prejudice, and respondent should have either disqualified herself or forwarded the matter to the Chief Justice. . . .

Questions

1. What methods can a tribal judge use to ensure confidentiality in sensitive cases involving children?
2. Should there be any exception to the prohibition of ex parte communications by a judge?
3. The sample judicial code of ethics in this chapter is based on codes of judicial ethics for judges in state and federal courts. Do you think that this code of ethics is realistic and appropriate for small tribal communities? If not, how would you modify the code?
4. How does the Navajo Nation Judicial Code of Conduct differ from other codes of conduct?

In Your Community

1. Does your tribe have a judicial code of ethics? If not, should there be one? If your tribe does have a current judicial code of ethics, is it appropriate for the needs of your community?
2. What do you think should be the reasons for a tribal judge to be recused from hearing a case in your tribe? Suppose you are the only judge for your tribe and an elder from your clan is a defendant in a case before you. Should you recuse yourself?
3. What are the reasons listed for recusal in your tribe's codes or rules? Do you agree with those reasons? Why?
4. Does your tribe's code list ways in which confidentiality in children's cases should be maintained?
5. How are tribal judges selected in your community? Do you think that the process allows judicial independence from other governmental entities?

Glossary

Avocational: Pertaining to an auxiliary (side) activity, such as a hobby, sport, or civic involvement.

Conclusory: Conclusive.

Contempt: An act that obstructs a court's work or lessens the dignity of the court.

Disposition: A final settlement or result.

Ex parte: (Latin) Having discussions with one party to a dispute without the other party being present.

Impropriety: An improper act.

Incumbent: A person who presently holds office.

Partisan: Devoted to or biased in support of a party, group, or cause.

Recusal: Disqualification or removal of a judge from hearing a case due to actual or potential bias or conflict of interest.

Stipulated: Laid down as a condition of an agreement.

CHAPTER 29

Ethics for Tribal Court Personnel

M OST OF THE ethical issues that tribal judges face are also faced by tribal court personnel. Tribal court personnel include court administrators, clerks, bailiffs, probation officers, court planners, and other tribal court employees. Since tribal court personnel, like tribal court judges, have access to confidential information and are in a position to affect the community's perception of the tribal court, they should also meet a high ethical standard of living, reflect impartiality, and avoid conflicts of interest. Court personnel may know and interact with more members of the community than the judge, and thus it is important that court personnel not allow their personal relations to interfere with carrying out their duties to the court and the public. Like judges, it is important that court personnel ensure that the laws and traditions of the tribe be carried out. Obtaining proper training in the laws and traditions of the tribe by all court personnel will help the tribal court ensure that the community is being properly served.

In 1978, the National American Indian Court Judges Association (NAICJA) promulgated some model (sample) rules for tribal court personnel. They provide a useful starting point for a discussion of ethical concerns.

NAICJA STANDARDS: COURT PERSONNEL

*National American Indian Court Judges Association**

A. Ethics
  1. An ethical code should be enacted by the tribe to cover the actions and relationships of all personnel connected with tribal court operations.
  2. Conflicts of interest and preference for any party should be eliminated.
  3. Confidentiality of the court's business should be stressed, especially in the juvenile area.
  4. Court personnel should be educated about the role of the court in the Indian community, and a public relations effort should be conducted to improve the image of the court in the community.
B. Training
  1. All court personnel shall receive available training in courtroom procedures and operations and other duties relevant to their position.
  2. All court personnel should receive training in tribal customs and law.
  3. Training should be made a mandatory requirement for holding a court support office.
C. Legal advisors
  1. The duty of the legal advisor is to advise the judges on points of law and to discuss hypothetical situations.
  2. The legal advisor shall not advise the tribal judge on the merits of a specific case.
  3. The tribal court's legal advisor should be available to judges at least by telephone for day-to-day consultation.
  4. The legal advisor should have knowledge of tribal law and custom and should have a working knowledge of the tribal language if it is regularly used in court proceedings.
  5. The tribal legal advisor shall not be the tribal attorney because of conflict of interest problems.
  6. The tribal judge's independence as a decision maker shall not be influenced by the legal advisor.

---

* National American Indian Court Judges Association, *Model Standards for Indian Judicial Systems,* in *Indian Courts and the Future: Report of the NAICJA Long Range Planning Project* 133–37 (1978).

D. Court clerks
1. The clerk shall respect the confidentiality of the business conducted by the court, and shall perform the duties of his/her office in a professional manner.
2. If there is a sufficient caseload, there should be separate clerks for the tribal juvenile court and appellate courts.
3. The clerk is responsible for maintaining the records of the court and supervising the court calendar.
4. The clerk should be qualified to perform the duties of his/her office. The clerk should have the business skills of filing, shorthand, typing and the organizational ability to administer the office efficiently. The clerk's salary should be adequate to attract qualified personnel.

E. Court reporter
1. The reporter's function is to record all court proceedings, and to transcribe those proceedings when required for an appeal or enforcement of a tribal judgment outside the tribe's jurisdiction.
2. The court reporter should be in the courtroom whenever court is in session.

F. Probation officer
1. Probation officers (male and female) shall be hired to supervise those persons placed on probation by the tribal court, or who are released from incarceration subject to some condition, such as enrolling in an alcohol rehabilitation program.
2. A separate probation officer should have social work training. An understanding of police operations and tribal customs also is necessary for proper performance of probation duties.
3. Probation officers should have social work training. An understanding of police operations and tribal customs also is necessary for proper performance of probation duties.
4. Probation officers should be subject to the control of the tribal court.
    a. They should be required to report violations of probation to the tribal judge.
    b. They should be required to report monthly on the progress of [t]heir cases.

G. Court administrator
1. When the size of a court warrants, a court administrator should be hired to coordinate and administer the tribal court. Otherwise, the functions of the court administrator can be combined with the court planner or if necessary, the chief judge or clerk.

2. The tribal court administrator should have the following responsibilities:
   a. Hiring and firing of all court personnel except for the tribal judges, under authority delegated by the chief judge.
   b. Planning and administration of the court budget.
   c. Oversight of all record keeping and reporting.
3. The tribal court administrator should be required to have training in the areas of office and court management.

H. Court planner
   1. The tribal court should have access to a court planner to organize court operations and plan for the needs of the court.
   2. The planner should conduct periodic review of court operations, suggest alterations in structure where necessary, and apply for funding for the court.
   3. The tribal court planner should have responsibility for:
      a. Planning for the court.
      b. Writing federal grant applications.
   4. The tribal court planner should be required to have training in court management and planning.

Explanation

Adequate court personnel are necessary to ensure the proper and efficient working of the tribal court. A sufficient number of trained court personnel would help eliminate many of the problems that now exist in Indian courts. Individual tribal policy and customs will determine which of the personnel recommended above should be hired. Costs can be saved by combining some job functions when possible. An example would be combination of court clerk and court reporter functions in one person. A position like court planner could be merged with the job of court administrator, performed part time by a judge or clerk, or shared in a circuit riding arrangement with several tribes. A national entity should draw up model ethical standards for court personnel.

The expectations for tribal personnel concerning appearances of impropriety are often very similar to those of tribal judges. The Blue Lake Rancheria Tribal Court provides some specific requirements in its Rules Governing the Conduct of Clerks, excerpted below.

RULES GOVERNING THE CONDUCT OF CLERKS

*Blue Lake Rancheria Tribal Court**

Chapter 2

Impropriety or Appearance of Impropriety

Rule 7. Avoid Impropriety or Appearance of Impropriety.

The Court Clerk shall not engage in any activities which are reasonably likely to be perceived as improper.
    (a) The Clerk shall not:

1. Use the position of the office for his/her own personal gain;
2. Allow family, social or other relationships to influence his/her official conduct or judgment;
3. Lend the authority or prestige of the Clerk's Office to advance the private interests of others;
4. Convey or assist others to convey the impression that they or anyone else is in a special position to influence the Clerk.

Rule 8. Sexual harassment.

    (a) The Clerk shall not make unwanted sexual advances, comments, or innuendos that would constitute sexual harassment.
    (b) The Clerk shall not sexually harass any tribal staff, attorney, party, or witness.

Rule 11. Acceptance of Gifts.

Neither the Tribal Court Clerk nor a family member residing in the Clerk's household shall accept any gift, bequest, favor, or loan from any person whose interests have come or are likely to come before the Clerk in the performance of his/her official duties as Tribal Court Clerk, or from any other person under circumstances which might reasonably be regarded as influ-

---

* Blue Lake Rancheria Tribal Court, *Rules Governing the Conduct of Clerks* (2007) at www.bluelakerancheria-nsn.gov/BLR_Tribal_Court_Clerk_Conduct_Rules.pdf.

encing the performance of the duties of the office. The Clerk shall report the value of any gift or bequest, other than from a relative of the first degree by blood, marriage, or custom, in the same manner compensation is reported under Rule 15(B) of these Rules.

Rule 12. Nondisclosure of Confidential Communications.

The Clerk shall abstain from public comment about a pending or impending proceeding in Tribal Court, and shall require all court personnel or staff to similarly abstain. The Clerk shall not disclose to any person any confidential information received in the course of official business, nor shall such information be used by the Clerk for personal gain.

Rule 13. Undue Influence.

The Clerk shall not influence or attempt to influence the outcome or assignment of any case or perform any discretionary or ministerial function of the Court in a manner which improperly favors or disfavors any litigant, party, witness or attorney, nor imply that the Clerk is in the position to do so. The Clerk shall resist all attempts by any Tribal Member, Council Member, Tribal Staff, party or witness to apply undue influence in the Clerk's performance of his/her duties as Clerk including any attempt to censor the Clerk's advocacy for and/or defense of the Court and the judiciary. The Clerk shall promptly report any such attempt at undue influence to the Chief Judge of the Tribal Court and/or to the members of the Business Council.

Tribal Court Personnel and the
Unauthorized Practice of Law

In some communities, there may be very few lawyers licensed to practice in tribal courts. Members of the general public often have legal questions and understandably go to the tribal court for answers. However, as you will read in the following chapter, there are strict guidelines as to who can offer legal advice. Because of this important distinction, tribal court personnel (particularly those who have a great deal of interaction with the public) should be very clear about their job descriptions. For example, a tribal court secretary might be able to provide a legal form to someone, but should not assist that person in completing the form. In 1998, the Coquille tribal chief judge issued the following point of clarification for his tribal court clerks.

COURT CLERK ASSISTANCE IN DRAFTING DOCUMENTS

*Coquille Indian Tribal Court**

The Coquille Indian Tribal Code provides in pertinent part that the Court Clerk shall ". . . give assistance to the Tribal Court, Tribal Police, and to residents of the Coquille Indian Community and other Tribal members in drafting complaints, summons, warrants and other documents as required . . ." (CITC 610.400.3[b]). The Coquille Code of Judicial Conduct provides that a Judge, and the Court Clerk, ". . . shall not act in a way that the Judge knows, or reasonably should know, would be perceived by a reasonable person as biased or prejudiced toward any of the litigants, jurors, witnesses, lawyers or members of the public" (Judicial Rule 2-110[B][C]). The Court Clerk therefore is required to assist in drafting documents only in a manner which would not be perceived by a reasonable person as biased or prejudiced toward any person or entity. Accordingly, in giving assistance in drafting documents pursuant to CITC 610.400.3(b), the Court Clerk is required to adhere to the following criteria:

1. The Court Clerk may not advise a party. Advice generally consists of rendering an opinion, judgment or recommendation regarding a decision to be made or a course of conduct to be taken by a party.
2. The Court Clerk may inform a party by directing or guiding a party to available resources which the party may choose to utilize in making decisions and in determining a course of conduct to be followed by the party.

Illustrative examples of common situations which clarify the distinction between advice and information, as that distinction applies to drafting of documents, and court-authorized forms with instructions, will be available at the Court Clerk's office.

---

* Coquille Indian Tribal Court, Supplemental Court Order, *Court Clerk Assistance in Drafting Documents* (1998) at www.tribalresourcecenter.org/ccfolder/coquille_clerkdrafting .htm.

Ethics and Law Clerks

It is becoming more common for tribal judges to hire law students and lawyers as clerks or research assistants. Clerks provide invaluable support to the judiciary by reviewing briefs, researching cases, and developing draft motions and decisions.

In 2007, the University of Colorado Law School developed a comprehensive guidebook for tribal judges and clerks. The following excerpt explores the ethical issues for tribal law clerks.

ETHICAL DUTIES

Massey K. Mayo and Jill E. Tompkins[*]

Lawyers are bound by particular rules of ethics. These rules ensure that a lawyer is acting honesty and with loyalty towards his or her clients and is providing competent representation. Even though you may not be working for a particular client, clerkships are bound by similar ethical rules. Maintaining your loyalty to your judge is critical. Integrity and discretion are key attributes of a successful law clerk. Tribal judges are held to the highest of ethical standards. Judicial law clerks are held to the same standards. A good rule of thumb is that if the judge himself or herself would be ethically prohibited from engaging in particular conduct or conversations so are you.

There might be a special code of ethics, or even a court employee handbook, that applies to your judicial system and you will benefit from finding out the acceptable codes of conduct as early as possible. There are several resources regarding applicable rules of ethics that you should read on your own and become familiar with prior to your clerkship. At the very start of your clerkship, you will want to ask your judge about the existence of any particular standards of conduct applicable to your court, including tribal codes of ethics or professional responsibility, tribal rules of judicial conduct, tribal rules governing tribal court employee conduct or even general tribal government employee handbooks. Most tribal courts possess narrowly tailored guidelines concerning your ethical duties and conduct and you will want to familiarize yourself with the rules.

---

[*] Massey K. Mayo & Jill E. Tompkins, *Ethical Duties,* in *A Guide for Tribal Court Law Clerks and Judges* (2007) at www.colorado.edu/iece/docs/Thompson/Final_version _Guide.pdf.

Even if the tribal court or tribe does not possess formal written rules, it does not mean you are free from standards. If the tribal court has not formally adopted rules of conduct then you might wish to review the Federal Judicial Center's publication, *Maintaining the Public Trust: Ethics for Federal Judicial Law Clerks* (https://lawclerks.ao.uscourts.gov/ethics_for_lawclerks.pdf) to help develop a compass for your behavior.

Throughout your entire career as a lawyer, the rules of guarding confidentiality and prohibiting conflicts of interest will apply. In the judiciary, these rules arise in different contexts but are no less binding. As a law clerk, you must comply with these rules. For example, you will always want to be cautious about conversation related to your work. You never know who may be listening in the hallway, elevator or even at the next restaurant table. They could be litigants, attorneys, jurors, witnesses, and even family members or friends of the parties involved. The same is true for your conversations with the law clerks, judges, and staff of other chambers.

Your judge must be able to rely on your absolute discretion about cases, opinions, debates and procedures in his or her chambers. The same discretion applies to your own notes and work product, as this protects the integrity of and respect for the tribal court. On the subject of papers, you should never bring the original documents home with you—use "courtesy copies" provided by the attorneys for this purpose or make your own copies. Your worst nightmare is to take originals home and lose them or have your new puppy gnaw on them.

If you are working remotely for a judge, the issue of ethics might be complicated. Be sure to develop an email privacy policy (like the need for a disclaimer of confidentiality on each email sent or using only first names within emails). Additionally, talk to your judge about the use of web-casting or video conferences. You would not want to host such a meeting from your dining room table where the rest of your family is able to hear the details of a particular case. If you do have files at home, your judge may request that you keep them in a secure place where only you are able to access the information. Or, if you send files over the internet you may need additional software to ensure privacy and complete deletion once the clerkship has ended. Your duties of confidentiality with regard to your clerkship are life-long. You can never divulge the deliberative and draft work with which you were involved.

While working in the tribal court, you might have to restrict the habits of your outside life while clerking. For example, if you take a clerkship in a United States federal court, your personal political involvement must be limited. This might be true for tribal courts as well. Certain tribal courts that hear cases involving the tribe's gaming enterprise may prohibit tribal judges and, by extension, law clerks, from gambling at tribal facilities to avoid the appearance of impropriety. It would be difficult for a plaintiff to have confidence in the impartiality of the court if the judge or his or her law clerk wins a jackpot from the very entity that is being sued.

Your judge might restrict your socializing (including drinking of alcohol) with the larger tribal community to avoid any appearance of impropriety. You are a representative of the tribal court 24 hours a day during your clerkship and must be mindful to rise to that responsibility. Also, you may not be able to work on files connected with a law firm in which you have a possible offer of employment pending.

Know what the ethical rules are in regard to cultural matters. It may be custom or tribal tradition to give a gift as a way of welcoming you or showing gratitude for your assistance, but this may be problematic if the gift is from a person who is a party in a suit pending before the tribal court. You may be offered the opportunity to sit in on tribal council meetings, which is an honor, but depending upon the structure of the tribal government or the cases present before your judge, this may pose a possible ethical concern regarding prohibited out-of-court communications about the case or risk the tribal court's appearance of impartiality and independence.

A law clerk is considered to be an officer of the court with a responsibility to maintain the integrity and decorum of the proceedings. You may have a duty in your position to inform the presiding judge if you have reason to believe that a defendant, litigant, witness, juror, attorney or courtroom spectator is under the influence of drugs or alcohol. This may be particularly relevant if you are clerking in a trial-level court. It would be prudent to discuss the possibility of this situation with your judge at the outset of your relationship and obtain direction from the judge as to whether and how such information about possible intoxication should be communicated.

As a representative of the tribal court, you must be aware of the ethical implications of your conduct and always clear questions with your judge prior to acting. As stated earlier, your integrity and discretion will be the key to the success of not just your clerkship, but your entire legal career and the tribal court that you serve.

Questions

1. Now that you have read about ethical issues that face tribal judges and court personnel, what do you find to be the differences between the two groups?

2. Why should tribes create a code of ethics for court personnel? Is one over-all code of ethics for court personnel adequate, or are these issues differ-ent for different court positions?

In Your Community

1. Does your tribe have a code of ethics for tribal court personnel? If so, do you think the rules are comprehensive enough to address all possible issues?
2. If your tribe does not have a code of ethics for court personnel, should one be adopted?
3. Does your tribe have codes of ethics for other tribal governmental officials (such as tribal council members)? If not, should your tribe have such codes? If you do, how do they differ from the code for tribal court personnel?

Glossary

Fiduciary: A person who manages money or property for another person and in whom that other person has a right to place great trust.

Ministerial: Done by carrying out orders rather than personally deciding how to act.

Nepotism: Favoritism shown to relatives.

CHAPTER 30

Ethics for Tribal
Court Advocates

L
AWYERS AND advocates are critical players in tribal legal systems. In order to enter an appearance in a court of law, most jurisdictions require that advocates have a license to practice law (sometimes called "being admitted to the bar"). Unlike state governments, however, many tribal governments have established rules that allow specially trained nonattorneys to be licensed to practice in tribal court. There are several reasons for this allowance. First, there have historically not been many Native attorneys available to practice law in tribal courts. In order to have sufficient numbers of Native attorneys to represent parties, tribal governments have sometimes allowed nonattorneys to practice. Second, as we have seen, many tribal governments are very interested in incorporating their unique legal heritage, including their traditions and customs, into the contemporary court systems. Often, an Anglo-American legal education is not the best test for ensuring that these traditional values are represented in tribal court. Therefore, some tribal governments have established other standards for admission to practice, including familiarity with tribal beliefs and an understanding of tribal kinship systems. Advocates who are admitted to practice before a tribal court but who do not have a formal Western legal education are often referred to as "lay" advocates.

Some tribal governments require a tribal bar examination for admission to practice. For example, the Colville Tribal Court requires that all applicants—whether they have passed a state bar examination or not—take the Colville Bar Exam.

The following provisions from the Sault Ste. Marie Tribe of Chippewa Indians provide an example of how one tribal government sets standards for admission to practice in its tribal court.

REQUIREMENTS TO PRACTICE LAW IN TRIBAL COURT

Sault Ste. Marie Tribe of Chippewa Indians

Chapter 87. Admissions to Practice

Adopted December 15, 1998, Resolution No: 98-163

87.101 Purpose.

The purpose of this Chapter is to provide standards relating to the admission to practice before the Sault Ste. Marie Chippewa Tribal Court ("Court"). The Tribe has a legitimate interest in protecting prospective parties and in the quality of justice within the tribal judicial system. Consequently, this Chapter imposes requirements relative to these interests on anyone seeking to represent clients/parties in the Sault Ste. Marie Chippewa Tribal Court.

87.102 Definitions.

When used in this Chapter, unless the context otherwise indicates:

1. "Attorney" means an individual who is a current member of the State Bar of Michigan or some other State. The term "attorney" is synonymous with the term "lawyer."
2. "Court" means the Sault Ste. Marie Chippewa Tribal Court.
3. "Lawyer" means an individual who is a current member of the State Bar of Michigan or some other State. The term "lawyer" shall be synonymous with the term "attorney."
4. "Lay Advocate" means a person who is a non-lawyer and who has been qualified by the Court to serve as an Advocate on behalf of a party.

87.103 Representation by Attorney.

Any party to a civil or criminal action shall have the right to be represented by an attorney of her own choice and at her own expense pursuant to the admission procedures set forth herein.

87.104 Representation by Lay Advocate.

Any party to a civil or criminal action shall have the right to be represented by a lay advocate of her own choice and at her own expense pursuant to the admission procedures set forth herein.

87.105 Right to Represent Themselves.

Nothing in this Chapter shall be construed to deprive a person of their right to represent themselves.

87.106 Standards of Conduct and Obligations for Attorneys and Lay Advocates.

Every attorney and lay advocate admitted to practice before this Court, and every attorney or lay advocate employed or appointed to represent another by this Court, shall conform her conduct in every respect to the requirements of the Code of Ethics or Code of Professional Responsibility for the State in which said lawyer is currently licensed or authorized to practice law. Further, every attorney and lay advocate, who has been admitted to practice before this Court, shall be deemed officers of the Court for purposes of their representation of a party and shall be subjected to the disciplinary and enforcement provisions of the Court.

87.107 Practice before the Court.

A lawyer may represent any person in an action before this Court upon being duly admitted in accordance with 87.108.

87.108 Admission Procedure.

A lawyer as defined in 87.102(3) who desires to practice before this Court shall submit to the Court:

1. An Application for Admission to Practice (as provided by the Court) accompanied by a Certificate of Good Standing or other appropriate documentation from the State Bar or Supreme Court of the State in which such lawyer is duly licensed to practice law; and further, such application must be signed and dated by the lawyer applicant in the presence of a Notary Public;
2. A Certification that she shall conform to the Code of Ethics or Code of Professional Responsibility for the State in which said lawyer is currently licensed as she performs her duties as a lawyer before this Court;
3. A sworn Oath of Admission (as provided by the Court), which must be signed and dated by the lawyer applicant in the presence of a Notary Public; and
4. An application fee for admission as set by the Chief Judge of the Court.

87.109 Lay Advocate Practice before Tribal Court.

A lay advocate may represent any person in an action before this Court upon being duly admitted in accordance 87.110.

87.110 Admission Procedures of Lay Advocates.

A lay advocate who desires to practice before this Court shall submit to the Court:

1. An application for Admission to Practice (as provided by the Court), which shall be signed and dated by the lay advocate applicant in the presence of a Notary Public; and further, said application shall provide information with regard to the following criteria for admission and/or append appropriate documentation which shows that said applicant:

   a. Is at least Twenty-One (21) years of age;
   b. Possesses at least a high school diploma or GED Certificate;
   c. Possesses good communication skills, both written and verbal and has the ability to express her position clearly and concisely;
   d. Has legal or law-related education and/or training;
   e. Has legal or law-related work experience including but not limited to experience and practice before Tribal Courts;
   f. Knows and understands tribal traditions and customs;
   g. Has the knowledge and understanding of the Tribal Constitution, Tribal Code, Tribal Court Rules and Procedures, Evidentiary Rules, and the Indian Civil Rights Act;

h. Knows and understands Tribal Court jurisdiction and the history, structure and function of the Tribal Court;

i. Has the ability to perform legal research and use the law library;

j. Possesses good character and moral fitness to represent clients, including supporting affidavits from at least two people familiar with the applicant's integrity, honesty, moral character, judgment, courtesy and self-reliance as well as providing background information and permission to contact other references in the Court's discretion.

2. Certification that she shall conform to the Code of Ethics or Code of Professional Responsibility for the State in which said Lay Advocate may be currently licensed as she performs her duties as a Lay Advocate before this Court;

3. A sworn Oath of Admission (as provided by the Court), which must be signed and dated by the lay advocate applicant in the presence of a Notary Public; and

4. An application fee for admission in the amount set by the Chief Judge of the Court.

87.111 Approval or Disapproval of Application for Admission to Practice.

(1) Upon the filing of the required documents and fee, the Court shall approve the Application for Admission to Practice provided said lawyer or lay advocate has complied with the admission procedures set forth above. If so approved, the lawyer's name shall be entered on the roster of lawyers admitted to practice before this Court and the lay advocate's name shall be entered on the roster of lay advocates admitted to practice before this Court.

Each shall be provided with a Certificate of Admission to Practice from this Court.

(2) An applicant for Admission to Practice shall respond to any additional requests for information or documentation from this Court within twenty (20) days of the date of said request.

(3) An applicant who was denied Admission to Practice shall receive written notice of the basis for the denial and the applicant may then submit a response within twenty (20) days of the date of said notice. The Court will then review the application materials, the basis for denial, and the applicant's response, and then notify the applicant in writing of the subsequent decision. Also, in the Court's discretion, a hearing may be held to elicit tes-

timony bearing on the basis for the denial prior to making such decision. There is no further appeal in the Admission Procedure.

(4) A disapproval for Admission to Practice may include, but are not limited to, the following:

1. Failure to meet the Admission requirements set forth herein;
2. Refusal to furnish available information or answer questions relating to the applicant's qualifications for Admission to Practice;
3. Knowingly making a false statement of a material fact or failure to disclose a fact necessary to correct a misapprehension or misrepresentation in connection with her application; or
4. Is the subject of disciplinary action as an attorney in the jurisdiction for the State in which the attorney is so licensed.

87.112 Annual Renewal to Practice of Lawyer.

Once admitted to practice before this Court, a lawyer may continue to practice before the Court each year thereafter provided said lawyer certifies that she continues to be a lawyer in good standing from her respective State Bar and submits an annual membership fee as set by the chief Judge of the Court.

87.113 Annual Renewal to Practice of Lay Advocate.

Once admitted to practice before this Court, a lay advocate may continue to practice before the Court each year thereafter provided said lay advocate certifies she continues to meet the criteria for admissions set forth herein and submits an annual membership fee as set by the chief Judge.

The issue of licensing advocates who do not have formal law school training raises important issues for tribal governments. The following case illustrates the importance of having clear, unambiguous guidelines for the admission to practice in tribal courts.

TAFOYA V. NAVAJO NATION BAR ASSOCIATION

Supreme Court of the Navajo Nation[*]

The opinion of the court was delivered by: Austin, Associate Justice.

Opinion

Appealed from a decision of the Board of Bar Commissioners of the Navajo Nation Bar Association.

This is an appeal from a Navajo Nation Bar Association administrative ruling revoking the bar membership of the appellant, Mehl Tafoya. The Navajo Nation Bar Association Board of Bar Commissioners affirmed the revocation, and Tafoya appealed to this Court.

In May 1987, Tafoya applied for admission to the Navajo Nation Bar Association (NNBA). At the time Tafoya applied, the NNBA By-Laws required state bar membership for all non-Indian applicants. Tafoya, a non-Indian, failed to satisfy this criterion. He had never attended law school and was not a member of any state bar association nor licensed to practice before any state court. Tafoya never claimed to possess such credentials. In fact, he clearly indicated on his NNBA application that he had never received a formal legal education.

On July 13, 1987, Tafoya successfully completed a legal training course approved by the NNBA. The next day, July 14, Tafoya was notified by Norman Cadman, then Vice President of the NNBA, that his application had been provisionally approved and he would be allowed to sit for the Navajo Nation Bar Examination. Tafoya was notified on September 8, 1987 that he had passed the bar examination, and was sworn in by this Court on September 11, 1987.

After practicing law for approximately two months, Tafoya received a letter from Donna Chavez, successor Vice President of the NNBA, informing him that his membership in the NNBA and his license were revoked by the NNBA Admissions Committee. The letter apprised Tafoya of his

---

[*] Supreme Court of the Navajo Nation, *Tafoya v. Navajo Nation Bar Association* (1989), 1989.NANN.0000014 at www.versuslaw.com.

right to appeal the decision to the Board of Bar Commissioners, which he did on December 9, 1987.

On December 10, 1987, Albert Hale, then President of the NNBA, remanded Tafoya's case to the Admissions Committee for a hearing after finding that the letter of revocation had violated Tafoya's due process rights. A motion for a stay of execution, which Tafoya had filed, was also directed to the Admissions Committee for their consideration. The stay was granted.

On January 6, 1988, the Admissions Committee held a hearing in which Tafoya appeared and gave testimony. He was also allowed to present evidence and witnesses in his defense, although he chose not to do so. No brief was filed.

Tafoya's lack of state bar membership and legal education were never points of contention in the Admissions Committee hearing, and no allegation of fraud or misrepresentation was leveled against him. In fact, testimony from NNBA witnesses indicated that Norman Cadman was aware of Tafoya's lack of qualifications.

In its decision on remand, the Admissions Committee rejected Tafoya's argument in equity and affirmed the revocation determination. Tafoya appealed to the NNBA Board of Bar Commissioners, which affirmed the Committee's decision of July 27, 1988. We now affirm.

Four issues are raised on appeal:

1. Whether the approval of Tafoya's NNBA application and licensing by the Navajo Supreme Court constitute actions which equitably estop the NNBA from raising Tafoya's lack of state bar membership as grounds for revocation.
2. Whether Tafoya was afforded due process of law in the NNBA revocation proceedings.
3. Whether Tafoya has been denied equal protection of the law.
4. Whether the NNBA Articles of Association, §§ 101–604, empower the NNBA Board of Bar Commissioners to conduct bar revocation proceedings.

The NNBA rules governing admissions are quite explicit. Section III(B)(3) of the By-Laws establishes two categories of applicants: those who are state bar members and those who are not state bar members. Different standards apply to the two categories. This bifurcated admissions structure is not arbitrary or capricious, but rather designed to improve the Navajo court system and enhance the quality of the Navajo Bar. As members of the tribe, Navajo advocates are familiar with the customs and traditions of their people. They can speak the tribal language, thereby communicating with those seeking legal help who rely upon their native tongue. An understanding of the Navajo life-style and culture is indispensable to the practice of law within the Navajo Nation, and Navajo advocates advance the development of a modern judicial system which retains traditional legal norms.

The NNBA has also realized, however, that a formal legal education serves as a catalyst in the process of Navajo legal evolution. Trained attorneys serve an important function: they elevate the level of trial and appellate practice by introducing new legal concepts and techniques into the legal community. Furthermore, law school uniquely trains an attorney to appreciate different legal values within an analytical framework. Although an outsider, a non-Navajo attorney is trained to study and decipher Navajo law in a manner few layman could emulate. The non-Navajo attorney is therefore crucial to the jurisprudential development of Navajo society.

Tafoya fits neither category. In Navajo tradition, an advocate spoke for the person accused, as a sort of character witness, with knowledge of the man, his family, and his upbringing. The Navajo advocate knows Navajo life-style, culture, clan relationships and the language. Tafoya does not possess this knowledge. At the same time, he is unable to perform as a non-Navajo attorney, because he lacks a formal legal education and he is not a state bar member. While he successfully completed a legal training course approved by the NNBA, the course is not the equivalent of law school. Law school provides an individual with an arsenal of analytical skills which no six-week course could offer. Due to his failure to satisfy one of the categories under Section III(B)(3) of the By-Laws, Tafoya is patently unqualified for membership in the NNBA.

Tafoya argues that although he failed to meet the criterion of section III(B)(3), the requirements were waived in his case. Tafoya argues that the NNBA is equitably estopped from revoking his membership because his application was approved by the NNBA, he took and passed the bar examination, and was ultimately sworn in by this Court.

The rules for membership in the NNBA may be waived for non-Indians in certain circumstances. See *In re: Elkins*, 4 Nav.R. 63, 64 (1983); *In re: Practice of Law*, 4 Nav.R. 75, 76 (1983). In these cases, however, the non-Indian attorney was a state bar member who was hired by the Navajo Department of Justice. She was granted associate status prior to taking the bar examination because she was needed by the tribe to present pressing issues in Navajo courts. Although she had not yet passed the Navajo Nation Bar Examination, Elkins was an attorney filling a needed role. Tafoya, however, is not a law school graduate and is not an attorney for the Navajo Department of Justice. His case, therefore, is quite different.

The question, though, is not whether section III(B)(3) can be waived, but rather who is authorized to make such a decision. This Court is ultimately responsible for all admissions to the bar, and is vested with the authority to waive NNBA rules. We have, however, delegated certain responsibilities to the Board of Bar Commissioners (NNBA Articles of Association, §§ 101–604).

It is clear, however, that Norman Cadman lacked the authority to issue a waiver on his own. Nowhere in the By-Laws is such a power delegated to the Vice President. Although he was entrusted with the responsibility of enforcing admissions criteria, he was not empowered to flout them. The NNBA is free to enforce their guidelines. The NNBA is not bound by the unauthorized acts of its agents. While an administrative agency like the NNBA may be faulted for "failure to police the actions of its own personnel, [it] as a whole cannot be held accountable for, nor required to perpetuate the . . . unauthorized practice. . . ." (*Huntway Refining Co. v. United States Dept. of Energy*, 586 F.Supp. 569, 573 [C.D.Cal. 1984]). Cadman's action in admitting Tafoya was unauthorized. That being the case, the NNBA is not prevented from repudiating that act and enforcing the rule.

Tafoya also argues that the revocation proceedings violated his due process rights. It is true that the Admissions Committee initially revoked Tafoya's membership without notice. The Committee's decision, however, was subsequently vacated and remanded for a full hearing. All evidence from the record below indicates that Tafoya, on remand, was given an opportunity to present a defense, including witnesses and evidence if he so chose. Referring Chavez's letter back to the Admissions Committee effectively negated previous error in favor of a de novo adjudication on the issue remanded. The record from the hearing on remand shows that Tafoya was given due process.

Tafoya draws a parallel between himself and William Battles in *In re: Practice of Law of Battles*, 3 Nav.R. 92 (1982), where Battles, a non-Indian, was allowed to maintain his NNBA membership. If Battles was now applying for admission he would not meet the qualifications established by the NNBA. The Battles case, however, is distinguishable. There, Battles became a member of the NNBA in 1976, which was prior to adoption of the rule (section III(B)(3)) which required non-Indians to be members of a state bar. Battles met all the qualifications for membership on the day he was admitted to the bar, while Tafoya was never eligible according to the admissions criterion. By allowing Battles to continue to practice before the Navajo courts, this Court simply refused to retroactively enforce a new rule. Here, the rule was in effect even before Tafoya took the bar examination.

Tafoya also argues that the NNBA lacks the authority to conduct bar membership and license revocation proceedings because this function has not been explicitly delegated by the Supreme Court. In fact, the Bar Association not only has been delegated the power but also the responsibility to conduct such proceedings.

Section 203 of the NNBA Articles of Association empowers the NNBA to "promulgate and enforce any and all appropriate rules and regulations, including ethical standards" (NNBA Articles of Association, § 203; emphasis added). This section makes it clear that ethical violations are not all-inclusive. Other considerations are implicit, as indicated by the phrasing "all appropriate rules."

Furthermore, the fact that this Court is the ultimate authority on bar membership does not mean that the Bar Association lacks power to conduct revocation hearings. This Court has previously determined that "while the bar association screens . . . the ultimate responsibility and authority for the admission and non-admission of an individual . . . is that of the courts. Occasionally, situations will arise in which an individual does not meet the standards fixed by the bar, and [those] individuals cannot be barred from directly petitioning the courts for admission" (*In re: Practice of Law*, 4 Nav.R. 75, 76 [1983]).

Tafoya has not been denied his right to appeal to this Court. At the same time, however, this Court lacks the time and resources to hear each case *de novo*. Judicial economy demands that the fact-finding begin at a lower level. The practice has been to remand bar proceedings which were improperly filed with this Court to the NNBA for screening. See order in *In re: Practice of Law of Stuhff*, 1 Nav.R. 267 (1978).

While the NNBA does possess the power to conduct revocation proceedings, only the Navajo Supreme Court has the ultimate power to revoke a practitioner's license and membership in the NNBA. Generally, this Court is also the ultimate arbiter of Bar Association membership. The administrative determination made by the NNBA is reviewable by this Court. When an appeal is taken, the NNBA's function is to preserve testimony for this Court's later review. Of course, if no appeal is filed within the time allowed, the NNBA decision becomes final. Revocation of bar membership constructively denies an attorney of his practice. Therefore, only this Court ultimately can deprive an individual of full NNBA membership.

Tafoya's appeal has been based on equitable considerations from the outset. Under these circumstances, the equities of the respective parties must be balanced (*American Savings v. Bell*, 562 F.Supp. 4 [D.D.C. 1981]). While Tafoya has an interest in maintaining his privilege to practice law, the NNBA has a far stronger interest in excluding Tafoya from membership. An individual unqualified to practice before the Navajo courts has been allowed to hang up his shingle through an unauthorized act of an NNBA official. Nothing less than the integrity of the bar is at stake.

Finally, there is the public's interest in the availability of competent and ethical legal counsel. The NNBA has a fiduciary obligation to the residents of the Navajo Nation, a responsibility it cannot abdicate. The impact Tafoya's practice will have on the public must be considered, because its interest is always paramount. An attorney is engaged in a highly specialized profession in which he is entrusted with the livelihood of a client. This Court has an obligation to the public to ensure that those certified to practice law within the Navajo Nation have met the standards for admission. Given the facts of this case, we have no choice but to conclude that Tafoya does not meet the standards necessary for admission to the NNBA.

Tafoya had a responsibility to determine what the standards for practice were before the Navajo courts (*Emery Mining Corp. v. Secretary of Labor*, 744 F.2d 1411, 1416 [10th Cir. 1984]). Every state in the Union requires a law degree for practice before their courts, and such a fundamental assumption cannot be wished away or ignored. It is not unreasonable to expect one in Tafoya's position to make a basic inquiry into his eligibility to practice law. Tafoya was admitted to the practice of law in the courts of the Navajo Nation due to an unauthorized waiver of an NNBA regulation.

We affirm the decision of the Board of Bar Commissioners.

Ethical Standards

Lawyers and advocates must be held to high ethical standards. Practicing law is a serious responsibility—individual lives and community well-being may be affected by one seemingly minor court proceeding.

The following excerpt is from the Bay Mills Tribal Code. It establishes standards for the lawyer–client relationship in tribal court.

CLIENT–LAWYER RELATIONSHIP

Bay Mills Indian Community Tribal Court

Rule 105.2 (2004)

2.303 *Client–Lawyer Relationship*. The following provisions apply to the client–lawyer relationship:

(A) *Competence*. A lawyer shall provide competent representation to a client. A lawyer shall not:

1. Handle a legal matter which the lawyer knows or should know that the lawyer is not competent to handle, without associating with a lawyer who is competent to handle it;
2. Handle a legal matter without preparation adequate in the circumstances; or
3. Neglect a legal matter entrusted to the lawyer.

(B) *Scope of Representation*.

(1) A lawyer shall seek the lawful objectives of a client through reasonably available means permitted by law and this Code. A lawyer does not violate this rule by acceding to reasonable requests of opposing counsel which do not prejudice the rights of the client, by being punctual in fulfilling all professional commitments, by avoiding offensive tactics, or by treating with courtesy and consideration all persons involved in the legal process. A lawyer shall abide by a client's decision whether to accept an offer of settlement or mediation evaluation of a matter. In a criminal case, the lawyer shall abide by the client's decision, after consultation with the lawyer, as to a plea to be entered, whether to waive a jury trial, and whether the client will testify. In representing a client, a lawyer may, where permissible, exercise professional judgment to waive or fail to assert a right or position of the client.

(2) A lawyer may limit the objectives of the representation if the client consents after consultation.

(3) A lawyer shall not counsel a client to engage, or assist a client, in conduct that the lawyer knows is illegal or fraudulent, but a lawyer may discuss the legal consequences of any proposed course of conduct with a client and may counselor assist a client to make a good-faith effort to determine the validity, scope, meaning, or application of the law.

When a lawyer knows that a client expects assistance not permitted by this Code or other law, the lawyer shall consult with the client regarding the relevant limitations on the lawyer's conduct.

(C) *Diligence*. A lawyer shall act with reasonable diligence and promptness in representing a client.

(D) *Communication*.

(1) A lawyer shall keep a client reasonably informed about the status of a matter and comply promptly with reasonable requests for information.

A lawyer shall notify the client promptly of all settlement offers, mediation evaluations, and proposed plea bargains.

(2) A lawyer shall explain a matter to the extent reasonably necessary to permit the client to make informed decisions regarding the representation.

(E) *Confidentiality of Information.*

(1) "Confidence" refers to information protected by the client–lawyer privilege under applicable law, and "secret" refers to other information gained in the professional relationship that the client has requested be held inviolate or the disclosure of which would be embarrassing or would be likely to be detrimental to the client.

(2) Except when permitted under paragraph (3) below, a lawyer shall not knowingly:

a.   reveal a confidence or secret of a client;
b.   use a confidence or secret of a client to the disadvantage of the client; or
c.   use a confidence or secret of a client to the disadvantage of the lawyer or of a third person, unless the client consents after full disclosure.

(3) A lawyer may reveal:

a.   confidences or secrets with the consent of the client or clients affected, but only after full disclosure to them;
b.   confidences or secrets when permitted or required by these rules, or when required by law or by court order;
c.   confidences and secrets to the extent reasonably necessary to rectify the consequences of a client's illegal or fraudulent act in the furtherance of which the lawyer's services have been used;
d.   the intention of a client to commit a crime and the information necessary to prevent the crime; and
e.   confidences or secrets necessary to establish or collect a fee, or to defend the lawyer or the lawyer's employees or associates against an accusation of wrongful conduct.

(4) A lawyer shall exercise reasonable care to prevent employees, associates, and others whose services are utilized by the lawyer from disclosing or using confidences or secrets of a client, except that a lawyer may reveal the information allowed by Subparagraph (E)(3) above through an employee.

(F) *Conflict of Interest: General Rule.*

(1) A lawyer shall not represent a client if the representation of that client will be directly adverse to another client, unless:

a. the lawyer reasonably believes the representation will not adversely affect the relationship with the other client; and
b. each client consents after consultation.

(2) A lawyer shall not represent a client if the representation of that client may be materially limited by the lawyer's responsibilities to another client or to a third person, or by the lawyer's own interest unless:

a. the lawyer reasonably believes the representation will not be adversely affected; and
b. the client consents after consultation. When representation of multiple clients in a single matter is undertaken, the consultation shall include explanation of the implications of the common representation and the advantages and risks involved.

(G) *Client Under a Disability.*

(1) When a client's ability to make adequately considered decisions in connection with the representation is impaired, whether because of minority or mental disability or for some other reason, the lawyer shall, as far as reasonably possible, maintain a normal client–lawyer relationship with the client.

(2) A lawyer may seek the appointment of a guardian or take other protective action with respect to a client only when the lawyer reasonably believes that the client cannot adequately act in the client's own interest.

(H) *Declining or Terminating Representation.*

(1) Except as stated in Subparagraph (3) below, a lawyer shall not represent a client or, where representation has commenced, shall withdraw from the representation of a client if:

a. the representation will result in violation of this Code of Ethics or other law;
b. the lawyer's physical or mental condition materially impairs the lawyer's ability to represent the client; or
c. the lawyer is discharged.

(2) Except as stated in Subparagraph (3) below, a lawyer may withdraw from representing a client if withdrawal can be accomplished without material adverse effect on the interests of the client, or if:

a. the client persists in a course of action involving the lawyer's services that the lawyer reasonably believes is criminal or fraudulent;
b. the client has used the lawyer's services to perpetrate a crime or fraud;
c. the client insists upon pursing an objective that the lawyer considers repugnant or imprudent;
d. the client fails substantially to fulfill an obligation to the lawyer regarding the lawyer's services and has been given reasonable warning that the lawyer will withdraw unless the obligation is fulfilled;
e. the representation will result in an unreasonable financial burden on the lawyer or has been rendered unreasonably difficult by the client; or
f. other good cause for withdrawal exists.

(3) When ordered to do so by this Court, a lawyer shall continue representation notwithstanding good cause for terminating the representation.

Upon termination of representation, a lawyer should take reasonable steps to protect a client's interests, such as giving reasonable notice to the client, allowing time for employment of other counsel, surrendering papers and property to which the client is entitled, and refunding any advance payment of fee that has not been earned. The lawyer may retain papers relating to the client to the extent permitted by law.

The following excerpt is from the Court rules for the Sac and Fox Tribe of the Mississippi in Iowa. It provides the oath to which all advocates must subscribe and provides authority for suspension, disbarment, and discipline of advocates who do not maintain their professional responsibility.

TRIBAL COURT RULES

Sac and Fox Tribe of the Mississippi in Iowa

Oath.

After admission, and prior to taking any action in any matter, applicant must subscribe to the following oath or affirmation: "I, _____ do solemnly swear [or affirm] that I will conduct myself as an attorney and coun-selor of the Court of the Sac and Fox Tribe of the Mississippi in Iowa, uprightly and according to law, that in every proceeding I will comply with my duty to ensure that all necessary, helpful, and relevant facts are discovered such that the Court can determine the truth and make a proper, informed, and just decision, and that I will uphold and support the Constitution of the Sac and Fox Tribe of the Mississippi in Iowa and the laws of the Tribe."

Suspension, Disbarment, or Discipline.

i. *Standard*. A member of the Bar is subject to suspension or disbarment by the Court if the member is guilty of conduct unbecoming a member of the Court's bar.

ii. *Procedure*. The member must be given notice and an opportunity to show good cause, within the time prescribed by the Court of Appeals, why the member should not be suspended or disbarred.

iii. *Order*. In any case where the Court of Appeals provides notice under subsection (ii), it shall subsequently issue a written order, appropriate under the facts of the case. There shall be no right to appeal from such order.

Discipline.

i. *Standard*. Any Court may discipline counsel who practices before it for conduct unbecoming a member of the Bar or for failure to comply with any Court rule.

ii. *Procedure*. The Court may impose appropriate discipline immediately only if the conduct occurs in open Court. In all other cases, the Bar mem-ber must be provided notice and an opportunity to show cause why disci-plinary measures should not be taken.

iii. *Order*. In any case where the Court provides notice under subsection (ii), it shall subsequently issue a written order, appropriate under the facts of the case. There shall be no right to appeal when the order is issued by the Court of Appeals, but appeal from orders of the Trial Court are permitted.

Cases

The following tribal court cases focus primarily on tribal lay advocates' ethi-cal standards within the tribe. Each case portrays how the court handles such situations and determines different sanctions and rulings for violations of the code of ethics of the tribe.

IN THE MATTER OF WAYNE WEBSTER

Fort Peck Court of Appeals

Fort Peck Court of Appeals No. 037 (1987)
In the matter of Wayne Webster, an Attorney Licensed to Practice before the Fort Peck Tribal Court System, Respondent.
Appeal No. 037

This matter was a proceeding initiated upon an Order to Show Cause and Notice of Hearing dated May 22, 1987, and filed by the Fort Peck Court of Appeals ordering Respondent to show cause why he should not be suspended or disbarred from practice as a Lay Counselor before the Fort Peck Tribal Court system pursuant to Title I, Section 504, of the Comprehensive Code of Justice of the Assiniboine and Sioux Tribes (hereinafter CCOJ), on the grounds that his conduct has violated Rules 1.3, 1.4(a), 1.5(a), 3.2, 8.4(a), (b), (c), and (d) of the ABA [American Bar Association] Rules of Professional Conduct or any other applicable rule.

For respondent: Wayne Webster, Lay Counselor, Brockton, Montana 59213.

On June 2, 1987, a hearing was held on the Fort Peck Court of Appeal's Order to Show Cause and Notice of Hearing dated May 22, 1987. At the hearing, testimony and evidence was presented by witnesses called by the Court and Respondent.

Opinion by Arnie A. Hove, Chief Justice, joined by Daniel R. Schauer, Justice and Gary James Melbourne, Justice.

Held: Respondent's conduct has violated rules 1.3, 1.4(a), 1.5(a), 3.2, 8.4(a), (b), (c), and (d) of the ABA rules of professional conduct. Respondent is disbarred from practice as a lay counselor before the Fort Peck Tribal Court system for a period of one (1) year. Respondent is ordered to make restitution to Deborah Macdonald, Valerie Simmons and Shari Swanson, obtain an alcohol evaluation and follow the recommendations or obtain the recommended treatment. Notice of respondent's disbarment is to be published to protect the public from further professional misconduct by respondent.

This Court received complaints from various sources within the Tribal Court system that the Respondent had taken money from several parties to perform legal work and failed to do the work for which he was retained. The complaints against Respondent were in the form of unsolicited letters to the Tribal Court judges and administrator. These letters were from Valerie Simmons, Deborah A. Tattoo, and Shari Swanson.

The above-referenced letters contained basically the same complaints. The parties hired Respondent to do their divorces and paid him a retainer. The Respondent failed to maintain any contact with his clients, prepare and file the necessary papers to start and finish the divorces or refund their money after the parties terminated Respondent's legal services.

This Court solicited affidavits from the parties who wrote the letters and two affidavits were received. Violet Martell, who is Valerie Simmons' mother and had personal knowledge surrounding the employment of Respondent by her daughter, gave an affidavit as to the truth of the allegations in Valerie Simmons' letter since Valerie Simmons was in the hospital. Deborah (Tattoo) Macdonald also gave an affidavit as to the truth of the allegations in her letter to Judge Brown dated March 20, 1987.

On May 22, 1987, an Order to Show Cause and Notice of Rearing was issued to and served upon Respondent. Respondent was ordered to appear before the Fort Peck Tribal Court of Appeals at 9:00 a.m. on June 2, 1987, in the Courtroom of the Fort Peck Tribal Court in Poplar, Montana, to show cause why he should not be suspended or disbarred from practice as a Lay Counselor before the Fort Peck Tribal Court system pursuant to Title I, Section 504, of the Comprehensive Code of Justice of the Assiniboine and Sioux Tribes (I CCOJ 504), on the grounds that his conduct has violated Rules 1.3, 1.4. 1.5(a), 3.2, 8.4(a), (b), (c) and (d) of the ABA Rules of Professional Conduct or any other applicable ABA rule. This hearing was ordered by the Fort Court of Appeals on its own motion as a result of the two (2) affidavits attached thereto.

The issues to be addressed in this opinion are as follows:

1. Whether this Court has jurisdiction to hear this matter.
2. Whether the allegations against Respondent are supported by evidence and are violations of Rules 1.3, 1.4(a), 1.5(a), 3.2, 8.4(a), (b), (c) and (d) of the ABA Rules of Professional Conduct or any other applicable rule.
3. If Respondent's conduct did violate ABA Rules of Professional Conduct, should Respondent be suspended or disbarred from practice as a Lay Counselor before the Fort Peck Tribal Court system.

I.

Whether this Court has jurisdiction to hear this matter and disbar or suspend the Respondent.

The law granting jurisdiction of this matter to this Court is Title I, Section 504 of the Fort Peck Comprehensive Code of Justice (hereinafter cited as I CCOJ 504). This section reads in full as possible:

Sec. 504. *Disbarment*.

a. The Tribal Court or the Court of Appeals may disbar an attorney or lay counselor from practice before the courts, or impose suspension from practice for such time as the Court deems appropriate, pursuant to rules adopted by the Court, provided that the Court shall give such attorney or lay counselor reasonable prior notice of the charges against him and an opportunity to respond to them.

b. Any person who is disbarred or suspended by the Tribal Court may appeal that determination to the Fort Peck Court of Appeals within 15 days of the disbarment or suspension. The Fort Peck Court of Appeals shall request a statement of the reasons for the disbarment or suspension from the Chief Judge, and after receiving such statement shall review the record which was before the Tribal Court and may, in its discretion, hear oral argument by the applicant. The Court of Appeals shall determine de novo whether the applicant shall be disbarred or suspended and its determination shall be final.

c. Any person who is disbarred or suspended by a Justice of the Court of Appeals may appeal that determination to the Fort Peck Court of Appeals within 15 days of the disbarment or suspension. The appeal shall be determined by those Justices of the Court not involved in the initial determination. The Court shall request a statement of the reasons for the disbarment or suspension from the Justice who took the initial action, and after receiving such statement shall review the record which was before the Justice and may, in its discretion, hear oral argument by the applicant. The Court of Appeals shall determine de novo whether the applicant shall be disbarred or suspended and its determination shall be final.

This Court adopted the American Bar Association Rules of Professional Conduct (hereinafter cited as ABA Rule) in *Tribes vs. Mary Cleland* (1986) AP-004 until the Fort Peck Assiniboine and Sioux Tribes adopt their own code of legal ethics for the Tribal Court system. Therefore, this Court has jurisdiction to hear this matter and determine whether Respondent should be disbarred or suspended and this Court's determination shall be final.

II.

Whether the allegations against Respondent are supported by evidence and are violations of ABA Rules 1.3, 1.4(a), 1.5(a), 3.2, 8.4(a), (b), (c) and (d) of the ABA Rules of Professional Conduct or any other applicable rule.

On June 2, 1987, several of Respondent's former clients and Tribal Court judges testified.

The first witness was Deborah Macdonald, who was one of Respondent's former clients. Deborah Macdonald testified that she was to pay Respondent $150.00 for her divorce and had paid Respondent $100.00. Deborah Macdonald claimed that she had contacted Respondent to determine the status of her divorce. Deborah Macdonald testified Respondent on one occasion claimed the papers he was to have filed were lost and on another occasion assured her the papers were filed. Deborah Macdonald further testified that, "I requested a refund from Mr. Webster on March 19, 1987 if he didn't want to do the divorce. He said no no no I want to do it but how do I get to town when I don't have a vehicle." Deborah Macdonald testified that Respondent did no work in her divorce and that she retained the services of an attorney to complete her divorce. Deborah Macdonald requested a refund from Respondent and he refused.

Respondent cross-examined Deborah Macdonald as to the fact he requested $150.00 to do the divorce. Deborah Macdonald did not deny that she was to pay $150.00 for Respondent's services to complete her divorce. . . .

[The second and third witnesses testified to similar complaints, their testimony is omitted.]

The fourth witness was Debbie Martell. Debbie Martell heard parts of the conversation between Valerie Simmons and Respondent in which she observed he acted intoxicated. Debbie Martell believed she heard Respondent asking Valerie Simmons for a date.

The fifth witness was Judge McAnnally. Judge McAnnally indicated that he felt Respondent performed his duties to the best of his ability and that Respondent was highly qualified as a lay counselor. While Judge McAnnally indicated that Respondent had done well in the juvenile court, on occasion Respondent was to have been abrupt with Judge McAnnally. In addition, Judge McAnnally indicated that while Respondent was present in juvenile court there was the aroma of alcohol and that more recently, Respondent's practice has slipped.

The sixth witness was Judge McClammy. Judge McClammy informed this Court that Respondent had entered a guilty plea to the charge of Simple Assault on April 27, 1987. Judge McClammy sentenced Respondent to 90 days and ordered him to refrain from drinking. The 90 days were suspended. Judge McClammy also testified that when Respondent had first appeared in his court he had been drinking and Judge McClammy had warned him not to appear before him when drinking. Judge McClammy did testify that Respondent represented clients to the best of his ability.

The seventh witness was Judge Gourneau. Judge Gourneau testified that when Respondent appeared in her court he smelled of liquor and appeared intoxicated before her at arraignments and when she was the acting juvenile judge. Judge Gourneau feels that Respondent has acted professional, however, she felt that he had done good and bad in his representation of clients before her court. Judge Gourneau testified that she had been informed by a dispatcher Respondent was at the jail "hustling" clients. Finally, Judge Gourneau indicated her daughter Roxanne Gourneau' s divorce was not properly completed.

The eighth witness was Judge Violet Hamilton. Judge Hamilton testified that on numerous occasions Respondent would inform her of his client's side of the matter. Judge Hamilton testified that a Zelma Mason had informed the Judge that she had retained Wayne Webster to represent her in an action involving a car company and he had filed nothing in the action. The Judge, Zelma Mason and Respondent had a conference call and it was established Respondent was not representing her. Finally, Judge Hamilton testified that she was present when Respondent was soliciting business before arraignments by asking defendants if he could represent them.

The ninth witness was Lawyer Judge Brown. Lawyer Judge Brown testified that Respondent was presently charged in his court with a criminal offense of Aggravated or Simple Assault against a minor, Patrick McKay.

The tenth and final witness was Lillian Webster. Lillian Webster, who was the mother of Respondent, was called by Respondent. Mrs. Webster testified that she had the same phone number as Respondent and that she did not receive any calls from Violet Martell or Valerie Simmons. When questioned further by this Court regarding her knowledge of Respondent's past and pending criminal charges, she had no knowledge of the same.

The testimony of Respondent's former clients, Deborah Macdonald and Valerie Simmons, establish clear violations of ABA Rule 1.3 which states, "A lawyer shall act with reasonable diligence and promptness in representing a client." Deborah Macdonald testified that Respondent failed to file divorce papers for her after continued assurances that the petition was being prepared and would be filed. Deborah Macdonald testified of receiving excuses from Respondent and eventually hiring an attorney to do her divorce. Valerie Simmons' case is a more extreme violation of this rule in that over a year had past before she obtained any relief and it was necessary to obtain that relief through this Court.

The testimony of Deborah Macdonald and Valerie Simmons also establish violations of ABA Rule 1.4(a) which states, "A lawyer shall keep a client reasonably informed about the status of a matter and promptly comply with reasonable requests for information." The testimony of both witnesses establish that Respondent neither informed them of the status of their cases or promptly complied with their reasonable requests for information.

The testimony of Deborah Macdonald and Valerie Simmons also establish violations of ABA Rule 1.5(a) which in part states, "A lawyer's fees shall be reasonable. . . ." In both cases, Respondent did not perform any services. Therefore, Respondent's fees were not reasonable and he should have refunded the same.

The testimony of Valerie Simmons establishes a violation of ABA Rule 3.2 which states, "A lawyer shall make reasonable efforts to expedite litigation consistent with the interests of the client." The previous discussion of Respondent's violation of ABA Rule 1.3 in his representation of Valerie Simmons is sufficient to and does establish a violation of ABA Rule 3.2.

The testimony of Deborah Macdonald, Valerie Simmons, Violet Martell, Debbie Martell, Judge McAnnally, Judge McClammy and Judge Gourneau, Judge Hamilton and Judge Brown establish violations of ABA Rule 8.4(a), (b), (c), and (d).

The applicable portions of this rule read in full as follows:

It is professional misconduct for a lawyer to:

a. violate or attempt to violate the Rules of Professional Conduct, knowingly assist or induce another to do so, or do so through the acts of another;

b. commit a criminal act that reflects adversely on the lawyer's honesty, trustworthiness or fitness as a lawyer in other respects;

c. engage in conduct involving dishonesty, fraud, deceit or misrepresentation;

d. engage in conduct that is prejudicial to the administration of justice; . . .

Respondent has violated paragraphs (a), (b), (c), and (d) of ABA Rule 8.4 and is guilty of professional misconduct. In the discussion of Issue No. II, Respondent was found to have violated ABA Rules 1.3, 1.4(a), 1.5(a), and 3.2. Therefore, Respondent has violated Rule 8.4(a) by violating several Rules of Professional Conduct.

Respondent has violated ABA Rule 8.4(b) as evidenced in his recent conviction for a simple assault and his alleged participation in an assault on a minor which is pending before Tribal Court. Respondent's recent conviction for a simple assault and pending charges for the same offense obviously does reflect adversely on Respondent's fitness as a lay counselor. Attorneys and lay counselors are not to be engaging in criminal acts against persons.

Respondent has violated ABA Rule 8.4(c) by engaging in conduct involving dishonesty, fraud, deceit or misrepresentation in his dealings with Deborah Macdonald, Valerie Simmons and Shari Swanson.

Respondent's handling of Valerie Simmons' divorce can be construed as a clear violation of ABA Rule 8.4(d). As a direct result of Respondent's conduct, there resulted a delay of over a year in Valerie Simmons' divorce and therefore was prejudicial to the administration of justice and her obtaining a divorce.

Therefore, the testimony of the witnesses and evidence of a recent conviction and pending charge, establish Respondent's violations of several ABA Rules. Furthermore, Respondent admitted receiving retainers from Deborah Macdonald and Valerie Simmons and not completing their divorces.

III.

If Respondent's conduct did violate ABA Rules of Professional Conduct, should Respondent be suspended or disbarred from practice as a lay counselor before the Fort Peck Tribal Court system.

The testimony presented to and evidence received by this Court, established that serious and numerous violations of the ABA Rules of Professional Conduct were committed by Respondent. The testimony and evidence also established that Respondent has a drinking problem which is affecting his performance as a lay counselor. Because of the above, this Court determined that it was necessary to protect the public from further professional misconduct by Respondent as well as attempt to rehabilitate him for possible readmission to the Tribal Bar.

Therefore, It is the unanimous decision of this court to disbar respondent from practice as a lay counselor before the Fort Peck Tribal Court system for a period of one (1) year. It is ordered that respondent shall make Restitution to Deborah Macdonald, Valerie Simmons and Shari Swanson and that respondent shall obtain an alcohol evaluation and follow the recommendations or obtain the recommended treatment. It is further ordered that notice of respondent's disbarment be published to protect the public from further professional misconduct by respondent. Respondent is put on notice that his failure to comply with all or any part of this order is a contempt of court.

Respondent is also put on notice that after one (1) year from this date and after providing proof of his compliance with the orders herein, respondent shall be allowed to take the Tribal Bar Exam and apply for readmission to practice in the Tribal Court System.

IN THE MATTER OF JERRY R. SEKAYUMPTEWA

*Appellate Court of the Hopi Tribe**

Before Sekaquaptewa, Chief Justice and Lomayesva and Abbey, Justices

Opinion and Order

This case asks whether the Hopi Trial Court may condition the terms under which a legal advocate may practice before the Courts of the Hopi Tribe.

Factual and Procedural Background

On July 6, 1990, the Hopi Tribal Court ("Court") found Jerry R. Sekayumptewa, Sr. ("Sekayumptewa") to be in contempt of court for failing to appear with his clients for their trials on that date.

On July 11, 1990, in *In the Matter of Sekayumptewa, Jerry R.*, the Court found that Sekayumptewa had "demonstrated a flagrant disregard and disrespect for the integrity of his profession and the courts," and suspended him from practice as a legal advocate for six months. See *In the Matter of Sekayumptewa. Jerry R.*, S-01-90 No. 18957 (1990) (hereinafter, "*Sekayumptewa* (1990)").

The Court permitted him to apply for reinstatement after six months and when he had "shown that he will desist from such behavior that caused him to be suspended from practice before the courts." *Id.*

On May 17, 1994, the Court denied Sekayumptewa's first application for reinstatement. The Court ruled that before he would be reinstated, he must complete a professional responsibility class and submit recommendations of two Hopi Bar members.

On September 19, 1997, the Court denied another request for reinstatement, noting that the conditions of the 1994 ruling had not been met.

On March 4, 1999, Chief Judge of the Hopi Trial Court responded to a letter from Sekayumptewa asking for reinstatement. The Chief Judge denied the request, also noting that the conditions of the 1994 ruling had not been met. The Chief Judge added the further condition that

---

* Appellate Court of the Hopi Tribe, *In the Matter of Jerry R. Sekayumptewa*, 2000.NAHT.0000009 (2000).

Sekayumptewa must obtain treatment for alcohol abuse before he would be reinstated.

On February 15, 2000, Sekayumptewa appealed to this Court.

Issues Presented on Appeal

1. Whether the Trial Court's initial order suspending Petitioner from practice became void when the case upon which his contempt charges were based was dismissed with prejudice.
2. Whether the Trial Court overstepped its authority by setting conditions under which Petitioner may practice as a legal advocate.
3. Whether the Trial Court violated Petitioner's due process rights in 1994 by stating new conditions he would have to meet to be reinstated.
4. Whether the Chief Judge violated Petitioner's due process rights in 1999 by stating out of court new conditions would have to meet to be reinstated.

Standard and Scope of Review

Sekayumptewa phrases his case in terms of a question of law pursuant to Hopi Tribal Ordinance ("H.T.O.") 21 § 1.2.8. H.T.O. 21 § 1.2.8 grants the Court jurisdiction to answer questions of law certified to it from any tribal, state, or federal court or administrative agency as well as the Hopi Tribal Council. This Court has no jurisdiction to hear questions of law certified to it by individuals.

This case will be construed as a petition for an extraordinary writ. This Court reviews petitions for writ under H.T.O. 21 § 1.2.6.

Discussion

I. The Hopi Trial Court's Initial Order Suspending Petitioner from Practice Is Not Void.

Petitioner asserts that the 1990 contempt order is void because the criminal case in which his contempt charges arose was dismissed. This argument is without merit. The contempt order stemmed from Petitioner's misconduct when he failed to appear with his clients. See Sekayumptewa (1990). The criminal case, *Hopi Tribe v. Koyiyumtewa, et al.*, was ultimately dismissed with prejudice on March 4, 1994 for reasons unrelated to Petitioner's conduct. See *Hopi Tribe v. Koyiyumtewa, et al.*, CIV-020-89 (March 4, 1994). Petitioner's conduct or misconduct, as an advocate, is grounds for contempt independent of the underlying case. In any event, the Trial Court noted that multiple contempt citations had been issued against Petitioner. See *Sekayumptewa* (1990). Any one of those citations, including the one stemming from Koyiyumtewa, would be sufficient grounds to punish Petitioner.

II. The Hopi Tribal Court Has Authority to Set Conditions under Which Petitioner May Practice as a Legal Advocate.

Petitioner contends that the Trial Court does not have authority to suspend a legal advocate. In contrast to Petitioner's position, H.T.O. 21 § 1.8.1(e) gives both the trial and appellate courts the authority "to control . . . the conduct of its ministerial officers. . . ." Section 1.9.1(C) defines officers of the court to include "Attorneys who are members of the Bar of the Hopi Tribe." This Court has held that "a statute that prescribes punishment for contempt for attorneys must apply equally to lay advocates." *In the Matter of Sekayumptewa et al.* at 16 (1997). Taken together, these sections provide the court's authority to regulate the conduct of attorneys and lay advocates.

In this case the Trial Court did not overstep its authority. It cited Petitioner with contempt of court five times before it took the extra step of suspending him from practice. The conditions set by the Court in 1990 and clarified in 1994 were narrowly tailored to address the conduct of Petitioner. So long as the Trial Court's discipline is reasonable and appropriate to restore the conduct of its officers to the furtherance of justice, it is within its power as defined in H.T.O. 21.

III. The Hopi Trial Court Did Not Violate Petitioner's Due Process Rights in 1994.

The Court in 1994 did not violate Petitioner's due process rights. Petitioner flagrantly disregarded his responsibilities as a member of the Hopi Bar. See *Sekayumptewa* (1990). Admission to the Bar is "a privilege burdened with conditions." *Theard v. United States*, 354 U.S. 278, 281 (1957). H.T.O. 21 gives the courts the authority to control, and implicitly, to punish members of the Bar. In punishing Petitioner, the Court did not violate the limited process due an individual in Petitioner's position.

The U. S. and Arizona Supreme Courts have recognized that bar disciplinary proceedings require procedural due process. See *In re Ruffalo*, 390 U.S. 544, 552 (1968). Similarly, Hopi requires due process of law pursuant to the Indian Civil Rights Act in the disciplining of attorneys and lay advocates practicing before the Hopi Courts.

In this case, the Court provided Petitioner a hearing in 1994. That hearing was sufficient process, wherein Petitioner was provided notice and an opportunity to be heard. Then the Court clarified its condition, imposed in 1990, that Petitioner must show "that he will desist from such behavior that caused him to be suspended from practice before the courts." See *Sekayumptewa* (1990). The Court in 1994 ruled that Petitioner must complete a class in professional ethics and responsibilities and submit two recommendations before he could be reinstated to the Bar. These conditions fit within the meaning of the original terms stated in 1990. They are clear directions how the Petitioner could show the Court that he met the concerns of the original order. Thus the Court did not violate Petitioner's due process rights.

IV. The Chief Judge Violated Petitioner's Due Process Rights in 1999 by Stating out of Court New Conditions Petitioner Would Have to Meet to Be Reinstated.

Petitioner contends that the Chief Judge violated his right to due process by adding a further condition to his reinstatement to the Bar. The Chief Judge added the condition in a letter to Petitioner outside of court. No hearing was granted. Although Hopi does not have to recognize due process standards of the United States or Arizona, it honors the due process clause of the Indian Civil Rights Act. As stated supra, the U.S. and Arizona Supreme Courts have recognized that bar disciplinary proceedings require procedural due process. Since Petitioner did not receive a hearing before the Chief Judge added the condition, due process was not satisfied.

H.T.O. 21 gives the trial and appellate courts the authority to control the conduct of attorneys. It does not give judges outside of court that authority. Even if it did, it would not allow judges to bypass due process requirements. This extra condition was added to Petitioner's punishment outside of the formal legal process and cannot now be enforced.

Order of the Court

Insofar as this petition asks the Court to bypass the Trial Court's previous rulings, it is denied. We affirm the Trial Court's disposition of Jerry R. Sekayumptewa, Sr. in its 1990 ruling, its 1994 ruling, and its 1997 ruling. However, this Court does not recognize the further condition added by Chief Judge outside of the formal judicial process.

We find that Jerry R. Sekayumptewa, Sr. may be reinstated to the Hopi Bar when he has met the conditions set forth by the Trial Court in the 1994 ruling.

Questions

1. In the *Tafoya* case, the Navajo Nation Supreme Court ultimately decided that Tafoya could not retain his bar membership. Why did the Court decide this?
2. In *In the Matter of Wayne Webster*, was the tribal court given sufficient testimony to determine that Webster had violated ABA regulations? Is a one-year suspension sufficient?
3. Do you agree with the way in which the Navajo Nation Bar Association has different requirements for Navajo and non-Navajos? Why or why not?
4. In the *Sekayumptewa* case, the Hopi Appellate Courts say, "Admission to the Bar is 'a privilege burdened with conditions.'" Do you agree?
5. Why did the Court uphold the revocation of Sekayumptewa's license to practice law?

In Your Community

1. What are the advantages and disadvantages of admitting nonlawyers to practice in tribal courts?
2. Who is eligible to practice before your tribal court? Are lay advocates allowed to practice before your tribal courts?
3. Does your tribal code provide any rules of professional responsibility or other ethics requirements for advocates? If so, do you think that these rules cover all of the necessary issues?

Glossary

Bifurcated: Divided into or made up of two parts.

Desist: To stop doing something.

Dismissed with prejudice: A case dismissed with prejudice cannot be brought back into court again.

Equity: Fairness; a court's power to do justice when specific laws do not cover the situation.

Estop: To preclude.

Provisionally: Temporarily; preliminarily.

Revoking: Reversing a legal decision.

Suggested Further Reading

Phyllis E. Bernard, *Community and Conscience: The Dynamic Challenge of Lawyers' Ethics in Tribal Peacemaking*, 27 University of Toledo Law Review 821 (1996).

James W. Zion, *Court Lawyering in the Navajo Nation*, The Navajo Supreme Court Clinical Program, Harvard Law School (2001).

Tracy N. Zlock, *The Native American Tribe as a Client: An Ethical Analysis*, 10 Georgia Journal of Legal Ethics 159 (1996).

Conclusion

PROFESSOR Steve Russell (Cherokee) authored the following "Indian Lawyer's Creed." We believe it provides a most fitting conclusion to this text. We encourage our readers to continue pursuing legal education. Your contribution is critical to the future of Native people.

AN INDIAN LAWYER'S CREED

Steve Russell

The other day, I read the "Texas Lawyer's Creed," which has been endorsed by the Bar. As I read it, all it appeared to say is "I will not lie, cheat, or steal, or be unnecessarily rude to my adversaries."

I wondered why something so simple would have to be written down.

But that led to thinking about what it meant, if anything, to be an *Indian* lawyer. Are we different? If so, how? What follows was a result of that meditation:

I am an Indian lawyer, a briefcase warrior. I stand between Indian people and those who would do them harm. The warrior's role is a duty and an honor.

I defend the few resources that have not been taken from us so Indian people may survive.

I defend the land and air and water on and off the reservations so all people may learn to live in harmony with the Creator's work.

I defend the right of Indian people to govern themselves, worship as they choose, and return their dead to the earth.

I will not use my skills against Indian people no matter how wrong I believe them to be. We suffer enough without causing each other to suffer.

I will not use unethical methods in the practice of law because that would dishonor the people I represent.

I will not accept fees from Indian people beyond my needs. If I receive fees from other people beyond my needs, I will remember that a wealthy Indian is one who can quickly forget duty and honor.

Whether I practice or teach [or] hold office, I will always remember the duty of an elder to share knowledge with young men and women who aspire to be warriors.

I am an Indian lawyer, a briefcase warrior. I stand between Indian people and those who would do them harm. When I do this, I bring honor to my tribe, my clan, and myself.

Glossary

Abrogated: Abolished by authority.

Acrimony: Harsh words, manner, or disposition.

Acquiesce: To agree; accept; go along with something.

Adversarial: Having opposite sides or interests.

Adversary system: The system of law in the United States in which a judge acts as a decision maker between opposite sides.

Absolution: Setting free from guilt.

Aggregation: Several things grouped together.

Alacrity: Cheerful eagerness; liveliness.

Allotment: An assigned portion. The Allotment Act (also known as the Dawes Act) authorized the U.S. president to allot (divide) portions of reservation land to individual Indians.

Amendment: An alteration, addition, or change in law.

Amicus Curiae: (Latin for "Friend of the Court.") A third party (not directly involved in the lawsuit) providing information to a court to assist the court in reaching a conclusion.

Anathema: Something that is intensely disliked.

Anglo-American: Someone or something of English American origin. The Anglo-American legal system is the system used by the majority of non-Indian legal systems operating in the United States today.

Anomalous: Out of the ordinary.

Anthropologist: A person who studies anthropology—the social science that studies the origins and social relationships of human beings.

Appellant: A person or party who appeals a court's decision.

Appropriation: A legislature's setting aside for a specific purpose a portion of money raised by the government; a governmental taking of land or property for public use; taking something wrongfully.

Arbiter: A person chosen to decide a disagreement.

Assignment: The act of transferring an interest in property or some right (such as contract benefits) to another.

Assimilate: To make similar; to cause to resemble. A tribal government is "assimilated" when it looks and operates exactly like an Anglo-American government.

Assimilation: The social process of one cultural group being absorbed by another.

Auspices: Support and approval.

Avocational: Pertaining to an auxiliary (side) activity, such as a hobby, sport, or civic involvement.

Banishment: Requiring someone to leave a country; driving out or removing someone from his or her home and society.

Bifurcated: Divided into or made up of two parts.

Bilateral family: Two sides or both sides of the family.

Bill of attainder: A legislative act pronouncing a person guilty without a trial and sentencing the person to death.

Blood feud: A feud in which members of the opposing parties murder each other.

Capricious: Not based on fact, law, or reason.

Castigate: To subject to severe punishment or criticism.

Cause of action: Facts sufficient to support a valid lawsuit; the legal theory on which a lawsuit is based.

Cede: To yield; surrender; give up ownership or responsibility.

Cession: Something ceded.

Civil justice system: The network of courts and tribunals that deal with laws concerned with civil or private rights and remedies, as contrasted by criminal laws.

Civil law: Law relating to private rights and remedies (as opposed to criminal law).

Clan: A social group made up of a number of families with a common ancestor. Matrilineal clans are organized on the basis of descent through female ancestors. Patrilineal clans are organized on the basis of descent through male ancestors.

Clearly erroneous: In Anglo-American law, a standard that appellate courts must apply when deciding whether to uphold or overturn a decision by a lower court. *Black's Law Dictionary* defines this standard as one whereby "a [lower court's] judgment is reversible if the appellate court is left with the firm conviction that an error has been committed."

Code of Federal Regulations (CFR): The compilation of all their rules and regulations put out by federal agencies.

Codified: Written down; organized; arranged. Included in an official and formal statement of law such as a legal code or statute.

Coercive: Restrained by force.

Cognizable: Knowable or perceivable.

Common law: A system of law that is derived from judges' decisions rather than legislation. Judge-made law.

Communitarian: Of or relating to social organization in small cooperative, partially collectivist communities.

Competent: Properly qualified; adequate.

Conclusory: Conclusive.

Concurrent: Together; at the same time. In legal parlance, having the same authority. Parallel; noncompeting, as authority.

Congressionally authorized: Sanctioned by the U.S. Congress and its administrative bodies asserting their authority over non-Indians.

Connotations: A set of associations implied by a word in addition to its literary meaning.

Consensus: General agreement.

Constituent: A citizen in a government who is represented by an official.

Contempt: An act that obstructs a court's work or lessens the dignity of the court.

Conveyance: Transfer of title (ownership papers) to property.

Covenant: A promise in a written contract or a deed of real property.

Criminal justice system: The network of courts and tribunals that deal with criminal law and its enforcement.

Custom: Regular behavior (of persons in a geographical area or type of business) that gradually takes on legal importance so that it will strongly influence a court's decision.

Customary law: A law based on custom or tradition.

Cylindrical: In the shape of a cylinder.

Decedent: A dead person.

Declaratory judgment: A judge's decision (about a real problem with legal consequences) that states the rights of the parties or answers a legal question without awarding any damages or ordering that anything be done.

Declination: A formal refusal.

Decree: A judgment of a court that announces the legal consequences of the facts found in a case.

Desist: To stop doing something.

Devise: A gift by will, especially of land or things on land.

Dichotomy: A division or the process of dividing into two mutually exclusive or contradictory groups.

Discretion: The power of a judge to make decisions on various matters based on his or her opinion, within general legal guidelines.

Discrimination: The act of exposing or discerning differences among individuals, usually used in a negative sense.

Dismissed with prejudice: A case dismissed with prejudice cannot be brought back into court again.

Disposition: A final settlement or result.

Dispute resolution: The process of resolving a disagreement between persons about their rights or their legal obligations to one another.

Divestiture: The act of divesting; the compulsory transfer of title or disposal of interests upon government order.

Doctrine of discovery: The legal theory that the Europeans gained title to the land in North American because they "discovered" the land.

Domestic dependent nations: A legal status describing tribal nations that retain some sovereignty but are also dependent on the United States for guidance and protection.

Domicile: A person's permanent home, legal home, or main residence.

Double jeopardy: Being prosecuted for the same crime twice by the same government.

Easement: The right to use the real property of another for a specific purpose.

Egalitarian: Marked by social equality. Promoting a belief in human equality with respect to social, political, and economic rights and privileges.

Equity: Fairness; a court's power to do justice when specific laws do not cover the situation.

Essentialism: The practice of categorizing a group based on an artificial social construction that imparts an "essence" of that group, which suggests that all members are the same and ignores individuality and difference.

Estop: To preclude.

Ethnocentric: Belief in the superiority of one's own ethnic group.

Ethnocide: The process of ridding a cultural group of its distinct ways of acting and believing.

Ethnographic: Relating to the branch of anthropology that deals with the scientific description of specific human cultures.

Ethnographic studies: The field of descriptive anthropology.

Evidentiary: Related to or constituting evidence.

Ex parte: (Latin) Having discussions with one party to a dispute without the other party being present.

Ex post facto: (Latin for "After the fact.") An ex post facto law attempts to make an action a crime even though it was not against the law at the time it was committed.

Exclusive jurisdiction: That power that a court or other tribunal exercises over an action or over a person to the exclusion of all other courts; that forum in which an action must be commenced because no other forum has the jurisdiction to hear and determine the action.

Exhaustion doctrine: When a non-Indian company or individual is seeking to challenge the civil jurisdiction of a tribal court, it must first raise those challenges in tribal court, not federal court. Even if the tribal court first rejects these challenges, the person making these claims must exhaust all chances to appeal that rejection in the tribal legal system before coming to the federal court.

Explicit: Fully developed or described.

Extended family relations: Family relations that extend beyond the nuclear family.

Faction: A group of people with similar political goals.

Fetish: An excessive or irrational devotion to an activity.

Fiduciary: A person who manages money or property for another person and in whom that other person has a right to place great trust.

Functional: Describing something based on what it *does* rather than what it *is*.

Fundamental: Basic; core; essential.

Generative: Having the ability to produce or generate.

Government-to-government: A relationship between equal or near-equal nations that prevents one from having control over the citizens of the other.

Habeas Corpus: (Latin for "You shall have the body.") A legal action filed to protect a person from unlawful detention. A judicial order to someone holding a person to bring that person to court.

Homogeneous: All of the same or similar kind or nature.

Heir: A person who inherits property.

Hierarchical: Classified according to certain criteria into successive levels.

Homogeneous: All of the same or similar kind or nature.

Idiosyncratic: A structural or behavioral characteristic peculiar to an individual or group.

Immaterial: Of no substantial consequence; unimportant.

Implied divestiture: A doctrine that tribes have been divested of powers without any direct action from the U.S. government.

Impropriety: An improper act.

Incumbent: A person who presently holds office.

Indebted: Owing gratitude or recognition to another.

Indictment: An accusation of wrongdoing.

Indigency: A level of poverty with real hardship and deprivation.

Individualistic: Relating to the character of persons as individuals rather than as members of a community.

Inherent sovereign power: National authority not derived from another; powers originating from the nature of government or sovereignty that are not dependent on being granted by another government.

Injunction: A legal command to prohibit someone from doing a specific activity. An injunction may be *preliminary* or *temporary* (until the issue can be fully tried in court), or it may be *final* or *permanent*.

Instrument: A formal or legal document.

Integrative: Tending to combine diverse elements into a whole.

Intervene: To voluntarily enter into a lawsuit between other persons.

Judicial notice: The act of a judge in recognizing the truth of certain facts.

Judicial review: A court's power to declare a law unconstitutional and to interpret state laws. The term also refers to an appeal from an administrative agency.

Judiciary: The branch of government that interprets the law; the branch that judges.

Jurisdiction: Legal authority. The geographical area within which a court (or a public official) has the right and power to operate; the persons about whom and the subject matters about which a court has the right and power to make decisions.

Jurisprudence: Legal philosophy.

Jurist: A person who works in the field of law such as scholars, lawyers, and judges.

Kinship: Biological and social relationships.

Kiva: A Pueblo Indian ceremonial building that is usually round and partly underground.

Legal actor: A person who participates in the legal system.

Legal system: Any system for addressing antisocial behavior or resolving disputes.

Legislative intent: The purpose for which a law is passed.

Legitimacy: Credibility.

Liability: Legal obligation, responsibility, or debt.

Litigant: A plaintiff or defendant in a lawsuit.

Maxim: A saying that is widely accepted.

Mediation: Outside help in settling a dispute.

Mediator: One who reconciles differences in a dispute.

Merits: Reward or punishment due; the intrinsic rights and wrongs of a legal case as determined by substance rather than form.

Metadiscursive: A stretch of talk or discourse whose subject is the talk or discourse of which it is a part.

Metaphorical: Using one thing to represent another; symbolic.

Milieu: Environment; setting.

Militia: A part of the organized armed forces of a country, liable to call-up only in an emergency.

Ministerial: Done by carrying out orders rather than personally deciding how to act.

Modicum: Small, moderate amount.

Moiety: Either of two kinship groups based on unilateral descent that together make up a tribe or society.

Morality tales: Stories relating the beliefs on what is right and wrong.

Negligent: Failing to exercise a reasonable amount of care in a situation that causes harm to someone or something. It can involve doing something carelessly or failing to do something that should have been done.

Negotiating power: The power the people in a dispute give the mediator and the dispute resolution process.

Nepotism: Favoritism shown to relatives.

Nonadversarial: Not having opposing interests against.

Non-Indian fee lands: Lands located within the tribes' territorial borders but owned by non-Indians.

Nonmember fee lands: Lands within Indian Country not owned by or held in trust for the tribe or its members.

Nonmember Indians: Indians who are not officially members of the tribe asserting jurisdiction over them.

Norms: Values and beliefs held by a community about the proper and improper ways to act toward other people, places, and things. See also *procedural norms* and *substantive norms.*

Notorious: Generally known and talked of by the public.

Nuclear family: Biological parents and children.

Nullified: No longer having any legal effect or validity.

Ostensibly: Apparently or visibly.

Ostracism: Banishment from society.

Ostracized: Exiled; excluded from a group by common consent.

Pan-Indianism: A political and social movement that became popular in the 1960s and 1970s and called for the alliance of all Native Americans despite traditional tribal animosities.

Paradigm: Outstanding clear or typical example; in social science, the way a theory and its parts are coherent.

Parliamentary: Pertaining to a supreme legislative body of cabinet members selected by and responsive to the legislature.

Partisan: Devoted to or biased in support of a party, group, or cause.

Paternalistic: Like a father; benevolent but intrusive.

Paternity: The state of being a father; fatherhood.

Patrilineal clan: A group united by relations or descent through the fathers' line.

Patronage: The privilege of some public officials to give out jobs on their own discretion, without going through civil service procedures.

Penal law: Law that provides for a penalty.

Penultimate: Next to the last.

Per capita: (Latin for "by head.") By the number of individual persons, each equally.

Perpetrator: One who commits an offense or crime.

Perpetuate: To cause to continue indefinitely; make perpetual.

Petition for habeas corpus: A request to the court for a judicial order requiring someone who is holding a person to bring that person to court.

Plea bargaining: In Anglo-American criminal law, when a person accused of a crime is given an opportunity to reduce his or her potential punishment by agreeing before the trial to admit being guilty of the crime.

Postulate: Fundamental element; basic principle.

Practices: What legal actors actually do when undertaking the operations of the legal system.

Prayer: In law, a request in a legal pleading.

Preamble: An introductory statement or preliminary explanation as to the purpose of a law.

Precepts: Rules of personal conduct.

Predecessor: Someone or something that goes before.

Presumptive: May be inferred.

Probate: Handling the will and estate of a deceased person.

Probation: Staying out of jail under supervised conditions.

Procedural norms: The norms that legal actors must themselves follow when handling a dispute.

Promontory: High point; prominent place.

Prosecutor: The public official who presents the government's case in criminal law.

Prototype: An original or model.

Provisionally: Temporarily; preliminarily.

Punitive: Inflicting or aiming to inflict punishment.

Putative: Generally regarded as such; supposed.

Ratified: Formally approved by authority.

Recidivism: Habitual relapse into crime.

Reciprocal: A relationship that involves mutual giving and receiving.

Reckless: Lacking proper caution; careless of consequences; negligent.

Recusal: Disqualification or removal of a judge from hearing a case due to actual or potential bias or conflict of interest.

Redress: To set right; to remedy; to compensate; to remove the cause of a grievance or complaint.

Reintegrative: Restoring to a condition of integration or unity.

Relinquish: To give up a possession, claim, or right.

Remedial: Intended to improve or make right.

Remedial law: A law passed to correct a defect in a prior law; a law passed to provide or modify a remedy.

Reparative: That which repairs.

Respondent: The person against whom an appeal is taken or against whom a motion is filed.

Restitution: Giving something back; making good for something.

Restorative: That which serves to restore, correct, or heal.

Retribution: The dispensing or receiving of reward or punishment, especially in the hereafter; something given or exacted in recompense.

Revoking: Reversing a legal decision.

Sachem: A chief of some Native American tribes or confederations.

Sanctioned: Agreed; accepted.

Secular: Not specifically relating to spirituality or religion.

Self-determination: Sovereignty; the right of a people to make their own laws and be governed by them.

Serendipitous: Being lucky in finding things one was not looking for.

Sovereign immunity: A government's freedom from being sued.

Stare decisis: (Latin for "To stand by the decision.") A legal principle under which judges are obligated to follow the precedents established in prior judicial decisions.

Stewardship: The careful and responsible management of something entrusted to one's care.

Stipulate: Specify as a condition or requirement in a contract or agreement.

Strident: Commanding by a harsh or obtrusive quality.

Structures: The roles played by people during the operation of a legal system and the institutions in which those operations occur.

Subjugation: Being brought under control; conquering.

Substantive norms: The norms about everyday life that legal actors think about when deciding how to handle a dispute or wrongdoing (e.g., "Do not murder," "Do not steal").

Termination: In federal Indian law, the era during which the United States stopped recognizing tribal governments.

Textual: Relating to a written text.

Theocracy: A government ruled by religious authority.

Title: A comprehensive term referring to the legal basis of the ownership of property.

Tiospaye: A group of related people.

Tort: A civil (as opposed to criminal) wrong other than a breach of contract.

Traditional dispute resolution: A nonadversarial style of resolving disputes through the use of cultural customs and traditions by tribal justice systems.

Transgress: To violate a law, command, or duty.

Transgression: Violation of a law, command, or duty.

Tribal civil jurisdiction: The power and authority that American Indian and Alaska Native tribal courts have to prosecute certain kinds of persons accused of committing certain kinds of crimes in certain locations and, if these people are found guilty, to punish them.

Tribal sovereignty: The capacity of a tribal people to express their own norms, practices, and structures.

Tripartite: Divided into three parts.

Trust relationship: A special legal relationship between the United States and Indian tribes, in which the U.S. government has a duty to protect and oversee affairs pertaining to tribes.

Unanimity: The condition of being unanimous; complete agreement within a group.

Unscrupulous: Without concern for the ethical treatment of others.

Vacate: Annul; set aside; take back.

Vest: To give to a person a fixed and immediate right of title.

Waive: To voluntarily give up a right. To give up a privilege, right, or benefit with full knowledge of what you are doing.

Ward: A person, especially a child, placed by the court under the care of a guardian.

Willful disregard: Acting in a manner known to be wrong; intentional or deliberate disregard of notice.

Worldview: The different beliefs, values, and meanings about the world that a particular society or people have that contribute to its unique culture, traditions, and ways of life.

Writ of habeas corpus: A judge's order requiring that someone holding a person bring that person to court.

Writ of mandamus: (Latin *mandamus*, "We command.") A judge's order requiring a public official or government department to do something.

Index